784.193 Rea
Read.
Compendium of modern
  instrumental techniques.

The Lorette Wilmot Library
Nazareth College of Rochester

Compendium of Modern Instrumental Techniques

Compendium of Modern Instrumental Techniques

GARDNER READ

Foreword by Gunther Schuller

Greenwood Press
Westport, Connecticut · London

Library of Congress Cataloging-in-Publication Data

Read, Gardner.
　　Compendium of modern instrumental techniques / by Gardner Read ; foreword by Gunther Schuller.
　　　　p. cm.
　　Includes bibliographical references and indexes.
　　ISBN 0-313-28512-8 (alk. paper)
　　1. Musical instruments—Instruction and study. 2. Music—20th century—History and criticism. 3. Instrumentation and orchestration. I. Title
MT170.R38 1993
784.193—dc20　　　　92-17854

British Library Cataloguing in Publication Data is available.

Copyright © 1993 by Gardner Read

All rights reserved. No portion of this book may be reproduced, by any process or technique, without the express written consent of the publisher.

Library of Congress Catalog Card Number: 92-17854
ISBN: 0-313-28512-8

First published in 1993

Greenwood Press, 88 Post Road West, Westport, CT 06881
An imprint of Greenwood Publishing Group, Inc.

Printed in the United States of America

The paper used in this book complies with the
Permanent Paper Standard issued by the National
Information Standards Organization (Z39.48-1984).

10 9 8 7 6 5 4 3 2 1

Every reasonable effort has been made to trace the owners of copyright materials in this book, but in some instances this has proven impossible. The author and publisher will be glad to receive information leading to more complete acknowledgments in subsequent printings of the book and in the meantime extend their apologies for any omissions.

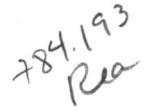

CONTENTS

FOREWORD BY GUNTHER SCHULLER — vii
ACKNOWLEDGMENTS — ix
PRELUDE — xi
LIST OF EXAMPLES — xiii

Part I: Generalized Techniques

INTRODUCTION — 3
1. Extended Ranges — 5
2. Muting — 15
3. Glissandi — 33
4. Harmonics — 55
5. Percussive Devices — 63
6. Microtones — 109
7. Amplification — 121
8. Extramusical Devices — 129

Part II: Idiomatic Techniques

9. Woodwinds and Brasses — 143
   Flutter-tonguing Variants, 143
   Vibrato, 144
   Fingering Devices, 146
   Breath and Air Sounds, 148
   Mouthpiece and Tubing Effects, 154
   Multiphonics, 158
   Vocalizations, 164
   Miscellaneous Effects, 166
   Hybrid and Modified Instruments, 168

10. Percussion ... 171
Tuning of Unpitched Instruments, 171
New Areas of Striking, 173
Unusual Agents of Attack, 174
New Methods of Striking, 184
Tremoli Variants, 191
Idiophone Clusters, 191
Miscellaneous Effects, 193

11. Harp and Other Plucked Instruments ... 195
Fingernail Plucking, 195
Pedal Glissandi and Trills, 196
Tuning-key and Tuning-pin Effects, 199
Guitar, Mandolin, and Banjo Techniques, 201

12. Keyboard Instruments ... 205
Piano and Harpsichord Clusters, 206
Key Attacks, 208
Pedal Effects, 209
Interior Devices, 210
Organ Clusters and Keyboard Effects, 213
Registration Devices, 217
Miscellaneous Effects, 218
Accordion Techniques, 219
Modified Keyboard Instruments, 219

13. Strings ... 221
Bowing Devices, 221
Sul Ponticello Variants, 227
Fingering Effects, 233
Pizzicato Variants, 235
Miscellaneous Effects, 244
Hybrid Instruments, 245

CODA ... 247
BIBLIOGRAPHY ... 249
INDEX OF INSTRUMENTAL REFERENCE ... 251
INDEX OF COMPOSERS AND WORKS ... 253
LIST OF PUBLISHERS ... 273

FOREWORD

The author of a compendium on "modern instrumental techniques" faces the disconcerting prospect that as soon as his tabulation is published, it is likely to be considered incomplete. For it is a reality of the mid- and late-twentieth century that the "progress" of music has been characterized by an unprecedented and bewildering amount of experimentation with the "techniques" of instruments. Almost every week it seems some composer somewhere is expanding or extending the capacities of traditional instruments. These efforts are often spurred on by attempts to identify with the relatively new sonoric potential of the various forms of electronic media (tape, synthesizer, computer, musique concrète, etc.). Composers are also, whether they are willing to admit it or not, very often inspired by the concept of "noise"—indeed, the *whole* world of sound—as a legitimate means of "musical" expression, first proposed by the Futurists early in the century, and definitely articulated by John Cage in the early 1940's.

To keep pace with these developments in anything approximating a comprehensive manner is an enormous task, and amongst American composers there is probably no one more suited to its accomplishment than Gardner Read. A veteran of encyclopedia cataloguing, as brilliantly evidenced in his *Thesaurus of Orchestral Devices,* Professor Read brings a composer's insights and expertise, a university professor's sense of history, and an experienced compiler's fanatic devotion to encyclopedic comprehensiveness. He has made available in a clear, concise, well-structured and handy compendium what must have taken untold hours of research and plowing through hundreds of scores.

When Read's earlier volume on this subject, *Contemporary Instrumental Techniques,* was published in 1976, many of the "modern" techniques and notational specifications collated in it were still relatively new and were certainly considered so even by performing musicians and composers. Thus the book was of immense value to the professionally interested.

Since 1976 a veritable revolution in performing standards of new music has occurred, much to the benefit of composers everywhere, in whatever style or conception. But new techniques and therefore new notational devices have also come into being in the intervening years. The present volume is thus a very welcome bringing-up-to-date of what has happened in the world of contemporary music.

What composers' ingenuity and drive for invention will yield in the future is, of course, hard to foretell. After some eighty years of nearly unrelenting experimentation—often it seemed for experimentation's sake—one might think that the pace would by now have slowed a little. And perhaps that is what has happened in the recent decade and a half. Perhaps we have now moved into a period when the innovations of the past are being assessed, weighed for their *real* value and long-term durability; and then, hopefully, the residue will be assimilated into the mainstream of compositional creativity.

If such evaluations are to take place, they will be made all the easier by Gardner Read's monumental efforts to tell us what in fact we have wrought in the last eighty years. For this we are a grateful community of composers, performers, conductors, listeners, and readers.

Gunther Schuller

ACKNOWLEDGMENTS

Books are customarily dedicated to persons, living or dead, and seldom to inanimate objects. This book, however, is dedicated to a ship: the Norwegian freighter *Tagaytay,* on which I enjoyed an extended trip to the Far East in 1972. Between exotic ports of call—Manila, Singapore, Kuala Lumpur, Belewan, Hong Kong, Taipei, Pusan, Yokohama—this survey of contemporary instrumental techniques took concrete shape. In welcome privacy and tacitly encouraged by discreet ship's personnel and understanding fellow passengers, voluminous notes were transformed into organized chapters and unfocused thoughts and impressions were honed into specific observation and critical commentary.

The original edition of this compendium contained the names of a number of individuals and publishers' representatives to whom I was greatly indebted for their welcome advice and concrete assistance in gathering the information essential to my research efforts. For this revised and expanded version of my book I am, in addition to the individuals previously cited, grateful for the unstinting cooperation and cheerful tolerance of the following Boston area music librarians: Millard Irion (Edna Kuhn Loeb Music Library, Harvard University), Holly Mockovac (Mugar Memorial Library, Boston University), and Diane Ota (Boston Public Library). Kindest thanks are also owed Gunther Schuller for his willingness to revise and update his original Foreword.

Grateful acknowledgment is hereby extended to the following music publishers for either supplying recent and relevant score publications or granting formal permission to quote examples from works under their control: Associated Music Publishers (agents for G. Schirmer, Inc., Editions Salabert, and Bote & Bock); Berandol Music Limited; Boosey & Hawkes, Inc.; Bowdoin College Music Press; M. M. Cole Publishing Company; Carl Fischer, Inc.; European American Music (agents for Schott & Co., Ltd. and Universal Edition A. G.); Hal Leonard Publishing Corporation (agents for Edward B. Marks and MCA Music); Margun Music, Inc. (agents for Aldo Bruzzichelli); Moeck Verlag; Oxford University Press; C. F. Peters Corporation (agents for Henmar Press and Henry Litolff's Verlag); Theodore Presser Company; Polskie Wydawnictwo Muzyczne; E. C. Schirmer Company; Seesaw Music Corporation; Shawnee Press, Inc.; Source: Music of the Avant-Garde.

PRELUDE

Composers of the late twentieth century are acutely aware of the bewildering multiplicity of styles and related techniques that are shaping the musical expression of our time. They are in general agreement, however, that sound per se is now of primary importance in the instrumentator's arsenal of techniques. Indeed, contemporary composers en masse have transferred to musical timbre the painter Kandinsky's belief that "Color makes a more insidious attack on the emotions than form."

Whereas self-expression, whether in music, in painting, or in literature, was the paradigm of the nineteenth-century Romantics, musical means have now become almost as important and as relevant to the composers' requirements as artistic ends. Compositional and instrumental techniques frequently exist in many of today's scores for their own intrinsic sakes rather than merely serving, as they did in the past, as vehicles of highly personalized sentiment.

A significant development and refinement of instrumental potential has taken place during recent years. Effects undreamed of, or once thought impossible by the early twentieth-century orchestrators, are now commonplaces in the vanguard scores of the present day; yet not all composers are fully aware of these developments nor of their pervasive influence on the kinds of music now being composed. Some instrumental techniques are understood only dimly or are utilized only tentatively, if at all. Indeed, certain new instrumentational devices are widely misunderstood, both as to the physical procedures involved and the results in terms of sound. It is, therefore, the primary purpose of this compendium, as it was in the original edition, to codify these techniques, to explain their production in terms of idiomatic peculiarity and limitation, and to cite representative scores in which the new devices form an integral part of the composer's concepts.

My initial survey of modern instrumental potential and utilization was published in 1976. Shortly after the book went out of print I determined that due to further significant instrumental exploration and to refinements of the techniques first discussed, as well as some entirely new sonic effects discovered in recently published scores, a considerably revised and expanded edition of the book was both desirable and essential. Many additional composers and their works are cited here and the number of excerpts from full scores has been increased. Furthermore, some 140 notational symbols for certain of the technical stipulations by the composers are now included.

The immanent value of both the original and this expanded edition of the book does not depend, of course, upon the prolific citation of bizarre instrumental effects—often more interesting as notations than as sounds—but on the systematic and detailed codification of modern instrumental potentiality. How, and under what compositional circumstances or in what stylistic context these techniques can be most felicitous, are decisions every composer must make for himself.

Even thoroughly experienced composers are sometimes apt to forget that their performers are not robots; they are human beings with human limitations of physical endowment and perception. If the avant-gardist is frequently impatient with these limitations, his solution is to create his music solely for the tape recorder, which knows no limitations other than its source of power. But if the composer utilizes conventional instruments played by human beings, he should not demand the physically impossible but only the realistically attainable from his performers.

All composers, whether experimental or basically conservative, deal with commonly shared materials—tonal, rhythmic, timbral, and formalistic. But no modern materials available to the contemporary orchestrator, it is safe to assert, are more fruitful than the current expansion of instrumental capability. Perhaps in the pages to follow both the composer and the performer may find as yet unexplored means towards the achievement of their common artistic ends as well as some unsuspected insights into modern instrumental potentiality.

LIST OF EXAMPLES

1. Claire Polin: *The Death of Procris* — 6
2. Donald Martino: *B.A.B.B.IT.T* — 8
3. Karel Husa: *String Quartet No. 3* — 12
4. Iannis Xenakis: *ST/4-1, 080262* — 13
5. Tomasz Sikorski: *Prologues* — 19
6. Luciano Berio: *Sequenza II* — 23
7. Toshiro Mayuzumi: *Pieces for Prepared Piano and Strings* — 27
8. Michael Colgrass: *As Quiet As* — 30
9. David Bedford: *Music for Albion Moonlight* — 34
10. Merrill Ellis: *Mutations* — 35
11. Larry Austin: *The Maze* — 37
12. Kazimierz Serocki: *Continuum* — 38
13. Mauricio Kagel: *Sonant* — 43
14. Roger Reynolds: *Blind Men* — 47
15. Krzysztof Penderecki: *Fluorescences* — 53
16. Heinz Holliger: *Siebengesang* — 56
17. Elliott Carter: *Eight Pieces for Four Timpani* — 57
18. George Crumb: *Ancient Voices of Children* — 60
19. Paul Chihara: *Branches* — 66
20. Istvan Anhalt: *Foci* — 79
21. Lukas Foss: *Ni bruit ni vitesse* — 86
22. William Albright: *Danse Macabre* — 89
23. Mel Powell: *Filigree Setting* — 93
24. Tadeusz Baird: *Espressioni varianti* — 105
25. Julián Carrillo: *Balbuceos* — 111
26. Alois Hába: *String Quartet No. 14* — 111
27. Harry Partch: *And on the 7th Day Petals Fell in Petaluma* — 112
28. Brian Ferneyhough: *Unity Capsule* — 115
29. Stephen Albert: *Cathedral Music* — 122
30. Bernard Rands: *Memo 1* — 127
31. Elliott Schwartz: *Music for Napoleon and Beethoven* — 132
32. Carlos Alsina: *Trio 1967* — 133
33. Gardner Read: *Diabolic Dialogue* — 139
34. Bruno Bartolozzi: *Collage* — 162
35. Witold Szalonek: *Aarhus Music* — 163

36.	Jacob Druckman: *Animus 1*	165
37.	David Reck: *Five Studies for Tuba Alone*	166
38.	Gardner Read: *Los Dioses Aztecas*	180
39.	Wlodsimierz Kotonski: *a battere*	181
40.	Cristobal Halffter: *Planto por las victimas de la violencia*	183
41.	Donald Erb: *The Seventh Trumpet*	192
42.	Francis Miroglio: *Réseaux pour harpe et orchestre*	198
43.	Sylvano Bussotti: *Fragmentations*	199
44.	Sven-David Sandström: *Surrounded*	203
45.	Stanley Lunetta: *Piano Music*	207
46.	Milko Kelemen: *Olifant*	211
47.	György Ligeti: *Volumina*	215
48.	William Bolcom: *Hydraulis*	216
49.	Jon Deak: *Color Studies for Contrabass*	223
50.	David Cope: *Angel's Camp II*	229
51.	Hans Werner Henze: *Sinfonia N. 6*	231
52.	Sergio Cervetti: *Zinctum*	241
53.	Luc Ferrari: *Société II*	243

I
GENERALIZED TECHNIQUES

INTRODUCTION

Many so-called "new" instrumental devices have developed from well-established techniques; they are extensions of, or refinements of, procedures long considered part of a composer's repertorium of expressive devices. The newness, then, is not one of kind but of degree, a further and more extensive development of basic effects found in scores from the late nineteenth century to the present day. Muting, glissandi, harmonics, and even certain percussive devices (as applied to nonpercussion instruments) are instrumental techniques common to the late Romantics (Mahler, in particular), the Impressionists (primarily Debussy and, to a lesser extent, Ravel), the Expressionists (beginning with Schoenberg, Berg, and Webern), and most certainly including the Neo-Romantics (Prokofiev, Bartók, and Britten, to name a few outstanding representatives).

More patently new, in conception and in method of individual production, are the techniques of microtones and of sound amplification, the latter applied to conventional instruments in live performance rather than referring to electronic composition. Newest and most radical in artistic conceptualization are the diverse theatrical effects now demanded of the instrumentalist (and vocalist, too)—extramusical devices injected to enhance the composer's avant-gardism.

Because all of the foregoing devices apply to all kinds of instruments, they are considered in Part I as generalized procedures that with but slight modification apply to all orchestral or ensemble members. In Part II the new devices and instrumental techniques discussed are exclusively idiomatic in nature; that is, they are conditioned by the individual constructions, basic performance procedures, and inherent limitations of the separate instruments. The effects catalogued are thus confined to similarities of instrumental type or family: fluttertonguing, for example, is a unique wind-instrument technique and cannot be achieved on percussion, keyboard, and stringed instruments; mechanical pedal effects are possible only on harp and certain keyboard instruments; similarly, *sul ponticello* is a manner of playing restricted to the bowed strings and plucked instruments such as guitar and mandolin.

The order of instrumental discussion in each section of Parts I and II, whether inter- or intra-choir, is always according to the traditional vertical format of the printed orchestral score page: woodwinds first, then brasses, followed by percussion, harp and other plucked instruments, keyboard instruments, and ending with the strings. And within each choir the instruments are generally referred to in similar verticality, according to their normal contiguous positions on the score page.

Purely in the interests of space, references to a composer's works in the many sectional listings throughout the book have been restricted to two citations. It should be understood that other but uncited scores by the same composer frequently utilize the identical technique—or at least one closely allied to it.

The choice of any particular work for citation or for illustration was governed by two criteria: 1) the clear and unequivocal demonstration of the instrumental or coloristic technique being analyzed, and 2) the availability of the score. Few manuscripts have been included and these only when they presented "one-of-a-kind" technical demonstrations or were otherwise unique in their utilization of the established devices.

The majority of the quoted musical examples serve a multiple purpose: that is, they frequently illustrate more than one unusual technical or expressive device. Hence the reader will often find cross-references to one or another of the score illustrations in chapters and sections other than those in which the examples are placed.

It should be evident that, of necessity, a rather rigorous and self-imposed selectivity resulted in a modest number of significant musical illustrations rather than a plethora of more routine examples that would serve a less useful purpose.

Because the primary focus of the book is on instrumental performance techniques, purely compositional or stylistic concepts are referred to, if at all, only peripherally. Consequently, there is no discussion here of aleatoric music, nor of improvisation, nor of formalistic considerations, except as they impinge directly on the performing techniques and the all-important parameter of tone color.

Although this survey of new instrumental devices was not designed expressly to be a textbook of contemporary orchestration, it could advantageously serve that purpose. It might also be profitably utilized as supplementary reference material in courses of basic instrumentation and of advanced composition and analysis. Performers, too, will find herein information regarding novel playing effects on their instruments not generally available elsewhere—certainly not within the confines of a single volume.

The multiplicity of new and experimental instrumental techniques has been equaled, if not surpassed, by a corresponding proliferation of new instrumental symbology. Because a consensus among composers and performers on the new notations is conspicuously lacking, it seemed inadvisable to include detailed discussion regarding the best choice among the existing notations. Just as each composer must determine subjectively the compositional and stylistic feasibility of any technique described in this book, so must he make a subjective choice among the concomitant symbologies currently in use.

1
EXTENDED RANGES

In the phenomenal development of late twentieth-century instrumental techniques it was inevitable that the total range of many of the orchestral and band instruments would be extended. Although these extensions are certainly not available to all instrumentalists, they form an important segment of modern instrumental potentiality. Range extensions are made possible by several means: first, by mechanical resources—longer tubing and extra keys on wind instruments; larger models of tuned percussion members; lengthened strings or the employment of scordatura on stringed instruments, and so on; second, by the development of individual performer technique.

WOODWINDS

Among the woodwind instruments whose ranges have now been notably increased, the flute has for many years been enabled to sound a low B by means of an extra key,[1] and to sound pitches higher than d^4, formerly considered the uppermost limit of the instrument. By means of embouchure manipulation and diaphragm control, certain flutists have recently been able to extend this limit to f^4—even on rare occasions to $f\sharp^4$, though the quality of sound is predictably rough and breathy. On the other hand, e^4 is both "safe" and of acceptable quality. For examples of the altissimo register see:

R. Barrett: *Anatomy* (e♭)
P. Boulez: *Sonatine pour flûte* (e♭,f)
B. Childs: *Music for Two Flute Players* (e♭)
A. Gilbert: *The Incredible Flute Music* (f)
T. Harsanyi: *Suite pour orchestre* (e)
J. Heiss: *Four Movements for Three Flutes* (e♭,e)

M. Kelemen: *Passionato* (f); *Studie für Flöte Solo* (e)
W. Kotonski: *Spring Music* (e,f♯,g♯)
P. Lawson: *Valentia Extramaterial* (f)
D. Martino: *Notturno; Quodlibets II* (f)
J. Mekeel: *The Shape of Silence* (e)
D. Milhaud: *IIe Symphonie* (e♭,f♯,g♯)
C. Wuorinen: *Flute Variations* (e♭,e,f)

A normally blown low B♭ is now possible by pulling out the head-joint about an inch and fingering low B. Thus the several B♭'s in three of Mahler's symphonies and the one in Ravel's orchestration of the Mussorgsky *Pictures at an Exhibition* (see page 139 of the pocket score) can no longer be regarded as notational errors. But whether the several low B♭'s notated in the third movement (at letter B) of Tchaikovsky's *Symphony No. 3* (1875) should be regarded as errors on the composer's part, or as intended pitch extensions, is inconclusive in retrospect.

Stokes and Condon maintain that the flute range can be extended downward by an octave (from c^1) through the use of so-called subtones;[2] that is, buzzing with the lips into the aperture as though it were a brass mouthpiece. They also suggest stopping the open end of the flute with a cork or pressing it against the player's leg to produce a soft pitch one octave lower than the blown note.

Key slaps, although primarily a percussive device (see pages 64–66), can also lower the pitches fingered into the octave below the instrument's normal range. Vigorously slapping the G-key with the left-hand fourth finger, while at the same time covering the blowhole with the tongue or the chin and fingering any one of the pitches from b to a♯[1] with the right hand, results in a percussive tone a major seventh below the fingered note. This effect was used successfully by:

D. Harris: *Ludus II*
J. Heiss: *Four Movements for Three Flutes*
B. Levy: *Orbs with Flute*
C. Polin: *The Death of Procris* (Example 1)

Example 1
Claire Polin: from *The Death of Procris* (p. 8)

© Copyright 1973 by Seesaw Music Corp., New York. Reproduced by permission.

George Crumb instructs the alto flute player in *Night of the Four Moons* to cover the air hole with the mouth while clicking the keys of certain specified pitches to produce tones an *octave* lower than notated. Anthony Gilbert includes

EXTENDED RANGES

a parallel directive in his *The Incredible Flute Music:* "Block head-joint hole with tongue and finger energetically an 8va above notated pitch."

Under normal circumstances it is not possible to lower the bottom B♭ of the oboe, but Barney Childs in his *Nonet* tells the player to insert a long cardboard tube in the bell and use the B♭-fingering; the resultant pitch is indeterminately lower than B♭ and is extremely rough and blatant. At the opposite end of the range, high B♭, B, and C are now available to certain oboists, the result of special fingerings and an ultratight embouchure. Both the *Spring Music* of Wlodsimierz Kotonski and Brian Ferneyhough's *Etudes Transcendanteles* require these stratospheric oboe pitches.

Bass-clef C, B, and A for clarinet, low A, A♭, and G for bassoon, as well as the bottom A for contrabassoon are achieved mechanically by means of cardboard tubing or a rolled cylinder of stiff drawing paper, about a foot in length, inserted into the bell of the instrument. Otherwise, the pitch extension is produced by embouchure adjustment, as in Alban Berg's *Chamber Concerto* (the bassoon part on page 52 of the Philharmonia score).[3] For further examples refer to:

P. Chihara: *Branches* (Example 19)
B. Conyngham: *Mirages*
D. Erb: *Symphony of Overtures*
A. Gilbert: *Spell Respell*
G. Ligeti: *Requiem*

D. Martino: *B.A.B.B.IT.T* (Example 2)
R. Shapey: *Concerto Grosso*
D. Shostakovich: *Symphony No. 3*
I. Stravinsky: *Chant du Rossignol; Symphony in C*

In Donald Martino's solo clarinet work listed above, nine cylinders of different lengths are required at various times to enable the player to lower drastically the normal range of the instrument, the nadir being B♭ below the bass staff. According to the composer, the instrument bell is to be removed and the cylinders inserted into the end-joint as needed, held in position with masking tape. A more modest requirement appears in Theodore Antoniou's *3 Likes for Solo Clarinet:* only four cardboard tubes are specified to lower the instrument's range.

The bass clarinet in William Albright's *Danse Macabre* is given a low C, achieved by pulling out the instrument neck a half-step and fingering D. Even lower pitches, however, have been requisitioned by other composers, as shown in the following score references.

R. Barrett: *Anatomy* (B)
R. R. Bennett: *Commedia I* (B,B♭)
J. Harvey: *Inner Light III* (C,B,B♭)
L. Janáček: *Sinifonietta* (B,B♭,A,A♭, G♭,F)

A. Khachaturian: *Gayne Ballet Suite; Piano Concerto* (B,B♭)
W. Piston: *Second Symphony* (B,B♭,A, A♭)
D. Shostakovich: *Symphonies Nos. 6, 7, 11* (B)

Presumably these composers had especially constructed instruments in mind or else the players resorted to mechanical extensions to produce such subterranean pitches.

Example 2
Donald Martino: from *B.A.B.B.IT.T* (p. 5)

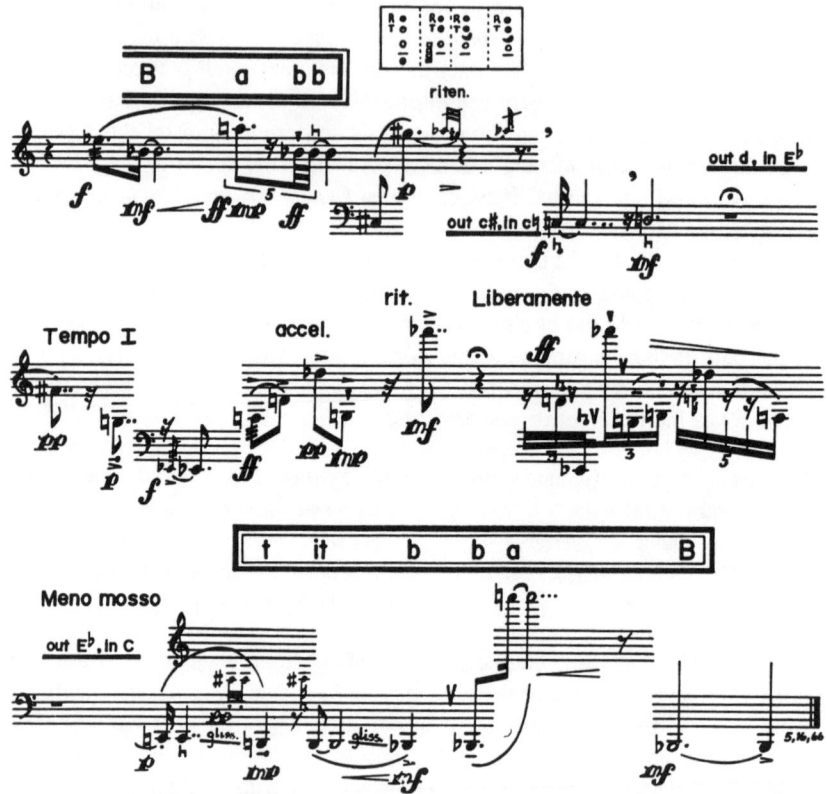

© Copyright 1970 by Ione Press, Inc. Used by permission. Sole selling agent: E. C. Schirmer-Boston.

Normally capable of producing pitches an octave lower than bass clarinet, the contrabass clarinet in Martino's *The White Island* must descend below its usual range to C♯ and C♮.

Pitches higher than the conventional limits of oboe, English horn, clarinet, and bass clarinet are achieved by ultratight embouchure and/or unusual fingerings worked out by the individual player; hence they vary in quality according to the performer's ability. Altissimo pitches for the clarinet are called for in Edward Cowie's *Clarinet Concerto* (g), William O. Smith's *Variants for Solo Clarinet* (d,e,a—the instrument muted), and Gilbert's *Brighton Piece* (c,d♭,f♭). For instances of extended upper notes on bass clarinet, see *Harry's Musike* by H-J. Hespos and Barrett's *Anatomy* (e in both works).

Without specifying a precise pitch, several composers have requested the

EXTENDED RANGES

highest note possible on a reed instrument, the player biting with clenched teeth on the reed while blowing. See:

B. Bartolozzi: *Collage* (oboe, bassoon)
J. Fox: *All Things Fancy* (clarinet)
H. Holliger: *"H" for Wind Quintet* (oboe, clarinet, bassoon)

According to Lester Weil (see Bibliography), the complete range of the bassoon may now be considered as $E\flat_2$ to c^3—an astonishing expansion of the instrument's traditional limits. It is achieved by the use of unorthodox ventings and fingerings, which produce difference tones. The altissimo register also requires considerable embouchure modification and almost superhuman lip control. A composer would be well advised to consult with an experienced performer before attempting to utilize such a drastic expansion of the bassoon range.

The upper ranges of the several saxophones have now been extended by a full octave and the lower ranges by a minor second.[4] On the baritone saxophone an added whole-step below the normally available low concert $D\flat$ is attainable by placing a specially designed cone in the instrument bell. Though the use of this device slightly dampens the resonance, it does provide a welcome extension to the bottom area of the instrument.

In all of the above-cited instances of expanded range, intonation is apt to be shaky, tone quality strained and rough, and pitch frequently approximate rather than precise. Nonetheless, if these conditions can be regarded as desirable from the vanguardist's point of view, there is no reason why they cannot be exploited in his works.

BRASSES

As with woodwinds, extended ranges in the brass instruments are accomplished through combinations of embouchure control and special fingerings. Although f^2 should still be regarded as the highest feasible pitch available to the average hornist, some players can achieve up to d^2 but only at a relatively high dynamic level. In point of fact, none of the brasses can exceed their normal upper limits at a moderate amplitude, nor without a progressive loss of stable intonation. Both Richard Barrett and Anthony Gilbert call for $g\flat^2$ in their scores just cited, while Donald Erb notates a $g\natural^2$ in his *Concerto for Brass and Orchestra*, but wisely indicates a lower optional pitch.

Both trumpet and trombone are now frequently required to exceed their traditional upper frequency boundaries. One cannot assign a precise and fixed limit for these stratospheric pitches; it depends almost wholly upon the individual player's embouchure and breath control. Certain jazz trumpeters can reach c^4 without undue difficulty, and $b\flat^2$ is available to skilled trombonists. Beyond these demonstrated possibilities, however, lies *terra incognita*.

The lower ranges of all the brass instruments have likewise been extended. The horn can now descend to G_1, as in György Ligeti's *Ten Pieces for Wind Quintet,* though the tonal quality is quite rough. To enable his trumpet player to go lower than the conventional f♯ or e, Barney Childs in *Nonet* instructs the player to insert a cardboard tube in the bell. Pedal tones (down to E_1) have been required of trombonists since the early part of the twentieth century, but composers must remember that the sound quality of these notes is far less focused than for those low pitches available by means of the modern F-attachment. As for tuba, although both ends of its total range have been somewhat extended, no specific boundary-notes can be cited; they vary according to individual performer techniques. Whereas b♭^{1} is available to most players, even higher pitches can be obtained by certain virtuoso performers on the instrument.

PERCUSSION

Among the pitched membranophones whose compasses can be mechanically enlarged, the timpani can now achieve tones on the plastic-headed drums somewhat beyond the traditional limits dictated by the older membrane-covered drum heads (see Example 17). These extreme pitches, however, are rather unreliable in intonation and of dubious quality.

Newcomers to the percussion section are the Roto-toms—a set of mounted tom-toms (usually up to five) which can be tuned like timpani to specific pitches. They may, as a consequence, be considered as extensions of the timpani in a higher range, a fact that greatly enlarges the instrumentator's tuned percussive resources.

Extended ranges on the keyed idiophones are entirely a matter of physical construction. That is, pitches higher or lower than those given in standard orchestration manuals as normal limits are available only on larger models of glockenspiel, xylophone, vibraphone, or marimba. Inasmuch as such nonstandard models are not everywhere available, idiophone range extensions cannot yet be regarded as feasible by contemporary orchestrators.

HARP AND OTHER PLUCKED INSTRUMENTS

The harp, guitar, and mandolin can have their extreme ranges enlarged only by means of scordatura. The highest string of these instruments can be tuned up a half—at the very most, a whole—scale-degree, and their lowest string tuned down by no more than a major second, possibly a minor third. To raise a string higher would be to risk breaking it, and to slacken a string further would be to deprive it of resonance and hence of specific pitch. Both Berg's opera *Wozzeck* and Maurice Ravel's ballet *Daphnis et Chloé,* as well as the more recent cello concerto of Ligeti, offer instances of low B♭ for the harp achieved by pretuning the bottom C-string, as the pedal mechanism does not affect this string.

Instances of returning the lowest string of the acoustic guitar to extend its range below the open E-string are to be found in the following scores:

G. Crumb: *Songs, Drones and Refrains of Death* (D)
J. Encinar: *Abhava* (E♭)
H. Shimoyama: *Dialogo No. 2* (D)
R. Smith Brindle: *Do Not Go Gentle* (C)
G. B. Wilson: *Concatenations* (C)

Because the neck of the electric guitar is thinner than that of the standard instrument and the frets closer together, its range extends an octave higher than the acoustic guitar. The lower range has also been extended, and both Tim Darter in *Dual* and Pelle Gundmundsen-Holmgreen in *Solo for Electric Guitar* have called for E an octave below the open string.

STRINGS

Extending the upper ranges of the various stringed instruments is almost entirely a matter of the performer's ability; it requires playing in an exceedingly high position, with fingers cramped together, and with little room on the string to maneuver. Intonation is invariably wobbly and tones are tense and strained; yet these sounds are considered viable and are deliberately exploited in much experimental composition today. Rather than specify actual pitches in the stratospheric positions, many composers have adopted the device of merely calling for the highest pitch(es) the player is capable of producing. Notationally, this is now quite generally indicated with a solid arrowhead or x-shaped notehead placed somewhat above the staff (see Example 3). Dieter Schnebel in *Versuche* tells his string players: "Sometimes extremely high tones are notated which are hardly possible. They are to be played regardless of the beauty or clearness of the result." The same comment might be applied to the altitudinous pitches required in Karel Husa's *String Quartet No. 3* (Example 3); at such a rarified height specific pitches are not within the realm of possibility, a fact that the composer acknowledges. On the other hand, Bernard Rands in his *Étendre* specifically notates c^3 and $f\#^3$—even $d\flat^4$—for the solo doublebass, an incredible instance of pitch expansion for this instrument.

As far as the lower ranges of all the string instruments are concerned, extensions of pitch are accomplished by means of the time-honored device of scordatura. Violins are seldom required to have their fourth strings lowered by more than a whole step, although there is at least one exception, indicated below.

A. Bax: *First Symphony* (f)
P. Hindemith: *Symphonische Tänze* (f)
R. Reynolds: *Aether* (f♯)
W. Riegger: *Study in Sonority* (e)
R. Strauss: *Ein Heldenleben; Elektra* (f)

The viola also is rarely directed to have its C-string lowered by more than a half step; Iannis Xenakis's score demonstrates a more extreme instance of extension.

Example 3
Karel Husa: from *String Quartet No. 3* (p. 16)

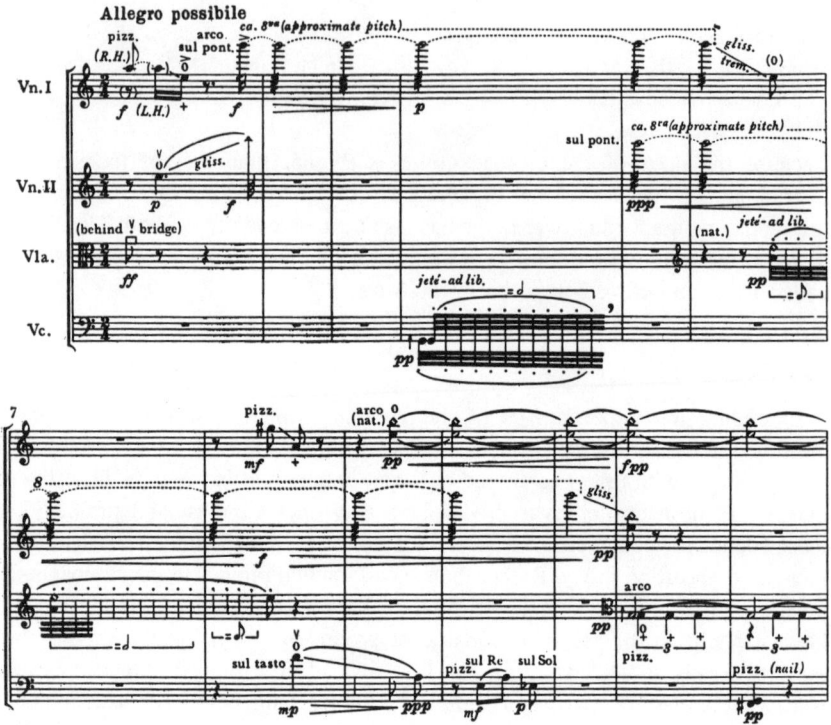

Copyright © 1970 Associated Music Publishers, Inc. International Copyright Secured. All Rights Reserved. Used by Permission.

- A. Bax: *First Symphony* (B)
- R. Strauss: *Don Quixote* (B)
- I. Xenakis: *ST/4-1, 080262* (G) (Example 4)

Scordatura for the cello and/or doublebass has been notably radical in several contemporary works. Although most composers have been content with lowering the C-string by only a half or whole step, certain others have called for a more drastic extension:

- T. Antoniou: *Parastasis II* (B)
- A. Honegger: *Concertino pour Piano et Orchestre* (B♭)
- M. Ravel: *Ma mère l'oye; Piano Concerto in G* (B)
- O. Respighi: *The Pines of Rome* (B)
- R. Reynolds: *The Promises of Darkness* (B)
- K. Serocki: *Swinging Music* (G)
- R. Strauss: *Also Sprach Zarathustra; Die Frau ohne Schatten* (B)
- I. Stravinsky: *Le Sacre du Printemps* (B)
- J. Wytennbach: *Divisions* (B)

EXTENDED RANGES

Example 4
Iannis Xenakis: from *ST/4-1, 080262* (p. 16)

© Copyright 1967 by Boosey & Hawkes Music Publishers Ltd. Reprinted by permission of Boosey & Hawkes, Inc.

There are several instances in twentieth-century published scores of notated pitches (usually B) in parentheses, as found in Berg's opera *Wozzeck*, for example. These are not scordatura pitches but are given only as the continued or concluding notes of a phrase, and are not intended to be played.

A tuning requirement quite generally restricted to the lower string instruments is achieved by the players lowering the C-strings by gradually turning the tuning peg; this device is a feature of the following works:

W. Albright: *Danse Macabre* (to C_1)
T. Antoniou: *Jeux for Violoncello and String Orchestra* (to Ab_1)
C. Ung: *Spiral* (to F_1)

I. Xenakis: *ST/4-1, 080262* (to F_1)
B. A. Zimmermann: *Intercommunicazione* (to G_1)

Two recent works contain directives to lower the doublebass C-string as far as possible: *Strobo I* of Alcides Lanza and Krzysztof Penderecki's *Fluorescences*

(Example 15). All four cello strings in Kazimierz Serocki's *Swinging Music* must be pretuned a perfect fourth lower—an unusual instance of extended scordatura.

Although the device known as the "Kapo-bar" does not extend the overall range of a string instrument, either higher or lower, its use in Joseph Schwantner's *In Aeternum* enables the cellist to produce a double-stop of a tenth, several tones higher than any normally fingered interval.

Further extensions of certain instrumental ranges may well be feasible, yet there surely must be a physical limit beyond which frequency increments cannot be successfully attained. Even now the expansions of instrumental pitch boundaries have in some instances entered the realm of "white noise"—valid in its own right but limited in its relevance to recognizable pitch distinction. It would seem that the law of diminishing returns would operate decisively in curtailing further significant range expansion—at least among traditional instruments. For new or for hybrid instruments the problem of increasing their total gamut may perhaps be solved more satisfactorily.

NOTES

1. Possibly the earliest example of low B occurs in the *Intermezzo* (measure 118) of Mendelssohn's incidental music to *A Midsummer Night's Dream* (1843).
2. Sheridon Stokes and Richard Condon, *Special Effects for Flute* (Culver City: Trio Associates, 1970).
3. All note references are at concert pitch.
4. See *The Art of Saxophone Playing* by Larry Teal (Evanston: Summy-Birchard Company, 1963) for fingering charts.

2

MUTING

WOODWINDS AND BRASSES

Whereas the muting of a brass instrument in contemporary music is almost too common to warrant mention, the device is encountered far more rarely in parts for woodwind instruments—and for good reason. More effective in theory than in practice, woodwind muting is limited in application and only moderately successful as a timbral agent. The basic reason is that the tube opening or bell of the instrument is not the sole avenue of blown sound; to close the bell artificially affects only a relatively few pitches at the lower end of the instrument range. Generally speaking, woodwind mutes affect only the fingerings that are closest to the position of the mute itself.

The flute and alto flute may be partially muted by inserting a piece of soft tissue or cloth in the tubing after removing the foot-joint, but only c^1 and $c\sharp^1$ are slightly affected. Somewhat higher pitches can be muted by employing the technique of spread tones. These are delicate alterations of normal timbre accomplished by closing the finger holes below the one open hole which produces the required pitch; they may be used to "mute" the tones from $d\sharp^1$ to $a\sharp^1$. Spread tones are actually more successful as a muting device than the artificial, and limited, closing of the tube end.

Stokes and Condon, in their *Special Effects for Flute*,[1] suggest muting the instrument with a piece of masking tape partially covering the embouchure hole. The muting is thus achieved by reducing the air flow rather than by blocking its egress as a specific tone.

The remaining woodwind instruments may have a cloth, wadded-up handkerchief, or large cork stuffed into the bell, but again only the fingerings closest to the mute itself are affected, thus precluding an even, overall scale of muted tones. It has been demonstrated that a clarinetist can simulate muting by producing a "wah-wah" effect with the left hand over the instrument bell if fingering is not required. A more complex muting effect appears in Martino's *Notturno:* the player is to rest the clarinet bell on his left knee with the upper part of the instrument against his left shoulder, thus muffling the normal tone.

An equally unusual muting device is required in Ligeti's *Lontano:* the contrabassoon is muffled with a horn mute that is placed in the tube end by the player seated next to the contrabassoonist. In the *Sinfonia N. 6* of Hans Werner Henze the saxophone is briefly muted, presumably with a specially designed ring, looking like an oversized doughnut, and covered with a velvet ribbon. Its primary advantage over a cloth or cork mute is that the bell tones (the lowest three pitches) can still be sounded when the instrument is muted with this agent. A less specific directive for woodwind muting occurs in Sir Michael Tippett's *Symphony No. 1;* the oboe is told to play "as if muted."

The instruments listed below are to be muted with pieces of cloth or, in a few instances, with corks or felt plugs:

Oboe and/or English horn:

P. Boulez: *Éclat*
K. Huber: *Tenebrae*
C. M. Loeffler: *Five Irish Fantasies*
D. Martino: *Cinque Framenti*
P. Méfano: *Interférences*
R. Reynolds: *Quick are the Mouths of Earth*

K. Stockhausen: *Adieu*
I. Stravinsky: *Petrouchka*
W. Szalonek: *Aarhus Music*
A. de la Vega: *Exospheres for Oboe and Piano*

Clarinet and/or bass clarinet:

R. Laneri: *Esorcismi II*
G. Perle: *Sonata quasi una fantasia*
W. O. Smith: *Variants for Solo Clarinet*

W. Szalonek: *Aarhus Music*
A. de la Vega: *Interpolation for Solo Clarinet*

Saxophone:

C. Delvincourt: *Pamir*
J. Fortner: *S pr ING*
S. Hodkinson: *Interplay*

Bassoon and/or contrabassoon:

C. Ballif: *Voyage de mon oreille*
K. Huber: *Tenebrae*
G. Ligeti: *Lontano; Requiem*

S-D. Sandström: *Just a Bit*
K. Stockhausen: *Adieu*
W. Szalonek: *Aarhus Music*

An interesting simulation of muting is requested of the oboist in Witold Szalonek's *Les Sons:* the player is to enclose the mouthpiece (staple) tightly with the clenched fist, gradually unclenching the hand during playing. The woodwind equivalent of brass instrument stopped-open (+ −o) procedures, the same technique is to be applied to oboe, English horn, and bassoon in Donald Erb's *The Seventh Trumpet.*

More feasible on brass than on woodwind instruments is the device of inserting a mute gradually in the bell of the instrument while playing. The effect,

MUTING 17

possible on all the brasses save tuba, and analogous to gradual handstopping on the horn, has been requested by:

D. Banks: *Horn Concerto*
H. W. Henze: *4. Sinfonie*

H. Holliger: *Siebengesang*
G. Rochberg: *Tableaux*

Conversely, the mute may be removed gradually from the bell, just as the hornist's clenched hand may be slowly withdrawn from inside the bell; see:

D. Bedford: *Pentomino*
E. Brown: *Available Forms 2*
N. T. Dao: *Phū-Dông*
D. Erb: *Concerto for Brass and Orchestra; Concerto for Solo Percussionist*

T. Ichiyanagi: *Activities*
L. de Pablo: *Modulos III*
E. Schwartz: *Essays; Rip*
K. Serocki: *Symphonic Frescoes*
K. Stockhausen: *Punkte*

The requisition of differently constituted brass mute types is a common requirement in twentieth-century scores. Those that have been specifically stipulated are as follows:

Bol (Robison)
Brass
Bucket
Buzz
Cardboard
Cleartone
Cup
Felt
Fiber
Hand
Hard
Harmon (with or without stem)
Hat (Derby)
Jazz
Mel-wa

Metal
Plunger
Ray Robison
Stone-lined cup
Stone-lined derby
Straight (ordinary, regular)
Tuxedo plunger
Velvet
Velve-tone (bucket)
Solotone
Stop
Wa-wa (wah-wah)
Whisper (wispa)
Wow-wow

Irwin Bazelon modifies his brass muting in *De-Tonations for Brass Quintet and Orchestra* by requesting "tight cup mutes," while in William Russo's *Three Pieces for Blues Band and Orchestra* the trumpets and trombones must use "loose plunger mutes." As a mute substitute, a toilet-paper cone is to be inserted in the trombone bell in William Bergsma's *Blatant Hypotheses,* so as to produce "a soft, delicate sound."

Other composers have made similar requests. Michael Colgrass in *As Quiet As* suggests that a Harmon mute with a piece of felt stuffed in the pinhole would be an acceptable surrogate for "whisper" mute. Similarly, Gunther Schuller in *Study in Textures* requests his brass players to cover their cup mutes with a cloth to simulate solotone mutes. And Barbara Kolb tells her trombonists in *Trobar Clus* to use a cup mute with extra felt if bucket mutes are not available. In *Remembrances* Lawrence Moss asks that a cup mute be further softened by winding a handkerchief around the cup before inserting it in the instrument bell.

Of the more commonly available mute types, the tone of a Harmon mute can be variously altered by pulling out the stem, by degrees or completely (as required in *Éclat* of Pierre Boulez and in Schuller's *Study in Textures,* for example).

Some composers have requested adjustments of the normal muting technique on the horn by way of half- or quarter-stopping with the hand in the bell, as in:

R. Barrett: *Anatomy*　　　　　　　　J. Schwantner: *Canticle of the Evening*
D. Martino: *Ritorno; Triple Concerto*　　　　*Bells*
W. Schuman: *Violin Concerto*

Rather exotic mute substitutes have on occasion been designated by certain avant-gardists: for example, in both *Apparitions* and *Aventures* Ligeti asks that the horn be muted with a cloth stuffed tightly into the bell (also required of trumpet in the *Double Concerto for ondes Martenot, Percussion and Orchestra* of Josep Mestres-Quadreny). Furthermore, Ligeti directs (in *Aventures*) that the hornist also use a large round vase with a narrow neck for muting purposes; he does not, however, explain how the vase is to be made secure in the bell opening. One presumes that it must be held in place with the hand, somewhat awkward for the player.

A muting trick borrowed from early jazz performance technique is to muffle the open tones of trumpet and trombone by playing directly into the music stand, the bell held as close as possible in front of the music on the rack. For examples refer to the following works:

S. Albert: *Voices Within*　　　　　　P. Phillips: *Novasonic for Orchestra*
W. Benson: *Star Edge*　　　　　　　M. Richter: *Blackberry Vines and*
M. Ellis: *Mutations*　　　　　　　　　　*Winter Fruit*
D. Martino: *Ritorno*　　　　　　　　D. Schnebel: *Versuche*
P. Méfano: *Paraboles*

An analogous effect is present in Warren Benson's *Helix:* trumpets and trombones are to play into a hat, gradually withdraw the instrument bell, then slowly return it into the hat.

Example 5
Tomasz Sikorski: from *Prologues* (p. 3)

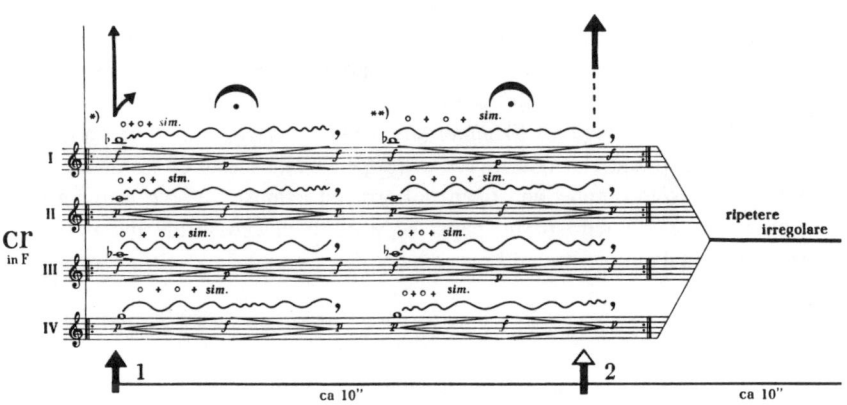

© Copyright 1967 by PWM-Edition, Kraków, Poland. Used by permission.

A rapid interchange of stopped/open tones on the horn is a requirement found in many contemporary scores, most notably in Tomasz Sikorski's *Prologues* (Example 5), where the effect is combined with varying degrees of vibrato and dynamic levels. The same technique, but employed slowly, is evident in Anthony Gilbert's *Brighton Piece*. An intriguing variation of this device is prominent in Christopher Rouse's *The Infernal Machine:* the hornist stops and opens the bell of his instrument without altering the embouchure, labeled by the composer the "Star Trek" effect. A trombonist can obtain a comparable effect by either rapidly or slowly opening or closing a plunger mute in the instrument bell; refer to the following scores:

D. Bedford: *Trona*
L. Berio: *Sequenza V*
J. Druckman: *Animus 1* (Example 36)
D. Erb: *Concerto for Brass and Orchestra; The Seventh Trumpet*

V. Globokar: *Accord; Discours II*
W. Heider: *-einander*
J. Heinke: *Music for Trombone and Percussion*

Feasible and highly effective, though strangely not a conspicuous requisition in contemporary scores, is the simultaneous use by similar brass instruments of different mute types. In his *Sinfonia,* for instance, Luciano Berio requires one trumpet to use plunger mute, one to use Harmon mute, and two others to employ straight mutes—all playing concurrently. And in *Epifanie* four trumpets synchronistically employ wa-wa, cup, straight, and plunger mutes—a fascinating amalgam of muted brass tone. (See also Jacob Druckman's *Windows* and two scores of Erb's, both listed above, as well as the *Finis Coronet Opus* of Costin Miereanu.)

Mixing both mute types and different brass instruments, Bernard Rands contrasts Harmon mutes for trumpet and trombone with straight fiber and metal mutes for the same instruments in *Canti lunatici,* while in *Étendre* he mixes straight metal mute for horn, whisper mute for trumpet, and Harmon mute for trombone. Karl-Birger Blomdahl pits ordinary horn mutes (non-transposing) against wa-wa trumpet and cup trombone mutes in *Forma Ferritonans*. Finally, in Karel Husa's *Concerto for Trumpet and Wind Orchestra* the three orchestral trumpets mix cup and Harmon mutes with open while the three trombones use straight and Harmon mutes and open, all arrayed against the solo trumpet employing a cup mute with tissue paper or a cloth placed inside the mute—a provocative amalgam of muted brass sonority.

PERCUSSION

Muting is a technical and timbral device that would not seem to have much relevance when applied to percussion instruments, but this is not the case. The various membranophones, timpani and tuned drums included, can all be muted in at least two different ways. First, a piece of cloth, a folded handkerchief, or a felt pad may be laid on the drum surface to muffle its normal resonance:

P. D. Q. Bach: *Grand Serenade*
H. Badings: *Symphonic Scherzo*
J. Cage: *First Construction (in Metal)*
M. Colgrass: *As Quiet As*
H. Ebenhöh: *4 Szenen für 10*
P. Hindemith: *Konzert für Violoncello und Orchester*
S. Hodkinson: *Imagind Quarter*
M. Kagel: *Anagrama*
L. Kupkovik: *Das Fleisch des Kreuzes*
D. Martino: *The White Island*
J. M. Mestres-Quadreny: *Tramesa a Tapies*
W. Pijper: *Six Symphonic Epigrams*
G. Read: *Los Dioses Aztecas*
E. Rubbra: *Symphony No. 6*
W. Russell: *Fugue for Eight Percussion Instruments*
D. Shostakovich: *Violin Concerto*
V. Thomson: *Symphony No. 2*
T-t. Tiêt: *Ngũ Hãnh II*
B. A. Zimmermann: *Canto di speranza*

In Walter Ross's trombone concerto, one timpano is muted by laying the protective cardboard cover on the head; this is struck with a bass drum beater instead of with normal timpani mallets. In *Windows* Jacob Druckman mutes a timpano by asking the player to lay a cymbal, rim down, on the surface.

For the second manner of muting, the flat hand or spread fingers are pressed against the membrane before striking, so as to deaden the normal vibration of the drumhead:

D. Bedford: *Piece for Mo*
P. Boulez: *Le marteau sans maître*
E. Carter: *Eight Pieces for Four Timpani*
V. Globokar: *Voie*
H-J. Hespos: *Passagen*
M. Kagel: *Anagrama; Sonant*
J. McKenzie: *Paths I*

R. Reynolds: *Quick are the Mouths of Earth*
Z. Rudzinski: *Impromptu for Orchestra*
W. Russell: *Fugue for Eight Percussion Instruments*
Y. Sadai: *Nuances*
B. Schäffer: *Scultura*
W. Schuman: *Symphony No. 7*
K. Serocki: *Episodes; Musica concertante*
B. A. Zimmermann: *Canto di speranza*

A snare drum may, in addition, be muted by laying a cloth or handkerchief on the snares themselves, with the drum turned upside down (required in Kagel's *Anagrama*).

Pitched mallet instruments—marimba, xylophone, vibraphone, and glockenspiel—can be effectively muted by pressing the fingers of one hand on the bars while striking with a mallet in the other; these requirements appear in:

P. Boulez: *Le marteau sans maître*
S. Hodkinson: *Fresco; Imagind Quarter*
J. McKenzie: *Paths I*
Y. Sadai: *Nuances*
B. Schäffer: *Scultura*

These instruments may also be muted by the player laying a cloth or felt pad, even a folded handkerchief, on the plates to be struck, as designated in:

N. T. Dao: *Máy*
G. Heussenstamm: *Seventeen Impressions*
K. Huber: *Tenebrae*
B. Maderna: *III Concerto per Oboe*

A percussionist mutes chimes and triangle by grasping the metal tubing or bar with one hand, while playing with the other:

R. Barrett: *Anatomy*
P. Boulez: *Le marteau sans maître*
N. Castiglioni: *A Solemn Music II*
M. Kagel: *Anagrama*
G. Read: *Los Dioses Aztecas*
Z. Rudzinski: *Impromptu for Orchestra*
W. Russell: *Fugue for Eight Percussion Instruments*
W. Schuman: *Credendum*
K. Serocki: *Continuum; Episodes*

In *Gulliver—His Voyage to Lilliput* by Edgar Stillman-Kelley, the triangle is not only held tightly in the player's hand while being struck but the instrument itself is wrapped in a cloth. It is safe to assume that the sound so produced is quite satisfactorily muffled.

Suspended cymbals, gongs, and tam-tams are customarily muted by holding their edges between the fingers of one hand, while playing on the surface with some agent in the other hand:

B. Bartók: *Deux Portraits*
D. Bedford: *Piece for Mo*
H. Birtwistle: *Nomos*
D. Erb: *Concerto for Brass and Orchestra*
L. Foss: *Echoi; Fragments of Archilochos*

J. Harvey: *Inner Light III*
H-J. Hespos: *Passagen*
M. Kagel: *Anagrama; Sonant*
W. Russell: *Three Dance Movements*
W. Schuman: *Symphony No. 7*
T. Sikorski: *Echa II*

In William Hellermann's *Formata* the suspended cymbal is to be muffled by laying or taping a piece of paper on the cymbal surface. A similar effect is obtained in the *Tramesa a Tapies* of José Maria Mestres-Quadreny by draping a cloth over the cymbal. Several composers have called for gongs to be muted by laying them flat on a large pad (or blanket) spread on the floor or a table and then striking them; this stipulation appears in Cage's *First Construction (in Metal)* and in Henry Cowell's *Set of Five*.

Maracas can be dampened in sound by holding them by the heads rather than by the handles when shaking or rotating them; both Anthony Gilbert in his *Introit, Gradual and Two Chorals* and Mauricio Kagel in *Anagrama* request this action. Finally, cowbells may be muffled by stuffing a cloth into their openings.

Orchestrators should be reminded that none of the foregoing muted effects should be confused with ordinary muffling of the vibrations of a percussion instrument after it has been struck.

HARP

Hand muffling of the harp strings is a routine performance technique and therefore does not constitute a bona fide muting device. Nor are "isolated sounds" and "xyloharmonic sounds" (so named by the French composer-harpist Carlos Salzedo) genuine muting effects. "Isolated sounds" result from muffling a string at the precise moment of plucking the next string required, and "xyloharmonic-sounds" are the immediate muffling of harmonics. Properly qualified as harp string muting is the technique of muffling the string at the actual moment of plucking it. One such procedure is Salzedo's "snare drum effect": the left hand is laid flat along the tops of a limited number of strings near the tuning pins while the right hand plays so-called "gushing chords" (see page 41). Many of Salzedo's solo harp pieces call for this effect, as do the following works:

L. Berio: *Sequenza II* (Example 6-d)
J. Druckman: *Windows*
V. Globokar: *Voie*
M. D. Levy: *Kyros*

V. Persichetti: *Sinfonia: Janiculum*
J. Serebrier: *Colores Mágicos*
T. Takemitsu: *Eucalypts (I)*

Another, and closely related, effect entails dampening a single string with a finger of one hand—or a group of contiguous strings with the flat hand—close to the soundboard while playing with the other hand in normal position. This effect,

MUTING   23

termed "xylophonic sounds" in the Salzedo lexicon, appears in the following scores:

L. Berio: *Circles; Sequenza II*
  (Example 6-a)
P. Boulez: *Le Soleil des Eaux*
V. Globokar: *Voie*
H. Holliger: *Glühende Rätsel*
B. Jolas: *Tranche pour harpe seule*

M. Kagel: *Anagrama; Sonant*
  (Example 13-c)
W. Kotonski: *Concerto per quattro*
B. Rands: *Formants 1*
C. Salzedo: *Sonata for Harp and Piano*

Example 6
Luciano Berio: from *Sequenza II* (p. 4)

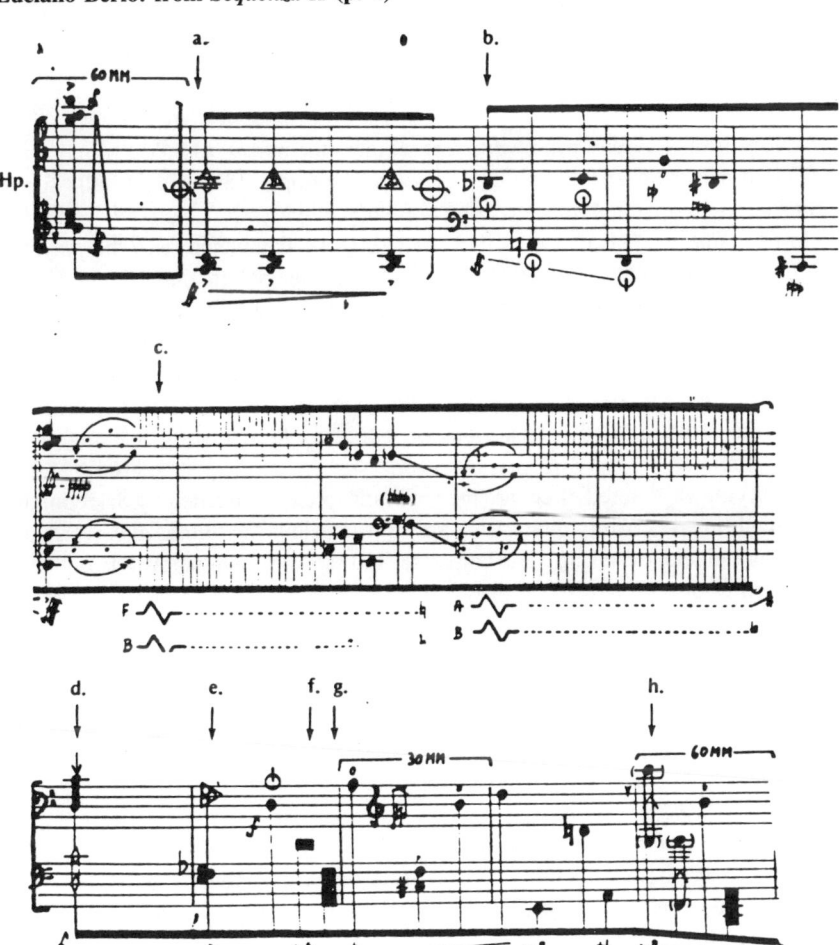

© Copyright 1965 by Universal Edition (London) Ltd., London. All rights reserved. Used by permission of European American Music Distributors Corporation, sole U.S. and Canadian agent for Universal Edition (London) Ltd.

Conversely, the harp strings can be muffled at their midpoint and plucked near to the soundboard, *a la guitarra:*

L. Berio: *Chemins I; Sequenza II* (Example 6-e)
B. Rands: *Formants 1*
T. Takemitsu: *Eucalypts (I)*

A harp string may also be dampened with the fingernail pressed against it; when the string is plucked by the other hand, it vibrates against the nail, producing a faint metallic "buzz." This technique is required in:

S. Bussotti: *Fragmentations; Memoria*
M. Kagel: *Sonant*
T. de Leeuw: *The Four Seasons*
R. Lomon: *Celebrations*

B. Rands: *Formants 1*
B. Van Nostrand: *Ventilation Manual*
I. Xenakis: *ST/10-1, 080262*

Donald Erb (in *Symphony of Overtures*) requires the harpist to hold a tuning fork against a vibrating string, while in *Sonant* (Example 13-t) Kagel calls for a drumstick and a triangle beater to be similarly employed.

In the same work Kagel asks that the strings be dampened with the player's whole arm, laid flat, while the other hand is engaged in playing. In Heinz Holliger's *Siebengesang* the harpist muffles the strings with his flat left hand while sliding across the strings with a plectrum in the right hand. In Gilbert Amy's *Trajectoires* the player dampens the strings with the palm while striking them with a triangle beater. A final unorthodox muting action: certain of the harp strings are to be muffled with a block of wood in *The Crown of Ariadne* of R. Murray Schafer.

Qualifying as a muted effect are the "vibrant sounds" invented by Salzedo: the left thumb presses firmly against the string just below the tuning pins while the right hand plucks the string. The composer's notation shown below has not been improved upon:

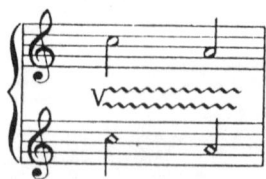

In addition to the muting procedures just discussed, the normal timbre of the harp can be altered by threading a piece of tissue paper (about ¾" wide) or a thin ribbon through the plastic strings. The tone thus created is remarkably akin to that of the harpsichord or, less obviously perhaps, of the lute. This type of muting is required in Sylvano Bussotti's *Fragmentations,* in George Crumb's *Ancient Voices of Children,* and in Edgard Varèse's *Ameriques.* The same effect can be produced by threading a strip of newspaper through the strings, as stipulated in Karen Ervin's *Five Little Pieces*. Szalonek asks that six narrow strips of cardboard be pressed on the harp strings in his *Three Sketches,* while an even more unorthodox request is made by Donald Wilson in *Decisions, Decisions!:* an IBM or a plastic credit card is to be inserted between certain contiguous strings so as to muffle their normal vibrations.

Muting the guitar is accomplished in two ways: first, by placing the right-hand heel on the strings at the bridge; second, by placing a soft cloth or piece of foam rubber under the strings. These muting actions are designated by terms that may confuse the nonguitarist composer: "pizzicato," which customarily means to pluck a string, and "étouffé," which to a harpist or percussionist means to muffle the instrument's vibrations.

KEYBOARD INSTRUMENTS

Of the several keyboard instruments, only the piano and the harpsichord can be mechanically muted so as to alter the natural sound of the instrument. There are several ways in which the alteration of piano tone-color can be accomplished: first, the pianist dampens the string(s) with the fingertips or the palm of one hand while playing on the keys with the other hand. By means of varying pressures on the string the sound can be further modified: a very light finger pressure changes the tone minimally, while a firm and heavy pressure results in a dead, thudding tone ("bass drum effect" on the very lowest strings). There are far too many contemporary works utilizing these muting procedures to justify a complete individual listing, but a few might be mentioned:

E. Brown: *Hodograph I; Music for Cello and Piano*
D. Burge: *Aeolian Music*
S. Bussotti: *Couple; Il Nudo*
J. Cage: *Concert for Piano and Orchestra*
F. Cerha: *Formation et Solution*
S. Cervetti: *Five Episodes; Six Sequences for Dance*
B. Childs: *Jack's New Bag*
G. Crumb: *Echoes of Time and the River; Eleven Echoes of Autumn*
L. Ferrari: *Société II*
R. L. Finney: *Divertissement*
L. Foss: *Echoi*
A. Gilbert: *Sonata No. 2*
M. Ishii: *Aphorismen*
M. Kagel: *Anagrama; Transición II*
H. Lazarof: *Textures*
B. Maderna: *Oboe Concerto III*
H. Pousseur: *Honeyrêves*
B. Rands: *Espressione IV; Wildtrack 1*
R. Reynolds: *Blind Men; The Emperor of Ice Cream*
B. Schäffer: *Modell III*
E. Schwartz: *Music for Prince Albert*
A. de la Vega: *Structures for Piano and String Quartet*

Composers have often requested a gradual increase or decrease of finger pressure on the string while the key is being depressed (as in Gilbert's *Sonata No. 2*). Not infrequently they have specified exact areas of the strings where the fingers or flat hand are to be placed. A slight variation of this technique is stipulated by Crumb in his *A Little Suite for Christmas:* the pianist mutes certain strings with the hand turned sideways. Recent scores that illustrate these various actions include:

1. At the end of the string

J. Cage: *Pastorale for Piano Solo*
G. Crumb: *Echoes of Time and the River; Makrokosmos—Vol. 1*

2. Near the pinboard (pegs, nut)

W. Albright: *Pianoagogo*
D. Burge: *Aeolian Music*

G. Crumb: *Eleven Echoes of Autumn*
H. Hartwell: *Soul Piece*

3. Close to the dampers

M. Finnissy: *As When Upon a Tranced Summer Night*
A. Lanza: *Plectros II*

4. Between the hammers (dampers) and the pegs (pinboard)

D. Cope: *Parallax*
D. Erb: *The Seventh Trumpet*

5. Near the bridge

E. Brown: *From Here*
F. Cerha: *Spiegel II*
Chou Wen-chung: *Cursive*

W. Hellermann: *Formata*
R. Reynolds: *Mosaic; Quick are the Mouths of Earth*

    A piano string (or series of contiguous strings) can also be finger-muted *after* the key has been depressed or struck with the sustaining pedal held down (as in William Albright's *Pianoagogo,* Kagel's *Anagrama* and Joel Spiegelman's *Morsels*). In Christian Wolff's *Duet I* the composer asks that the pianist mute a certain string with his finger but at the same time allow the fingernail to lightly touch an adjacent string; when the key of this string is struck, the resulting vibration against the nail creates a delicate buzzing.
    Muting the piano strings in a somewhat different manner is accomplished by preperformance preparation: the player inserts such objects as screws, bolts, nuts, nails, erasers or rubber wedges, paper clips, pencils, coins, and the like, between certain preselected strings. John Cage, of course, is the uncontested pioneer in the field of "prepared piano" (in *Amores* and other early pieces).[2] Later composers, including those listed below, have been quick to adapt the technique to their own peculiar requirements:

L. Austin: *Accidents*
Z. Bargielski: *Parades*
D. Bedford: *Piano Piece 2*
B. Childs: *Jack's New Bag*
L. Hiller: *Machine Music*
T. Mayuzumi: *Pieces for Prepared Piano and Strings* (Example 7)

C. Miereanu: *Finis Coronet Opus*
S. Montague: *At the white edge of phrygia*
A. Pärt: *Tabula Rosa*
E. Schwartz: *Music for Napoleon and Beethoven*
C. Wolff: *Suite 1 for Prepared Piano*

Example 7
Toshiro Mayuzumi: from *Pieces for Prepared Piano and Strings* **(p. 3)**

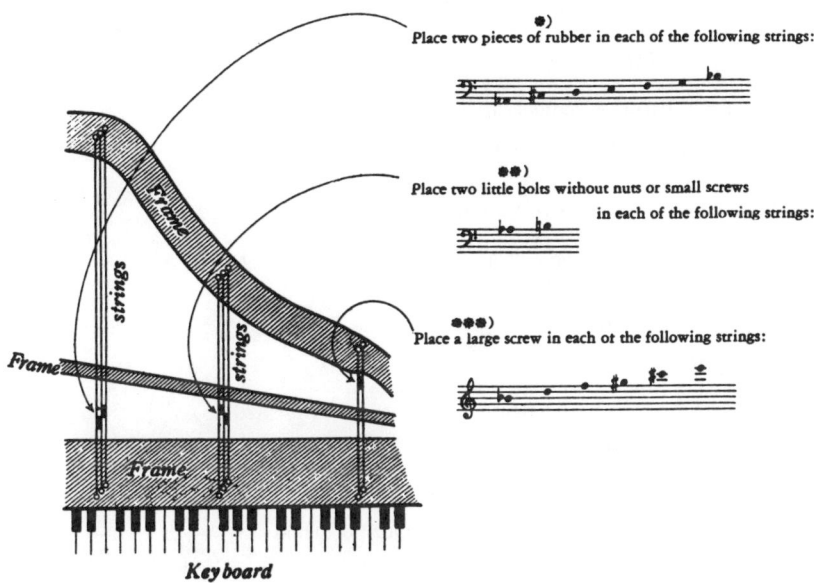

© Copyright 1958 by C. F. Peters Corporation. Reprinted by permission of the publisher.

A curious effect: at one point in Lejaren Hiller's work a rubber band is to be tied around several of the low strings, thus muting them when the corresponding keys are struck; at the same time, one hand stretches the rubber band and lets it snap against the strings, creating an explosive crack.

A specialized version of prepared piano is the so-called "tack piano." As used by Lou Harrison in his *Concerto in Slendro* and *Suite for Violin, Piano and Small Orchestra,* this is an ordinary upright having thumbtacks driven into the felt hammers; the resulting sound is remarkably akin to that of the harpsichord. On the other hand, the "Luthéal" piano, as required in Maurice Ravel's opera, *L'enfant et les sortilèges* and by Maurice Delannoy in his *Grande Suite de la Pantoufle de Vair,* is a standard model having a strip of tissue paper woven through the strings to modify their normal resonance. The sound is somewhat like that of a clavichord.

Any piano string, or group of strings, can also be muted by placing various objects on top of the string(s). The following list is testimony to the vanguardist's sonic imagination:

1. A pad or soft cloth, such as a wadded-up handkerchief

A. Gilbert: *Sonata No. 2*
G. Ligeti: *Nouvelles Aventures*

2. A thick towel

A. Janson: *Canon*

3. A felt or rubber mat

M. Kagel: *Transición II*

4. A strip of paper or cardboard

G. Crumb: *Music for a Summer Evening*
A. Gilbert: *Sonata No. 2*
R. Reynolds: *The Emperor of Ice Cream*

5. A strip (or several strips) of adhesive, masking, or duct tape

D. Erb: *The Seventh Trumpet*
W. Szalonek: *Proporzioni II*
R. Zupko: *Fixations*

6. Sticks of plasticine, laid lightly on the strings or pressed down

K. Serocki: *Fantasmagoria*
W. Szalonek: *Mutanza per pianoforte*

7. A pencil, dowel, drumstick, or small piece of wood

B. Childs: *Nonet*
G. Crumb: *Night Music I*
L. Ferrari: *Société II*

8. A coin or small piece of metal

B. Childs: *Jack's New Bag*

9. A common artgum eraser

B. Childs: *Music for Singer*

10. A tambourine

G. Crumb: *Echoes of Time and the River*

11. A heavy hardbound book

T. Antoniou: *Lyrics*
D. Cope: *Parallax*

12. a 7"–8" pocket comb

D. Cope: *Parallax*

13. Four milk bottles, side by side, about an inch apart

D. Bedford: *Piano Piece 2*

In his orchestral work *The Jerusalem Chagall Windows*, Jacob Gilboa directs the pianist to prepare the strings of the lowest section by covering them with a number of antique cymbals; later he places a single large cymbal on the strings, and also several small pieces of metal—presumably bolts or screws. Szalonek in *Proporzioni II* requires a metal rod (triangle beater) to be laid across the strings, as well as wood slabs and iron chains, requirements partially duplicated in Chou Wen-chung's *Cursive* for flute and piano. And in Werner Heider's *-einander,* the piano strings are to be fitted with several rulers (or strips made of plastic or celluloid); when the keys are struck, a clashing (though muted) sound is produced. The same device is also required by Roger Reynolds in his *Mosaic.*

Other players in an ensemble are sometimes directed to "prepare" the piano strings while the pianist is playing at the keyboard. In *Music for Napoleon and Beethoven,* Elliott Schwartz asks the trumpet soloist to alternate playing improvisatory sections on his instrument with preparing the piano strings. He stands in the curve of the piano to play and, during moments of rest, inserts between certain strings a number of objects previously placed in a container inside the piano.

STRINGS

Composers of the past had no need to call for different types of mutes for the string instruments. There was basically only one kind in general use, usually made of ebony. Today, however, the composer can requisition a number of dissimilar mute types; these are not as numerous, of course, as are available to brass players, but are still varied enough to satisfy the composer's penchant for subtle string tone modification. They include: three-pronged mutes made of aluminum, ebony, or rosewood; mutes made of leather ("Meroff"), plastic ("Menuhin"), metal ("Tonwolf"), rubber ("Tourte"), and so-called "slide-on" mutes. The timbral differences created by these assorted agents can only be fully evaluated by personal contact with experienced string players and performance demonstration.

Several curious stringed instrument muting effects have recently been devised by orchestrators of experimental music; these are as follows:

1. Violins and violas place their mutes *behind* rather than on the bridge

J. Rodrigo: *Zarabanda Lejana y Villancico*

2. The left-hand fingers press the strings down to the fingerboard, deadening the normal resonance, whether played arco or *col legno,* as in:

E. Brown: *String Quartet*   F. Miroglio: *Réfractions*
L. Hiller: *String Quartet No. 5* K. M-Nazar: *Variazioni concertanti*

3. A "skittering" effect is produced by deadening the strings as just described and bouncing the bow *col legno battuto,* from high on the fingerboard to the bridge

M. Colgrass: *As Quiet As* (Example 8)

Example 8
Michael Colgrass: from *As Quiet As* (p. 20)

*Strings: skittering effect: jeté col legno batt. from fingerboard to bridge (deaden strings).

© Copyright 1969 by MCA MUSIC PUBLISHING, A Division of MCA INC., 1755 Broadway, New York, NY 10019. International Copyright Secured. All Rights Reserved, MCA MUSIC PUBLISHING.

4. The strings, muffled by grasping them with the left-hand fingers, are played upon either arco or *col legno*

D. Wilson: *Doubles*

5. The doublebass strings are muted by laying the left-hand palm across them

G. Read: *Diabolic Dialogue*

6. A doublebass mute is placed on the cello strings between the bridge and the end of the fingerboard; the player bows on either side of the mute—that is to say, on either the upper or the lower part of the string

M. von Biel: *1. Quartett*

That one genius of orchestration can easily appropriate an instrumentational device from another master orchestrator is verified by the extraordinary technique used by Richard Strauss in *Salome:* a solo doublebass player pinches the G-string between his thumb and forefinger while bowing a high B♭ with short, violent bow strokes. Called the "Langlois" effect after the Italian performer who invented it, this was commented upon by Hector Berlioz in his pioneering instrumentation treatise—enlarged and revised, of course, by Strauss in later years.

MUTING

More recently this device has been utilized by both Ligeti in his *Requiem* and by Sydney Hodkinson in *November Voices*. The latter composer directs the doublebass player to pinch both the D- and G-strings with thumb and forefinger, leaving only enough room on the two strings for the bow.

SPATIAL MUTING

Distance can also soften and muffle normal instrumental tone, an acoustical fact that many composers have applied to their sonic requirements. All instruments, singly or collectively, can be stationed off-stage or in remote parts of the auditorium to provide distant ("lontano") effects. Although the basic timbre of an instrument is not drastically altered by remote placement, it is attenuated and softened to a considerable degree. Thus offstage positioning of instruments produces a different, but entirely viable, kind of muting.[3]

Twentieth-century works that have called for this procedure include the following, categorized by orchestral section:

Woodwinds

D. Burge: *Sources III* (clarinet)
G. Crumb: *Echoes of Time and the River* (flutes; clarinets)
M. Gould: *Family Album* (clarinet)
P. Graener: *Flute of Sanssouci* (flute)
O. Knussen: *Masks* (flute)

S. Prokofiev: *Alexander Nevsky* (oboe, English horn)
R. M. Schafer: *East* (oboes, clarinets, bassoons)
G. Schuller: *Seven Studies on Themes of Paul Klee* (flute)

Brasses

G. Crumb: *Echoes of Time and the River* (horns; trumpets; trombones)
M. Gould: *Family Album* (horn; trumpet; trombone)
P. Hindemith: *When lilacs last in the door-yard bloom'd* (Army bugle)
C. Ives: *The Unanswered Question* (trumpet)

S. Prokofiev: *Alexander Nevsky* (trumpet, trombone)
M. Ravel: *Daphnis et Chloé* (horn, trumpet)
E. Schelling: *A Victory Ball* (trumpet)
J. Serebrier: *Momento Psicologico* (trumpet)
P. Standford: *Notte* (horns)

Percussion

G. Crumb: *Echoes of Time and the River* (crotales; glockenspiel plates; suspended cymbals; tam-tams).
D. E. Ingelbrecht: *Rapsodie de Printemps* (triangle)

Plucked and keyboard instruments

G. Crumb: *Echoes of Time and the River* (mandolin)
G. Crumb: *Night of the Four Moons* (banjo)

L. Foss: *Baroque Variations* (harpsichord)
D. E. Ingelbrecht: *Rapsodie de Printemps* (harmonium)

Strings

H. Brant: *Voyage Four* (all strings)
P. Hindemith: *Symphonia Serena* (solo violin; solo viola)

D. E. Ingelbrecht: *Rapsodie de Printemps* (solo viola)
H. Tircuit: *String Quartet No. 3* (all strings)

The ultimate in spatial alteration of instrumental timbre occurs in Henry Brant's *Antiphony One;* the full orchestra is divided into five groups, each to be situated in a different part of the concert space. The combined sonic effect is perhaps more stereophonic than an illusion of distance muting. The visual element of the dispersed orchestra, furthermore, adds an unmistakable dimension to the performance of Brant's work.

It is tempting to speculate on further novel, as yet undiscovered, methods of muting the various instruments. Whatever may be brought to light, we may be sure that our experimental and adventurous composers will do their part in exploiting the new techniques.

NOTES

1. Sheridon Stokes and Richard Condon, *Special Effects for Flute* (Culver City: Trio Associates, 1970).
2. A comprehensive and amply illustrated discussion of piano interior preparation will be found in Richard Bunger's *The Well-Prepared Piano*.
3. Henry Brant's article in *Contemporary Composers on Contemporary Music* on aspects of spatial composition is especially informative.

3

GLISSANDI

WOODWINDS AND BRASSES

As glissando techniques in woodwind and brass instrument scoring have been fairly common since Mahler's time, they cannot qualify as indubitably "new" devices; their use, however, has become so prevalent in contemporary orchestration and their variants so extensive that special mention must be accorded this particular instrumental technique.

Glissandi are normally achieved on wind instruments through the tightening or relaxing of the embouchure, generally specified by composers and performers as "lip glissandi." Among many works relying on this effect one might cite:

I. Bazelon: *Sound Dreams*
D. Bedford: *Music for Albion Moonlight* (Example 9)
Chou Wen-chung: *Pian*
B. Ferneyhough: *Unity Capsule* (Example 28)
R. L. Finney: *Divertissement*
V. Globokar: *Atemstudie für Oboe*
J. Harvey: *Inner Light II*
S. Hodkinson: *Fresco*
D. Martino: *Strata*
D. Reck: *Blues and Screamer; Five Studies for Tuba Alone*

By rolling the mouthpiece into the upper lip, flutists can somewhat extend the range of lip glissandi ("bends"), a directive specified in George Rochberg's *Apocalyptica* and Chou Wen-chung's *Cursive,* for example. Also, by removing the head-joint and inserting a finger in the tubing, then slowly removing it while blowing, one can get an extended glissando from $g\sharp^2$ down to b^1. This version of glissando was required by Boguslaw Schäffer in his *Scultura*. John Casken in *Music for the Crabbing Sun* (intriguing title!) requires the flutist to glissando a series of harmonics, with the lips tight.

The so-called "key glissando" is achieved on the flute by a gradual and smooth alteration of finger position, an effect more fully described in Robert Dick's *The Other Flute,* and effectively used in Brian Ferneyhough's *Unity Capsule.*

Example 9 David Bedford: from *Music for Albion Moonlight* (p. 18)

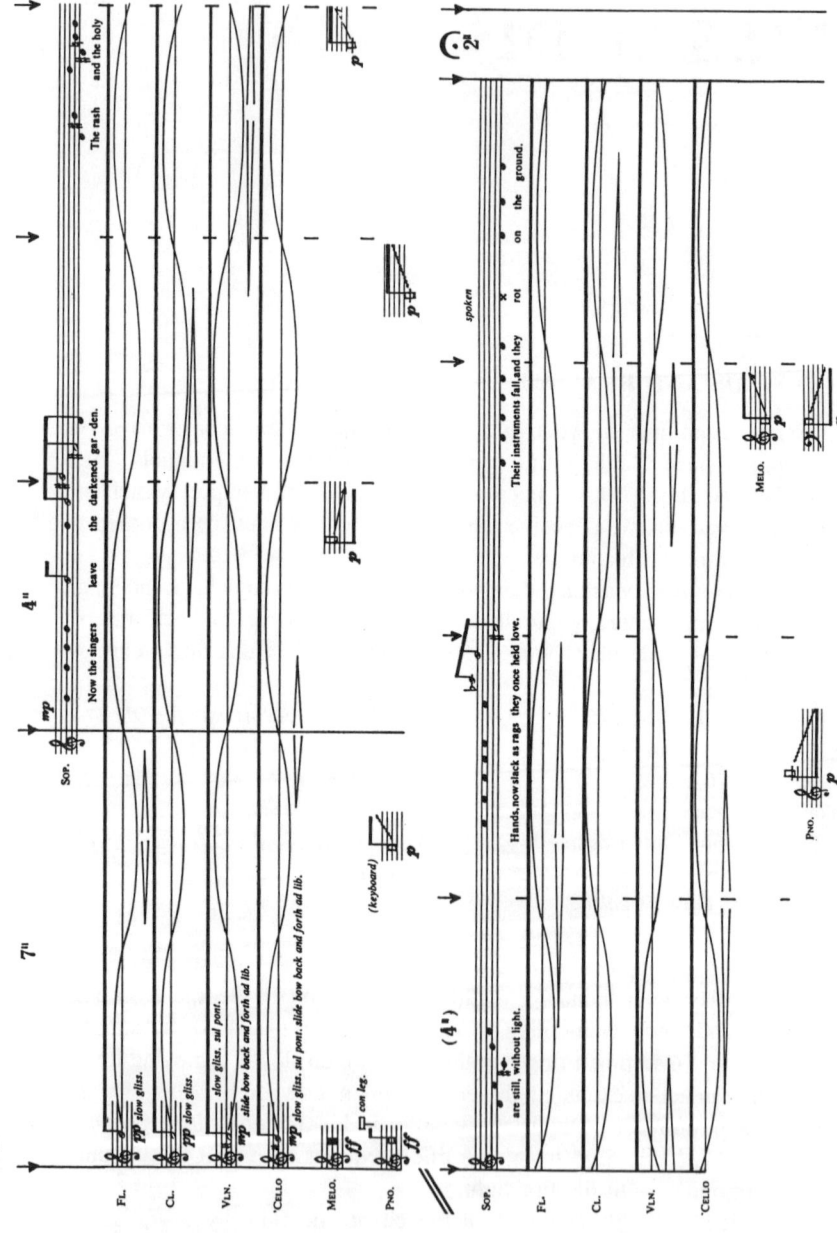

Poem—"Lament for the Makers of Songs" from *Red Wine and Yellow Hair*. Copyright 1949 by New Directions. Printed by permission. © Copyright 1966 by Universal Edition (London) Ltd., London. All rights reserved. Used by permission of European American Music Distributors Corporation, sole U.S. and Canadian agent for Universal Edition, London.

GLISSANDI

It is quite common for brass players to create a glissando over the harmonic series of a given fundamental, analogous to the string player's glissando on natural harmonics—the latter a favorite instrumentational device of Ravel and Stravinsky. A few recently published scores that call for the brass version of harmonic glissandi include:

J. Bark, F. Rabe: *Bolos*
J. Druckman: *Animus 1*
K. Huber: *Alveare vernat*

K. Kroeger: *Toccata for Clarinet, Trombone and Percussion*
G. Rochberg: *Tableaux*
B. A. Zimmermann: *Stille und Umkehr*

Another fairly common and characteristic brass technique is the half-valve glissando on horn, trumpet, or tuba, achieved by pushing down the required valves only half-way while blowing:

M. Ellis: *Mutations* (Example 10)
G. Schuller: *American Triptych; Spectra*
E. Schwartz: *Music for Napoleon and Beethoven; Rip*

Example 10
Merrill Ellis: from *Mutations* (p. 7)

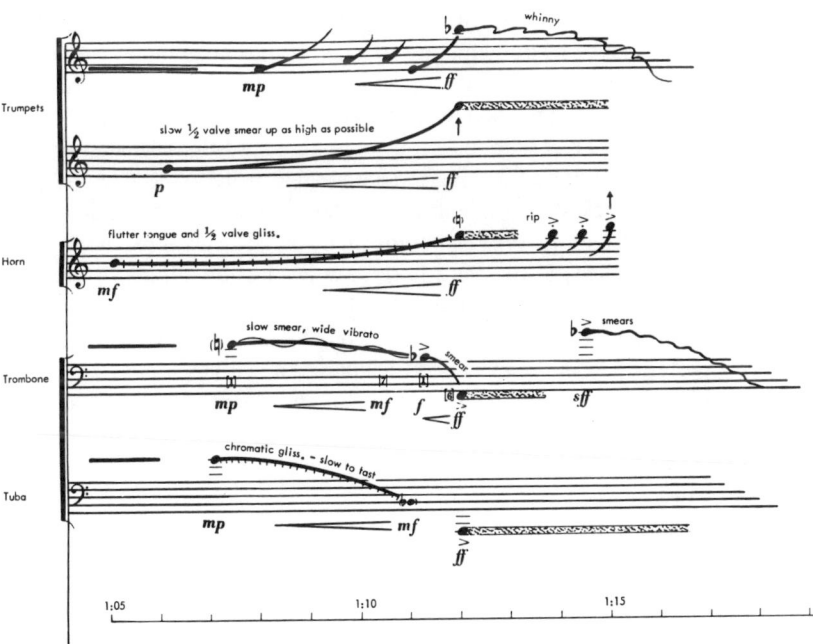

Copyright © 1972 Shawnee Press, Inc. International Copyright Secured. All Rights Reserved. Used by Permission.

An uneven glissando on the horn, effectuated by moving all the valves rapidly and randomly, is a technique stipulated in *Anatomy* by Richard Barrett.

In David Reck's *Five Studies for Tuba Alone* the composer calls for the player to produce a "bellowing" lip glissando. Other variants of the technique, resulting from combined lip, fingering, or slide manipulation are those staples of jazz performance—"rips," "smears," "squeals," "whinnies," and the like.[1] No longer, of course, are these techniques the exclusive province of jazz and popular expression; they are frequently incorporated into symphonic and chamber scores, even by some composers basically antipathetic to the more commercial forms of contemporary music:

B. Childs: *Jack's New Bag; Nonet*
M. Colgrass: *As Quiet As*
M. Ellis: *Mutations* (Example 10)
D. Erb: *Symphony of Overtures*
R. L. Finney: *Divertissement*
M. Gould: *Jekyll and Hyde Variations*
A. Jolivet: *Suite Transocéane*
W. Kotonski: *Midsummer*

G. Rochberg: *Tableaux*
G. Schuller: *Journey into Jazz; Seven Studies on Themes of Paul Klee*
E. Schwartz: *Music for Napoleon and Beethoven; Rip*
K. Stockhausen: *Adieu*
E. Varèse: *Arcana; Ecuatorial*

PERCUSSION

Conventional glissandi on timpani, first exploited by Béla Bartók, and glissandi on the pitched mallet instruments are too familiar to contemporary orchestrators to require further explication. Less conventional, and surprisingly effective, is the one-plate glissando available on glockenspiel or vibraphone. To achieve this effect the player with his left hand holds a hard-tipped mallet against the plate to be struck, lightly touching the metal about a half-inch from its end. When the plate is struck with a mallet in the player's other hand, the left-hand mallet is slowly moved to the very end of the metal bar. The aural result is a half-step bending of the pitch, always at a fairly low level of amplitude, it must be stressed. This device is used prominently in Crumb's *Echoes of Time and the River* and in George Rochberg's *Tableaux*. For obvious reasons the technique cannot be transferred to the wooden bars of marimba or xylophone.

A simulation of pitch "bend" can, surprisingly, be obtained on a clashed pair of cymbals or crotales; after being struck together the two plates are rapidly shaken in the air, resulting in a perceptible oscillation of frequency (as in the Crumb work just cited).

Qualifying perhaps more as a percussive noise-effect than as a genuine glissando variant is a rapid sweep with a hard mallet or wood stick over the resonators (metal tubes) of vibraphone and marimba; this stipulation appears in:

L. Austin: *The Maze*
F. Miroglio: *Réfractions*

W. Russell: *Fugue for Eight Percussion Instruments*
K. Serocki: *Continuum; Segmenti*

Example 11
Larry Austin: from *The Maze* (p. 21)

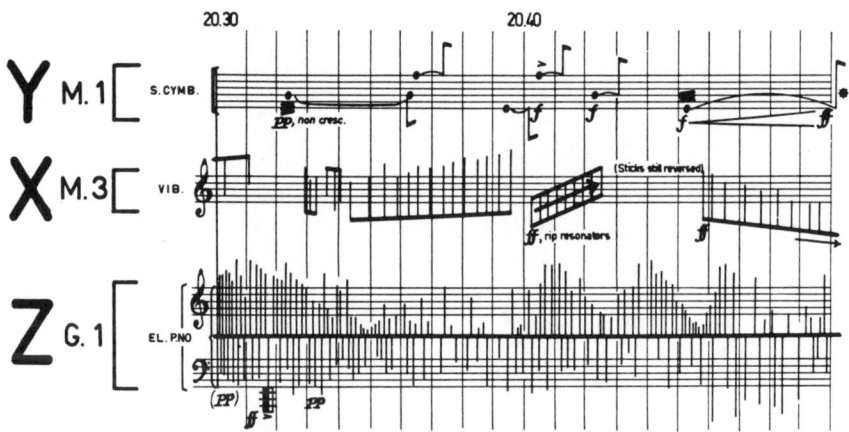

© Copyright 1967, SOURCE, Vol. 1, No. 1, January, 1967. By permission.

A point of notational interest is the comparison between Austin's symbology in *The Maze* (Example 11) and that favored by Serocki in *Continuum* for a resonator glissando (Example 12).

Whereas idiophone glissandi with differently headed mallets are extremely common in modern scores, less prevalent are glissandi with the backs of the fingernails across the metal plates of glockenspiel and vibraphone (as requested in Reginald Smith Brindle's *Orion M. 42,* for example). A number of vanguardists have designated that the entire range of the various idiophones be rubbed in ascending or descending spiral patterns with precisely specified stick types—wood, metal, or plastic mallets, wirebrushes, and so on:

L. Foss: *Fragments of Archilochos*
R. Reynolds: *Quick are the Mouths of Earth*
K. Serocki: *Continuum* (Example 12); *Segmenti*

Simultaneous "black-key" and "white-key" glissandi are by now clichés of contemporary percussion scoring, and their primary interest is notational rather than technical (see Example 12). In parallel or in contrary direction, such chromatic glissandi are prominently displayed in the following recent scores:

T. Baird: *Exhortation*
J. Barraqué: *Chant après chant*
L. Berio: *Circles*
E. Brown: *Available Forms 1*
G. Crumb: *Echoes of Time and the River; Night Music I*

L. Foss: *Fragments of Archilochos*
J. Gilboa: *The Jerusalem Chagall Windows*
A. Jolivet: *Piano Concerto*
M. Kagel: *Anagrama*
F. Miroglio: *Réfractions*

Example 12
Kazimierz Serocki: from *Continuum* **(p. 9)**

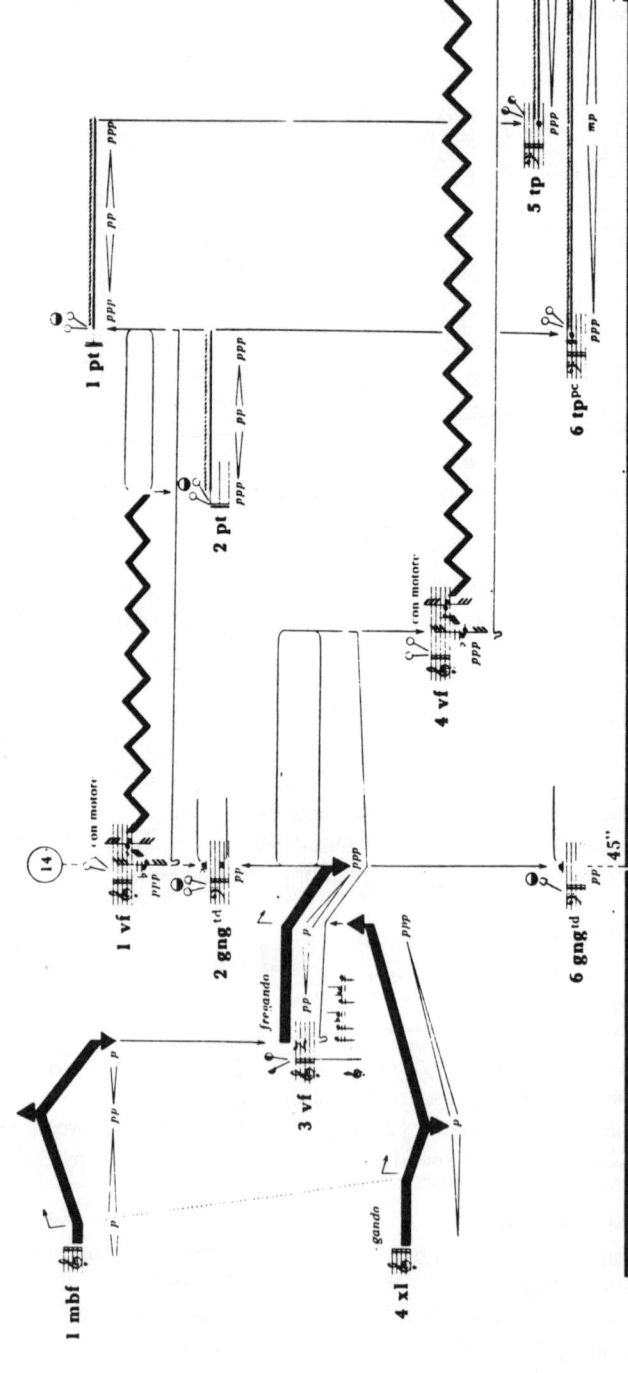

© Copyright 1968 by Moeck Verlag. Abdruck mit Genehmigung des Moeck Verlags, D-31, Celle.

GLISSANDI

A. Paccagnini: *Musica da Camera*
B. Rands: *Actions for six*
G. Read: *Galactic Novae*
R. Reynolds: *Quick are the Mouths of Earth; Wedge*
K. Serocki: *Fantasmagoria: Segmenti*
K. Stockhausen: *Kontakte; Zyklus*

A glissando across the chime tubes is ordinarily effectuated with the chime mallet or a hard stick, but in his *Concerto lirico per orchestra* Robert Wittinger calls for four triangle beaters, presumably two in each hand.

Not a true glissando but merely a simulation is achieved on the various drumheads (timpani, tenor drum, tom-toms, and the like) by the player exerting or relaxing pressure on the membrane with the hand or elbow while striking. For an example of this technique see *Concatenations* by George Wilson.

Though it cannot be considered a glissando in the ordinary sense of the term, Kagel's directive in *Sonant* to glissando on the snares of a snare drum deserves mention. The effect is achieved by sliding the stick across the taut snares, the drum turned upside down.

HARP AND OTHER PLUCKED INSTRUMENTS

Normally, harp glissandi are played with the fingers of either hand, but one of the earliest experiments of Carlos Salzedo was to slide on the strings with the fingernails—an effect he picturesquely termed "falling hail." As with many of Salzedo's inventions, this device appears frequently in today's scores, including:

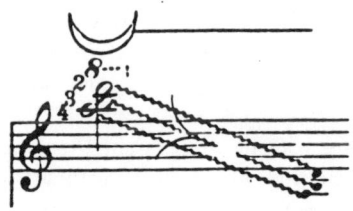

L. Berio: *Chemins II; Sequenza II*
D. Eberhard: *"Especially . . ."*
R. Felciano: *Background Music*
S. Hodkinson: *November Voices*
B. Jolas: *Tranche pour harpe seule*
M. Kagel: *Sonant*
M. Kelemen: *Changeant*
P. Méfano: *Paraboles*
B. Rands: *Wildtrack 1*
G. Read: *Haiku Seasons*
C. Salzedo: *Sonata for Harp and Piano*
G. Schuller: *Spectra*
B. Van Nostrand: *Ventilation Manual*
E. Varèse: *Offrandes*
Z. Wiszniewski: *Tre pezzi della tradizione*

Played close to the soundboard, the nail glissando becomes a "xyloflux" in Salzedo's terminology. Parenthetically, one might mention that he terms an ordinary glissando a "flux"; played close to the soundboard, it is an "oboic flux." Recent scores that contain this latter technique include:

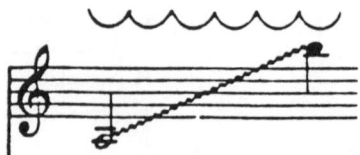

H. Gorecki: *Monologhi*
P. Méfano: *Paraboles*

G. Read: *Sonoric Fantasia No. 3*
C. Salzedo: Various solo harp works

In addition to fingernail glissandi, the strings of the instrument may be stroked or rubbed with the following:

1. The flat fingers

H. W. Henze: *Being Beauteous*
B. Rands: *Formants I*

G. Read: *Haiku Seasons*
K. Serocki: *Niobe; Segmenti*

2. The fingernails

S. Matsushita: *Fresque sonore*

3. The palm or flat hand (cluster effect)

G. Becker: *Moirologhi*
L. Berio: *Sequenza II* (Example 6-g)
S. Bussotti: *Fragmentations*
H. Gorecki: *Monologhi*
R. Haubenstock-Ramati: *Petite musique de nuit; Séquences*
M. D. Levy: *Kyros*

S. Matsushita: *Fresque sonore*
K. Penderecki: *Dimensions of Time and Silence*
B. Rands: *Actions for six*
G. Read: *Haiku Seasons*
Z. Wiszniewski: *Tre pezzi della tradizione*

Salzedo called rubbing with the fingers an "Aeolian tremolo" and with the palm pressing against the strings an "Aeolian rustling." This action is sometimes termed a "flutter" or a "palm" glissando, and is prominently featured in Toru Takemitsu's *Star Isle*. Related to this last technique is the "rolling surf" effect in which a glissando, at a slow tempo, is played with all the fingers bunched together, the normally unused little finger included. In addition to appearing in many of Salzedo's own works, the device has been requisitioned by:

GLISSANDI   **41**

    M. Colgrass: *Déja vu*　　　　　　B. Rands: *Formants 1*
    D. Eberhard: *"Especially . . ."*　　　K. Serocki: *Niobe*

More conventional variants are simultaneous upward and downward glissandi, usually encompassing the entire instrument range; as precise beginning and ending pitches are not important, composers usually content themselves with writing stems attached to arrow heads below and above the two staves. See, for instance:

    K. Serocki: *Segmenti; Symphonic Frescoes*
    C. Surinach: *Feria Mágica; Melorhythmic Melodramas*
    P. Turok: *Chartres West*

Also frequently used in avant-garde scores are Salzedo's "gushing chords," which are very rapid and short-range bursts of glissandi:

    S. Barber: *Souvenirs*　　　　　　　　C. Surinach: *Feria Mágica;*
    L. Berio: *Sequenza II* (Example 6-h)　　　*Melorhythmic Melodramas*
    J. Serebrier: *Colores Mágicos*

"Gushing chords" can also be played with the thumb fingernail, an action for which Salzedo devised the following notation:

More esoteric glissandi techniques include the following actions:

1. Rapid vertical gliding up on several adjacent wire bass strings with the flat hand ("whistling sounds" in the Salzedo harp manual)

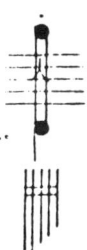

T. Antoniou: *Violin Concerto*
L. Berio: *Chemins I; Sequenza II*
S. Bussotti: *Fragmentations; Memoria*
E. Denisov: *Romantische Musik*
D. Erb: *Symphony of Overtures*
R. Felciano: *Background Music*
A. Ginastera: *Bomarzo Cantata*
S. Hodkinson: *November Voices*
B. Jolas: *Tranche pour harpe seule*

M. Kagel: *Anagrama; Sonant*
M. Kelemen: *Changeant*
A. Lanzi: *Quattro pezzi per arpa*
B. Rands: *Actions for six*
G. Read: *Sonoric Fantasia No. 3; Villon*
T. Takemitsu: *Eucalypts (I)*
D. Wilson: *Decisions, Decisions!*

2. Vertical sliding on the string(s) with the fingernail(s), either up from the soundboard to as high as the tuning pins, or the reverse, usually on the low wire strings

M. Kagel: *Sonant* (Example 13-h)

3. Same action, with a mallet or stick

D. Erb: *The Seventh Trumpet*
M. Kagel: *Sonant* (Example 13-m)

4. Same action, with a nail file

R. Felciano: *Background Music*

5. Same action, with the metal end of the tuning key (Salzedo's "fluidic glissando"), and notated as shown below

B. Beerman: *Polygraph VI*
L. Berio: *Chamber Music*
E. Brown: *Times Five*
S. Bussotti: *Fragmentations*
P. M. Davies: *Revelation and Fall*
J. Druckman: *Windows*
D. Erb: *Concerto for Solo Percussionist; The Seventh Trumpet* (Example 41)
R. Felciano: *Background Music*
L. Foss: *Orpheus*
S. Hodkinson: *November Voices*
H. Holliger: *Glühende Rätsel*

M. Kagel: *Sonant* (Example 13-g)
M. Kelemen: *Changeant; Olifant*
R. Kuhl: *Dreams Before Dark*
R. Loman: *Celebrations*
A. Mellnäs: *Transparence per orchestra*
F. Miroglio: *Réseaux pour harpe et orchestre*
G. Read: *Haiku Seasons*
R. M. Schafer: *The Crown of Ariadne*
L. Schidlowski: *Koloth*
T-t. Tiêt: *Ngũ Hãnh II*
D. Wilson: *Decisions, Decisions!*

6. Same action with a coin

R. M. Schafer: *The Crown of Ariadne*

Example 13
Mauricio Kagel: from *Sonant (Faites votre jeu ii)*

© Copyright 1964 by Henry Litolff's Verlag. Sole selling agents C. F. Peters Corporation, New York. Reprinted by permission of the publisher.

7. Same action with a chisel

G. Crumb: *Madrigals—Book I*

8. Same action with a plastic knife having a serrated edge

C. J. Sheppard: *Garden of Earthly Delights*

A metal string may also be scraped vertically with the back of a fingernail. In Crumb's *Ancient Voices of Children* the harpist is directed to make a single stroke along the string, lightly and rapidly, creating a nasal and whistling sound which is immediately to be muffled by touching the string with the other hand.

In addition to the glissandi variants just described, the harp strings may be rubbed or stroked horizontally with the following objects:

1. A metal (wire) brush

H. W. Henze: *Heliogabalus Imperator; Sinfonia N. 6* (Example 51)
M. Kagel: Sonant (Example 13-b, d)

K. Penderecki: *Anaklasis; The Devils of Loudun*
K. Serocki: *Niobe*

2. An ordinary hairbrush

T. Baird: *Espressioni varianti*
H. Gorecki: *Scontri*
H. W. Henze: *Heliogabalus Imperator; Sinfonia N. 6*

3. A wooden stick, pencil, or metal rod

T. Baird: *Espressioni varianti; Exhortation*
D. Banks: *Tirade*

B. Bartók: *Concerto for Orchestra*
G. Crumb: *Ancient Voices of Children*

4. A small board

H. Gorecki: *Scontri*

5. A plectrum or piece of hard cardboard

P. Maxwell Davies: *Revelation and Fall*
H. Holliger: *Siebengesang*

6. A soft rubber plectrum

R. Moeves: *Et Occidentem Illustra*

Finally, there is Salzedo's "thunder effect"—a rapid and violent glissando limited to the lowest range of the harp, the wire strings being allowed to clash together:

GLISSANDI

L. Berio: *Chemins I; Sequenza II*
S. Bussotti: *Mit einem gewissen sprechenden Ausdruck*
R. Felciano: *Background Music*
S. Hodkinson: *Fresco*
M. Kagel: *Sonant* (Example 13-a)
F. Miroglio: *Réseaux pour harpe et orchestre*
B. Rands: *Actions for six; Formants 1*
E. Raxach: *Paraphrase*
G. Read: *Haiku Seasons*

Among the other plucked instruments, George Crumb's "bottle-neck" technique on mandolin and banjo (discussed on page 202) qualifies as a quasi-do device, as does Sidney Hodkinson's directives to the guitarist in *Fresco* to glissando by means of turning the tuning peg of the string just plucked. In Siegfried Behrend's *Movimenti für Gitarre* the composer calls for a glissando with the right-hand little finger over the frets between two adjacent strings. Other current guitar techniques include the "bending" glissando: the player's left-hand finger stretches the string without moving from first position; the "scratch" glissando, achieved by scraping along the wire bass strings with a left-hand fingernail, and the so-called "Koto" glissando, possible only on instruments that have an added length of string between the bridge and tail-piece—the effect simulating the sound of the Japanese instrument.

KEYBOARD INSTRUMENTS

New glissando effects on the piano involve both the keyboard and the interior strings. Foremost among the several key-glissando procedures is a pitchless sliding over the white keys with the back of the fingernails, designated by:

S. Bussotti: *Couple; Pour Clavier*
B. Rands: *Espressione IV*
R. Reynolds: *Mosaic; Quick are the Mouths of Earth*

The same, with a coin held between the fingers

N. Castiglioni: *Consonante; A Solemn Music II*

A visually dramatic variant of a conventional key glissando occurs in Russell Peck's *Suspended Sentence:* a two-hand glissando effected with the arms crossed ends with a cluster as far up and down the keyboard as the crossed arms can reach.

In both performance techniques and resultant sounds, interior glissandi directly on the piano strings are immensely varied. They can be achieved laterally or horizontally; that is, the glissando can be along the length of a single string, from near the pinboard to as far up as the player can reach, or it can sweep across the successive strings within any one of the three or four inside sections of the instrument.

Lateral glissandi can be effectuated with the following:

1. The fingertip(s)

D. Banks: *Assemblies*
F. Cerha: *Formation et Solution*
H. Cowell: *The Banshee*

K. Penderecki: *Strophes*
K. Serocki: *Niobe*

2. The fingernail

W. Albright: *Danse Macabre*
D. Burge: *Aeolian Music*
S. Bussotti: *Couple*
D. Cope: *Indices*
G. Crumb: *Ancient Voices of Children; Echoes of Time and the River*
A. Gilbert: *Sonata No. 2*

A. Lanza: *Plectros I, II*
T. Lucas: *Aberrations No. VII*
K. Penderecki: *Strophes*
B. Sakač: *Struktur I*
E. Schwartz: *Music for Prince Albert*
A. de la Vega: *Antinomies for Piano*

3. The flat hand

F. Miroglio: *Réfractions*

4. A wood stick, end of a mallet, flat piece of wood, pencil, or similar object

I. Anhalt: *Foci*
E. Boguslawski: *Apokalypsis*
Z. Bujarski: *Kinoth*
R. Hannay: *Fantôme*
H. Heiss: *Bewegungspiel*

M. Kagel: *Transición II*
P. Maxwell Davies: *Vesalii Icones*
C. Miereanu: *Finis Coronet Opus*
Z. Rudzinski: *Contra Fidem*

5. A metal stick or wirebrush

J. Cage: *First Construction (in Metal)*
R. L. Finney: *Divertissement*
R. Hannay: *Fantôme*

W. Kotonski: *Pour quatre*
K. Penderecki: *Fluorescences*
E. Vercoe: *Herstory III*

6. A metal brush of the type used for brushing animals

I. Anhalt: *Foci*

7. A plectrum or pick

G. Crumb: *Makrokosmos—Vol. I*
R. Gerhard: *Concert for 8*
R. L. Finney: *Divertissement*

A. Lanza: *Plectros I, II*
R. Reynolds: *Blind Men* (Example 14); *Quick are the Mouths of Earth*

8. A dull knife-blade

B. Childs: *Music for Singer; Nonet*

9. A nail file

W. Albright: *Danse Macabre*

10. A coin held like a banjo or mandolin pick (a quarter is the most convenient to grasp)

GLISSANDI

Example 14
Roger Reynolds: from *Blind Men* (p. 1)

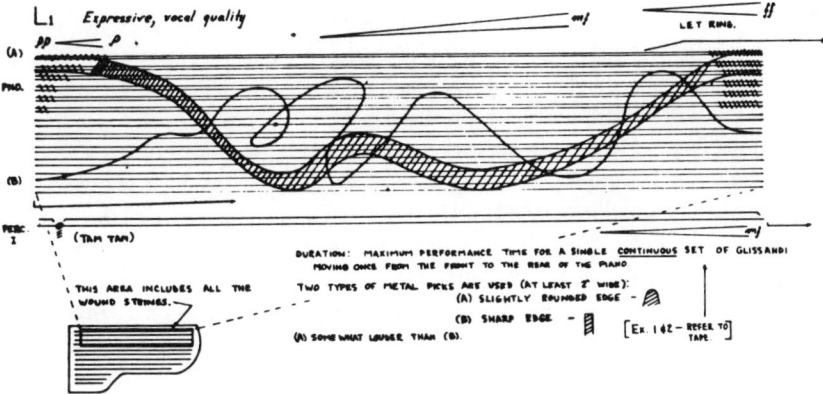

© Copyright 1967 by C. F. Peters Corporation. Reprinted by permission of the publisher.

R. Reynolds: *Traces*
W. Russell: *Fugue for Eight Percussion Instruments*

11. The four open edges of one half of a metal tea container (canister) of medium size

I. Anhalt: *Foci*

12. A cowbell

L. Foss: *Ni bruit ni vitesse*

13. The bottom edge of a pop bottle or glass tumbler

D. Erb: *Concerto for Solo Percussionist; The Seventh Trumpet*
P. Patterson: *Rebecca*

14. The open end of a bottle

V. Luti: *Mixed Quintet*

15. A plastic ruler

A. Janson: *Canon*
R. Reynolds: *The Emperor of Ice Cream*

16. A hammer head

V. Luti: *Mixed Quintet*

17. A lump of rosin

B. Childs: *Jack's New Bag*

Generally speaking, the low, wound bass strings of the piano are best for lateral glissandi, owing to their greater length and resonance. And nearly always the sustaining pedal is used in conjunction with glissandi on the strings, whether lateral or horizontal.

In the first volume of *Makrokosmos* for amplified piano, George Crumb combines an intriguing percussive effect with a lateral glissando over the metal winding of a low string. The pianist is directed to "pull plectrum very slowly over string (toward player) while gradually increasing pressure. A series of articulations will be produced by plectrum striking ridges of metal winding."

A curious form of lateral glissando is encountered in Anthony Gilbert's second piano sonata: the composer asks the pianist to strike a designated string centrally with the side of a small bottle or glass tumbler and then slide it toward the far end of the string. And David Bedford in *Come in here child* directs the player to push two milk bottles, one in either hand, up and down certain specified strings, creating a whistling glissando. A related effect is present in Crumb's *Makrokosmos II:* the pianist is to silently place two glass tumblers on the bass strings next to the dampers, then slowly move one tumbler laterally while pressing it against the strings. The left hand is to lightly strike the other tumbler with the flat fingers so as to produce sympathetic vibrations.

Further curiosities: both Stanley Lunetta in his *Piano Music* and Roger Reynolds in *The Emperor of Ice Cream* call for a metal object (triangle beater, large nail, for instance) to be held against a string; after the requisite key is struck, the object is slowly moved along the string, thus altering both timbre and pitch. In his *Proporzioni II* Szalonek requests the same procedure, except that the initial tone is produced by plucking the string rather than striking the key.

All of the objects listed in our discussion of lateral glissandi can be employed in horizontal sweeps across the sectional strings, plus those enumerated below. Today's composers have thus directed their keyboard players to glide, rasp, rub, scrape, stroke, or strum over the strings with the following:

1. The fingertips

L. Bassett: *Designs, Images and Textures*
Z. Bujarski: *Kinoth*
D. Burge: *Aeolian Music*
G. Crumb: *Echoes of Time and the River; Eleven Echoes of Autumn*
J. Gilboa: *The Jerusalem Chagall Windows*
W. Hellermann: *Formata*
H. Lazarof: *Textures*

J. Mills-Cockell: *Fragments*
R. Reynolds: *Blind Men; Wedge*
W. Russell: *Fugue for Eight Percussion Instruments*
E. Schwartz: *Music for Prince Albert; Texture*
A. Silsbee: *Spirals*
A. de la Vega: *Exospheres*
L. Widdoes: *From a Time of Snow*

2. The fingernails

D. Burge: *Aeolian Music*
S. Bussotti: *Couple; Il Nudo*
H. Cowell: *The Banshee*

G. Crumb: *Echoes of Time and the River; Night Music I*
L. Ferrari: *Société II*

GLISSANDI   **49**

L. Foss: *Orpheus*
A. Gilbert: *Sonata No. 2*
J. Gilboa: *The Jerusalem Chagall
   Windows*
J. M. Horvath: *Die Blinde*
A. Hrisanide: *Volumes*
A. Lanza: *Plectros I*
H. Lazarof: *Textures*
T. Lucas: *Aberrations No. VII*

J. Mills-Cockell: *Fragments*
K. Penderecki: *Strophes*
R. Reynolds: *Blind Men; Wedge*
W. Russell: *Fugue for Eight Percussion
   Instruments*
B. Sakač: *Struktur I*
K. Serocki: *Fantasmagoria; Segmenti*
A. de la Vega: *Antinomies; Structures*

3. The flat land

H. Cowell: *The Banshee*
L. Ferrari: *Société II*

4. A wirebrush

W. Albright: *Danse Macabre*
  (Example 22)
E. Brown: *Corroboree*
S. Cervetti: *Six Sequences for Dance*
R. Hannay: *Fantôme*
H. W. Henze: *Sinfonia N. 6*

S. Hodkinson: *Fresco*
J. M. Horvath: *Die Blinde*
A. Hrisanide: *Volumes*
K. Penderecki: *Anaklasis*
K. Serocki: *Segmenti*

5. A hairbrush or shoebrush

Z. Bujarski: *Chamber Piece; Kinoth*
D. Cope: *Iceberg Meadow*
H. W. Henze: *Sinfonia N. 6*
J. Kunst: *Ijzer*

G. Ligeti: *Atmospheres*
A. Mellnäs: *Aura*
W. Szalonek: *Mutanza per pianoforte*

6. A toothbrush

N. T. Dao: Tây Nguyên

7. A gong beater or soft lamb's wool mallet

J. Cage: *First Construction (in Metal);
   Imaginary Landscape No. 1*
J. Kunst: *Ijzer*

8. A piece of cloth, such as a wadded-up handkerchief

G. Ligeti: *Apparitions*

9. A wood stick or pencil

D. Cope: *Iceberg Meadow*
W. Eisma: *Affairs II*
J. Gilboa: *The Jerusalem Chagall
   Windows*
H. Heiss: *Bewegungspiel*
M. Kagel: *Transición II*

A. Lanza: *Plectros I*
P. Olsen: *Images*
K. Penderecki: *Anaklasis*
Z. Rudzinski: *Contra Fidem*
E. Schwartz: *Soliloquies*
E. Vercoe: *Herstory III*

10. The point of a lead pencil

L. Widdoes: *From a Time of Snow*

11. A metal stick or triangle rod

F. Miroglio: *Réfractions*
K. Penderecki: *Fluorescences; Sonata per Violoncello e Orchestra*

12. A steel rod held horizontally

F. Miroglio: *Réfractions*
W. Szalonek: *Mutanza*

13. A finger cymbal or crotale

B. Schäffer: *S'Alto*

14. A cowbell

L. Foss: *Orpheus*

15. A plectrum or guitar pick

R. L. Finney: *Divertissement*
H. Hartwell: *Soul Piece*
R. Reynolds: *Blind Men* (Example 14); *The Emperor of Ice Cream*

16. A coin, held like a pick

W. Russell: *Fugue for Eight Percussion Instruments*

17. A comb, of plastic or rubber

J. Gilboa: *The Jerusalem Chagall Windows*
P. Patterson: *Rebecca*
R. Reynolds: *Traces*

18. A large, soft eraser

W. Albright: *Seven Deadly Sins*
A. Silsbee: *Spirals*

19. A piece of hard rubber drawn along the string

G. Crumb: *Eleven Echoes of Autumn*

20. A knife blade, across the short portions of the strings between the tuning pins and front support

I. Anhalt: *Foci*

21. The bottom of a straight tumbler, water glass, or a glass ashtray

W. Albright: *Danse Macabre*
M. Mitrea-Celarianu: *Seth*

The pitchless key-glissando described on page 45 can also be utilized on the remaining standard keyboard instruments—harpsichord, celesta, and organ (the latter minus all registration). Only the various kinds of interior glissandi are limited to the piano, although the more delicate variants might possibly be transferred to the harpsichord interior.

On the organ it is possible to produce cluster glissandi on both the manuals and pedals, an effect prominently displayed in the following works:

W. Albright: *Organbook II*
G. Read: *Galactic Novae*
A. Stout: *Study in Densities*

ACCORDION

As the modern concert accordion is also a keyboard instrument, albeit a miniaturized version, its players can produce conventional glissandi on its limited bank of white and black keys, normally with the flat fingers or the palm. In his *Piece for Mo* David Bedford directs the accordionist to rub his knuckles up and down the keyboard, creating a rapid and continual "whoosh." Slight pitch bends can also be produced by partially depressing either the keys or the buttons, using maximum bellows pressure.

On the chromatic free-bass accordion, of course, one may glissando as well on the left-hand button keyboard. Each of the three rows of buttons outlines a diminished-seventh chord, progressively pitched a semitone higher, so that a glissando with the flat fingers on any one of the parallel rows would produce that harmonic structure. Although a rapid glissando can be effectuated on any one of the three rows of buttons, because of the necessarily awkward position of the left hand only a very slow slide with the palm can be made on all three rows simultaneously.

STRINGS

The symphonies of Gustav Mahler notwithstanding, glissando on the string instruments did not come into its own until Bartók made the device a primary aspect of his string writing (as in the last four string quartets among other works). Today the experimental composer has enlarged both his concept and his usage of string glissando to include the following refinements:

1. Glissando on the string, reducing the finger pressure until a harmonic is reached

A. Silsbee: *Spirals*

2. Glissando over the string(s) with a very light finger pressure (*glissando effleuré*), almost as though harmonics were to be produced

J. Casken: *Music for the Crabbing Sun*
T. de Leeuw: *Spatial Music III*

3. Glissando along the entire length of the string with the bowhair

D. Erb: *Concerto for Brass and Orchestra*
M. Kagel: *Sonant*
M. Kelemen: *Changeant*

4. Same, with the flat hand

S. Bussotti: *Mit einem gewissen sprechenden Ausdruck*
W. Rudzinski: *Pictures from the Holy-Cross Mountains*
B. Schäffer: *String Quartet*

5. Same, with the fingernail

D. Bedford: *Five for String Quintet; That White and Radiant Legend*

6. Same, with the edge of a coin or other small metal object

E. Raxach: *Paraphrase*

7. Same, with a small cymbal (crotale)

K. Penderecki: *Fluorescences*

8. Same, with a cloth (handkerchief)

T. Ichiyanagi: *Duet for Piano and String Instrument*

9. Glissando changing bows on each pitch

J. Casken: *Music for the Crabbing Sun*

10. Play rapidly arpeggiated down and up strokes across all four strings while fingering double-stop glissandi

J. Schwantner: *Consortium (I)*

11. Glissando *sul ponticello,* sliding the bow back and forth *ad libitum*

D. Bedford: *Music for Albion Moonlight* (Example 9)

12. Glissando *col legno,* the bow drawn *across* the strings as the left-hand finger slides up or down

I. Xenakis: *Syrmos*

13. Same, the bow gliding softly *along* the string

A. Woodbury: *Remembrances*

14. Pizzicato glissando, the sound continued arco glissando, the player overlapping the two sounds as smoothly as possible

W. Albright: *Danse Macabre*

15. Glissando in two directions simultaneously (possible only on the cello and doublebass); achieved by using the thumb on the lower and the third finger on the upper of a pair of adjacent strings

P. Phillips: *Sonata for String Bass*

Example 15
Krzysztof Penderecki: from *Fluorescences* (p. 33)

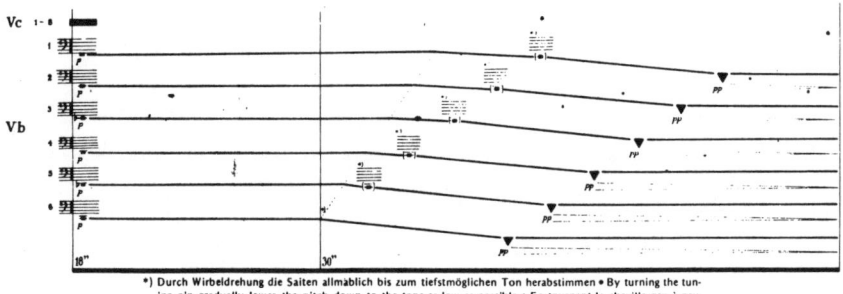

*) Durch Wirbeldrehung die Saiten allmählich bis zum tiefstmöglichen Ton herabstimmen • By turning the tuning pin gradually lower the pitch down to the tone as low as possible • En tournant la cheville peu à peu, relâcher les cordes jusqu'au son le plus bas possible.

© Copyright 1962 by Moeck Verlag. Abdruck mit Genehmigung des Moeck Verlags, D-31, Celle.

16. Glissando (arco or pizzicato) by means of turning the tuning peg with the left hand while bowing or plucking with the right hand. On cello and doublebass it is usually the lowest string that is so treated, the player lowering its pitch as far as possible. Obviously, a tuning-peg glissando can only be downward in pitch direction; a string may be relaxed to the point of total slackness but cannot, on the contrary, be drastically tightened without the danger of snapping. See:

L. Berio: *Chemins II*
L. Foss: *Orpheus*
H. Gorecki: *Elementi; Monodram*
G. Ligeti: *Apparitions*
A. Mellnäs: *Aura; Gestes sonores*
P. Nørgård: *Prism*
P. Patterson: *Rebecca*

K. Penderecki: *Emanationen;*
  Fluorescences (Example 15)
R. Reynolds: *Quick are the Mouths of Earth*
B. Schäffer: *Scultura; Violin Concerto*
I. Xenakis: *ST/4-1, 080262* (Example 4)
Y. Yannay: *preFIX-FIX-sufFIX*

17. Execute a double-stop tremolo glissando until the fingers push the bow off the string (of cello)

D. Martino: *From the Other Side*

The first use in orchestral literature of a normal glissando over the natural harmonic series on a string instrument has long been attributed to either Ravel (in the *Rapsodie espagnol* of 1907) or to Stravinsky (*The Firebird* of 1910). Actually, this device initially appeared in Rimsky-Korsakov's opera *Christmas Eve* of 1895. More currently, an unorthodox method of glissando on the series of natural harmonics has been stipulated by Roger Reynolds in *Aether:* the violinist is to slide along the string with his left-hand thumb.

Not an authentic glissando in harmonics but a repeated series of broken, gliding tones is the fancifully termed "seagull harmonic glissando." To produce this effect (on doublebass) the left-hand fingers are set in position for an artificial harmonic, the hand then sliding up and down the string, but not varying the finger position, while the right hand bows normally. At least four recent scores have exploited this device:

G. Crumb: *Vox Balaenae*
G. Heussenstamm: *Pentalogue*
G. Read: *Diabolic Dialogue*
C. Rouse: *Mitternachtlieder*

If further variants of conventional glissandi on all instruments capable of their production are forthcoming in the remaining years of the twentieth century, we may be sure that the experimental composer of the times will exploit the effects to the maximum in his new scores.

NOTE

1. Chapter 24 of this writer's *Music Notation: A Manual of Modern Practice* includes a more detailed discussion of various jazz instrumental techniques.

4

HARMONICS

WOODWINDS

By far the most common use of wind instrument overblowing is to produce harmonics on members of the flute and oboe families. Formerly, harmonics were overblown only at the twelfth from the fingered fundamental (as is required, for instance, in Ravel's *Daphnis et Chloé* and Stravinsky's *Le Sacre du Printemps*). More recently, flute harmonics have been available at the octave (from b^1 up to f^2; those at the twelfth begin with $f\#^2$). Even more recently, certain flutists have devised ways of producing "artificial" harmonics, beginning with $d\#^1$ and extending to b^1, when overblowing at the octave takes over.[1]

Octave partials on the flute often result in the harmonic sounding with its fundamental (termed a residual tone); they are produced by enclosing the blowhole tightly with rather loose lips and blowing with strong pressure. See, for example:

G. Amy: *⁵∕₁₆ pour flûte solo*
G. Ligeti: *Aventures*

H. Sollenberger: *2 Pieces for 2 Flutes*
W. Szalonek: *Aarhus Music; Les Sons*

The general effect of all harmonics on wind instruments is a weaker tone and a reduced amplitude.

For the closely related technique of "whistle (or whisper) tones" on piccolo, flute, and alto flute—very high and clear, but soft, pitches—the air column is directed over the mouthpiece without lip pressure. Actually, "whistle tones" are part of the harmonic series, being the fifth to tenth partials of the overblown fundamental; they have been used in the following works:

P. Chihara: *Willow, Willow*
J. Fortner: *S pr ING*
B. Levy: *Orbs with Flute*

R. Reynolds: *Quick are the Mouths of Earth*

Octave harmonics on oboe are produced by overblowing the fundamental (from b to d♯^{1}) and adding the octave key. Above d♯^{1} more complicated fingerings and octave key additions are required. Among recent scores requiring the use of oboe and/or English horn harmonics may be mentioned:

G. Amy: *Jeux*
T. Antoniou: *Five Likes*
S. Barber: *Souvenirs*
W. Hellermann: *One Into Another*
H. Holliger: *Mobile; Siebengesang*

K. Penderecki: *Capriccio per Oboe*
R. Reynolds: *Quick are the Mouths of Earth*
P. Zonn: *Chroma*

Certain double harmonics are also possible on the flute and oboe, and several composers have called for trills on these structures; both techniques are illustrated in:

G. Amy: *Jeux*
L. Berio: *Sequenza I; VII*
N. Castiglioni: *Alef*
V. Globokar: *Discours III*

H. Holliger: *Siebengesang* (Example 16)
T. de Kruyf: *Mosaico*
B. Levy: *Orbs with Flute*
K. Penderecki: *Capriccio per Oboe*

Example 16
Heinz Holliger: from *Siebengesang* (p. 1)

© Ars Viva Verlag, Mainz, 1967. All rights reserved. Used by permission of European American Music Distributors Corporation, sole U.S. and Canadian agent for Ars Viva Verlag.

Normally, harmonics are not available to the clarinet or bassoon, but in his *Concerto for Wind Quintet* Donald Martino asks the clarinetist to produce artificial harmonics by closing all the finger holes and muffling the instrument bell against his calf while overblowing the required fundamental of the harmonic. Hans Werner Henze also calls for clarinet harmonics in his orchestral *Heliogabalus Imperator,* as does Takemitsu in *Waves* and Jaromir Weinberger in *The Bird's Opera* (for saxophone). None of these composers, however, instructs the players as to the technical execution or tonal effect of the harmonics. On the other hand, certain other composers have been very precise in their directives to the woodwind players as to the production of the harmonics. For instance, in *Les Sons* Szalonek tells the flutist to cover the aperture with the lips as if to produce a

HARMONICS

harmonic, but then stop the sound abruptly with the tongue. Bruno Bartolozzi, in his *Concertazioni per oboe,* has distinguished degrees of timbre for various harmonics by way of the following symbols:

PERCUSSION

Harmonics are a technical device that would seem logically to be restricted to those instruments of a primarily harmonic and/or melodic nature; one would not ordinarily assume them to be feasible on, or characteristic of, the percussion instruments. Yet several of the tuned percussions can obtain certain partials from a struck fundamental. On timpani, for instance, octave harmonics are available by striking the head of the drum quite close to the rim:

E. Carter: *Eight Pieces for Four Timpani* (Example 17)
W. Kotonski: *Musica per fiati e timpani*
K. Penderecki: *Dimensions of Time and Silence*
G. Read: *Diabolic Dialogue*
K. Serocki: *Segmenti*

Example 17
Elliott Carter: from *Eight Pieces for Four Timpani* (p. 8)

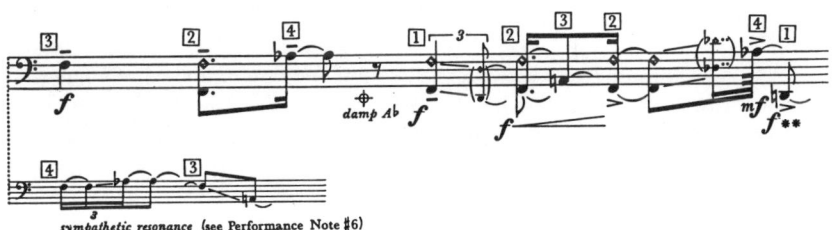

© Copyright 1968 by Associated Music Publishers, Inc. International Copyright Secured. All Rights Reserved. Used by permission.

Both the glockenspiel and vibraphone are capable of producing harmonics. The player places the tip of his left forefinger against the center (node) of the struck plate, using a hard mallet to strike the plate. The resulting sound is the third partial, or a pitch two octaves above the fundamental. Vibraphone harmonics can also be produced by striking the front or side edge of the bar with a brass mallet. See Crumb's *Madrigals—Book I* and Kagel's *Anagrama* for examples of vibraphone harmonics.

Oddly enough, even the suspended cymbal can create the effect of a harmonic, achieved by the player rubbing its surface with the edge of a cardboard tube, both the cymbal surface and the tube being lightly chalked.

HARP

There has been no significant change in the technique of producing harp harmonics other than the occasional requisition of harmonics at the twelfth in addition to those at the octave. As on the bowed string instruments, partials at the twelfth require the harpist to locate the node at one-third the string length instead of at the half-way point for octave harmonics. See, among other works, Mauricio Kagel's *Sonant* (Example 13-i).

Harpists today are still physically limited to producing only single harmonics with the right hand; double, triple, and even quadruple harmonics are possible with the left hand as long as the pitches created are on contiguous strings (demonstrated in Kagel's work).

KEYBOARD INSTRUMENTS

In contemporary piano writing, octave harmonics are extremely common. They are produced by silently depressing the key, or keys, and then sharply striking the key(s) an octave higher or lower than the depressed fundamental(s). Less common, however, are other partials possible—at the twelfth, the fifteenth, and the seventeenth; they are created by touching the proper node on the interior string with the fingertip of one hand while striking the corresponding key with the other hand. Some players facilitate their finding of the requisite node by marking the string with chalk or tape. Among the many recent works exploiting these harmonics are:

S. Bussotti: *Il Nudo; Memoria*
G. Cacioppo: *Time on Time in Miracles*
N. Castiglioni: *Sequenze*
F. Cerha: *Formation et Solution*
B. Childs: *Jack's New Bag*
D. Cope: *Parallax*
G. Crumb: *Ancient Voices of Children; Eleven Echoes of Autumn*
B. Ferneyhough: *Etudes Transcendantales*

R. L. Finney: *Divertissement*
A. Gilbert: *Sonata No. 2*
M. Kagel: *Anagrama*
A. Lanza: *Plectros I, II*
R. Reynolds: *The Emperor of Ice Cream*
G. Rochberg: *Contra Mortem et Tempus*
J. Spiegelman: *Morsels*
K. Stockhausen: *Klavierstück V*

It is possible to delay the sounding of a harmonic produced on an interior string by first striking the key and then pressing the fingertip lightly on the required node (as in Reynolds' *Blind Men*). In her *Spirals* Ann Silsbee has the pianist lightly touch the harmonic nodes on the interior strings with one hand while the other hand strikes the keys.

An unconventional manner of producing piano harmonics is used by George Crumb in his *Ancient Voices of Children* (Example 18) and *Vox Balaenae:* termed "chisel piano," the technique requires the player to apply the smooth edge of a ⅝″ chisel to a designated string at the node corresponding to the notated harmonic. The string is then plucked with the fingernail of the other hand and the chisel is then moved rapidly and decisively along the string so as to create a series of harmonic pitches. An identical effect is called for in Cage's *First Construction (in Metal)*, the pianist sliding a metal rod instead of a chisel along the string. In the *Eleven Echoes of Autumn*, Crumb instructs the player to "draw a piece of rather hard rubber very slowly along the indicated strings. When the correct pressure is exerted, a 7th-partial harmonic emerges."

STRINGS

As for new stringed-instrument concepts of harmonics, first we point out one or two current refinements, such as the half-harmonic; to achieve this the left-hand finger touches the string very lightly, but *not* at a harmonic node. Another method used to obtain a half-harmonic is to press the left-hand fourth finger on a harmonic node a little more firmly than usual. Both of these procedures produce a flutey sound, roughly akin to the timbers of *sul tasto* and of a genuine harmonic; one or the other of these techniques is displayed in:

J. Druckman: *Valentine* M. Kagel: *Match für drei Spieler*
H-J. Hespos: *Passagen* I. Yun: *Images*
J. M. Horvath: *Redundanz 2*

Harmonics are normally played with the tip or the middle of the bowhair, but in Michael Colgrass's *As Quiet As* the composer directs that the harmonics be played at the frog of the bow, imparting a rougher quality to the sound than usual. Furthermore, harmonics are not often played *col legno*, but Robert Gerhard includes such a directive to his doublebass player in *Concerto for 8*. The player extends his left hand in a flat position so that it lightly touches all four strings, sliding it up and down as the wood of the bow is bounced on the strings to produce a random series of harmonics.

Alternating a series of artificial harmonics and their fundamentals is a technique that is prominent in Donald Erb's *Concerto for Brass and Orchestra*. To achieve this effect the player's fourth finger periodically presses down on and lifts off the string node, thus causing a two-octave leap of pitch and a shift of timbre. Another alternation, this between producing the second and third har-

Example 18
George Crumb: from *Ancient Voices of Children* (p. 6)

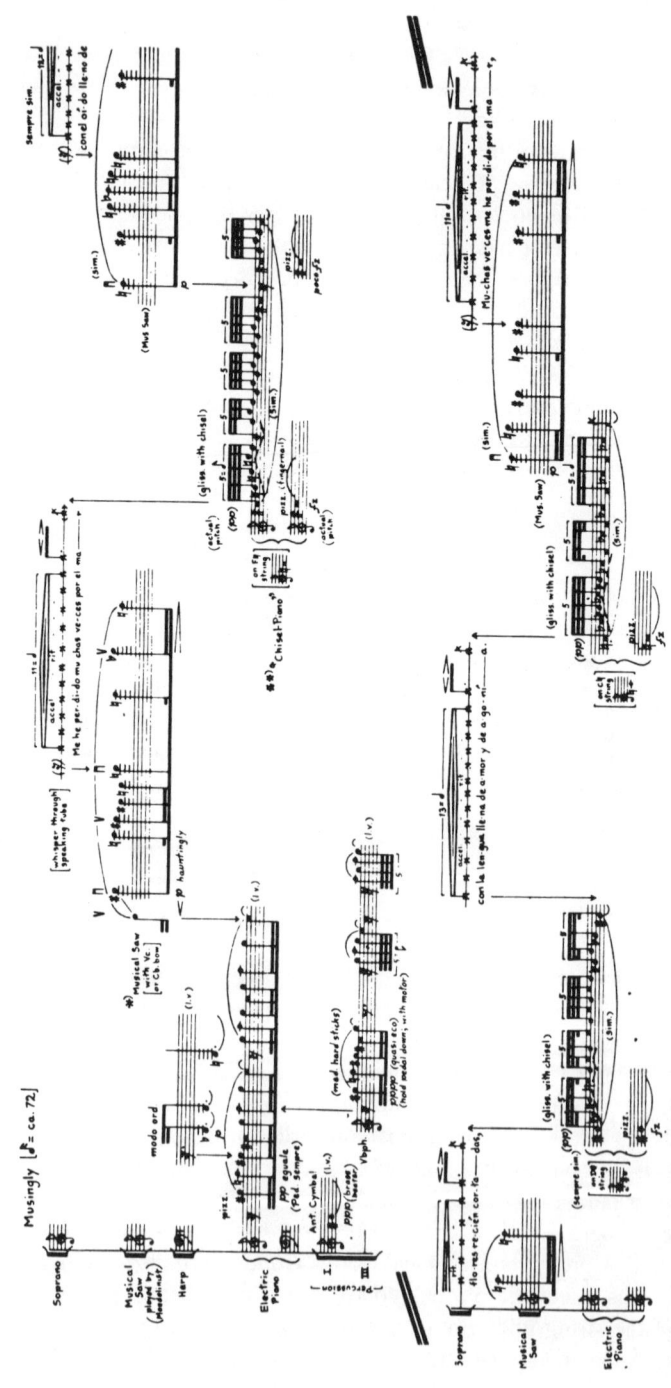

© Copyright 1971 by C. F. Peters Corporation. Reprinted by permission of the publisher.

monics on the string, is required in Richard Barrett's *Anatomy*—one more example of a systematic shifting of pitch and tone color.

Parenthetically, it may be added that artificial harmonics, formerly unplayable or inordinately difficult to achieve on the doublebass, are now gradually being utilized in solo and chamber literature for this instrument. Artificial harmonics are produced in the higher positions by using the thumb to stop the string and the stretched second or third finger to lightly touch the requisite node.[2] Among the new works conspicuously requiring doublebass artificial harmonics one might mention:

P. Chihara: *Logs*
G. Crumb: *Madrigals—I, IV*
J. Druckman: *Valentine*
M. Kagel: *Sonant*

G. Read: *Diabolic Dialogue*
B. Turetzky: *Poems, Portraits, Ballades and Blues*

On the cello and doublebass it is possible to produce what are called "pulled" harmonics; these are natural harmonics fingered in the customary manner, but the string is at the same time pulled sideways with another left-hand finger near the end of the fingerboard. The aural result of this action is a slight bending of the harmonic pitch. Paul Chihara's suggested notation for this effect (♭̂) cannot be bettered. Scores that have called for pulled harmonics include:

P. Chihara: *Ceremony II; Logs*
B. Childs: *Jack's New Bag; Nonet*
J. Druckman: *Valentine*

M. Kagel: *Sonant*
L. Moss: *Windows*
G. Read: *Diabolic Dialogue*

In some recent scores doublebass players have been required to produce the string equivalent of a wind instrument "enharmonic trill" (see page 146) on overtone pitches, both natural and artificial. This is accomplished by alternately or successively changing fingerings on a specific and repeated pitch, including the shifting of positions (as in Kagel's *Sonant* and Robert Aitken's *Kebyar*).

A recent phenomenon in the basic concept of string instrument harmonics is the discovery and compositional use of the undertone series (also called "subharmonics" and "pedal tones"). These are pitches in direct reversal of those obtained in the overtone series (the first partial, or octave, for instance, is *higher* than the open string in the overtone series and *lower* in the undertone series). Subharmonics are created by applying fairly heavy bowing pressure on the open string at one or another of the harmonic nodes, and moving the bow very slowly. They have been used conspicuously in at least two recent experimental scores: George Crumb's *Black Angels* and Arthur Woodbury's *Remembrances*.

Finally, it should be mentioned that many composers today call for the "highest harmonic possible" on the individual string instruments. In other words, the specific pitch is not as important as the peculiar and strained timbre of the stratospheric pitches so created (see Henze's *Sinfonia N. 6*, Example 51 and Karel Husa's third string quartet, Example 3).

NOTES

1. Refer to Bruno Bartolozzi's *New Sounds for Woodwind* for fingering charts.
2. See Bertram Turetzky's articles in *The Composer* and his recent book on the contemporary doublebass. Turetzky laments the fact that comparatively few composers have so far utilized doublebass artificial harmonics and even fewer players have mastered the technique of playing them.

5
PERCUSSIVE DEVICES

WOODWINDS AND BRASSES

Percussive effects on the wind instruments may be classified in two categories: those that are produced by the action of the tongue or the breath stream against reed or mouthpiece, and those produced by action of the fingers, hand, or an extraneous object on the body of the instrument. In the former category are sharp, explosive note attacks, with the player enunciating an exaggerated "t," as well as emphatic tongue clicks (velar sounds). Slap-tongue, a staple in older jazz performance techniques and occasionally used by vanguard composers, belongs to this category; it has been stipulated by:

R. Barrett: *Anatomy*
R. Erickson: *Ricercar à 5*
B. Ferneyhough: *Carceri d'Invenzione III; Etudes Transcendantales*
J. Fox: *All Things Fancy*
A. Hrisanide: *Clarinet Sonata*

W. Holab: *Woodshedding*
H. Holliger: *"H" for Wind Quintet*
D. Martino: *Strata; Trio for Violin, Clarinet, and Piano*
T. Olah: *Sonate pour Clarinette Seule*
T. Takemitsu: *Voice*

A prolonged use of slap-tongue is roughly akin to flutter-tonguing; it is achieved by letting the tongue come between the lips rather than keeping it behind the teeth as in normal fluttering.

"Tongue-stops" are additional percussive resources for flutists, produced by covering the embouchure hole with the lips and stopping it quickly with the tongue, combined with forceful breath exhalation. The sound is somewhat like key slaps with the mouthpiece covered; it is also markedly akin to string instrument pizzicato. Composers have sometimes designated the effect as "pizz.", or as a "tongue ram." This device has been prominently specified by Brian Ferneyhough in two solo flute works, *Cassandra's Dream Song* and *Unity Capsule* (Example 28).

Brass instrumentalists have been instructed by some composers to "pop" the tongue into the mouthpiece (as in Elliott Schwartz's *Rip*), or to produce a percussive tongue attack by pronouncing "fla" into the mouthpiece. See:

J. Bark, F. Rabe: *Bolos*
V. Globokar: *Discours II; Etude pour Folklora II*
R. Haubenstock-Ramati: *Credentials*

Among the recent works that call for either velar clicks or percussive tongue attacks by woodwind and brass instruments we might cite:

G. Crumb: *Night of the Four Moons*
J. Druckman: *Animus 1* (Example 36)
W. Eisma: *Non-lecture II*
J. Fulkerson: *Patterns III*
V. Globokar: *Discours II*

R. Haubenstock-Ramati: *Credentials*
H. Holliger: *"H" for Wind Quintet*
G. Ligeti: *Apparitions*
B. A. Zimmermann: *Tempus loquendi*

All the wind instruments have been called upon to strike the instrument body in some manner, the exact location being always indicated by the composer. Foremost among these possibilities are key or valve clicks: the player's fingers rattle, slap, strike, or tap the keys of woodwind and the valves of brass instruments in a highly audible manner, either combined with normal tone production or divorced from it.[1] A clear notational distinction should be made between these two approaches. Composers today are generally in agreement that an x-shaped notehead, either on or off the staff, is most appropriate for an unpitched key or valve click, while a small cross over the notehead (or under it) is the most logical symbol for a click combined with specific tone production. Two other current notations are lastly illustrated:

 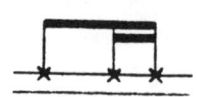 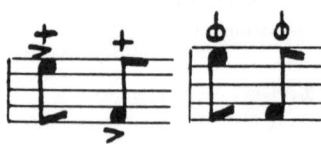 

A very few of the innumerable recent works requiring both varieties of key and valve claps are:

W. Albright: *Danse Macabre*
D. Amram: *Quintet for Winds*
E. Brown: *Available Forms 2; From Here*
J. Casken: *Music for the Crabbing Sun*
F. Cerha: *Enjambments*
P. Chihara: *Willow, Willow*
M. Davidovsky: *Synchronisms No. 1*

J. Fox: *All Things Fancy*
V. Globokar: *Accord*
E. Grosskopf: *Dialectics*
D. Harris: *Ludus II*
R. Haubenstock-Ramati: *Interpolation*
J. Heiss: *Four Movements for Three Flutes*
H-J. Hespos: *Passagen*

PERCUSSIVE DEVICES

S. Hodkinson: *Fresco*
H. Holliger: *Siebengesang*
A. Hrisanide: *A la recherche de la verticale*
M. Kelemen: *Entrances*
D. Martino: *From the Other Side*
A. Mellnäs: *Gestes sonores*
F. Miroglio: *Phases*
S. Montague: *At the white edge of phrygia*
K. Penderecki: *Fluorescences*
C. Polin: *The Death of Procris* (Example 1)
G. Read: *Sonoric Fantasia No. 3*

D. Reck: *Blues and Screamer*
R. Reynolds: *Ambages; Quick are the Mouths of Earth*
R. Romiti: *Palingenesis*
W. Rudzinski: *Pictures from the Holy-Cross Mountains*
E. Schwartz: *Soliloquies; Texture*
K. Serocki: *Segmenti*
H. Sollberger: *Grand Quartet for Flutes*
W. Sydeman: *Clarinet Duo*
W. Szalonek: *Concertino per flauto ed orchestra da camera*
A. de la Vega: *Exospheres*

Key and valve clicks, if long extended in duration, produce the percussive equivalent of trill or tremolo; this particular effect has been requisitioned in the following scores:

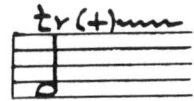

D. Bedford: *Music for Albion Moonlight*
A. Benvenuti: *Polymérie*
L. Berio: *Sequenza I*
S. Bussotti: *Couple*
F. Cerha: *Enjambments*
P. Chihara: *Branches* (Example 19)
B. Childs: *Nonet*
M. Constant: *Winds*
D. Erb: *Concerto for Solo Percussionist*
F. Evangelisti: *Proporzioni*
L. Ferrari: *Société II*
V. Globokar: *Atemstudie für Oboe*

C. Halffter: *Lineas y puntos*
S. Hodkinson: *Interplay*
M. Kelemen: *Equilibres*
D. Martino: *Strata*
D. Maves: *Oktoechos*
K. M-Nazar: *Variazioni concertanti*
C. Polin: *The Death of Procris* (Example 1)
M. Subotnick: *Lamination I*
W. Sydeman: *Concerto da Camera No. III; Texture Studies for Orchestra*
D. Wilson: *Doubles*
W. Witzerrmann: *Dedicazione a Herbert*

An unusual byproduct of this technique is described by William O. Smith in comments on his *Variants for Solo Clarinet:* "With the use of cross-fingerings certain two-note [key] tremolos produce a third tone, which changes pitch during expansion of the tremolo."

In Elliott Schwartz's *Soliloquies,* a gradual crescendo of the impact of the fingers on the keys of flute is coupled with a corresponding diminuendo of the

Example 19
Paul Chihara: from *Branches* (p. 6)

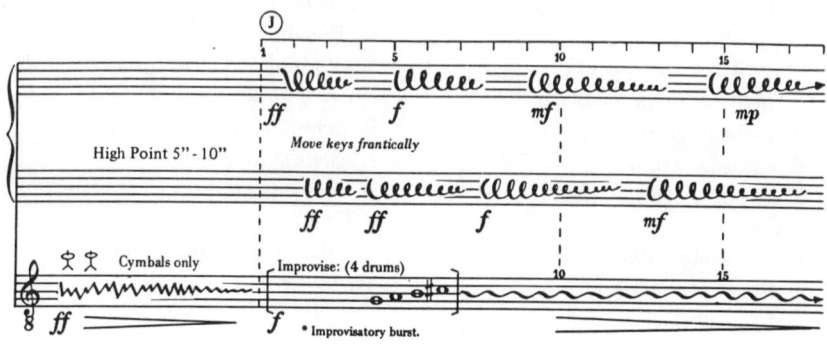

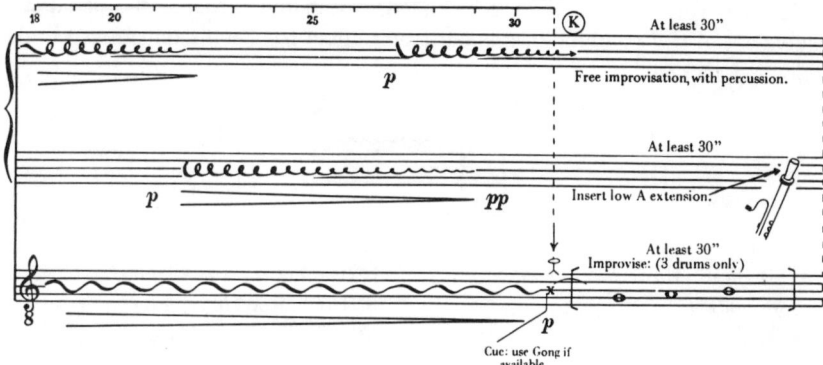

© Copyright 1968 by Henmar Press Inc. Sole selling agents C. F. Peters Corporation. Reprinted by permission of the publisher.

blown pitches to a total absence of tone. A related, delicate effect on all the woodwind members is achieved by lightly fingering a series of specific pitches but without blowing into the mouthpiece or vibrating the reed (as in de la Vega's *Interpolation*).

Though the trombone lacks valves to clack, the equivalent effect can be obtained by rapidly and audibly flipping the F-attachment lever (required in Vinko Globokar's *Accord* and *Discours II*). One wonders, however, how effective this action is on an instrument whose F-attachment lever is well oiled and hence relatively quiet when operated.

Among the available exterior areas of a woodwind instrument that can be lightly struck with the fingers, knuckles, or flat hand, the most obvious is the flaring bell of oboe, clarinet, bass clarinet, or saxophone. On members of the flute family the mouthpiece or the tube opening, with head-joint removed, offer the most convenient locales for striking (as in Zbigniew Bujarski's *Contraria*,

PERCUSSIVE DEVICES 67

Serocki's *Swinging Music* and *Symphonic Frescoes*, as well as Jim Fox's *All Things Fancy*).

An even more unusual action is requested in *Ring* of Toru Takemitsu: the flutist must knock between the mouthpiece and a joint with a finger ring. Obviously, the knocking must be done gently so that the flute surface is not scratched or dented.

English horn, bassoon, and contrabassoon may be struck *ad libitum* on their elongated tubings. The resultant sounds in all instances, however, are generally weak and inconclusive; no player is willing to strike his instrument with such force that it may be damaged. Exterior percussive effects on the woodwinds, therefore, must be regarded more as psychological visual gestures than as bona fide percussion.

In addition to the several works just cited, the following scores also contain directives for hand-striking on a woodwind instrument:

D. Bedford: *Gastrula*   A. Hrisanide: *Directions*
B. Childs: *Nonet*   W. Sydeman: *Texture Studies*

With the brass instruments, the most likely place for percussive blows with the hand is the bell, either outside on its rim or on the curved inside area. Certain vanguard composers have requested their brass players to rattle, strike, or tap on the instrument bell with the following agents:

1. The fingers, flat palm, or cupped hand

D. Bedford: *Gastrula; Trona*   A. Mellnäs: *Gestes sonores; Tombola*
R. Haubenstock-Ramati: *Credentials* K. Serocki: *Symphonic Frescoes*
M. Kelemen: *Olifant*

2. The fingernails

R. Aitken: *Kebyar*   R. Haubenstock-Ramati: *Credentials*
D. Cope: *Spirals*   A. Mellnäs: *Gestes sonores*
D. Erb: *The Seventh Trumpet*
   (Example 41)

3. A metal mute, coin, finger ring, or mouthpiece

R. Aitken: *Kebyar*   W. Heider: *-einander*
J. Bark, F. Rabe: *Bolos*   H-J. Hespos: *Passagen*
L. Berio: *Sequenza V*   S. Hodkinson: *Fresco*
J. Cage: *Solo for Sliding Trombone* E. Schwartz: *Rip*
B. Childs: *Jack's New Bag*   M. Stibilj: *Condensation*
V. Globokar: *Accord*

4. The wood end of a mallet, a plastic-headed stick, or a hard vibraphone mallet

L. Austin: *Changes*
B. Childs: *Music for Trombone*

R. Erickson: *Ricercar à 5*
E. Krenek: *Five Pieces for Trombone and Piano*

5. A felt-headed mallet, tapped on the bell rim

L. Austin: *Changes*

6. A wirebrush

R. Erickson: *Ricercar à 5*

7. A plastic knitting needle

B. Childs: *Nonet*

8. A metal rod

A. Hrisanide: *Directions*

Trombonists can also produce several percussive effects not possible on the other brasses. One of these is to stop the bell quickly with a plunger mute:

T. Albert: *Sound Frames*
C. Alsina: *Trio 1967*
V. Globokar: *Discours II; Fluide*

Another action is to close the slide abruptly so that a sharp metallic click is heard, as required in Vinko Globokar's *Discours II*. A rather special percussive sound can be obtained by rattling a small stick or a pencil inside the curves of the slide (as requested by Barney Childs in *Jack's New Bag* and *Music for Trombone*). And a unique percussive effect utilizing the instrument bell is to be found in both Ernst Krenek's *Five Pieces* and the *Options I* of Elliott Schwartz: the trombonist gently rolls the bell over the strings of a grand piano (with lid off).

The mouthpiece alone of the various brass instruments can also serve as the locale of percussive attack. In "popping" it, for instance, the player hits the cup with his flat palm, as in:

PERCUSSIVE DEVICES 69

R. Aitken: *Kebyar*
L. Austin: *Changes*
M. Bamert: *Inkblot*
J. Bark, F. Rabe: *Bolos*
D. Bedford: *Gastrula; Trona*
H. Budd: *III for Double Ensemble*
F. Cerha: *Enjambments; Relazioni fragili*
B. Childs: *Jack's New Bag; Music for Trombone*
M. Constant: *Winds*
R. Erickson: *Ricercar à 5*
J. Fulkerson: *Patterns III*
C. Halffter: *Anillos; Lineas y puntos*
R. Haubenstock-Ramati: *Credentials*
S. Hodkinson: *Fresco*
H. Holliger: *"H" for Wind Quintet*

B. Jolas: *How Now*
M. Kelemen: *Changeant*
W. Kotonski: *Pour quatre*
E. Krenek: *Five Pieces for Trombone and Piano*
G. Ligeti: *Apparitions*
A. Mellnäs: *Gestes sonores: Tombola*
S. Montague: *At the white edge of phrygia*
L. de Pablo: *Modulos III*
W. Rudzinski: *Pictures from the Holy-Cross Mountains*
E. Schwartz: *Options I*
K. Serocki: *Swinging Music; Symphonic Frescoes*
M. Subotnick: *Lamination I*
W. Sydeman: *Texture Studies*

In the Jan Bark, Folke Rabe *Bolos* for four trombones, the composers direct that the mouthpiece be struck with another mouthpiece, a very logical as well as effective agent of attack. A rather special tapping procedure is called for in Larry Austin's *Changes:* the trombonist places the end of the slide on the floor, holding it down with his foot; he then taps on the mouthpiece while slowly drawing the rest of the instrument upward, the slide being pulled out as he does so. The result is a descending "scale" of percussive pitches.

Finally, one cannot neglect to mention several other intriguing effects possible only on trombone: first, audibly sloshing the water in the slide (requested by Vinko Globokar in *Discours II* and by Mihai Mitrea-Celarianu in *Seth*); second, removing the outer slide from the instrument, covering the open ends with the palm and thumb to create a vacuum, and then pulling the tube rapidly out of the slide to make a sharp "vacuum smack" (most notably requisitioned in *Bolos*). Krenek requests the same sound in his *Five Pieces for Trombone and Piano*, but it is achieved by sharply pulling out the F-attachment slide, a gesture duplicated in Donald Erb's *The Seventh Trumpet*.

HARP AND OTHER PLUCKED INSTRUMENTS

Percussive devices for the harp are of two basic varieties: those produced on the strings and those effected by striking the frame of the instrument. Included in the first category are percussive attacks with the fingertips, knuckles, nails, or palm. The first usage of this technique was outlined in Carlos Salzedo's *Modern Study of the Harp*:[2] his "tam-tam sounds" were created by filliping a low string with the left-hand second or third finger (or, as a substitute, striking it with a small ivory stick).

GENERALIZED TECHNIQUES

Subsequent percussive innovations on the instrument call for flicking, slapping, striking, or tapping the strings with the following agents:

1. The flat fingers or the palm

L. Berio: *Chemins I; Sequenza II* (Example 6-g)
Z. Bujarski: *Chamber Piece*
S. Bussotti: *Fragmentations; Memoria*
D. Eberhard: *"Especially . . ."*
H. Gorecki: *Monologhi; Scontri*
B. Jolas: *Tranche pour harpe seule*
M. Kagel: *Anagrama; Sonant*
M. Kelemen: *Changeant; Olifant*
R. Maros: *Monumentum*
S. Matsushita: *Fresque sonore*
F. Miroglio: *Réseaux pour harpe et orchestre*
L. de Pablo: *Radial*

A. Paccagnini: *Musica da Camera*
K. Penderecki: *Dimensions of Time and Silence*
B. Rands: *Formants 1*
G. Read: *Sonoric Fantasia No. 3*
C. Salzedo: *Scintillation*
L. Schifrin: *Continuum*
K. Serocki: *Segmenti, Symphonic Frescoes*
T. Takemitsu: *Eucalypts (I)*
D. Welcher: *White Mares of the Moon*
D. Wilson: *Decisions, Decisions!*
I. Yun: *Fluktuationen*

2. The fingernails

S. Bussotti: *Fragmentations*
J. Fortner: *S pr ING*
M. Kagel: *Sonant* (Example 13-o)
C. Polin: *Summer Settings*

B. Rands: *Formants 1*
K. Stockhausen: *Kontra Punkte*
T. Takemitsu: *Eucalypts (I)*

PERCUSSIVE DEVICES

3. The knuckles

S. Bussotti: *Mit einem gewissen sprechenden Ausdruck*
C. Polin: *Summer Settings*

4. The two hands

M. Kagel: *Sonant* (Example 13-e)
G. Read: *Sonoric Fantasia No. 3*

In many experimental scores of the last several decades one also finds instructions to play on the harp strings (usually in the lowest octave and a fifth, which comprise the wire strings) with the following extraneous agents:

1. Timpani mallets (soft, medium, hard)

S. Bussotti: *Fragmentations*
G. Crumb: *Echoes of Time and the River*
H. Holliger: *Siebengesang*
M. Kagel: *Anagrama; Sonant* (Example 13-k)
S. Matsushita: *Fresque sonore*

K. Penderecki: *Anaklasis*
B. Rands: *Actions for six*
G. Read: *Haiku Seasons*
Z. Wiszniewski: *Tre pezzi della tradizione*

2. A wooden drumstick or piece of wood

M. Kagel: *Sonant* (Example 13-l)

3. A hammer or a chime mallet

Y. Sadai: *Nuances*

4. A metal stick (triangle rod)

G. Amy: *Trajectoires*
L. Berio: *Chemins I*
M. Kagel: *Sonant* (Example 13-s)

5. A rubber-covered metal rod

H. Holliger: *Siebengesang*

6. The tuning key (metal end)

D. Erb: *Symphony of Overtures*
S. Matsushita: *Fresque sonore*
F. Miroglio: *Réseaux pour harpe et orchestre*

7. A plectrum or guitar pick

G. Crumb: *Echoes of Time and the River*
H. W. Henze: *Heliogabalus Imperator*
K. Serocki: *Segmenti*
W. Szalonek: *Concertino per flauto*
I. Yun: *Symphonische Szene*

8. Wirebrushes

G. Arrigo: *Infrarosa*
M. Kagel: *Sonant* (Example 13-b,f)
K. Penderecki: *The Devils of Loudun*

9. Two bottle brushes about 1 cm in width

Borup-Jorgenson: *Nordisk Sommer Pastoral*

10. An antique cymbal (crotale)

L. Foss: *Elytres*

11. An 18" ruler

D. Erb: *Symphony of Overtures*

12. An ordinary pencil

B. Van Nostrand: *Ventilation Manual*

13. A 10-penny nail

R. Felciano: *Crasis*

14. Gloves having small sticks embedded in the fingers

J. Kapr: *Dialogues*

15. A woman's 9" comb with half dense and half sparse rows of teeth, and an ordinary 5" pocket comb

Y. Yannay: *Coloring Book for the Harpist*

Remarkably similar to a deep gong stroke is the sound of the low wire harp strings when struck with mallets or a hammer. Though not to be compared in resonance with this action, an intriguing direction to rattle a pencil between two wire strings occurs in Don Banks's *Tirade* and in R. Murray Schafer's *Requiems for the Party-Girl*. The resulting sound can be fairly violent or delicately restrained, depending upon the intensity of the rattling. An allied effect is that stipulated by Zolt Durkó in his *Serenata:* a metal plate, also a deep bell, are to be held against a low wire string before the harpist plucks it, resulting in a sharp metallic clash. Related to these several techniques is Salzedo's "thunder effect," achieved by violently sliding the second finger of the left hand on the low wire strings so that they strike each other. This action is displayed in several of Salzedo's solo harp pieces, as well as in Dennis Eberhard's *"Especially . . . ,"* Richard Felciano's *Crasis,* and *Réseaux pour harpe et orchestre* of Francis Miroglio. The so-called "dead-slap" technique requires the same action as the "thunder effect," except that the hand remains pressed against the strings.

When the player is seated at the instrument, not many areas of the harp frame are readily accessible for percussive striking. The most obvious locale, and the one most easily reached, is the wide soundboard; predictably, the majority of nonstring percussive effects are created in this area. As with the strings themselves, the soundboard can be drummed upon, struck sharply, or tapped lightly with the following agents:

1. The fingertips

S. Bussotti: *Fragmentations*
Z. Durkó: *Serenata*
J. Fortner: *S pr ING*
M. Kagel: *Anagrama; Sonant*
J. Kapr: *Dialogues*

F. Miroglio: *Réseaux pour harpe et orchestre*
B. Rands: *Formants 1*
G. Read: *Haiku Seasons*
D. Welcher: *White Mares of the Moon*

2. The palm or open hand

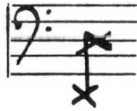

G. Becker: *Moirologhi*
L. Berio: *Circles*
S. Bussotti: *Fragmentations*
R. Felciano: *Background Music*
H. Holliger: *Siebengesang*
M. Kagel: *Anagrama; Sonant*

T. de Kruyf: *Einst den Grau*
A. LeBaron: *Memnon*
B. Maderna: *Stele per Diotima*
S. Matsushita: *Fresque sonore*
B. Rands: *Aum; Formants I*
W. Szalonek: *Three Sketches*

3. The knuckles

L. Berio: *Chemins I; Circles*
S. Bussotti: *Fragmentations*
D. Erb: *Symphony of Overtures*
R. Felciano: *Background Music*
S. Matsushita: *Fresque sonore*

F. Miroglio: *Réseaux pour harpe et orchestre*
B. Rands: *Formants 1; Wildtrack 1*
D. Welcher: *White Mares of the Moon*

4. The fingernails

A. Paccagnini: *Musica da Camera*   K. Stockhausen: *Kontra Punkte*
L. Schidlowsky: *Koloth*   W. Szalonek: *Three Sketches*

5. The tuning key

Y. Sadai: *Nuances*
B. Sakač: *Struktur I*

> The shank of the tuning key can also be made to slide across the tuning pegs (right side of the instrument), creating a violent clacking sound; this effect was used by Anne LeBaron in her *Memnon* for six harps.

6. A stick or mallet

S. Bussotti: *Fragmentations*
M. Kagel: *Sonant* (Example 13-1)
Y. Sadai: *Nuances*

Several closely related effects combine normal plucking of the strings with percussive blows on the soundboard. First—from a chronological standpoint, at least—are Salzedo's "timpanic sounds": the right hand taps the soundboard with the third finger while the left hand plucks the string(s). See various of Salzedo's solo harp pieces, as well as Bussotti's *Fragmentations,* Varèse's *Ameriques,* and *Kyros* of Martin David Levy. A variant of this technique is to pluck the string at its lower end and beat simultaneously on the soundboard with a finger of the same hand:

PERCUSSIVE DEVICES

G. Becker: *Moirologhi*
L. Berio: *Sequenza II*
V. Globokar: *Voie*
M. Kagel: *Anagrama; Sonant*
   (Example 13-q)
T. de Kruyf: *Einst den Grau*

B. Maderna: *Stele per Diotima*
S. Matsushita; *Fresque sonore*
F. Miroglio: *Réseaux pour harpe et orchestre*
B. Rands: *Formants 1*
T. Takemitsu: *Eucalypts (I)*

In his *Sequenza II* (Example 6-b) Berio directs the harpist to play *prés de la table,* letting the finger slide immediately and vigorously to the soundboard after plucking the string. This is also requested in:

E. Brown: *Available Forms* 2
S. Bussotti: *Fragmentations*
M. Kagel: *Sonant*

Two further refinements of this technique are specified in Kagel's *Anagrama:* the player strikes the soundboard immediately before and immediately after plucking the string, indicated by the following symbols:

The back of the soundboard—the rounded part that rests against the player's right shoulder—can be struck with the flat hand (as in Kagel's *Sonant*) or with the knuckles:

L. Berio: Sequenza II (Example 6-f)
S. Bussotti: *Mit einem gewissen sprechenden Ausdruck*
G. Crumb: *Ancient Voices of Children; Madrigals—III*

Striking the brass plate above the tuning pins with the end of the tuning key is another Salzedo invention. Termed the "anvil effect," the technique is appropriately identified by the following notational symbol:

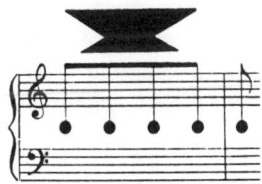

Surprisingly, relatively few contemporary instrumentators have availed themselves of this device; among the many works surveyed it showed up only in Bussotti's unique *Fragmentations* and in Sydney Hodkinson's orchestral *Fresco.*

A few composers, however, have designated that the metal front column be struck with the tuning key or other metal object. It should be pointed out that most harpists will strongly—and rightly—resist such a directive as being damaging to their instrument. Composers would be well advised, therefore, to restrict any metallic blows on the harp to the curving brass plate at the top of the instrument.

GUITAR, MANDOLIN, AND BANJO

In many avant-garde scores the guitar appears more frequently and performs more unconventionally than either the mandolin or banjo. Mainly, the newer guitar effects are percussive in nature and include actions both on the strings and the body. The most common directive in the first category is to slap the strings vigorously against the fingerboard with the left hand: this action has been stipulated by:

A. Bloch: *Dialoghi*	M. Kagel: *Sonant*
D. Erb: *String Trio*	W. Kotonski: *a battere*

A guitarist can also simulate "snap" pizzicato by plucking a string so violently that it rebounds against the fingerboard (see Cristobal Halffter's *Codex I* and Bartolozzi's *Concertazioni per Oboe*). He can also snap the thumbnail against a string to create a sharp metallic sound, as required in *Prisms II* of Gilbert Biberian.

In both his *a battere* and *Concerto per quattro,* Kotonski's guitarist must strike a string with a right-hand finger and then press it to the fingerboard. This action sets both segments of the string in vibration and produces a faint double-stop effect combined with a subtle percussive noise. In George Crumb's *Night of the Four Moons,* the banjo player obtains a delicate murmuring by trilling on one string with two thimble-capped fingers.

George Wilson asks his guitarist in *Concatenations* to dampen all the strings with his left hand while striking them with the flat right hand.

Other percussive effects on the guitar strings, as stipulated by various contemporary composers, include the following: tremolos with xylophone mallets and with triangle beaters (Kagel: *Tremens*); with a teaspoon (David Bedford: *You Asked for It*); with a tuning fork and with a felt-covered metal bar (Maurice Ohana: *Si le jour si le jour parait*); with ping-pong balls (Tomas Marco: *Albayalda für Gitarre*), and with the rubber end of a pencil (Keith Humble: *Arcade IV*).

The strings of all three instruments can be rubbed or stroked with the fingers or flat hand to create a soft percussive coloration (as in Sydney Hodkinson's *Fresco*): or a single string can be deadened with the left hand and then stroked with a fingernail of the right hand (requested in Lukas Foss's *Fragments of Archilochos*).

All three instruments can be struck on their backs, sides, top, or fingerboard with the player's fingers, thumb, knuckles, nails, or palm:

L. Foss: *Fragments of Archilochos;*
    Paradigm
R. Gerhard: *Concert for 8*
S. Hodkinson: *Fresco*

M. Kagel: *Sonant*
W. Kotonski: *a battere*
G. Read: *Canzone di Notte*

Tapping on the guitar soundboard near the bridge and also on the side of the instrument near the neck are both requirements found in David Leisner's *Dances in the Madhouse*.

In his *Nuances*, Yizhak Sadai asks the guitarist to strike the back of the instrument while pressing down all the strings. It is also possible (and effective) to strike the bridge of either guitar or mandolin with the hand; see the following works:

G. Arrigo: *Tre Occasioni*
L. Foss: *Fragments of Archilochos*
G. Read: *Canzone di Notte*

Today's composers might find it profitable to examine the very elaborate notation devised by the noted guitarist-composer Alvaro Company in his treatise, *Las Seis Cuerdas,* for designating both agents and locales for percussive effects on the instrument.

KEYBOARD INSTRUMENTS

Of the several keyboard instruments available to the contemporary composer, the piano offers the greatest possibility for percussive use. Sounds so produced may originate on various areas of the interior—the strings or the metal frame—or on the exterior body of the instrument.[3] Without a doubt, the most common method of interior playing is to pluck a string, quasi-pizzicato, with the following diverse agents:

1. The fingertip

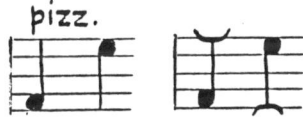

W. Albright: *Danse Macabre*
E. Brown: *Hodograph I; Music for Cello and Piano*
T. Bruins: *Sei Studie*
E. Bujarski: *Kinoth*
S. Bussotti: *Five Pieces for David Tudor; Il Nudo*
J. Cage: *Pastorale for Piano Solo*
R. Cordero: *Cello Sonata*
H. Cowell: *The Banshee*
G. Crumb: *Eleven Echoes of Autumn; Five Pieces*
W. Eisma: *Affairs II*
F. Evangelisti: *Ordini*
R. L. Finney: *Divertissement*
A. Gilbert: *Sonata No. 2*
R. Haubenstock-Ramati: *Credentials*

J. M. Horvath: *Die Blinde*
A. Hrisanide: *Volumes*
M. Ishii: *Sieben Stücke*
A. Lanza: *Plectros II*
H. Lazarof: *Textures*
I. Lidholm: *Poesis*
B. Maderna: *Concerto for Oboe*
K. Penderecki: *Anaklasis; Sonata per Violoncello e Orchestra*
B. Schäffer: *Modell III*
E. Schwartz: *Music for Prince Albert*
K. Serocki: *Fantasmagoria*
A. Silsbee: *Spirals*
J. Spiegelman: *Morsels*
A. de la Vega: *Antinomies*
S. Wiechowicz: *Lettre à Marc Chagall*
C. Wolff: *Duet I for Piano 4 Hands*

2. Two fingers

M. Ishii: *Aphorismen*

3. The thumb

A. Silsbee: *Spirals*

4. The fingernail

W. Albright: *Danse Macabre*
D. Banks: *Assemblies*
R. du Bois: *Pour faire chanter*
S. Bussotti: *Couple; Il Nudo*
Chou Wen-chung: *Cursive*
R. Cordero: *Cello Sonata*
G. Crumb: *Eleven Echoes of Autumn; Night Music I, II*
M. Davidovsky: *Inflexions*
A. Gilbert: *Sonata No. 2*

R. Haubenstock-Ramati: *Credentials*
W. Hellermann: *Formata*
J. Horvath: *Die Blinde*
P. R. Olsen: *Images*
G. Read: *Haiku Seasons*
E. Schwartz: *Music for Prince Albert*
K. Serocki: *Segmenti*
A. Silsbee: *Spirals*
A. de la Vega: *Antinomies; Structures*
C. Wolff: *Duet I*

Example 20
Istvan Anhalt: from *Foci* (p. 110)

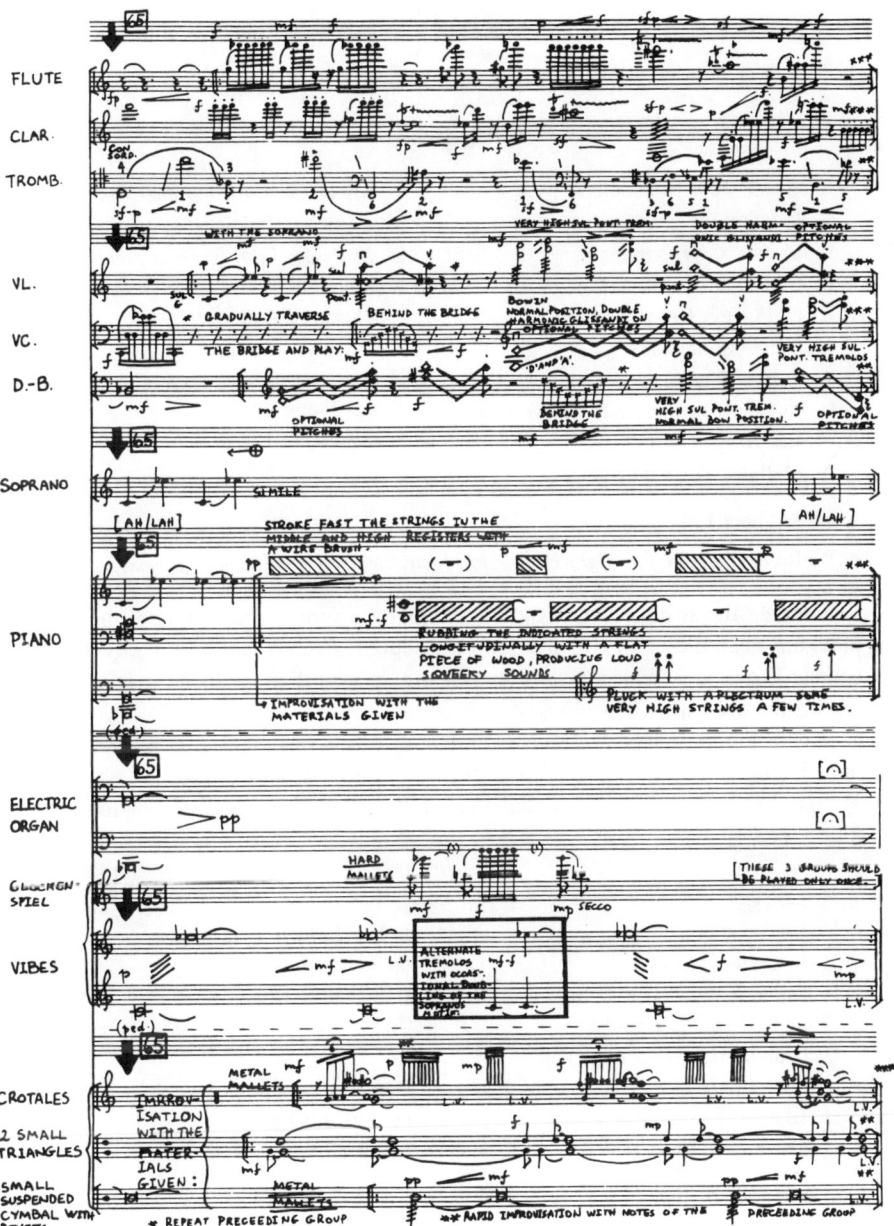

© Copyright 1972 by Berandol Music Limited. Used by permission.

5. A plectrum or pick (or an ordinary paperclip)

I. Anhalt: *Foci* (Example 20)
T. Antoniou: *Nenikikamen*
E. Brown: *Corroboree*
B. Childs: *Jack's New Bag; Nonet*
R. L. Finney: *Divertissement*
M. Ishii: *Aphorismen*
A. Lanza: *Plectros I, II*
P. Maxwell Davies: *Eight Songs for a Mad King*
A. Mellnäs: *Tombola*

C. Miereanu: *Finis Coronet Opus*
M. Mitrea-Celarianu: *Seth*
L. de Pablo: *Libro para el pianista*
R. Reynolds: *Blind Men; Quick are the Mouths of Earth*
B. Schäffer: *Scultura*
H. Shimoyama: *Dialog for Violoncello and Piano*
W. Szalonek: *Les Sons*

6. A dinner fork

W. Russell: *Fugue for Eight Percussion Instruments; Three Dance Movements*

Plucking the string close to the pegs imparts a hard, metallic bite to the tone; plucking near the center of the string produces a more mellow quality to the sound. The higher strings have less sustaining power than the lower octaves, and are brittle and thin when plucked.

In addition to the above-described methods of interior pizzicato, the strings of the piano can be patted, slapped, struck, or tapped with a wide selection of agents. Methods that rely on the use of the player's two hands include the following:

1. The fingertips

   D. Banks: *Assemblies*
   S. Bussotti: *Memoria*
   F. Cerha: *Formation et Solution*
   Chou Wen-chung: *Cursive*
   G. Crumb: *Makrokosmos—Vol. I; Night Music I*
   H. Dianda: *Estructuras*
   D. Eberhard: *Parody*

   J. M. Horvath: *Die Blinde*
   A. Lanza: *Plectros I, II*
   H. Lazarof: *Textures*
   C. Miereanu: *Finis Coronet Opus*
   K. Penderecki: *Strophes*
   R. Reynolds: *Wedge*
   K. Serocki: *Niobe*
   J. Spiegelman: *Morsels*

2. The fingernails

   S. Bussotti: *Five Pieces for David Tudor; Il Nudo*
   G. Crumb: *Five Pieces for Piano; Night Music*

   A. Gilbert: *Sonata No. 2*
   R. Reynolds: *Quick are the Mouths of Earth*
   A. de la Vega: *Antinomies for Piano*

PERCUSSIVE DEVICES   **81**

In *Makrokosmos—Vol. II*, George Crumb directs the pianist to strike the strings sharply with the curved fingers, so that the fingernails contact the strings. Roger Hannay calls for an allied effect in *Fantôme:* the pianist drops the tips of his left-hand fingernails directly onto the strings. *Parody* by Dennis Eberhard includes a directive to slap a string with a fingernail while simultaneously hitting the corresponding key, then releasing it suddenly.

3. The knuckles

J. Mills-Cockell: *Fragments*
A. de la Vega: *Antinomies for Piano*

4. The palm or open hand

T. Antoniou: *Fluxus I*
D. Burge: *Aeolian Music*
S. Bussotti: *Il Nudo; Mit einem gewissen sprechenden Ausdruck*
J. Casken: *Music for a Tawny-Gold Day*
G. Crumb: *Echoes of Time and the River; Night Music I*
D. Eberhard: *Parody*
D. Erb: *The Seventh Trumpet*
L. Ferrari: *Société II*
R. L. Finney: *Divertissement*
J. Gilboa: *The Jerusalem Chagall Windows*
R. Hannay: *Fantôme*
R. Haubenstock-Ramati: *Credentials*
M. Kagel: *Transición II*
W. Kilar: *Dipthongos*

W. Kotonski: *Pour quatre*
A. Lanza: *Plectros, I, II*
I. Lidholm: *Poesis*
T. Lucas: *Aberrations No. VII*
A. Mellnäs: *Tombola*
L. de Pablo: *Reciprico*
R. Reynolds: *Wedge*
R. Romiti: *Palingenesis*
E. Schwartz: *Music for Napoleon and Beethoven* (Example 31)
K. Serocki: *Niobe; Symphonic Frescoes*
W. Szalonek: *Proporzioni II*
A. de la Vega: *Antinomies for Piano; Exospheres for Oboe and Piano*
L. Widdoes: *From a Time of Snow*
R. Wittinger: *Espressioni*

5. The edge of the open hand

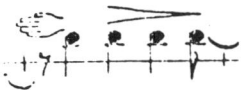

H. Dianda: *Estructuras*
A. Lanza: *Plectros I*
B. Rands: *Wildtrack 1*

6. The clenched fist

N. T. Dao: *Tây Nguyên*
A. Lanza: *Plectros I, II*
V. Luti: *Mixed Quintet*

G. Read: *Haiku Seasons*
A. de la Vega: *Exospheres for Oboe and Piano; Structures for Piano and String Quartet*

Extraneous objects used in playing upon the piano strings, as found in recently published scores, include:

1. Mallets or drumsticks (such as soft timpani, hard rubber, sponge-headed, medium plastic, bamboo, and so on)

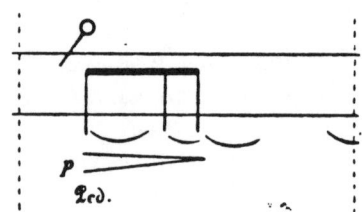 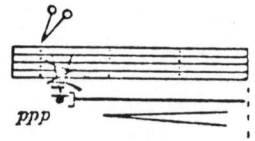

I. Anhalt: *Foci*
R. du Bois: *Pour faire chanter*
E. Brown: *Music for Cello and Piano*
E. Bujarski: *Kinoth*
G. Crumb: *Echoes of Time and the River; Night Music I*
D. Eberhard: *Parody*
H-U. Engelmann: *Cadenza*
D. Erb: *Symphony of Overtures*
J. Gilboa: *The Jerusalem Chagall Windows*
C. Halffter: *Planto por las victimas de la violencia*
H. Hartwell: *Soul Piece*
R. Herder: *Requiem II*
H. Holliger: *Siebengesang*
A. Hovhaness: *Jhala*
A. Lanza: *Plectros I, II*
H. Lazarof: *Espaces*

D. Martino: *Notturno*
A. Mellnäs: *Tombola*
K. M-Nazar: *Variazioni concertanti*
P. Nørgård: *Symphony No. 2*
M. Ohana: *Sorôn-Ngô*
K. Penderecki: *De Natura Sonoris (I); Dimensions of Time and Silence*
H. Pousseur: *Honeyrêves*
R. Reynolds: *Blind Men; The Emperor of Ice Cream*
W. Russell: *Fugue for Eight Percussion Instruments*
E. Schwartz: *Music for Napoleon and Beethoven; Soliloquies*
H. Shimoyama: *Dialog for Violoncello and Piano*
A. de la Vega: *Antinomies for Piano; Exospheres for Oboe and Piano*
R. Wittinger: *Espressioni*

2. Wirebrushes

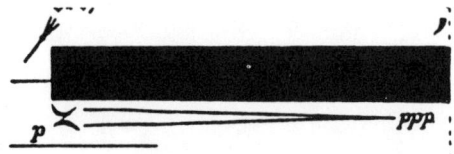

I. Anhalt: *Foci* (Example 20)
G. Crumb: *Night Music II*
H. W. Henze: *Sinfonia N. 6*
J. M. Horvath: *Die Blinde*
A. Janson: *Canon*
K. M-Nazar: *Variazioni concertanti*

L. de Pablo: *Libro para el pianista;*
  Modulos III
K. Penderecki: *Dimensions of Time*
  and Silence
R. Reynolds: *The Emperor of Ice*
  Cream

3. Triangle beaters or thin metal rods

L. Foss: *Ni bruit ni vitesse*

4. A steel rod held vertically

W. Szalonek: *Mutanza*

5. Knitting needles

A. Mellnäs: *Tombola*

6. Pencils (with the wood or the metal end)

D. Cope: *Iceberg Meadow*
J. Gilboa: *The Jerusalem Chagall*
  Windows
G. Heussenstamm: *Seventeen*
  Impressions

J. M. Horvath: *Die Blinde*
T. Lucas: *Aberrations No. VII*
R. Swift: *Piano Concerto*

7. A clave or piece of wood

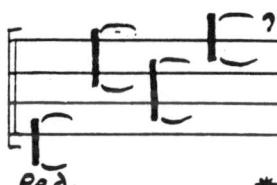

M. Finnissy: *As When Upon a Tranced Summer Night*
C. Halffter: *Planto por las victimas de la violencia*
E. Vercoe: *Herstory III*

8. A xylophone mallet and a clave

R. Hannay: *Fantôme*

9. Four cimbalom sticks

A. Gilbert: *Spell Respell*

10. A plectrum or pick

I. Anhalt: *Foci* (Example 20)
R. L. Finney: *Divertissement*
H. Shimoyama: *Dialog for Violoncello and Piano*

11. Teaspoons

J. Kunst: *Ijzer*
L. Moss: *Omaggio*

12. A metal plate or a cymbal

K. Penderecki: *Fluorescences*
B. Schäffer: *S'Alto*
R. Wittinger: *Concentrazione*

13. An antique cymbal (crotale)

G. Crumb: *Music for a Summer Evening; Night Music I*

14. A well-rosined cello bow

T. Marco: *Jetztzeit*

15. A plastic fly swatter or ruler

B. Childs: *Jack's New Bag*
C. Halffter: *Noche Pasiva del Sentido; Planto por las victimas de la violencia*
P. Patterson: *Rebecca*

16. A screwdriver

N. T. Dao: *Tây Nguyên*

17. A hammer

Y. Sadai: *Nuances*

18. A hairbrush

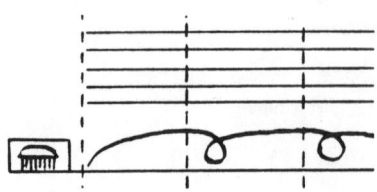

PERCUSSIVE DEVICES 85

E. Bujarski: *Kinoth*
H. W. Henze: *Sinfonia N. 6*

J. Kunst: *Ijzer*
A. Mellnäs: *Tombola*

19. A clothes brush and a toothbrush

N. T. Dao: *Tây Nguyên*

20. A water glass or small bottle

M. Mitrea-Celarianu: *Seth*

21. The metal edge of a wooden ruler

D. Cope: *Parallax*

22. Thimble-capped fingers

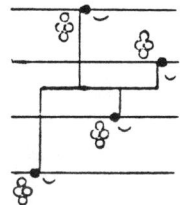

Chou Wen-chung: *Yu Ko*
G. Crumb: *Makrokosmos—Vol. I*

J. M. Horvath: *Die Blinde*
A. Lanza: *Plectros I, II*

23. The fingers of a leather glove (not worn!)

G. Ligeti: *Nouvelles Aventures*

A threefold percussive effect is demonstrated in Matthias Bamert's *Introduction and Tarantella:* a tambourine is to be laid on the strings and struck with a soft mallet, resulting in the simultaneous sounds of the tambourine jingles and struck membrane plus reverberations of the piano strings.

Indubitably effective as a percussive device but patently hard on the piano strings is the directive to drop a large piece of wood or a heavy metal bar onto the strings of the lowest section, leaving the sustaining pedal down and allowing the sound to vibrate until it dies away. Somewhat more delicate effects are to be obtained by dropping such lighter objects as pencils, a snare drum stick, or several bamboo sticks onto the strings. One or the other of these various actions can be seen in the following works:

H-U. Engelmann: *Cadenza*
M. Kagel: *Transición II*
A. Lanza: *Plectros II*

K. Penderecki: *Anaklasis; Cantata in Honorem Alma Matris*
W. Szalonek: *Mutanza*
R. Wittinger: *Espressioni*

In Penderecki's *Dies Irae,* and *Grablegung Christi* a similar result is obtained by dropping a hand cymbal onto the strings. And Szalonek in his *Mutanza* also requests that steel balls, 15 to 20 cm in diameter, be poured onto the strings of one section; ordinary marbles could also be used for this action, though the

Example 21
Lukas Foss: from *Ni bruit ni vitesse* (p. 10)

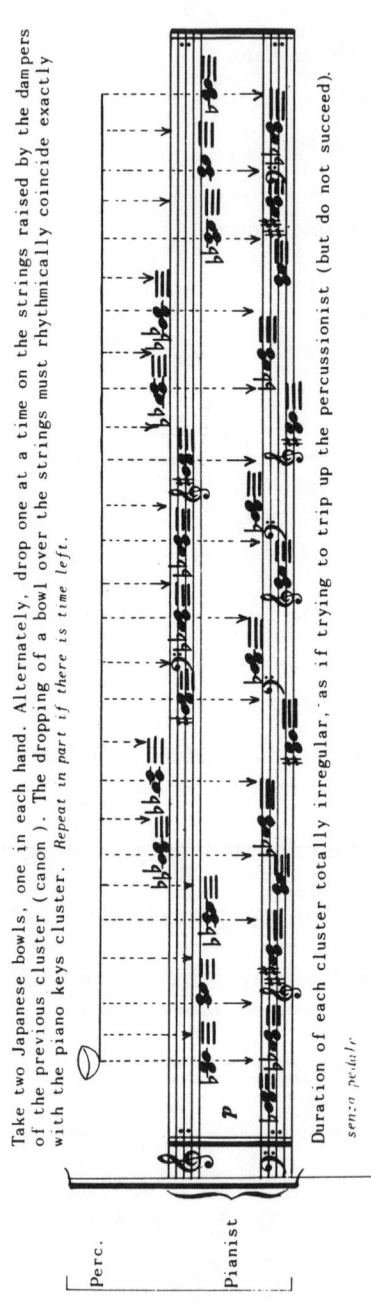

Copyright © 1973 Editions Salabert (France). All rights for the U.S. & Canada controlled by G. Schirmer, Inc. (New York). International Copyright Secured. All Rights Reserved. Used by Permission.

resulting sound might be less sharp and decisive. Equally effective as an auditory as well as a visual experience is Pauline Oliveros's directive in her *Theatre Piece* to the trombonist to roll the instrument bell over the piano strings.

In *Ni bruit ni vitesse* (Example 21) Lukas Foss has the pianist play upon the keyboard while an assistant drops a pair of Japanese lacquer bowls on the strings. In the same work, the bowls—gently placed on certain strings—are shoved with the pianist's hand to produce a faint sound, or the piano itself is pushed by the player to reactivate the lingering sound.

There is an amusing 30-second sequence in Paul Patterson's *Rebecca* in which the pianist continuously drops several tennis balls onto the interior strings, the pedal depressed, to the accompaniment of deflating balloons. Tennis balls are also utilized for a similar purpose in Mireanu's *Finis Coronet Opus,* and there is a command in *Superball!* of Raymond Wilding-White that the pianist drop five sizes of ping-pong balls onto the interior strings as well as on the soundboard and metal frame. On the other hand, Tomas Marco in *Jetztzeit* requires only one ping-pong ball be dropped onto the strings.

Pitchless percussive noises can be produced on the exterior surfaces or various interior parts of the piano. Avant-gardists are usually quite precise in designating areas to be struck in some manner. On the outside of the instrument these include the sides next to the keyboard, under the keyboard, the top surfaces, or the music rack if one is used. These areas may be struck with the flat fingers, palm, fingernails, knuckles, clenched fist, or with a stick or similar object. Such requirements are prominently displayed in:

W. Albright: *Danse Macabre*
D. Banks: *Tirade*
D. Bedford: *Music for Albion Moonlight*
R. du Bois: *Pour faire chanter*
D. Burge: *Aeolian Music*
S. Bussotti: *Couple; Five Pieces for David Tudor*
J. Cage: *The Wonderful Widow of Eighteen Springs*
B. Childs: *Jack's New Bag; Music for Trombone*
G. Crumb: *Echoes of Time and the River; Night Music I*
L. Ferrari: *Société II*
S. Garant: *Cage d'Oiseau; Piece for Piano No. 2*
V. Globokar: *Vendre le nuit*
W. Heider: *Landschaftspartitur*
S. Hodkinson: *Fresco*
M. Ishii: *Aphorismen*

M. Kelemen: *Changeant*
I. Lidholm: *Poesis*
G. Ligeti: *Apparitions*
T. Lucas: *Aberrations No. VII*
B. Maderna: *Stele per Diotima*
J. Mills-Cockell: *Fragments*
P. Olson: *Images*
B. Rands: *Espressione IV*
R. Reynolds: *The Emperor of Ice Cream*

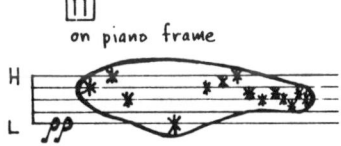

B. Schäffer: *Scultura*
E. Schwartz: *Septet; Soliloquies*
K. Serocki: *Fantasmagoria*
A. de la Vega: *Antinomies for Piano; Exospheres for Oboe and Piano*

Other agents required in recent works have included a coin (denomination unspecified, in Krenek's *Sonata for Flute*); a wood ruler (in *Société II* of Luc Ferrari), a plastic fly swatter (in Barney Child's musical catch-all, *Jack's New Bag*), a knife blade (in Maxwell Davies' *Vesalii Icones*), and a wooden hammer (in Haubenstock-Ramati's *Jeux 6 für zwei Schlagzeuger*).

The piano pedal can also be utilized percussively: it can be sharply depressed so that one hears not only a noise but the added resonance of the strings vibrating; or the foot can strike the pedal forcibly without depressing it fully. These several usages can be seen in the following scores:

D. Bedford: *Music for Albion Moonlight*
B. Ferneyhough: *Sonata for Two Pianos*
M. Finnissey: *As When Upon a Tranced Summer Night*
A. Gilbert: *Sonata No. 2*
V. Globokar: *Vendre le nuit*

M. Kagel: *Transición II*
A. Lanza: *Plectros I, II*
P. Lewis: *Sweets for Piano*
T. Marco: *Jetztzeit*
F. Miroglio: *Réfractions*
B. Schäffer: *Musica per pianoforte*

In his orchestral *Heterophonie,* Kagel requests a percussive pedal effect on the celesta; no examples for harpsichord pedals have so far been observed.

Much favored by today's avant-gardist, possibly for visual as well as for auditory shock value, is slamming down the keyboard cover:

W. Albright: *Seven Deadly Sins*
S. Bussotti: *Couple; Il Nudo*
J. Cage: *Music of Changes IV*
J. Christou: *Enantiodromia*
S. Hodkinson: *Fresco*
A. Hrisanide: *Volumes*
M. Kelemen: *Olifant*

T. Mayuzumi: *Metamusic*
P. Patterson: *Rebecca*
R. Reynolds: *Wedge*
B. Schäffer: *Musica per pianoforte*
E. Schwartz: *Septet; Soliloquies*
R. Wilding-White: *Whatzit No. 1*

Interior piano areas available for percussion use include the metal frame or cross-beams, the tuning pins, the wooden sides, and the soundboard—the latter struck through the largest hole in the metal frame; see the following works for examples of interior percussion:

W. Albright: *Danse Macabre* (Example 22)
R. Ashley: *Maneuvers for Small Hands*
D. Burge: *Aeolian Music*
S. Bussotti: *Mit einem gewissen sprechenden Ausdruck*

G. Crumb: *Echoes of Time and the River; Night Music I*
L. Foss: *Orpheus*
R. Hannay: *Fantôme*
C. Miereanu: *Finis Coronet Opus*
P. Nørgård: *Symphony No. 2*

PERCUSSIVE DEVICES

Example 22
William Albright: from *Danse Macabre* (p. 14)

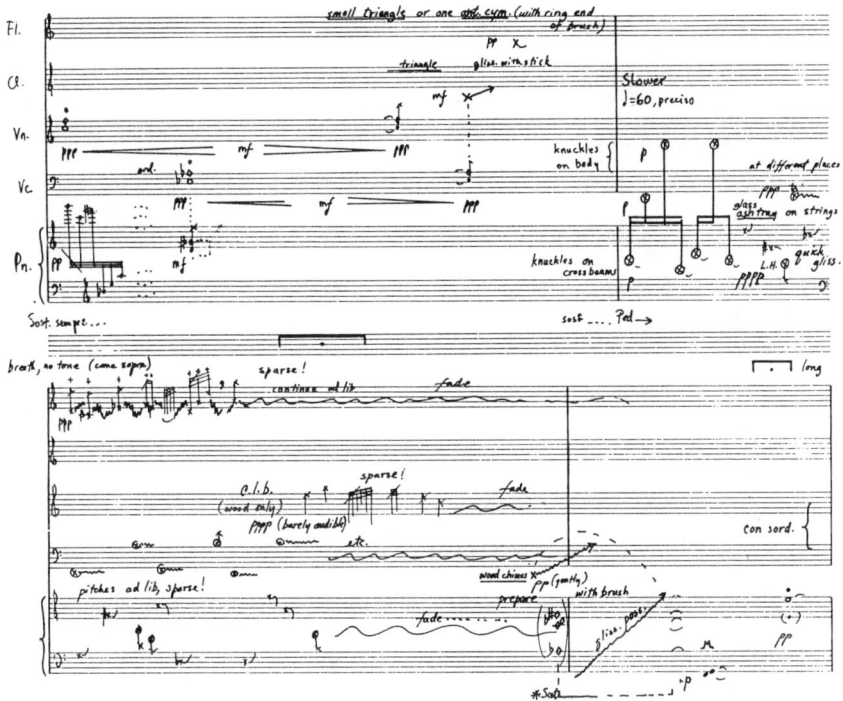

Bowdoin College Music Press. © Copyright 1972 by the President and Trustees of Bowdoin College. Quoted by permission of the copyright owner.

Although, strictly speaking, it is not a percussive effect, mention should be made of Witold Szalonek's directive in *Mutanza* to rub the surface of the soundboard with a nylon cork. Foss includes a parallel direction to the keyboard player in *Orpheus* to rub a wooden chime mallet along the soundboard.

As with the other interior techniques on piano, contemporary composers have generally been careful to designate specific agents of attack on cross-beams, tuning pegs, and related areas:

1. The fingers

E. Schwartz: *Septet; Soliloquies*

2. The fingernails

S. Bussotti: *Couple*
G. Crumb: *Night Music I*

3. The knuckles

W. Albright: *Danse Macabre* (Example 22)
D. Burge: *Aeolian Music*
G. Crumb: *Eleven Echoes of Autumn; Makrokosmos—Vol. 1*
L. Ferrari: *Société II*
A. Janson: *Canon*
E. Schwartz: *Septet; Soliloquies*

4. A stick or mallet

D. Burge: *Aeolian Music*
S. Bussotti: *Il Nudo*
D. Cope: *Parallax*
G. Crumb: *Night Music I*
R. Hannay: *Fantôme*
B. Maderna: *Stele per Diotima*
R. Reynolds: *Wedge*
E. Schwartz: *Music for Napoleon and Beethoven* (Example 31)
H. Shimoyama: *Dialog for Violoncello and Piano*

5. A coin or small metal object

M. Ishii: *Aphorismen*
W. Szalonek: *Proporzioni II*

6. A crotale beater

G. Crumb: *Music for a Summer Evening*

7. A hammer

B. Childs: *Jack's New Bag*
V. Luti: *Mixed Quintet*

8. The spine of a heavy hardbound book

D. Cope: *Indices*

In his fancifully titled *Mit einem gewissen sprechenden Ausdruck,* Bussotti directs the pianist to draw a metal stick heavily along the tuning pins, an action that produces an impressive clatter.

In addition to the pitchless glissando over the white keys (mentioned on page 45), Roger Reynolds further stipulated in *Blind Men* that the player rasp the wood end of a mallet across the edges of both white and black keys, resulting in a rhythmic clacking. Similarly, in Barney Child's work cited above the pianist is to glissando along the fronts of the white keys with a wood stick.

Three closely allied percussive key effects have been utilized by Kagel in *Anagrama:* an already depressed key is struck sharply with the finger, making an audible click; a key is struck with a ring on the player's finger; and a key is held by the fingers of one hand (without being depressed) and then struck with a finger ring. Another action stipulated by Kagel is for the pianist to strike a key sharply and then depress it silently.

In his various piano works Bussotti invariably requests that the keys be tapped or trilled upon with the fingertips or nails, but so lightly that the keys are not depressed and one hears only faint percussive clickings (as in the *Five Pieces for David Tudor*). These same actions are also requested by Niccolo Castiglioni in *Consonante* and by Kagel in his solo organ *Improvisation ajoutée*, as well as in Bernard Rands' *Espressioni IV*.

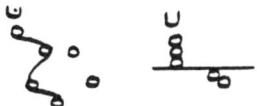

The accordion—especially the modern free-bass model—is capable of some unusual percussive effects, although to date few composers for the instrument have notably availed themselves of these particular sound resources. Among the several possibilities one might list: 1) slapping the keys very lightly to create a percussive impact to the pitch(es) sounded; 2) audibly clicking the registration switches, rather akin to the sound of woodwind instrument key clacks; 3) flicking the nail on the bellows snaps; 4) running the finger, or a stick or pencil, along the opened bellows; 5) knocking with the fingers or knuckles on various parts of the instrument; 6) tapping with the palm on the front side of the opened bellows—a sound that is remarkably drumlike and resonant.

STRINGS

Possibly no avant-garde string technique is more varied in production or more intriguing sonically than the concept—currently high in favor—of the bowed strings as percussion rather than lyric instruments. As with the keyboard instruments, there are basically two modes of producing percussive sounds: the strings themselves are struck in various manners, or the body of the individual instrument becomes the locale for varied attack. Precise areas on the strings or on the instrument frame are indicated and the striking agents are specifically designated by the great majority of composers.

In point of historical development, *col legno* was the earliest percussive technique applied to the bowed string instruments. Although striking the strings with the wood of the bow was first utilized by composers as early as 1605, it was rare even in nineteenth-century string literature.[4] Not until the early part of the present century did the technique become firmly rooted in orchestrational practice; at the same time it assumed an increasingly important role in chamber music for strings (the quartets of Schönberg, Berg, and Webern, for instance). Today a number of viable variations of the *col legno* technique have appeared in vanguard scores; these may be catalogued as follows:

1. The string is struck or rubbed with the hair and wood of the bow simultaneously, the bow being turned on its side; whether specifically requested or not, this is the manner in which most string players respond to *col legno* directives

   M. Colgrass: *Rhapsodic Fantasy*
   K. Gaburo: *Antiphony IV; Two*
   W. Haupt: *CSS1 (Cellosolosonate)*
   M. Kagel: *Match; Sonant*

   M. Seiber: *Pastorale and Burlesque*
   W. Sydeman: *Projections I; Texture Studies for Orchestra*

2. The strings are struck over the fingerboard with the wood of the bow (*col legno battuto*)

   C. Halffter: *Anillos*
   M. Kagel: *Sexteto de cuerdas*

3. The strings are struck directly over the bridge, *col legno*

   M. Davidovsky: *Synchronisms No. 3*
   L. Harrison: *Suite for Symphonic Strings*
   A. Lanza: *Cuarteto V*

   S. Matsushita: *Fresque sonore*
   P. Méfano: *Paraboles*
   S. Wiechowicz: *Lettre à Marc Chagall*

4. The strings are gently stroked or rubbed with the back of the bow (*col legno frotté*)

   F. Evangelisti: *Aleatorio*
   R. Kayn: *Galaxis*
   H. Pousseur: *Ode pour quatuor à cordes*

   W. Rudzinski: *Pictures from the Holy-Cross Mountains*

5. The left-hand fingernail strikes the string at the same time that the back of the bow taps the same string

   M. Kagel: *Match*

6. *Col legno battuto* is combined simultaneously with left-hand pizzicato on the same string

   S. Cervetti: *Zinctum*

7. The same, combined with glissando on the string

   D. Erb: *Trio for Two*
   M. Kagel: *Sexteto de cuerdas*

8. The strings are deadened with the left-hand fingers or palm, the wood of the bow then bouncing from the fingerboard to the bridge, creating a "skittering" effect

   M. Colgrass: *As Quiet As*
   J. Druckman: *Animus 2; String Quartet No. 2*

   L. Ferrari: *Société II*
   V. Globokar: *Accord*
   K. M-Nazar: *Variazioni concertanti*

Example 23
Mel Powell: from *Filigree Setting* (p. 2)

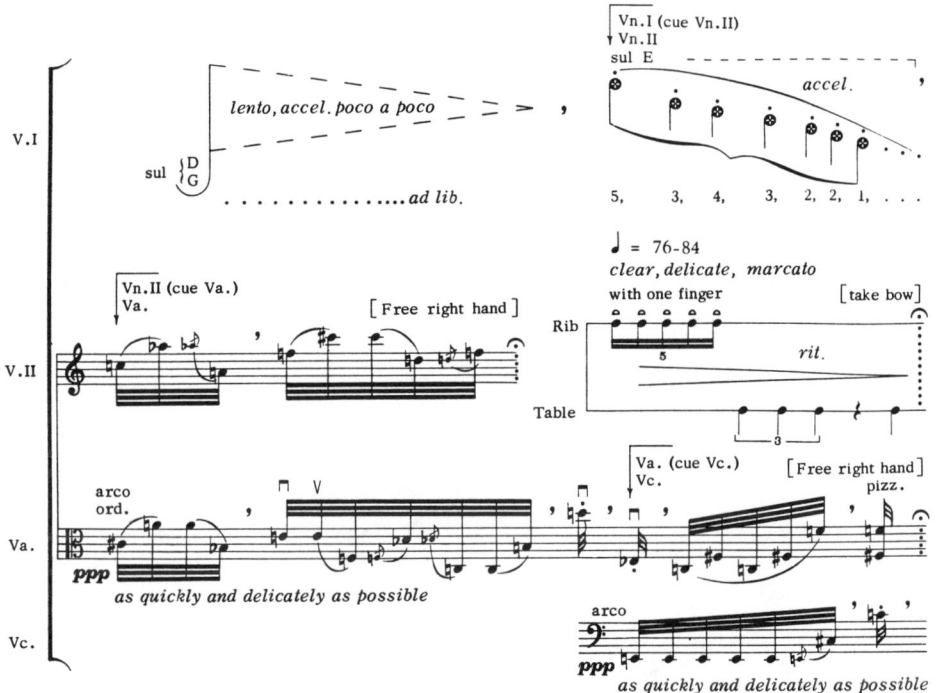

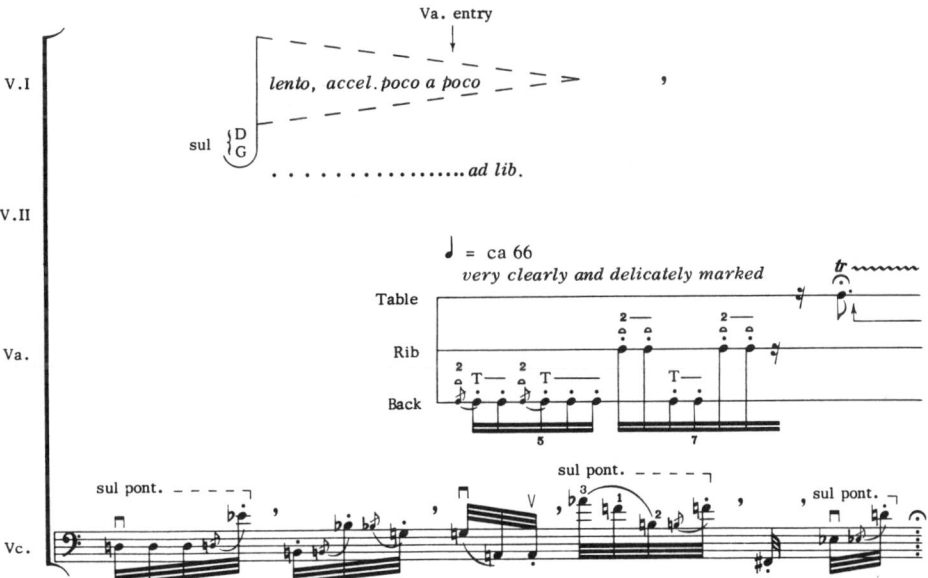

© Copyright 1965 by G. Schirmer, Inc. International Copyright Secured. All Rights Reserved. Used by permission.

9. With the left-hand fingers in first position (on violin and viola), lightly touching the strings as for harmonics, the bow-wood is bounced freely along the length of a pair of strings; the motion is from on or near the bridge toward the fingers

W. Kilar: *Générique*
M. Kopelent: *3. Quartetto*

M. Powell: *Filigree Setting* (Example 23)
R. Reynolds: *Quick are the Mouths of Earth*

10. Same, on cello (possible also on doublebass); the motion is from the end of the fingerboard to the bridge

J. Druckman: *Incenters*
M. Powell: *Filigree Setting*

11. *Col legno battuto* on the strings behind the bridge; according to Lou Harrison, on the doublebass this will produce "a slightly 'pingy' semi-pitched drumming, whose sound will suggest both that of the marimbula and that of certain Oriental drums."

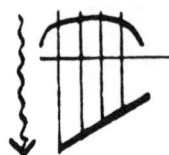

G. Bacewicz: *In una parte*
L. Berio: *Epifanie*
E. Brown: *String Quartet*
B. Childs: *Nonet*
M. Davidovsky: *Synchronisms No. 3*
D. Erb: *Reconnaissance*
R. Gerhard: *Concerto for Orchestra*
A. Ginastera: *Bomarzo Cantata*
L. Harrison: *Suite for Symphonic Strings*
A. Lanza: *Cuarteto V*

S. Matsushita: *Fresque sonore*
A. Mellnäs: *Gestes sonores; Per caso*
K. M-Nazar: *Variazioni concertanti*
K. Penderecki: *The Devils of Loudun; Fluorescences*
A. de la Vega: *Segments for Violin and Piano: Structures for Piano and String Quartet*
G. Wilson: *Concatenations*

12. The player arpeggiates with the back of the bow across the four strings behind the bridge

M. Mitrea-Celarianu: *Seth*

13. The fingerboard is struck or tapped *col legno*

S. Bussotti: *Il Nudo*
M. Davidovsky: *Synchronisms No. 3*

S. Matsushita: *Fresque sonore*
F. Raxach: *Estrofas*

14. The tailpiece is struck, tapped, or stroked *col legno;* the graphic symbol devised by Penderecki for this effect cannot be bettered

PERCUSSIVE DEVICES

B. Conyngham: *Ice Carving*
R. Gerhard: *Concerto for 8; Concerto for Orchestra*
J. Harvey: *Inner Light III*
H-J. Hespos: *Passagen*
S. Hodkinson: *Fresco*
M. Ishii: *Aphorismen*

M. Kelemen: *Changeant; Surprise*
M. Mamiya: *String Quartet No. 1*
D. Martino: *Parisonatina al' dodecafonia*
K. Penderecki: *The Devils of Loudun; Polymorphia*
D. Reck: *Blues and Screamer*

15. *Col legno battuto* on the chin rest

R. Gerhard: *Concerto for Orchestra*

16. The undersides of the strings are rubbed with the wood of the bow just over the end of the fingerboard; the effect is obviously most feasible on cello and doublebass

B. Sakač: *Struktur I*

17. A tri-dimensional effect is obtained on cello by striking the two lower strings *col legno* while at the same time sliding the thumb and index finger on the strings, and plucking the C-string with the third or fourth finger

C. Alsina: *Trio 1967*

18. The doublebass player lightly stops the open strings to prevent clear pitches from sounding, the bow-wood bouncing from near the bridge to the fingerboard (*ricochet legno*); the aural result is a rapidly descending figure of indeterminate pitches

D. Bedford: *Music for Albion Moonlight; Piece for Mo*
J. Druckman: *Incenters; Valentine*

It has been suggested that a potential solution to the ever-present danger that a string player seriously scratches the varnish on his bow when playing *col legno* is to have at hand a second and cheaper bow. This suggestion, however, does not take into consideration the time factor involved in quickly switching from arco or pizzicato to *col legno*. Obviously, it would be impossible for any string player to change from one bow to another with undue speed; thus this solution cannot be considered truly feasible, however highly desirable.

In addition to *col legno* there are a number of other and highly favored modes of percussive attack on the string(s) of the family members. In the listings that follow, the devices first enumerated apply to all the stringed instruments; those more or less limited to the cello and doublebass follow in separate listings. Certain manners of playing are only feasible on these latter instruments, owing to their size, shape, and the physical relationship of player to instrument. Devices applicable to all the instruments include:

1. Slap or strike the strings with the flat left-hand fingers over the fingerboard

C. Alsina: *Trio 1967*
G. Arrigo: *Infrarosa*
D. Bedford: *Piece for Mo*
S. Bussotti: *Mit einem gewissen sprechenden Ausdruck; Phase à trois*
S. Cervetti: *Six Sequences for Dance; Zinctum*
D. Cope: *Angel's Camp II* (Example 50)
A. Curran: *Home-made*
M. Davidovsky: *Synchronisms No. 2*
H-J. Hespos: *Passagen*
M. Kagel: *Anagrama; Sonant*
M. Kelemen: *Changeant*
W. Kilar: *Dipthongos*
W. Kotonski: *a battere*
G. Ligeti: *Apparitions*
V. Luti: *Mixed Quintet*
M. Mamiya: *String Quartet No. 1*
A. Mellnäs: *Aura*
K. Meyer: *Concerto da Camera*
L. Nono: *Canto di vita e d'amore*
P. Nørgård: *Prism*
L. de Pablo: *Radial*
K. Penderecki: *Dimensions of Time and Silence; Fluoresences*
E. Raxach: *Estrofas*
G. Read: *Diabolic Dialogue*
R. Reynolds: *Quick are the Mouths of Earth*
Z. Rudzinski: *Moments Musicaux II*
R. M. Schafer: *Requiems for the Party-Girl*
B. Schäffer: *Scultura; String Quartet*
H. Schramm: *Shilappadikaram*
R. Sender: *Balances*
W. Szalonek: *Concertino per flauto*
K. E. Welin: *Nr.3-1961*
G. B. Wilson: *Concantenations*

2. Same, with the left hand, across the bridge

J. Fortner: *Quartet*
R. M. Schafer: *Requiems for the Party-Girl*
W. Sydeman: *Texture Studies*

3. Tap the string(s) with the left-hand finger(s)

G. Becker: *Diaglyphen*
S. Bussotti: *Il Nudo; Phrase à trois*
F. Cerha: *Enjambments*
R. Haubenstock-Ramati: *Tableau III*
A. Hrisanide: *Volumes*
M. Kagel: *Match; Sonant*
G. Ligeti: *Apparitions*
M. Mamiya: *String Quartet No. 1*
L. Nono: *Canti di vita e d'amore*
L. de Pablo: *Radial*
G. Read: *Diabolic Dialogue*
R. Reynolds: *Quick are the Mouths of Earth*
W. Sydeman: *Texture Studies*
W. Szalonek: *Concertino per flauto*
A. Vieru: *Clepsidra II*
R. Wittinger: *Irreversibilitazione*

4. Trill on the strings with the left-hand fingers (no bow)

PERCUSSIVE DEVICES

G. Becker: *Diaglyphen*
B. Brosch: *Prolations*
C. Halffter: *Pourquoi für Streicher*
M. Kupferman: *Infinities 24*

5. Tap on the string with a left-hand fingernail

M. Davidovsky: *Synchronisms No. 3*

6. Tap on string with two right-hand fingers (quasi-trill)

M. Babbitt: *String Quartet No. 4*
W. Haupt: *CSS1* (Cellosolosonate)

7. Trill or tremolo with the fingernails of the right hand

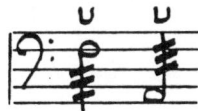

S. Cervetti: *Six Sequences for Dance*
B. Rands: *Memo 1*

8. Tap on the string with a right-hand fingernail

M. Subotnick: *Lamination I*
W. Sydeman: *Projections I*

9. Tap the string(s) with the right-hand knuckles

M. Kupferman: *Infinities 24*
R. Sender: *Balances*

10. Strike open strings with palm of right hand

D. Bedford: *Piece for Mo*
S. Cervetti: *Six Sequences for Dance*
A. Curran: *Home-made*
W. Haupt. *CSS1 (Cellosolosonate)*
H-J. Hespos: *Passagen*
M. Kagel: *Sonant*
M. Kelemen: *Abecedarium; Surprise*
W. Kilar: *Dipthongos*
E. Kurtz: *Improvisation for Contrabass*

A. Mellnäs: *Aura*
K. Meyer: *Concerto da camera*
K. Penderecki: *Dimensions of Time and Silence*
E. Raxach: *Estrofas*
B. Schäffer: *Scultura*
H. Schramm: *Shilappadikaram*
K. E. Welin: *Nr.3—1961*

11. Slap the four strings across the bridge with the right-hand flat fingers

W. Kotonski: *a battere*

12. Strike the four strings between the bridge and tailpiece

J. M. Horvath: *Redundanz 3*

13. Tap or trill with the right-hand fingers on the string(s) behind the bridge

Z. Bujarski: *Kinoth*
K. Penderecki: *Polymorphia*

14. Use both hands to slap strings quickly and loudly

W. Sydeman: *Texture Studies for Orchestra*

15. Trill on the string(s) with two thimble-capped fingers

G. Crumb: *Black Angels*

16. Tap on the string(s) with the ivory tip of the bow

I. Bazelon: *De-Tonations for Brass Quintet and Orchestra*

H. W. Henze: *Heliogabalus Imperator*

P. Phillips: *Divertimento for Three String Basses*

G. Read: *Symphony No. 3*

17. Use the metal (and wood) part of a pencil to bounce (*jeté*) on the string

B. Schäffer: *String Quartet*

W. Sydeman: *Projections I; Texture Studies*

18. Muffle the strings with the left hand; play on them with a pocket comb

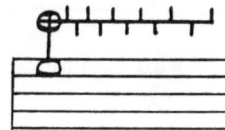

Y. Sadai: *Nuances*

19. Same, behind the bridge

Y. Sadai: *Nuances*

20. Hold the instrument like a mandolin; strike the string with a glass rod held in the left hand; the open string sounds automatically as the rod rebounds from the string

G. Crumb: *Black Angels*

21. Hold instrument (violin and viola) in the lap and play on the strings with a small stick

S. Montague: *At the white edge of phrygia*

22. Scrape with the fingernail up and down the lowest string of the instrument

D. Bedford: *That White and Radiant Legend*

Devices mainly applicable to cello and/or doublebass include:

1. Slap the four strings with the left-hand flat fingers near to or on the instrument neck

I. Anhalt: *Foci*

E. Kurtz: *Improvisation for Solo Contrabass*

2. Roll on the strings with a mallet

J. Druckman: *Valentine*

L. Harrison: *Labyrinth No. 3*

M. Kupferman: *Infinities 24*

W. Sydeman: *Texture Studies*

PERCUSSIVE DEVICES

3. Same, the mallets wielded by a percussionist

G. Crumb: *Madrigals—I*

4. Drum on the strings with a pencil

G. Rochberg: *Tableaux*

5. Same, with a metal stick

H. Ebenhöh: *4 Szenen für 10*

6. Hit a string with a wooden stick; let it bounce while squeezing it against the string, creating a fast, tight roll

J. Druckman: *Valentine*

7. Rattle a pencil, stick, or small dowel between two strings; close to the bridge this action picks up random harmonics

B. Childs: *Mr. T., His Fancy*
R. Erickson: *Ricercar à 3*

8. Same, with the tip of the bow

R. Aitken: *Kebyar*

9. Insert the handle of a mallet between two strings; beat rapidly from side to side while moving the handle from near the bridge to over the fingerboard

J. Druckman: *Valentine*

10. Arpeggiate rapidly across the strings behind the bridge with a wooden stick

J. Druckman: *Valentine*
J. Yuasa: *Triplicity for Contrabass*

11. With a large wooden salad-tossing spoon in the left hand, strike the strings behind the bridge

W. Sydeman: *Duo for Trumpet and Amplified Doublebass*

12. Same, with a tablespoon

W. Sydeman: *Texture Studies for Orchestra*

13. Lay the doublebass flat between two padded supports; play on the open strings with two rods

L. Harrison: *Violin Concerto*

14. Strike string(s) with a maraca

D. Erb: *Reconnaissance*

15. Same, with a wood stick

W. Albright: *Marginal Worlds*

16. Same, with a chopstick

B. Turetzky: *Poems, Portraits, Ballades and Blues*

17. Flick right-hand fingernail against the string

G. Read: *Diabolic Dialogue*

For percussion on the body of a string instrument the player may, of course, employ the same agents used for striking the strings, plus additional objects listed below. Furthermore, the diversity of locale is quite extensive, particularly on cello and doublebass, whose surface areas are both larger and more easily accessible to the players than those of violin and viola. Though not all composers are as specific in pinpointing the areas to be struck as they are in designating the agent of attack, the areas available include the following: the fingerboard, front or belly, sides or ribs, back, top or shoulders, neck, nut, and scroll—as well as the more commonly designated bridge and tailpiece. The following is a fairly comprehensive cataloguing of the percussive effects possible on the body of a string instrument:

1. Knock, strike, or tap on the body of the instrument (exact locale unspecified by the composer) with the fingers or thumb

C. Alsina: *Trio 1967*
D. Bedford: *Gastrula*
A. Blatter: *A Study of Time and Space*
D. Burge: *Aeolian Music*
S. Bussotti: *Il Nudo*
S. Cervetti: *Six Sequences for Dance; Zinctum*
B. Childs: *Jack's New Bag; Nonet*
G. Crumb: *Madrigals—Book I; Night Music II*
M. Davidovsky: *Synchronisms No. 3*
E. Denisov: *Crescendo e diminuendo*
J. Druckman: *Incenters; Valentine*
J. Fortner: *Quartet*
L. Harrison: *Suite for Symphonic Strings*
H. W. Henze: *Sinfonia N. 6*
A. Hrisanide: *Volumes*
M. Ishii: *Aphorismen*
M. Kagel: *Match für drei Spieler*
M. Kelemen: *Changeant*
M. Kopelent: *3. Quartetto*
A. Lanza: *Cuarteto V*
G. Ligeti: *Apparitions*
B. Maderna: *Quartetto per archi in due tempi*
T. Marco: *Aura*
D. Martino: *Parisonatina al' dodecafonia*
S. Matsushita: *Fresque sonore*
B. Nilsson: *Versuchungen*
K. Penderecki; *Capriccio per Siegfried Palm; Dimensions of Time and Silence*
B. Rands: *Actions for Six; Étendre*
D. Reck: *Blues and Screamer*
W. Rudzinski: *Pictures from the Holy-Cross Mountains*
Y. Sadai: *Nuances*
B. Schäffer: *4 Pieces for String Trio; Scultura*
W. Szalonek: *Concertino per flauto*

PERCUSSIVE DEVICES

2. Roll with the fingers, "quasi-tamburo," on the body (locale unspecified)

J. Fortner: *S pr ING*
A. Janson: *Canon*
C. Whittenberg: *Conversations for Solo Doublebass*

3. Strike or tap on body of instrument (locale unspecified) with the fingernails

R. Aitken: *Kebyar*
D. Burge: *Aeolian Music*
G. Darvas: *Sectio Aurea*
R. Haubenstock-Ramati: *Tableau III*
L. Widdoes: *From a Time of Snow*

4. Same, with the knuckles

W. Albright: *Danse Macabre*
  (Example 22)
D. Burge: *Aeolian Music*
F. Cerha: *Enjambments*
S. Cervetti: *Six Sequences: Zinctum*
G. Crumb: *Black Angels; Echoes of Time and the River*
W. Fortner: *Immagini*
L. Hiller: *String Quartet No. 5*
L. Hiller, L. M. Isaacson: *Illiac Suite*
D. Reck: *Blues and Screamer*
H. Schramm: *Shilappadikaram*
W. Szalonek: *Concertino per flauto*
D. Wilson: *Seventeen Views*

5. Same, with the flat hand

C. Alsina: *Trio 1967*
B. Bartolozzi: *Quartetto per archi*
D. Burge: *Aeolian Music*
W. Fortner: *Immagini*
C. Halffter: *Anillos*
M. Kagel: *Match; Sonant*
A. Lanza: *Cuarteto V*
A. Mellnäs: *Aura*
H. Schramm: *Shilappadikaram*
B. Schäffer: *Scultura; Trio*
C. Whittenberg: *Conversations for Solo Doublebass*

6. Same, with the wood of the bow

P. Chihara: *Driftwood*
Y. Claoue: *Mutations*
W. Fortner: *Immagini*
A. Lanza: *Cuarteto V*
B. Nilsson: *Versuchungen*
D. Reck: *Blues and Screamer*
Y. Sadai: *Nuances*

7. Same, with the nut (heel) of the bow

K. Penderecki: *Dimensions of Time and Silence; Threnody*
W. Rudzinski: *Pictures from the Holy-Cross Mountains*

8. Roll, tap, or trill with the fingers on the fingerboard

A. Bancquart: *Ecorces III*
G. Becker: *Diaglyphen*
D. Bedford: *Five for String Quintet; Music for Albion Moonlight*
L. Berio: *Sinfonia*
A. Curran: *Home-made*
J. Druckman: *Incenters*
D. Erb: *String Trio*
F. Evangelist: *Aleatorio*
B. Ferneyhough: *Sonatas for String Quartet*
J. Fortner: *Quartet*
R. Gerhard: *Concerto for Orchestra*
V. Globokar: *Accord*

C. Halffter: *Fibonaciana*
W. Haupt: *CSS1 (Cellosolosonate)*
H. W. Henze: *Sinfonia N. 6*
A. Hrisanide: *Volumes*
K. Huber: *Tenebrae*
D. Martino: *Parisonatina al' dodecafonia*
A. Mellnäs: *Capriccio per Orchestra*
K. Penderecki: *Fluorescences; Polymorphia*

M. Powell: *Filigree Setting* (Example 23)
D. Reck: *Blues and Screamer*
W. Rudzinski: *Pictures from the Holy-Cross Mountains*
R. Sender: *Balances*
B. Turetzky: *Poems, Portraits, Ballades and Blues*
A. Vieru: *Clepsidra II*

9. Same, with the fingernails

R. Sender: *Balances*

10. Same, with the knuckles

P. Chihara: *Logs*

11. Same, with the bowhair

M. Davidovsky: *Synchronisms No. 3*
E. Raxach: *Estrofas*

12. Rub the fingerboard with the fingers or flat hand

A. Hrisanide: *Volumes*
M. Ishii: *Aphorismen*
K. Penderecki: *Fluorescences*

W. Rudzinski: *Pictures from the Holy-Cross Mountains*
B. Schäffer: *Scultura*

13. Strike the fingerboard with the flat hand

C. Alsina: *Trio 1967*
E. Kurtz: *Improvisation for Contrabass*

D. Wilson: *Seventeen Views*
I. Xenakis: *Pithoprakta*

14. Same, with the cupped hand or fist

A. Bancquart: *Ecorces III*
T. Fredrickson: *Music for Five Instruments*

15. Snap the finger against the fingerboard

D. Erb: *Concerto for Solo Percussionist; The Seventh Trumpet*

16. Tap on the bridge with the finger(s)

M. Kagel: *Match für drei Spieler*
K. Penderecki: *Capriccio per Siegfried Palm; String Quartet No. 2*

PERCUSSIVE DEVICES

17. Same, with the hand

M. Davidovsky: *Synchronisms No. 3*

18. Strike the bridge (of cello or doublebass) with a mallet, stick, or pencil

B. Childs: *Nonet*

19. Tap horizontally on the bridge (between the strings) with the bowhair

D. Bedford: *That White and Radiant Legend*
J. Fortner: *Quartet*

L. Harrison: *Suite for Symphonic Strings*
S. Matsushita: *Fresque sonore*
D. Wilson: *Concatenations*

20. Tap on the tailpiece with the finger(s)

K. Huber: *Tenebrae*
B. Rands: *Étendre*

21. Strike the tailpiece with the fingernail

R. Sender: *Balances*

22. Rap, strike, or tap on the front (belly or box) of the instrument with the fingertips

G. Burt: *Exit Music*
B. Childs: *Mr. T., His Fancy*
G. Crumb: *Madrigals—I; Night Music II*
R. Gerhard: *Concerto for Orchestra*
R. Goeb: *Fantasy for Oboe*
L. Harrison: *Suite for Symphonic Strings*
S. Hodkinson: *Interplay*
D. Martino: *Notturno; Parisonatina al' dodecafonia*

P. Phillips: *Divertimento for Three String Basses*
G. Read: *Diabolic Dialogue*
G. Rochberg: *Music for the Magic Theatre*
R. Sender: *Balances*
W. Sydeman: *Projections I*

23. Same, with the fingernails

B. Childs: *Mr. T., His Fancy*
D. Martino: *Notturno*
R. Sender: *Balances*

24. Same, with the knuckles

S. Cervetti: *Zinctum*
B. Childs: *Mr. T., His Fancy*
G. Crumb: *Night of the Four Moons*

R. Gerhard: *String Quartet No. 2*
E. Kurtz: *Improvisation for Contrabass*

25. Same, with the flat hand

E. Kurtz: *Improvisation for Contrabass*
K. Penderecki: *Capriccio per Oboe*
I. Xenakis: *Pithoprakta*

26. Same, with cupped hand

T. Fredrickson: *Music for Five Instruments*

27. Same, with the bowstick

S. Cervetti: *Zinctum*

28. Tap on rim of the side and belly with the tip of the bow, moving toward the scroll

W. Sydeman: *Texture Studies for Orchestra*

29. Tap on one side of the instrument with the fingertips

B. Childs: *Mr. T., His Fancy*
M. Kagel: *Match für drei Spieler*
D. Martino: *Notturno*

30. Same, with the fingernails

T. Baird: *Espressioni varianti* (Example 24)
P. Chihara: *Logs*

B. Childs: *Mr. T., His Fancy*
R. Erickson: *Ricercar à 3*

31. Same, with the thumb

B. Childs: *Mr. T., His Fancy*

32. Same, with the knuckles

D. Burge: *Aeolian Music*
F. Cerha: *Enjambments*
P. Chihara: *Ceremony I: Logs*
B. Childs: *Mr. T., His Fancy*

A. Curran: *Home-made*
A. de la Vega: *Structures for Piano and String Quartet*

33. Same, with the bowstick

H. Haufrecht: *Square Set*

34. Same, with a pencil

B. Childs: *Mr. T., His Fancy*

35. Rub ("caress") the side of the doublebass

J. Deak: *Color Studies for Contrabass*

36. Rub back of the rib (of doublebass), producing a high squeak

J. Deak: *Color Studies for Contrabass*

37. Strike or tap on the back of the instrument with the fingers or thumb

P. Chihara: *Ceremony I; Logs*
T. Fredrickson: *Music for Five Instruments*
L. Harrison: *Suite for Symphonic Strings*

K. Huber: *Tenebrae*
D. Martino: *Notturno*
M. Powell: *Filigree Setting* (Example 23)
I. Xenakis: *ST/4-1, 080262*

PERCUSSIVE DEVICES   105

Example 24
Tadeusz Baird: from *Espressioni varianti* (p. 31)

*)uderzać paznokciem w bok instrumentów
Frapper avec l'ongle le côté de l'instrument

© Copyright 1961 by PWM-Edition, Kraków, Poland. Renewed 1988. Used by permission.

38. Same, with the knuckles

T. Fredrickson: *Music for Five Instruments*
C. Santoro: *Três Abstrações*
A. de la Vega: *Structures for Piano and String Quartet*

39. Same, with the flat hand

D. Cope: *Angel's Camp II* (Example 50)
M. Subotnick: *Lamination I*

40. Same, with the bowstick *(col legno)*

B. Sakač: *Struktur I*

41. Same, with a timpani stick (on doublebass)

Y. Sadai: *Nuances*

42. Rattle fingernails against the back of the instrument

D. Erb: *The Seventh Trumpet* (Example 41)

43. Turn the instrument over (violin or viola) and strike on the center of the back with the flat hand

I. Xenakis: *ST/4-1, 080262*

44. Slap, strike, or tap on the top (shoulders) of the instrument (cello or doublebass) with the cupped hand

R. Erickson: *Ricercar à 3*
K. Gaburo: *Inside*

45. Same, with the fingernails

R. Erickson: *Ricercar à 3*
K. Gaburo: *Inside*

46. Same, with the left-hand fingers

K. Gaburo: *Inside*
M. Kelemen: *Abecedarium*
I. Lang: *Impulsioni*

D. Martino: *Parisonatina al' dodecafonia*

47. Strike scroll with the finger(s)

G. Read: *Diabolic Dialogue*
R. Sender: *Balances*

48. Same, with the fingernail(s)

R. Sender: *Balances*

49. Snap the fingernail on the back of the instrument neck

B. Childs: *Nonet*

50. Trill with the fingernails on the chinrest (of the violin)

D. Martino: *Notturno*

51. Strike edge of the fingerboard with the side of the bow nut

B. Ferneyhough: *Sonatas for String Quartet*

52. Tap (agent unspecified) on the most resonant part of the instrument body

B. Conyngham: *Three*

The tuning pegs of a string instrument can also be struck with either the bow or the player's hand, an action that sets up sympathetic vibration of the strings. Tapping on the soundboard with a finger while simultaneously bowing on the strings is also possible, a technique required in Maurice Ohana's *Cinq Séquences* for string quartet and the solo cello *Intercommunicazione* of Bernd Alois Zimmermann.

Indubitably a percussive device, though not effected on the instrument body, is the stipulation to strike or tap rhythmically on the music stand with the bowtip (*col legno*), this appears in:

G. Burt: *Exit Music*
V. Globokar: *Accord*
K. Penderecki: *Fluorescences; Polymorphia*

R. M. Schafer: *Requiems for the Party-Girl*
W. Szalonek: *Concertino per flauto*

This practice (the traditional, but dubious, interpretation of the "*col legno*" directive in Rossini's 1813 overture to *Il Signor Bruschino*) is related to another avant-garde device: the player lightly strikes his chair with the nut of the bow. This is an alternative action for the music-stand tappings in the Penderecki works mentioned above.

It does not seem likely that the ultimate of percussive potential of the strings— indeed, of all nonpercussion instruments—has been discovered, let alone exploited by the avant-garde composer of the late twentieth century. Predictions are suspect, but one ventures to say that in the years to come experimentally minded composers will bring to light new and intriguing ways in which to coax percussive sounds from the standard instruments, as well as to foster novel percussive effects on instruments yet to be invented. As Lou Harrison once said, "I think that any sound that can be generated by a musical instrument is legitimate so long as that method does not injure the instrument." It is an opinion with which no reasoning musician, whether composer or performer, can disagree.

NOTES

1. It is generally acknowledged that the first use of key slaps occurred in Edgard Varèse's solo flute piece *Density 21.5* (1936).

2. Carlos Salzedo, *Modern Studies of the Harp* (New York: G. Schirmer, Inc., 1921).

3. It should be readily understood that all of the effects catalogued here are feasible only on a grand piano, usually with the lid and music rack removed.

4. In Tobias Hume's *Musical Humors,* according to Bertram Turetzky (*The Contemporary Contrabass*). Turetzky's book, incidentally, contains not only a veritable goldmine of information on his instrument but, like Bartolozzi's *New Sounds for Woodwind,* is a pioneer in the whole area of research into contemporary instrumental techniques.

6

MICROTONES

Historically, the development of microtonal composition in the twentieth century can be said to have begun in 1895 with the experiments of the Mexican theorist-composer Julián Carrillo. In many of his orchestral, vocal, and chamber works, such as *Balbuceos* for string quartet (Example 25), Carrillo sought to infuse his music with a systematic microtonalism. In the early decades of this century Alois Hába pursued the same goals in the majority of his works, his string quartets representing the most concentrated application of the technique (see Example 26). Later experiments in extended microtonalism reached an extraordinary degree of complexity in Harry Partch's research that led to the creation of his 43-tone scale and construction of a number of unique instruments designed solely to play his equally unique music (Example 27). More current efforts to expand the parameters of microtonal techniques include the contributions of such musicians as Easley Blackwood, John Eaton, and Ben Johnston.

Generally speaking, other than the specialists committed to extended microtonalism, the vast majority of the composers using microtones in their music do so as embellishments of the standard chromatic pitches rather than as components of an integrated system. Notationally, there is still a notable absence of any consensus on a standardized form of microtonal delineation, whether of quarter-, of third-, of fifth-tones, or of any other possible division of the half or whole step.[1] If any preference is to be discerned in quarter-tone symbology—the fractional interval most favored—the following signs are those most frequently encountered in recent published scores. The first eight examples are all based on varied modifications of the flat and sharp signs, while the final two examples illustrate the next most accepted symbology—simple arrows attached to the standard accidentals:

Example 25
Julián Carrillo: from *Balbuceos* (p. 1)

© 1957 by Julián Carrillo.

Example 26
Alois Hába: from *String Quartet No. 14* (p. 2)

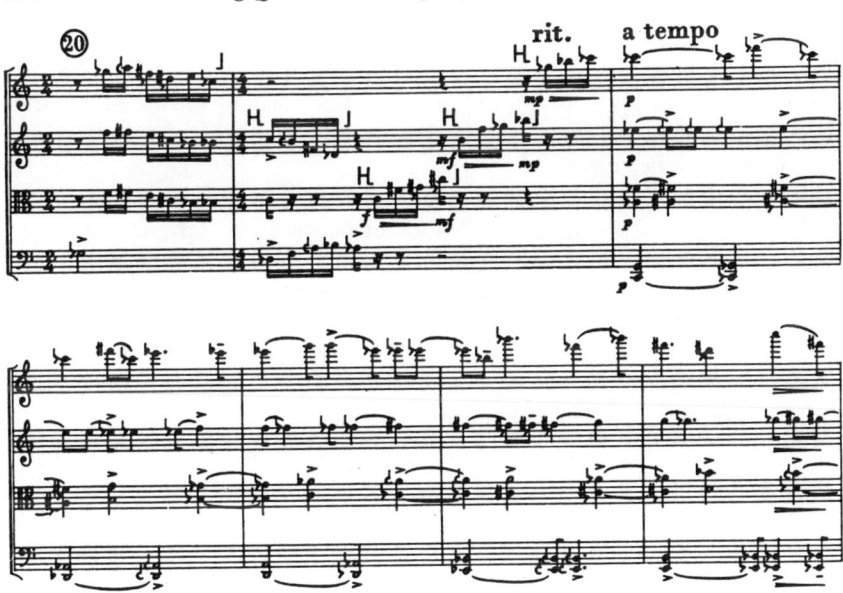

© 1967 PANTON, Praha. By permission.

Example 27
Harry Partch: from *And on the 7th Day Petals Fell in Petaluma* (p. 100)

© Copyright 1967. SOURCE, Vol. 1, No. 2, July, 1967. By permission.

WOODWINDS AND BRASSES

Microtonal pitch inflection is a staple of the current avant-garde in both instrumental and vocal music. Formerly restricted to the string instruments and sparingly used even in the serious music of the early twentieth century, quarter-tones and even smaller subdivisions of the half-step are now an integral part of wind-instrument techniques. According to Bruno Bartolozzi, quarter-tones on the woodwind instruments are more and more to be obtained by the use of specific fingerings, thus moving from an approximate to a determinate manner of achieving microtonal inflection.[2]

Microtonal bends—the gradual flatting or sharping of a given note—are achieved by the woodwinds through the embouchure, the lip pressure being tightened or relaxed according to the designated direction of the minute pitch inflection. Flute players generally roll the instrument slowly away from the lips, for upward bends, or into the lips, for downward bends, thus minutely altering the degree and angle of the air stream directed into the mouthpiece. This action affects the blown and fingered pitch, causing it to rise or sink by a quarter-tone, a third-tone, or other designated fractional interval, according to the distance the instrument is moved. Microtonal bends on the oboe are stipulated in Roger Reynolds' *Islands from Archipelago: I. Summer Island* by way of the following directive: "Raise pitch while moving the jaw irregularly." On clarinet a bend is usually produced by varying the lip pressure on the reed as well as by altering the throat position.

Next to the bend the most common usage of microtonal variance within a

MICROTONES

chromatic context is the quarter-tone vibrato: the player produces a slow and greatly exaggerated vibrato on his instrument, in which pitches a quarter-tone above or below (or both) the principle tone can be readily heard. The requisite notation devised by Penderecki in *Fluorescences* and other scores is clear and succinct:

Among a great many contemporary works requiring some kind of microtonal inflection (bends, glissandi, and the like) we might cite:

1. Flute and/or alto flute

W. Albright: *Danse Macabre*
Z. Bujarski: *Chamber Piece*
S. Bussotti: *Couple*
Chou Wen-chung: *Cursive*
M. Colgrass: *As Quiet As*
G. Crumb: *Eleven Echoes of Autumn; Night of the Four Moons*
B. Ferneyhough: *Unity Capsule* (Example 28)
H. Gaber: *Voce II*
B. Hambraeus: *Introduzione, Sequenze, Coda*
H. W. Henze: *El Cimarrón*
G. Heussenstamm: *Poikilos*
S. Hodkinson: *Fresco; Interplay*
K. Korte: *Remembrances*
W. Kotonski: *Musica per fiati e timpani*
H. Kox: *Cyclofonie V*
J. Mekeel: *The Shape of Silence*

C. Polin: *The Death of Procris*
G. Read: *Sonoric Fantasia No. 3*
D. Reck: *Blues and Screamer*
R. Reynolds: *Ambages; Traces*
G. Rochberg: *Music for the Magic Theatre; Tableaux*
W. Rudzinski: *Pictures from the Holy-Cross Mountains*
B. Schäffer: *Azione a due*
G. Schuller: *Contours; Seven Studies on Themes of Paul Klee*
E. Schwartz: *Texture*
H. Sollberger: *Grand Quartet for Flutes*
T. Takemitsu: *Masque pour deux flûtes; Voice*
D. Welcher: *White Mares of the Moon*
L. Widdoes: *From a Time of Snow*
B. A. Zimmermann: *Stille und Umkehr; Tempus loquendi*

2. Recorder

W. Heider: *Katalog*

3. Oboe and/or English horn

T. Antoniou: *Five Likes*
B. Bartolozzi: *Concertazioni per oboe*
L. Berio: *Sequenza VII*
B. Childs: *Four Inventions*
G. Crumb: *Ancient Voices of Children*
W. Kotonski: *Musica per fiati e timpani*

R. Reynolds: *Quick are the Mouths of Earth*
G. Schuller: *Seven Studies on Themes of Paul Klee*
W. Sydeman: *Texture Studies*
S. Walden: *Coronach; A Kaddish*
I. Yun: *Dimensionen*

4. Clarinet and/or bass clarinet

L. Austin: *Current for Clarinet and Piano*
B. Childs: *Trio for Clarinet, Cello and Piano*
G. Crumb: *Eleven Echoes of Autumn*
I. Dahl: *Five Duets for Clarinets*
L. Foss: *For 24 Winds*
A. Hába: *Suite for ¼-tone Clarinet and ¼-tone Piano*

H. W. Henze: *Sinfonia N. 6*
W. Kotonski: *Pour quatre*
D. Martino: *Strata*
G. Rochberg: *Music for the Magic Theatre*
W. Sydeman: *Texture Studies for Orchestra*
B. A. Zimmermann: *Stille und Umkehr*

5. Saxophone

K. Husa: *Apotheosis of This Earth*
C. Polin: *O, Aderyn Pur*

6. Bassoon and/or contrabassoon

P. Chihara: *Branches*

7. Flute, oboe, clarinet and bassoon

B. Bartolozzi: *Collage* (Example 34)
L. Foss: *For 24 Winds*
H. W. Henze: *Sinfonia N. 6*

K. Penderecki: *De Natura Sonoris (I)*
I. Xenakis: *Polytope*
B. A. Zimmermann: *Photoptosis*

A slight change in normal embouchure is usually sufficient to produce microtonal bends on the horn; the effect can also be obtained by partial hand-stopping. On trumpet, quarter-tone inflections are produced by adjustments of the tuning slides, and on trombone by maneuvering the slide between positions. Embouchure adjustment takes care of microtonal inflections on tuba.

The following scores all require the use of these techniques on the various brass instruments:

1. Horn

G. Crumb: *Echoes of Time and the River*
D. Erb: *Symphony of Overtures*
V. Globokar: *Etude pour Folklora II*
K. Huber: *Tenebrae*

K. Penderecki: *Dies Irae*
G. Rochberg: *Tableaux*
W. Szalonek: *Aarhus Music*
I. Xenakis: *Akrata; Metastaseis*

2. Trumpet

D. Erb: *Symphony of Overtures*
I. Xenakis: *Eonta*
B. A. Zimmermann: *Stille und Umkehr*

Example 28 Brian Ferneyhough: from *Unity Capsule* (p. 4)

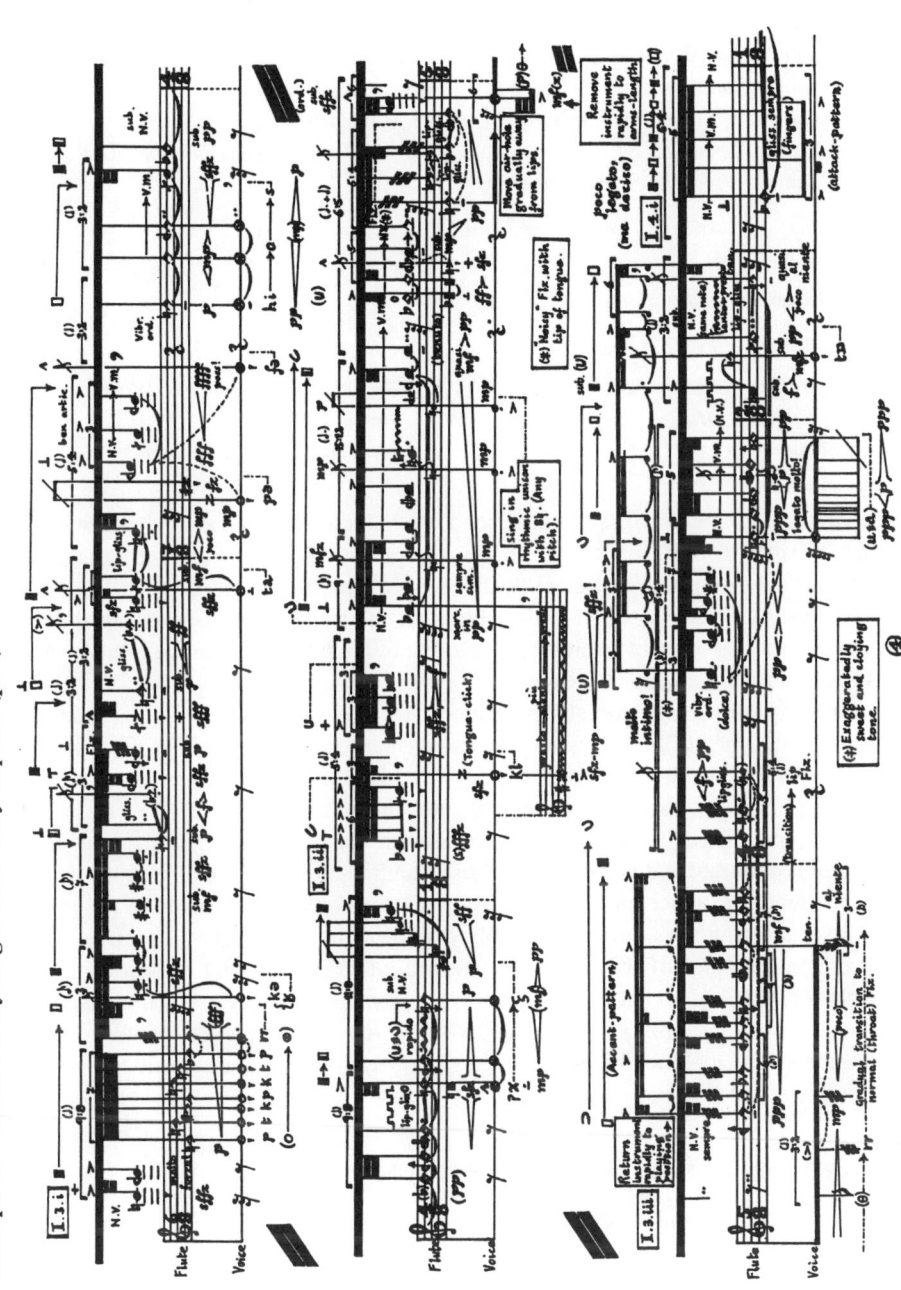

© 1975 by Peters Edition, Ltd. Used by permission of C. F. Peters Corporation, New York.

3. Trombone

L. Austin: *Changes*
B. Childs: *Jack's New Bag*
B. Conyngham: *Mirages*
V. Globokar: *Etude pour Folklora II*
K. Huber: *Tenebrae*
E. Krenek: *Five Pieces for Trombone and Piano*

G. Rochberg: *Tableaux*
M. Stibilj: *Condensation*
A. Strange: *Scapes*
I. Xenakis: *Eonta*
B. A. Zimmermann: *Stille und Umkehr*

4. Tuba

I. Xenakis: *Linaia-Agon*

5. Horn, trumpet and trombone

A. Gilbert: *Brighton Piece*
W. Kotonski: *Musica per fiati e timpani*

L. Nono: *Canti di vita e d'amore*
I. Xenakis: *Polytope*
B. A. Zimmermann: *Photoptosis*

An effect allied to the microtonal bend, available to both woodwind and brass instruments, is the quarter-tone vibrato: the player's normal vibrato is exaggerated to the extent that an actual quarter-tone "beat" is perceived (as in Husa's *Apotheosis of this Earth*). A wide vibrato on the trombone, produced by slide action, can also create a microtonal wavering of pitch (required in the *Eonta* and *Metastaseis* of Xenakis, for example).

Furthermore, many composers request passages of unstable pitch, timbre, and/or frequency from their wind players. Unstable pitch would be accomplished by liberal recourse to microtonal bendings, while unstable timbre results from a flexible mixing of tonguing techniques, embouchure control (irregular pressure of lips and varied breath force), fingering variants, and rapid alternations of degrees of vibrato and non-vibrato. These requirements form a conspicuous part of the technical procedures in Earle Brown's *Available Forms 1* and *2*.

To date composers have not notably exploited the possibilities of consistent microtonal tunings of the brass instruments, either individually or sectionally. Only a handful of recent experimental works exhibit this special tonal concept, such as Alcides Lanza's *Eidesis II*, in which the second players of horn and trombone are to tune their instruments a quarter-tone flat in relation to the instruments of the first players.

HARP AND OTHER PLUCKED INSTRUMENTS

Few twentieth-century works, to date, have required microtonal harp tunings; Sylvano Bussotti's *Fragmentations* for two harps, one tuned unconventionally, and Alain Bancquart's orchestral *Palimpsestes* are notable examples of this tuning procedure.[3] Other recent works that require microtonal tunings of certain selected strings include:

MICROTONES

B. Beerman: *Polygraph VI* S-D. Sandström: *Just a Bit*
R. Loman: *Celebrations* R. M. Schafer: *The Crown of Ariadne*

Quarter-tone "bends," nonetheless, can be created on normally tuned harp strings; they are effectuated in two ways: first, the tuning key may be lightly pressed against a string to be plucked and then moved slowly up or down the string (as in Harrison Birtwistle's *Entr'actes and Sappho Fragments*). Second, the left hand presses hard against the plucked string quite close to the tuning pins (as specified in George Crumb's *Ancient Voices of Children* and in Vinko Globokar's *Voie*). A quarter-tone slide is achieved in Dennis Eberhard's "*Especially . . .* " by the harpist squeezing the string between the tuning peg and tuning disc, then slowly releasing the pressure.

Quarter-tone slides have also been requisitioned of guitar and mandolin by certain vanguardists. They are accomplished on these plucked instruments by pulling the string laterally with a left-hand finger immediately after the string is plucked normally with the right hand. For examples, refer to the following works:

J. Carrillo: *Sonata in Quarter-Tones for Solo Guitar* A. Gilardino: *Abrenana*
G. Crumb: *Ancient Voices of Children* A. Hába: *Suite für Vierteltonguitarre*
L. Foss: *Fragments of Archilochos* M. Ohana: *Tiento*

Quarter-tone trills on these plucked instruments are in reality vibratos of such width that a microtonal pitch variance can be perceived, an effect that was specified in Crumb's score just cited.

An interesting example of guitar strings tuned microtonally occurs in Sandström's *Surrounded:* the low E- and B-strings are pitched a quarter-tone low and the D-string a quarter-tone high.[4] In a similar vein, the E-, A-, and G-strings in *Mikrotonos* of John Winiarz are tuned a quarter-tone flat while the remaining three strings are pitched normally.

KEYBOARD INSTRUMENTS

Even in the highly experimental milieu of late twentieth-century composition, the use of quarter-tone piano is comparatively rare. The early microtonal experiments of Hába, Hans Barth, and Carrillo, which led to the construction of keyboard instruments capable of producing quarter-tones, did not create a sizable corresponding body of literature for these innovative instruments. Aside from a few works by these three composers, and some occasional oddities such as the *Three Quarter-Tone Pieces* of Charles Ives, we lack a significant corpus of keyboard microtonal music. It is, therefore, a novelty of some note when one comes across such a work as Donald Lybbert's *Lines for the Fallen,* which requires that one of its two pianos be tuned a quarter-tone low. Also, in Jean-

Etienne Marie's *Tombeau de Julián Carrillo,* one of two pianos required is—appropriately enough—tuned a third-tone higher than the other. Works of more recent vintage for two pianos, one of which is tuned either a quarter-tone flat or sharp, include:

G. Boziwick: *Red Skies at Night*
M. Couper: *Dirge for Two Pianos*
J. Eaton: *Microtonal Fantasy*
T. St. George Tucker: *Little Pieces*

Solo piano compositions designed for a microtonally tuned instrument are most notably represented by Ben Johnston's *Sonata for Microtonal Piano.* In this work all 88 notes of the standard keyboard are retuned in just intonation, for which the composer utilizes an elaborate and highly personalized notation.

Current interest in microtonal composition has fostered the invention and development of entirely new instruments capable of reproducing various microtonal tunings. Chief among these are the several organs built to 31-tone-per-octave specifications, notably the so-called *31-toonsorgel* of the Dutch physicist-musician Adriaan Fokker, and the even more recent *arcifoon.* Also a five-manual piano has been designed by Ervin Wilson to produce fifth-tones, but there is no information currently available as to its use by today's composers. On the other hand, a number of composers have written works expressly for the 31-tone organs, including:

H. Badings: *Praeludium en fuga*
A. Fokker: *New Music with 31 Notes*
H. Kox: *Passacaglia en Koraal*
T. de Kruyf: *Quahquahtinchen in Foreign Lands*
J. Mandelbaum: *Ten Studies for 31-tone Keyboard*
P. Schat: *Collages voor 31-toonsorgel*

STRINGS

String players have long produced minute differences in notated pitch by means of wide vibrato or by finger and position shifting on enharmonic tones (G♭ and F♯, for example). But such fractional colorings of pitch were never actually specified by the composers until the early twentieth century, when microtones became an integral part of string technique—especially quarter-tones, which are both theoretically and practically the most feasible. Spurred by the experiments of such theorists as Carrillo and Hába, and espoused by composers as diverse in style as Alban Berg, Ernest Bloch, and Béla Bartók, string instrument microtones are now designated by orchestrators with increasing frequency.

Microtonal bends, glissandi, trills, and vibratos are all as effective on the string instruments as they are on the woodwinds and brasses—and as frequently

MICROTONES

specified. Among a great many recent works calling for quarter-tone vibratos we may cite the following:

S. Cervetti: *Zinctum*
L. Foss: *Echoi; Elytres*
A. Hrisanide: *Volumes*
K. Huber: *Alveare vernat*
M. Kagel: *Match für drei Spieler; Sexteto de cuerdas*
T. de Leeuw: *Second String Quartet*

W. Lutoslawski: *Cello Concerto; Livre pour orchestre*
P. Maxwell Davies: *Vesalii Icones*
A. Mellnäs: *Quasi nienti*
P. Nørgård: *Symphony No. 2*
K. Penderecki: *Emanationen; Miniatures*

Quarter- or third-tone glissandi of brief extent are other ways in which minute pitch fluctuations can be achieved on strings, the finger sliding almost imperceptibly up or down from normal full or half position; such requirements appear in:

D. Bedford: *That White and Radiant Legend*
W. Benson: *The Dream Net*
J. Deak: *Color Studies for Contrabass*
F. Evangelisti: *Aleatorio*

K. Penderecki: *Emanationen*
D. Reck: *Blues and Screamer*
G. Rochberg: *Duo Concertante*
W. Sydeman: *Texture Studies*
R. Wittinger: *Quartetto per archi No. 3*

In his *Incenters* Jacob Druckman requests a trill a quarter-tone both above and below a specified pitch; the result is what he aptly describes as a "whimpering and whining sound." Quarter-tone bends are produced by the doublebass player in George Crumb's *Madrigals—IV* by turning slightly the tuning peg of the string played, rather than by finger shifting.

Just as quarter-tone "beats" can be produced on single woodwind instruments playing certain multiphonic structures (see page 116), so can microtonal beating tones be created by individual stringed instruments playing double-stopped unisons, the higher of the two strings fingered a quarter-tone above the lower string. This action is called for, and with striking results, in Peter Maxwell Davies' *Revelation and Fall*.

Xenakis in *Nomos* calls for a quarter-tone inflection to be produced in a curious manner: the cellist stops G on the C-string with his first finger, then plucks the string with his thumb between the instrument nut and the finger on the string; the resultant sound is an octave higher plus a quarter-tone.

Relatively few composers have asked for preperformance tunings of string instruments in microtones, either of individual instruments or of whole sections within the string choir. To cite one outstanding example, in Ligeti's *Ramifications for Double String Orchestra* the violins, violas, and cellos of one group are tuned a quarter-tone higher than the members of the other ensemble. Alcides Lanza's *Eidesis II* requires one cello to be pretuned a quarter-tone high and one cello and one doublebass a quarter-tone low. In the *Monodram (Genesis III)* of

Gorecki all the members of the string section are to be tuned flat, presumably by a quarter-tone, more or less. Among other works calling for selective retunings of the string instruments are the following:

- H. Barth: *Piano Concerto; Piano Quintet*
- C. Ives: *Quarter-Tone Chorale for Strings*
- A. Lanza: *Cuarteto V para cuerdas*
- M. Poncs: *Suite für zwei Streichengruppen*
- S-D. Sandström: *Just a Bit*
- M. Subotnick: *Before the Butterfly*

Finally, for the composer or performer especially interested in all the various microtonal techniques and tuning systems, there are numerous publications that deal with the subject from historical, aesthetic, technical, and/or notational perspectives; most of these sources are included in the extensive Bibliography of this writer's *20th-Century Microtonal Notation*. But whatever the degree of interest any composer or performer may have in the potential of microtonalism, its influence is already quite considerable in the music being composed in these remaining years of the present century.

NOTES

1. See Read's *20th-Century Microtonal Notation* for a comprehensive survey of current symbology.
2. Refer to the technical treatises by Bartolozzi, Robert Dick, and Phillip Rehfeldt (listed in the Bibliography) for detailed information regarding microtonal fingerings on the woodwind instruments.
3. Most theorists know, of course, that Julián Carrillo's 1922 *Preludio a Colón* includes a part for a harp specially tuned in 16th-tones; the work, however, was not published until 1969, and so remained largely unknown to composers.
4. See Example 41 for the composer's tuning chart.

7
AMPLIFICATION

In modern music-making the most obvious manifestation of electronic technology is tape recorder, synthesizer, and computer composition. But the basic science and various techniques of electronic sound manipulation have also affected nonelectronic music, mainly through live performance amplification. Contact microphones can be attached to certain instruments, or the players can direct their instrumental sounds into individual air microphones placed directly before them, suspended above them, or attached to their bodies. Normal amplitudes can thus be increased—even distorted—and characteristic timbres radically altered through the use of special filters (ring modulators) connected to the amplifiers. Microphones and amplifiers are, of course, hooked into one or more loudspeakers placed in different locations in the performance area. Spatial, or stereophonic, impressions are thus directed to the individual listeners, wherever they may be located in the auditorium.

Electronic amplification of instruments (or voices) is motivated by two factors: first, to obtain simple volume control of normal instrumental or vocal tone; second, to achieve radical timbral alteration. Among the several possibilities for tone-color manipulation are: feedback, distortion, reverberation, time-lapse, and the splitting of pitches through ring modulators. All have become viable new sound resources, independent of prerecorded or simultaneous tapings.

WOODWINDS AND BRASSES

As with any instrument of the symphonic orchestra or band, the woodwinds and brasses can be individually or collectively amplified by the procedures just described. For the flute an air microphone placed close to the lip plate gives best results, while a contact mike attached to the crook of the bassoon or under the wire of the reed is the most satisfactory placement on that instrument, providing optimum results. Recent compositions, mostly of an experimental nature, requiring woodwind amplification, include:

122 GENERALIZED TECHNIQUES

1. Flute

   S. Albert: *Cathedral Music* (Example 29)
   H. Birtwistle: *Nomos*
   P. Chihara: *Ceremony II*

   G. Crumb: *An Idyll for the Misbegotten; Vox Balaenae*
   B. Hambraeus: *Introduzione, Sequenze, Coda*
   T. Takemitsu: *Voice*

2. Bass flute

   P. Chihara: *Willow, Willow*

3. Bass recorder

   L. Andriessen: *Hoe het is*

4. Oboe

   H. Holliger: *Siebengesang*
   W. Kotonski: *Oboe Concerto*

5. English horn

   S. Hodkinson: *The Edge of the Olde One*

Example 29
Stephen Albert: from *Cathedral Music* (p. 7)

Copyright © 1977 by Carl Fischer, Inc., New York. International copyright secured. All rights reserved. Used by permission.

6. Clarinet

H. Birtwistle: *Nomos*	W. Kotonski: *Midsummer*
A. Gilbert: *Spell Respell*	E. Schwartz: *Extended Clarinet*
V. Globokar: *Airs de voyages vers l'intérieur*	E. Valcarcel: *Trio*

7. Saxophone

D. Del Tredici: *Pop-Pourri*

8. Bassoon

H. Birtwistle: *Nomos*

In Haubenstock-Ramati's *Multiple 5* all of the woodwinds are to be amplified, *ad libitum*—a decision presumably left to the conductor. Luc Ferrari in his *Tautologos III, Version No. 4*, however, specifically asks that all the orchestral instruments—woodwinds, brasses, strings—be amplified. In addition, his score calls for electric guitar and an electronic organ, surely the sum total constituting the ultimate in amplification requirements.

Scores that call for brass instrument amplification include:

1. Horn

H. Birtwistle: *Nomos*
G. Mumma: *Hornpipe* (the horn played with a bassoon reed!)

2. Trombone

S. Cervetti: *Raga II*	W. Heider: *-einander*
V. Globokar: *Airs de voyages vers l'intérieur*	J. Kramer: *Renascence*
	E. Valcarcel: *Trio*

PERCUSSION

Because most percussion instruments are inherently loud, few composers have called for their electronic amplification. Nonetheless, there are one or two quite recent works, highly exploratory in intent, that do require amplification of certain of the percussion instruments; they are:

1. Vibraphone

P. Chihara: *Willow, Willow* (amplified through a conventional air microphone connected to an Echo-plex)

2. Tubular bells

B. Hambraeus: *Introduzione, Sequenze, Coda*

3. Marimbula (African harp)

H. W. Henze: *Heliogabalus Imperator*

4. Cymbals

K. Stockhausen: *Mixtur*

5. Tam-tam

R. O'Donnell: *Microtimbre I*
K. Stockhausen: *Hymnen; Kurzwellen*

Cymbals, gongs, and tam-tams customarily have contact microphones taped onto their surfaces, tightly enough so that they do not rattle against the surface when the instrument is struck.

To date, the most notable example of percussion amplification occurs in Jani Christou's *Enantiodromia:* a separated group of percussion instruments consisting of tubular bells, gongs, sizzle cymbals, and bass drum (all amplified) are reserved for an impressive entry at the work's climax. In the composer's words: "When they are struck, the collective impact should result in an almost deafening explosion, capable of cutting through the full orchestra playing at its maximum loudness." Doubtless!

HARP AND OTHER PLUCKED INSTRUMENTS[1]

Instances of amplified harp are relatively few in the scores of contemporary composers. Research to date has brought to light only nine compositions requiring this technical device:

S. Albert: *Cathedral Music*
B. Beerman: *Polygraph VI*
A. Boucourechliev: *Anarchipel and Archipel 5*
M. Constant: *Candide*
P. Maxwell Davies: *Revelation and Fall*
P. Méfano: *La Cérémonie*
J. Nightingale: *Entente*
P. Nørgård: *Symphony No. 2*
T. Takemitsu: *Stanza II*

A few composers have called for optional amplification of the harp, including Martin Amlin in *The Black Riders,* Kagel in *Sonant,* and Yehudi Yannay in *Coloring Book for the Harpist.* As with all instances of optional amplification, presumably it is the conductor who makes the decision.

Electric guitars are, of course, staple ingredients of rock music, but amplification of the guitar in serious orchestral and chamber music is also an accepted modus operandi among vanguard composers, such as:

S. Albert: *Cathedral Music*
L. Berio: *Nones*
E. Brown: *From Here*
M. Constant: *14 Stations*
B. Conyngham: *Ice Carving*
G. Crumb: *Songs, Drones and Refrains of Death*
D. Del Tredici: *Pop-Pourri*
D. Erb: *String Trio*
R. L. Finney: *Nun's Priest's Tale*
L. Foss: *Fragments of Archilochos; Paradigm*
H. W. Henze: *Sinfonia N. 6* (also banjo)

AMPLIFICATION

S. Hodkinson: *Fresco*
M. Kagel: *Sonant*
E. Lutyens: *"Go, Said the Bird"*
A. Mellnäs: *Tombola*
A. Nordheim: *Partita II*
H. Partch: *Plectra and Percussion Dances*
K. Penderecki: *Partita*
B. Rands: *Aum*
E. Raxach: *Interface*
S. Silverman: *Elephant Steps*
K. Stockhausen: *Gruppen*
T. Takemitsu: *Cassiopeia*
J. Tavener: *Celtic Requiem*
G. Wilson: *Concatenations*
C. Wolff: *Electric Spring I; II; III*

The amplified guitar in Foss's *Paradigm* is equipped with a volume-control pedal; when a note is played with the pedal off, then faded in by depressing the pedal, the resultant sound is remarkably like that of a bowed string instrument. Other devices that have been applied to the electric or amplified guitar are the "fuzz-tone," "wah-wah," and "phaser" pedals. Also, some guitars are equipped with so-called "vibrato" arms attached to the tailpiece. This latter mechanism alters the tension on the strings, thus affecting pitch stability. An amplifier tremolo or amplitude modulator may be used as substitutes for this effect.

The zenith of amplified guitar requirement is convincingly exemplified by John McLaughlin's *Apocalypse,* in which the guitar is a member of an amplified rock group pitted against a conventional symphonic orchestra.

KEYBOARD INSTRUMENTS

Certain recent scores have called for amplification of both piano and harpsichord. Contact microphones can be attached to certain preselected interior strings, as in Mestres-Quadreny's *Double Concerto* and in Crumb's *Songs, Drones, and Refrains of Death* and *Vox Balaenae* (both using piano). They may also be placed in such a position in the piano or harpsichord interior as to pick up the vibrations of any or all of the struck or plucked strings; see, among other works:

S. Albert: *Cathedral Music* (Example 29)
I. Anhalt: *Foci*
L. Austin: *The Maze*
I. Bazelon: *Sound Dreams*
D. Bedford: *Come in here child*
J. Cage: *Cartridge Music; Hpschd*
M. Constant: *14 Stations*
G. Crumb: *Apparition; Makrokosmos— Vol. I, II*
D. Erb: *The Towers of Silence*
L. Foss: *Baroque Variations*
V. Globokar: *Vendre le vent*
H. W. Henze: *Compasses*
B. Kolb: *Trobar Clus*
W. Kotonski: *Midsummer*
K. Penderecki: *Partita*
G. Rochberg: *Electrakaleidoscope; Tableaux*
R. Romiti: *Palingenesis*
Y. Takahashi: *Bridges I*

A specific directive in Kotonski's cited score requires that a ring modulator, which is hooked up to the amplified piano, is to be turned on slowly rather than preset or activated suddenly. Cage's aptly titled *Hpschd* calls for between one and seven amplified harpsichords, while André Boucourechliev's *Anarchipel and Archipel 5* requires the use of an amplified cembalo, a singular instance of this early music instrument appearing in a contemporary score—as is the amplified clavichord specified in James Fulkerson's *Now II*.

A rare instance of amplified accordion, found in *Concatenations* of George Wilson, is a technical device that perhaps merits further exploitation by today's composers.

STRINGS

Amplification has been applied to various string instruments, quite generally in a solo context or in chamber music ensemble, in the following recent scores:

1. Violin

   M. Constant: *Candide*
   B. Conyngham: *Ice Carving*
   H. W. Henze: *Sinfonia N. 6*
   R. Laneri: *L'Arte del Violino*
   P. Maxwell Davies: *Revelation and Fall*
   M. Subotnick: *Before the Butterfly*

   W. Sydeman: *Projections I*
   Y. Takahashi: *Rosace I*
   E. Valcarcel: *Trio*
   C. Wuorinen: *Concerto for Amplified Violin and Orchestra*

Two contact microphones, one taped to the instrument body and one attached to the bowhair (!), are specified in Roberto Laneri's tongue-in-cheek work listed. And in Wuorinen's solo concerto a transducer, which is built into the violin bridge, is connected to a pre-amplifier controlled by an offstage technician.

2. Viola

   K. Stockhausen: *Hymnen; Kurzwellen*

3. Cello

   S. Albert: *Cathedral Music*
   P. Chihara: *Ceremony II*
   M. Constant: *Candide*
   G. Crumb: *Night of the Four Moons; Vox Balaenae*
   D. Erb: *The Towers of Silence*

   B. Ferneyhough: *Time and Motion Study II*
   W. Kotonski: *Midsummer*
   Y. Takahashi: *Bridges I*
   C. Wuorinen: *Five*

4. Doublebass

   A. Bloch: *Gilgamesz*
   P. Chihara: *Logs*
   G. Crumb: *Songs, Drones, and Refrains of Death*
   K. Huber: *Tenebrae*

   M. Karlins: *Reflux*
   P. Méfano: *Lignes*
   W. Sydeman: *Duo for Trumpet and Amplified Doublebass*

AMPLIFICATION

Example 30
Bernard Rands: from *Memo 1* (p. 1)

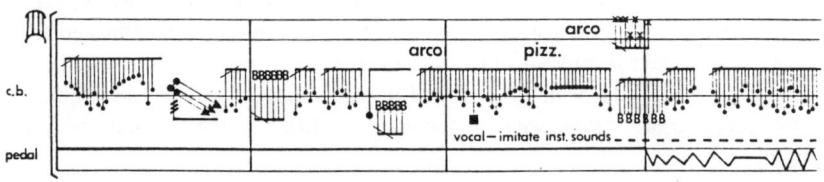

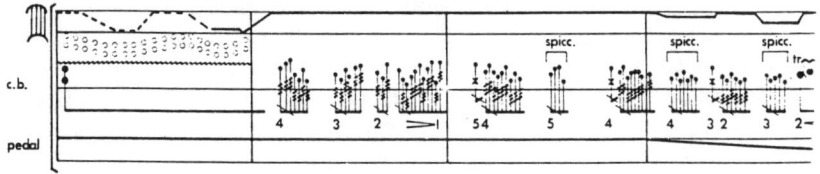

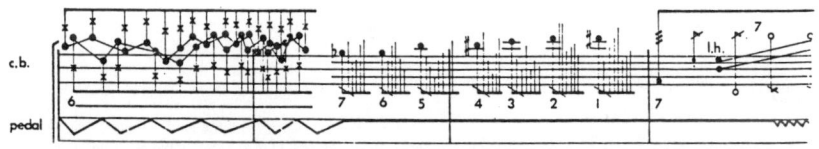

© Copyright 1973 by Universal Edition (London) Ltd., London. All rights reserved. Used by permission of European American Music Distributors Corporation, sole U.S. and Canadian agent for Universal Edition, London.

Bernard Rands is very specific as to amplification procedures in *Memo 1*: "A contact microphone should be firmly attached to the body of the instrument—preferably just in front of the bridge. This should be connected to an amplifier and two speakers placed stereophonically either side of the instrumentalist and as far away from him as is practicable. A foot pedal should be used to control the amplitude. The instrument should be placed as far away from the amplifier as possible to prevent feedback." (See Example 30.)

The electric doublebass used in Alcides Lanza's *Penetrations VI* is to have two paper clips attached to the two highest strings, which imparts a metallic buzz to the amplified string tone.

Amplification procedures have also been applied to all four members of the string quartet in the following works:

R. Ashley: *Describing the Motions of Large Real Bodies*
G. Crumb: *Black Angels*
D. Lentz: *Sermon*

In Crumb's unusual score the composer specifies instruments with a built-in pick-up, but indicates that conventional instruments with contact microphones attached to their bellies with rubber bands would be acceptable substitutes. Each player in Donald Lentz's work is to have a contact microphone attached to his instrument and an air mike in close proximity for the vocal effects required by the composer. Four loudspeakers separated from the players serve as a complementary second quartet, their sounds relayed to modifiers affecting the eight microphones.

Performance amplification of the standard orchestral and ensemble instruments is a new compositional device that is not invariably successful. Although one of the primary reasons for instrumental amplification is to produce a certain distortion of the instrument's normal tone, amplifying its sound often creates unwanted falsification of timbre as well as conspicuous dynamic imbalance. To put the matter bluntly, the composer must be aware of the often unpredictable behavior of amplification systems. Furthermore, he must prejudge whether unexpected degrees of electronic amplification during performance might help or harm his expression. He must determine whether novelty of amplified instrumental sound is worth the hazards of its technical production. If it is, of course he need have no reservations in applying this recent technological accommodation to his music.[2]

NOTES

1. Also refer to Ruth Inglefield's *Writing for the Pedal Harp* and John Schneider's *The Contemporary Guitar* (see Bibliography).

2. Although primarily discussing doublebass amplification, Chapter VII of Bertram Turetzky's *The Contemporary Contrabass* is a comprehensive discussion of instrumental amplification in all its aspects. Three other fruitful sources of information on the technique are: Philip Rehfeldt's *New Directions for Clarinet* (Chapter 5), *Experimental Music* by Michael Nyman (pages 84–87), and John Schneider's *The Contemporary Guitar* (Chapter VIII).

8
EXTRAMUSICAL DEVICES

The concepts of multimedia—in particular those pertaining to such avant-garde manifestations as Happenings, The Living Theatre, and similar experimental approaches to staging—directly influence a considerable body of vanguard musical expression today. Such music is not content to rely on aural perception alone from its listeners but demands visual, even tactile, communication as well to put its total message across. Indeed, the listener to much avant-garde music is required to be an active participant in extramusical activities.

It is not strange, then, that experimental compositions of the late twentieth century often demand a certain degree of theatricality from the performers—extracurricular activities, as it were, that include emphatic and exaggerated bodily movement, visible facial contortion, perambulation during performance, and vocal projection independent of instrumental playing. These concepts of performance cut right across the board; they are not confined to any one type or kind of instrumentalist (or singer), nor do they require special idiomatic attributes from any of the players involved other than a minimum sense of dramatics and a willingness to participate in such supra-musical requirements.

Whether the unconventional activities expected by the composer help or hinder the player in his labors, loosen up his reflexes or inhibit them, engage his lively interest or embarrass him, are moot points. But as theatricalities, perambulations, vocalizations, and related performance activities are basic to our avant-garde milieu; the instrumentalist and singer of today has to participate as wholeheartedly as he is able in the convincing performance of such new music.

The categories that follow represent the most commonly demanded extramusical activities found in current scores:

1. Instrumentalists are sometimes directed in their parts to stand up to play—as often, perhaps, for acoustical as for histrionic reasons. Not even cellists and harpists are

exempt from this stipulation, in spite of the physical awkwardness involved. Directives to stand while playing occur in:

Woodwinds

D. Bedford: *Pentomino* (quintet)
R. Felciano: *Contractions* (bassoon)

T. Musgrave: *Space Play* (flute, oboe, clarinet)
B. Rands: *Ballad 1* (flute)

Brasses

H. Birtwistle: *Verses for Ensemble* (horns)
J. Christou: *Enantiodromia* (all brasses)
T. Musgrave: *Night Music* (horns)

E. Schwartz: *Music for Napoleon and Beethoven* (trumpet)
I. Xenakis: *Eonta* (trumpets; trombones)

Plucked instruments

B. Beerman: *Polygraph VI* (harp)
G. Crumb: *Echoes of Time and the River* (mandolin)

R. Felciano: *Background Music* (harp)
W. Szalonek: *Three Sketches* (harp)

Strings

L. Berio: *Epifanie* (solo violins)
J. Christou: *Enantiodromia* (a few violins)
L. Foss: *Orpheus* (solo cello)

F. Miroglio: *Projections* (solo violin; viola)
T. Musgrave: *Viola Concerto* (violas)

All the orchestral players in *Cortège* by R. Murray Schafer are to stand up at one time or another during the course of the performance. In contrast, the quartet of players required in Martino's *From the Other Side* (flute, cello, percussionist, and pianist) are directed to stand only on the final beat of the work—a visual punctuation, as it were, to the composition's ending.

2. Perambulation, from off- to on-stage, or the reverse, or around the concert platform or the auditorium itself, is an integral and indispensable factor in the following works:

Woodwinds

I. Anhalt: *Foci*
W. Bolcom: *Duets for Quintet*
D. Burge: *Sources III*
J. Cage: *Variations IV*
G. Crumb: *Echoes of Time and the River*

L. Foss: *Echoi; Orpheus*
M. Kelemen: *Entrances*
O. Knussen: *Masks for Solo Flute*
T. de Leeuw: *Spatial Music IV*
J. Mekeel: *The Shape of Silence*

Brasses

I. Anhalt: *Foci*

E. Schwartz: *Music for Napoleon and*

G. Crumb: *Echoes of Time and the River*
V. Globokar: *Discours II*

Beethoven (Example 31)
I. Xenakis: *Eonta*

Percussion

L. Austin: *The Maze*

Keyboard Instruments

E. Schwartz: *Music for Napoleon and Beethoven* (Example 31)

Strings

I. Anhalt: *Foci*
W. Bolcom: *Duets for Quintet*
T. de Leeuw: *Spatial Music IV*

F. Miroglio: *Projections*
W. Sydeman: *Projections I*
H. Tircuit: *String Quartet No. 3*

Just as he had directed all his players to stand up periodically during *Cortège*, Schafer also devised a complex scenario for entering and leaving the concert space, various woodwinds, brasses, and the violins playing their instruments while perambulating to and from the stage. For percussionists, perambulation has severe limitations. The players of timpani, gongs, and tam-tam, and the idiophones, for example, can hardly be expected to function normally while moving about the concert platform. But the smaller and more portable instruments—woodblock, triangle, tambourine, maracas, finger cymbals, and the like—can all be played easily and effectively while the percussionist is moving about.

Keyboard players cannot, quite obviously, stroll about while performing. But one composer, at least, has directed his pianist to perform other functions while walking about. In Elliott Schwartz's *Music for Napoleon and Beethoven*, the pianist is required to get up from the keyboard and to circle about the solo trumpeter, who stands close to the piano. Each time the pianist passes in front of the trumpet bell he is to insert, or to remove, one of three different mute types which he carries in his hand. Before returning to the keyboard he obligingly turns the page for the trumpeter. (See Example 31.)

Rather elaborate scenarios of movement, including exchanging one seat for another, are found in Harrison Birtwistle's *Verses for Ensemble* and in George Crumb's orchestral *Echoes of Time and the River*. All stage action on the part of performers must be carefully plotted by the composer lest unnecessary collision and/or confusion result from haphazard movement.

3. Vocalizations of one kind or another—speaking, shouting, screaming, whistling, hissing, grunting, muttering, laughing, whispering, singing, humming—either completely independent of instrumental playing or else combined with various methods of sound production on the instruments, have been demanded with increasing frequency of performers, as in:

Example 31
Elliott Schwartz: from *Music for Napoleon and Beethoven* (p. 6)

Bowdoin College Music Press. © Copyright 1971 by the President and Trustees of Bowdoin College. Quoted by permission of the copyright owner.

EXTRAMUSICAL DEVICES

Woodwinds

- G. Amy: *⁵⁄₁₆ pour flûte solo*
- D. Bedford: *Music for Albion Moonlight*
- W. Benson: *The Dream Net; Helix*
- B. Childs: *Nonet*
- D. Cope: *Indices*
- G. Crumb: *Echoes of Time and the River; Eleven Echoes of Autumn*
- D. Eberhard: *Parody*
- B. Ferneyhough: *Unity Capsule* (Example 28)
- L. Foss: *Paradigm*
- J. Fox: *All Things Fancy*
- R. Haubenstock-Ramati: *Multiple 5*
- S. Hodkinson: *Fresco*
- W. Holab: *Woodshedding*
- K. Husa: *Apotheosis of this Earth*
- P. Maxwell Davies: *Vesalii Icones*
- B. Rands: *Wildtrack 1*
- D. Reck: *Blues and Screamer*
- C. Rouse: *Rotae Passionis*
- R. M. Schafer: *Requiems for the Party-Girl*
- W. O. Smith: *Variants for Solo Clarinet*
- T. Takemitsu: *Voice*

Brasses

- R. Aitken: *Kebyar*
- C. Alsina: *Trio 1967* (Example 32)
- J. Bark, F. Rabe: *Bolos*
- V. Globokar: *Discours II*
- S. Hodkinson: *Fresco*
- A. Lanza: *Eidesis II*

Example 32
Carlos Alsina: from *Trio 1967* (p. 9)

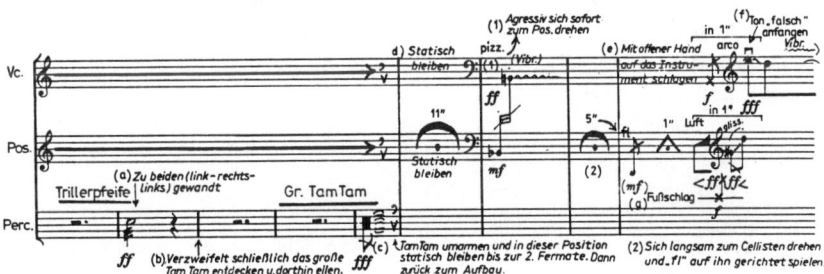

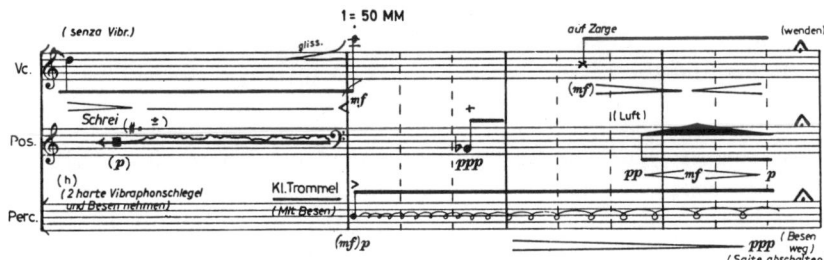

© Copyright 1969 by Bote & Bock. (Germany). All rights for the U.S. and Canada controlled by Associated Music Publishers, Inc. (New York). International Copyright Secured. All Rights Reserved. Used by Permission.

R. Barrett: *Anatomy*
G. Burt: *Exit Music*
N. T. Dao: *Phū-Dông*[1]
M. Ellis: *Mutations*
D. Erb: *The Seventh Trumpet*

P. Patterson: *Rebecca*
R. Reynolds: *"From Behind . . ."; The Promises of Darkness*
E. Schwartz: *Music for Napoleon and Beethoven* (Example 31); *Rip*

Brass players contend that because of tube bore and mouthpiece design on both the horn and the trumpet, vocal effects are somewhat more difficult on those instruments than on trombone or tuba.

Percussion

T. Antoniou: *Chorochronos I, II*
L. Berio: *Circles*
B. Childs: *Jack's New Bag; Nonet*
G. Crumb: *Echoes of Time and the River; Eleven Echoes of Autumn*
D. Eberhard: *Parody*
L. Foss: *Paradigm*
J. Hawkins: *Three Cavatinas*

M. Kagel: *Sonant*
A. Lanza: *Eidesis II*
B. Rands: *Ballad I; Wildtrack 1*
E. Raxach: *Paraphrase*
C. Rouse: *Ogoun Badagris*
J. Schwantner: *Canticle of the Evening Bells*

Harp and Other Plucked Instruments

B. Beerman: *Polygraph VI*
G. Crumb: *Songs, Drones and Refrains of Death*
D. Eberhard: *"Especially . . ."*
R. Felciano: *Background Music*
L. Foss: *Paradigm*
S. Hodkinson: *Drawings, Set No. 9*

M. Kagel: *Sonant*
A. LeBaron: *Memnon for Six Harps*
J. Nightingale: *Entente*
B. Rands: *Wildtrack 1*
R. M. Schafer: *Requiems for the Party-Girl*
D. Wilson: *Decisions, Decisions!*

Keyboard Instruments

D. Burge: *A Song of Sixpence; Sources III*
B. Childs: *Jack's New Bag: Nonet*
G. Crumb: *Echoes of Time and the River; Eleven Echoes of Autumn*
B. Rands: *Ballad 1*

R. M. Schafer: *Requiems for the Party-Girl*
B. Schaffer: *Musica per pianoforte*
E. Schwartz: *Music for Prince Albert*
K. Stockhausen: *Refrain*

Strings

D. Bedford: *Music for Albion Moonlight*
B. Childs: *Jack's New Bag; Mr. T., His Fancy*
J. Christou: *Enantiodromia*
D. Cope: *Angel's Camp II* (Example 50)

S. Montague: *At the white edge of phrygia*
P. Oliveros: *Doublebasses at Twenty Paces*
R. Peck: *Automobile; 1 db (1968)*
K. Penderecki: *Fluorescences; Polymorphia*

EXTRAMUSICAL DEVICES **135**

G. Crumb: *Black Angels; Madrigals—I*
I. Deak: *Color Studies for Contrabass*
D. Erb: *Trio for Two*
R. Erickson: *Ricercar à 5*
R. Felciano: *Spectra*
J. Fortner: *Quartet*
L. Foss: *Paradigm*
R. Haubenstock-Ramati: *Multiple 5*
G. Heussenstamm: *Pentalogue*
M. Kagel: *Sonant*
A. Lanza: *Eidesis II*
H. Lazarof: *Konkordia for String Orchestra*
D. Lentz: *Sermon*
F. Rabe: *Pajazzo*
B. Rands: *Memo 1* (Example 30)
D. Reck: *Night Sounds (and Dream)*
G. Rochberg: *Tableaux*
R. M. Schafer: *Requiems for the Party-Girl*
E. Schwartz: *Dialogue for Solo Contrabass*
H. Tircuit: *String Quartet No. 3*
B. Turetzky: *Poems, Portraits, Ballades and Blues*
C. Whittenberg: *Conversations for Solo Doublebass*

An unusual directive to a harpist occurs in Anne LeBaron's *Memnon:* "Tilt the harp slightly forward with the hands and hold it steady while cupping your mouth into the topmost hole." Presumably, the harpist then produces some kind of vocal sound into the hole. Another singular directive is present in Schafer's *East:* all the orchestral instrumentalists are to hum a pitch first produced on a tam-tam and a gong.

Parenthetically, it might be noted that a doublebass player could direct vocal sounds into the f-hole of his instrument while kneeling—an effect, however, not as yet encountered in this writer's research. But as anything and everything is grist in the mill of today's music, the action will no doubt be found in some score of the future.

4. Exaggerated body movements, facial contortions, and calculated theatrical gestures of one kind or another—foot stamping, finger snapping, hand clapping, and the like—supplement the performance contributions of various instrumentalists in the following scores:

Woodwinds

B. Childs: *Nonet*
R. Felciano: *Contractions*
V. Globokar: *Discours III*
S. Hodkinson: *Fresco*
B. Rands: *Ballad I*

Brasses

R. Aitken: *Kebyar*
C. Alsina: *Consequenza; Trio 1967* (Example 32)
B. Childs: *Nonet*
N. T. Dao: *Phū-Dông*
M. Ellis: *Mutations*
S. Hodkinson: *Fresco*
B. Jolas: *How Now*
A. Mellnäs: *Tombola*
E. Schwartz: *Music for Napoleon and Beethoven* (Example 31)

Percussion

D. Burge: *Sources III*
J. Hawkins: *Three Cavatinas*
S. Hodkinson: *Drawings, Set No. 9*

G. Ligeti: *Nouvelles Aventures*
P. Méfano: *Lignes*
L. de Pablo: *Prosodia*

Harp and Other Plucked Instruments

G. Crumb: *Songs, Drones and Refrains of Death*
R. Felciano: *Background Music*
H. W. Henze: *El Cimarrón*

J. Nightingale: *Entente*
R. M. Schafer: *The Crown of Ariadne*
W. Szalonek: *Proporzione II*

Keyboard Instruments

W. Albright: *Danse Macabre*
D. Burge: *Sources III*
B. Childs: *Nonet*
S. Lunetta: *Piano Music*
A. Mellnäs: *Tombola*

R. Roxbury: *Aria for Cello and Piano*
B. Schäffer: *Musica per pianoforte*
E. Schwartz: *Music for Prince Albert*
R. Wilding-White: *Whatzit No. 1*

Strings

B. Childs: *Nonet*
D. Cope: *Angel's Camp II* (Example 50); *Cedar Breaks*
G. Crumb: *Songs, Drones, and Refrains of Death*
J. Deak: *Color Studies for Contrabass*
K. Gaburo: *Inside*

G. Heussenstamm: *Pentalogue*
E. Kurtz: *Improvisation for Contrabass*
K. Penderecki: *Capriccio for Violin and Orchestra*
P. Phillips: *Divertimento for Three String Basses*
E. Schwartz: *Music for Prince Albert*

Even more theatrical effects are often demanded in experimental and multimedia works. Percussionists, for example, have been directed to smash bottles or plates of glass (in Ligeti's *Nouvelles Aventures* and William Russell's *Three Dance Movements*, for instance), or to pop inflated balloons with a pin, as in Nicolas Slonimsky's *My Toy Balloon* (see page 193). The brass players in *Aura* of Arne Mellnäs must attach balloons to their music stands and explode them with a pin at certain designated moments in the work. Balloon popping is also an intrusive feature of the *"Erotica" Variations* by a certain P. D. Q. Bach, a composer known far and wide for his shameless plagiarism.

Not primarily a theatrical but rather a sonic device is the "Doppler effect." One cannot deny, however, the visual contribution to any performance moment calling for this gesture. Named after its inventor, Christian Johann Doppler (1803–53), it is accomplished by rotating or pivoting the bell of a brass instrument from one side to the other, or from high to low, with varying speeds and angles of trajectory. Stuart Dempster's *Didjeridervish* for solo trombone demonstrates the Doppler effect applied to both the instrument and the performer.[2] The Doppler technique can also be applied to the clarinet and saxophone, and rather less successfully to the oboe and English horn. (See, for instance, *Verses for Ensemble* of Birtwistle and Philippe Boesmans' *Correlations*.)

In addition to the visual stimulation created by this action, an apparent shift in frequencies and in dynamics and/or timbre is produced, owing to the motion of the sound source. The following works request the use of this viable technique:

C. Alsina: *Trio 1967*
D. Burge: *Sources III*
J. Fulkerson: *Patterns III*

I. Xenakis: *Eonta*
R. Reynolds: *"From Behind . . ."*
T. Takemitsu: *Green*

The "Doppler effect" has also been used effectively by the horns, alternately stopping and opening the notated pitches at the same time as the instrument bell is pivoted (see Example 5).

AUXILIARY INSTRUMENTS

A final theatricality much in evidence in contemporary scores is the playing upon auxiliary instruments by various instrumentalists (and singers). Generally, the auxiliary instruments are percussion—finger cymbals, woodblocks, a tambourine, pair of maracas, and the like. Frequently, too, wind or string players must perform with mallets or their hands on the interior areas of the piano. These several requirements appear in:

W. Albright: *Danse Macabre*
C. Alsina: *Trio 1967*
I. Anhalt: *Foci*
D. Burge: *Sources III*

D. Cope: *Indices*
B. Johnston: *One Man*
E. Schwartz: *Options I*
L. Widdoes: *From a Time of Snow*

In Arne Mellnäs's *Aura* the woodwind and brass players are directed—in addition to popping balloons as previously mentioned—to hang small bottles from their music racks and to strike them with long-handled spoons. And manifestly unconventional auxiliary instruments are the three smoking pipes to be "played" by a flutist, horn player, and trumpeter at the outset of Yizhak Sadai's orchestral *Nuances*—not to mention the slide flutes and assorted bird-calls to be played by all the wind performers in Marius Constant's *Winds*.

Other instances of auxiliary instrument use by members of the wind section include:

M. Bamert: *Introduction and Tarantella* (flutist plays on two tam-tams)

G. Crumb: *Vox Balaenae* (flutist plays antique cymbals)

D. Erb: *The Rainbow Snake* (trombonist plays metal wind chimes)

T. Marco: *Rosa-Rosae* (flutist plays triangle and clarinetist plays crotales)

C. Rouse: *The Infernal Machine* (flutist and oboist rub a wetted finger around the wetted rims of crystal goblets)

J. Schwantner: *and the mountains rising nowhere* (oboist plays a glass harmonica)

Idem: *Canticle of the Evening Bells* (several woodwind and brass instrumentalists perform on glockenspiel and glass crystals)

In David Bedford's *Brighton Piece* the hornist is to strike together two walnut shells—or, as the composer says, "anything which makes a non-metallic click."

Percussionists are now quite frequently instructed to play inside a grand piano, its lid removed, with mallets or other striking agents. Nearly always the player stands at the left side of the piano in order to reach the bass strings with ease. The following scores have required this performance practice:

Z. Durko: *Iconography No. 2*

D. Erb: *Concerto for Solo Percussionist*

L. Kirchner: *Music for Orchestra*

G. Ligeti: *Aventures*

G. Read: *Haiku Seasons*

In the third book of *Madrigals* of George Crumb, a percussionist is directed to play with mallets on the wire bass strings of the harp; at the same time the harpist plays with both hands on the higher strings. A similar action is required in Crumb's *Songs, Drones, and Refrains of Death* on the open strings of a doublebass. In this composer's *Madrigals—I* the solo bassist fingers certain stipulated pitches while the percussionist plays on the four strings with mallets, an action also specified in this writer's *Diabolic Dialogue* for solo doublebass and timpani. (see Example 33)

The players of plucked instruments have also been directed to handle auxiliary sound producers, as in:

G. Crumb: *Songs, Drones and Refrains of Death* (guitarist plays a Jew's harp)

J. Hutcheson: *Three Things for Dr. Seuss* (harpist plays a guiro)

R. Kuhl: *Dreams Before Dark* (harpist plays antique cymbals)

R. M. Schafer: *The Crown of Ariadne* (harpist activates nine assorted percussion instruments)

Keyboard players, too, have been asked to perform on auxiliary, ready-to-hand percussion instruments. Those that are easily transportable or that can be comfortably handled while seated at the keyboard are most often designated. Tri-

Example 33
Gardner Read: from *Diabolic Dialogue* (p. 7)

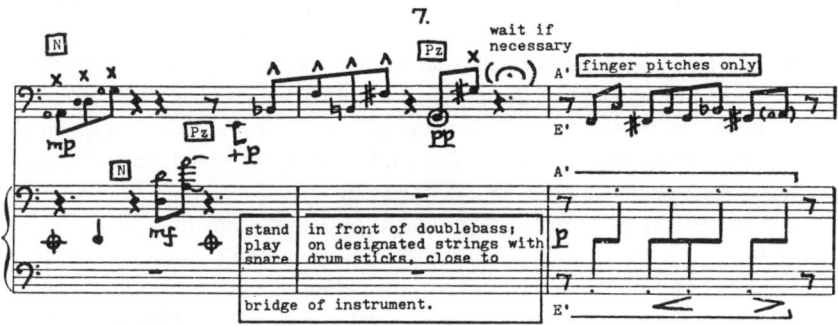

© 1979 by Gardner Read

angle, woodblock, cowbell or a crotale, for instance, are easily managed by a pianist, who can even play on the keyboard with one hand while shaking or beating upon an auxiliary instrument with the other. A good example of this action is to be found in Udo Kasemet's $\sqrt{5}$. Other examples include the pianist in Erb's *The Rainbow Snake,* who also plays a harmonica, and the keyboardist in Elizabeth Vercoe's *Herstory II* who must alternately play on the keys or interior strings and on a woodblock, finger cymbal, tambourine, triangle, maraca, and castanet. Finally, we find Gunther Schuller asking the pianist in his *Music for Violin, Piano and Percussion* to tap on a gourd, as well as directing the violinist to shake a maraca.

Two of Ligeti's works call for a harpsichordist to perform also on the strings of an adjacent piano: in *Aventures* he is to use soft timpani sticks, and in *Nouvelles Aventures* he must employ two clothes brushes. The organist in Istvan Anhalt's *Foci* is required at one point in the score to play with mallets in the piano interior.

An obvious auxiliary "instrument" for keyboard players, but one surprisingly seldom requisitioned, is a metronome. In Peter Lewis's solo piano *Sweets,* the pianist must turn it on and off, changing its rate of speed, as directed in the music. Both metronomes and alarm clocks are prominent requirements for the accompanying players in Xavier Benguerel's guitar concerto. All of the instrumentalists in *Tautologos III, Version No. 4* of Luc Ferrari are equipped with pocket metronomes, each one calibrated to a different tempo. When activated the resultant sound is a dense cloud of clickings superimposed on the musical pitches produced by the instrumentalists.

Serving not as an auxiliary instrument but rather as an extra performer is the page turner in Crumb's *Celestial Mechanics,* who joins in playing at the keyboard in several passages with the duo pianists.

Members of the string section are perhaps less frequently expected to perform on auxiliary instruments than other instrumentalists. But in Crumb's *Black Angels* for electrified string quartet the players all must handle various percussion, including bowing on the rim of a tam-tam and on the rims of a set of tuned crystal glasses. These requirements admirably complement the disembodied sounds produced by amplification of the strings in altissimo positions. The string players in Schwantner's *Canticle of the Evening Bells* also strike crotales and bow on a vibraphone bar, and in his *Magabunda* the first violins play on glass crystals.

One composer has solved the problem of simultaneous string and auxiliary percussive sound by having the violist and cellist of a string quartet attach small bells to their ankles and stamp their feet while playing; this requirement appears in Peter Apfelbaum's *Lanterns and Cathedrals*.

No doubt the ultimate in the requirement of auxiliary instruments occurs in *Terretektorh* of Xenakis: each of the eighty-eight orchestral instrumentalists must play, in addition to his own instrument, a woodblock, a whip, a maraca, and a siren whistle. The latter, in three sizes and with three correspondingly different registers, produces "sounds resembling flames," to quote the composer. An additional innovative feature of this work is that the orchestra members are to be seated amidst the audience, the performance area thus being integrated with that customarily occupied by the listeners.

Bizarre as many of the extramusical stipulations discussed in this chapter undoubtedly are, they yet form an integral part of the vanguard composer's aesthetic premise. As logical extensions of the concept of "total theatre" the histrionic effects must be assessed within the contexts of the specific compositions requiring them. If not all multimedia works demanding theatrical gestures from their participating instrumentalists are artistically viable, neither are all traditionally conceived and executed works. If some avant-garde musical essays are sophomoric and boring, then so are some earnest and well-meaning pieces in conventional idioms. The efficacy of any one, or all, of these extramusical devices depends not upon their mere presence in today's experimental vocal and instrumental scores but upon the conviction with which they are carried out by the performers involved and by their dramatic impact upon the totality of the musical experience.

NOTES

1. The horn player is directed to speak into the bell of the instrument.
2. This composer's book on the modern capabilities of the trombone lists 115 examples of effects now possible, offering startling evidence of what this brass member is able to contribute to the new music of our time.

II

IDIOMATIC TECHNIQUES

WOODWINDS AND BRASSES

9

FLUTTER-TONGUING VARIANTS

Neither new nor uncommon, the highly favored technique of flutter-tonguing appears in several new guises in vanguard scores. One is to request a gradual and measured shift from normal tonguing to fluttering, or the reverse—though both procedures are easier in theory than in actual practice. Many recent works have requested these tonguing shifts, among them:

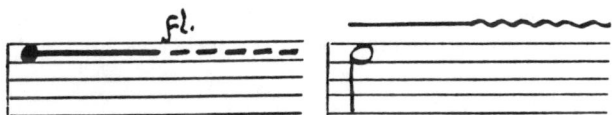

N. T. Dao: *Tây Nguyên*
J. Druckman: *Animus 1* (Example 36)
V. Globokar: *Etude pour Folklora II*
D. Kam: *Rendezvous II*

M. Kelemen: *Study for Flute Alone*
B. Schäffer: *Azione a due*
K. Stockhausen: *Momente*
W. Szalonek: *Les Sons*

Flutter-tonguing may also begin suddenly on a sustained note or, conversely, change abruptly into normal single-, double-, or triple-tonguing (as in the *Keime und Male* of Hans-Joachim Hespos). Also, flutter-tonguing, as with other tonguing patterns, may be combined with fingered and valve glissandi:

R. Aitken: *Kebyar*
M. Bamert: *Woodwind Quintet*
M. Ellis: *Mutations* (Example 19)
B. Ferneyhough: *Cassandra's Dream Song; Unity Capsule* (Example 28)

G. Read: *Sonoric Fantasia No. 3*
G. Schuller: *Spectra*
E. Varèse: *Ameriques*
I. Xenakis: *Eonta*

On oboe and English horn an authentic flutter-tonguing is impossible, but a "faked" variety can be obtained by diminishing the blowing pressure so as to produce a rough and tremulous sound resembling fluttering (see Szalonek's *Les Sons*). In his *Exospheres* Aurelio de la Vega directs the oboist to approximate flutter-tonguing by beating on the lower three keys while blowing the required pitch, while in *Interpolation* he calls for breath sound coupled with the same throat action required for flutter-tonguing. Elliott Carter appends a footnote to an oboe passage in his *8 Etudes and a Fantasy* suggesting alternating normal fingering with pressing down the low B♭-key to achieve an approximation of flutter-tongue.

For an authentic flutter on an approximate pitch, Witold Szalonek asks the flute soloist in his *Concertino* to enclose the mouthpiece tightly with the lips while trilling with the tongue, while Milko Kelemen in *Olifant* directs the flutist to flutter-tongue without producing any pitch, a technique also required in Sergio Cervetti's *Six Sequences for Dance*.

It has been pointed out that the ability of wind players to flutter-tongue is more hereditary than acquired, owing to the physical incapacity of some performers to trill with the tongue. When flutter-tonguing is required of such players, they usually substitute a throat "growl," though prolonged use of this device is rather tiring to the throat muscles. At times this latter technique has been explicitly stipulated:

J. Bark, F. Rabe: *Bolos*
J. Barraqué: *. . . au delà du hasard*
L. Berio: *Gesti*
J. Druckman: *Dark Upon the Harp*

D. Martino: *Strata*
D. Reck: *Blues and Screamer*
T. Takemitsu: *Voice*
I. Xenakis: *Linaia—Agon*

VIBRATO

Contemporary composers are usually quite specific in designating the complete absence of woodwind vibrato or, contrariwise, an exaggerated vibrato—both for coloristic reasons. Also, uneven or unstable vibratos are frequently requested in current scores: for example, either nonvibrato gradually moving to full normal or overemphasized vibrato, or a more sporadic shift from one condition to another, may be called for. Among the works requiring these various degrees of vibrato production are included:

WOODWINDS AND BRASSES

A. Bloch: *Erwartung*
Chou Wen-chung: *Cursive; Pien*
H. W. Henze: *Sinfonia N. 6*
G. Heussenstamm: *Poikilos*
M. Kagel: *Heterophonie*
B. Levy: *Orbs with Flute*
D. Martino: *Concerto for Wind Quintet*
P. Nørgård: *Symphony No. 2*

G. Read: *Sonoric Fantasia No. 3*
D. Reck: *Blues and Screamer*
R. Reynolds: *Quick are the Mouths of Earth; Wedge*
B. Sakač: *Struktur I*
A. de la Vega: *Structures*
C. Wuorinen: *Flute Variations*
I. Yun: *Images*

More fanciful vibrato requests have been forthcoming from some recent composers: for example, in his *Nonet* Barney Childs calls for a clarinet and bassoon "schmaltzy" vibrato "to sound like a Guy Lombardo saxophone player of the 1920's." A very slow vibrato, equal to one pulse per second, is stipulated by E. A. Alemann in his *Spectra for 4 Recorders;* this composer also asks for a "finger vibrato," achieved by closing one or more of the lower holes of the instrument with a trill movement according to the fingerings given below the pitches.

In Conrad de Jong's *Contact* the solo trombonist is to produce an exaggerated vibrato "like Tommy Dorsey," while in his *Changes* Larry Austin requires the trombonist to use a "nanny-goat" vibrato—as graphic a request as can be imagined.

Among the brass instruments, the trombone is frequently directed to produce a "slide vibrato," achieved by rapidly maneuvering the slide between positions so that an actual wavering of pitch is perceived—sometimes as much as a major third. The slide vibrato, it should be noted, is most effective in the middle to upper range of the instrument, where the player has more control of the slide. Works specifically requesting slide vibrato include:

R. Aitken: *Kebyar*
C. Alsina: *Consequenza*
R. du Bois: *Music for a Sliding Trombone*
M. Ellis: *Mutations*

W. Kotonski: *Pour quatre*
E. Krenek: *Five Pieces for Trombone and Piano*
I. Xenakis: *Eonta; Metastaseis*

A different kind of vibrato, one affecting amplitude rather than frequency, is requested in several works of recent composition; it is referred to as a "smorzato" effect in Bruno Bartolozzi's music. On the flute this is achieved by interrupting the blown tone with an excessive velocity of breath, and with lip or jaw rather than diaphragm action; on the reed instruments it is obtained by "squeezing" the reed with gentle movements of the lips or by momentarily pulling the jaw away from the reed. The result in both instances is a slight oscillation of dynamic level, more apparent in the instruments' lower range than in the higher; see the following:

- B. Bartolozzi: *Collage; Concertazioni per Oboe*
- J. Dillon: *Uberschreiten*
- B. Ferneyhough: *Cassandra's Dream Song; Etudes Transcendantales*
- V. Globokar: *Atemstudie für Oboe*
- G. Read: *Phantasmagoria*
- D. Rosenboom: *and come up dripping*
- L. Widdoes: *From a Time of Snow*

FINGERING DEVICES

Many new woodwind and brass effects relate primarily to fingering patterns or valve combinations rather than to embouchure or breath control. Possibly the most common of these is the single-pitch trill or "timbral tremolo," achieved by rapidly alternating the normal and the harmonic (or other alternative) fingering of the notated, unchanging pitch. Also referred to variously as an enharmonic trill, a "color trill," a unison tremolo, a key vibrato, and "bariolage" (from the string instrument technique of alternating an open string with a fingered note on the same pitch), the technique of alternate fingerings is most frequently demanded of flute and also flute players. It is less often required of oboists, clarinetists, bassoonists, and saxophonists. The following works all require the application of enharmonic trills from various woodwind instruments:

 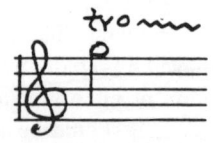

- R. Aitken: *Kebyar*
- E. A. Alemann: *Spectra for 4 Recorders*
- G. Amy: *Jeux*
- T. Antoniou: *Five Likes for Solo Oboe*
- L. Bassett: *Music for Saxophone and Piano*
- L. Berio: *Sequenza VII*
- J. van de Booren: *Chanson de Printemps*
- G. Braun: *Monologe I*
- R. Caravan: *Excursions for Clarinet*
- E. Carter: *Sonata for Flute, Oboe, Cello and Harpsichord*
- N. Castiglioni: *Alef*
- Chou Wen-chung: *Cursive*
- L. Foss: *Echoi*
- J. Fox: *All Things Fancy*
- A. Gilbert: *The Incredible Flute Music*
- V. Globokar: *Accord; Discours II*
- J. Harvey: *Persephone Dream*
- S. Hodkinson: *Interplay*
- K. Huber: *Alveare vernat*
- M. Kelemen: *Equilibres*
- K. Korte: *Remembrances*
- T. de Kruyf: *Mosaico*
- S. Montague: *At the white edge of phrygia*
- K. Penderecki: *Capriccio per Oboe*
- G. Read: *Sonoric Fantasia No. 3*

WOODWINDS AND BRASSES

G. Crumb: *Eleven Echoes of Autumn*
E. Denisov: *Romantische Musik*
J. Dillon: *Uberschreiten*
W. Eisma: *World Within World*
D. Erb: *Concerto for Solo Percussionist*
B. Ferneyhough: *Etudes Transcendantales; Unity Capsule*

D. Stalvey: *PLC-Extract*
T. Takemitsu: *Eucalypts (I), II*
L. Widdoes: *From a Time of Snow*
A. Woodbury: *Remembrances*
C. Wuorinen: *Flute Variations*

According to that authority on wind instrument techniques, Bruno Bartolozzi,[1] there are nearly 100 possible fingerings which would produce b^1 on the oboe, thus enabling the player to create a seemingly unending succession of subtle timbral changes on a single pitch. Not all the available notes on the oboe, nor on the other woodwinds, possess so many fingering alternates, but most wind players have not yet fully explored the impressive potential of this viable technique. Shown below are a few of the note symbols this composer devised for characterizing variable timbres on the pitch of b^1.

On the brass instruments, with the exception of trombone, the enharmonic trill is achieved by an alternation of different valve actions and minute embouchure adjustments (as in Schuller's *Five Pieces for Five Horns*). The trombone, of course, must rely on quick changes of slide position in conjunction with slight changes of embouchure. Examples of brass "bariolage" include:

L. Berio: *Sinfonia*
J. Druckman: *Animus 1*
D. Erb: *Symphony of Overtures*
V. Globokar: *Accord; Etude pour Folklora*
A. Imbrie: *Three Sketches for Trombone and Piano*

M. Kelemen: *Olifant*
E. Krenek: *Five Pieces for Trombone and Piano*
D. Reck: *Five Studies for Tuba Alone*
R. Reynolds: *"From Behind. . ."; The Promises of Darkness*
M. Stibilj: *Condensation*

Half-valving (on horn, trumpet, and tuba) is another fingering device in current use; the brass player gradually pushes down the valves half-way, an action that subtly but perceptibly changes both the blown pitch and its timbre (as requested in Ton de Leeuw's *Spatial Music III*, for example). It is an ideal way to "dirty up" a tone, and is highly favored by composers of jazz and rock music.

Another modern fingering device on woodwind and brass instruments is the double trill; it is achieved by rapidly alternating two fingers on a single key or valve of the instrument. The pitch produced is a unison but is slightly "broken" in effect; see:

R. Aitken: *Kebyar*
A. Gilbert: *The Incredible Flute Music*
G. Read: *Phantasmagoria*

An allied technique, termed "interrupted tones," and used by William O. Smith in his *Variants for Solo Clarinet,* is created by repeating the pitches as rapidly as possible using legato tonguing.

BREATH AND AIR SOUNDS

Just as late twentieth-century music exploits the percussive potential of wind instruments, so it has come to explore breath and air effects unrelated to normal tone production. For breath or wind sound alone on an instrument, the player contracts or relaxes his diaphragm without tonguing into mouthpiece or reed. The sounds are achieved by exaggerated emphasis of inhalant or exhalant effort, but without precise embouchure control or fingerings of specific pitches.

On the single- and double-reed instruments the player directs the air stream into the mouthpiece or reed; on members of the flute family the player slightly turns or rolls the instrument away from the lips while blowing air across the mouthpiece opening. This kind of effect was first specified in Heitor Villa-Lobos' *The Jet-Whistle* of 1953: the flutist is directed to close the blowhole tightly with the mouth and to blow violently while fingering low B; the result is a forceful downward "swoosh," without pitch. The same general effect is called for in the following works:

D. Eberhard: *Parody*
D. Erb: *Concerto for Brass and Orchestra*
H. Gaber: *Voce II*
S. Hodkinson: *Interplay*
S. Montague: *At the white edge of phrygia*
R. Reynolds: *Quick are the Mouths of Earth*
D. Welcher: *White Mares of the Moon*

Another flute technique is known as "edge tones;" they are achieved by the player fingering the pitches in the normal manner but blowing very lightly over the embouchure hole, best realized in the highest fifth of the instrument's range.

Brian Ferneyhough's *Unity Capsule* for solo flute is a veritable manual of contemporary techniques for the instrument. In addition to calling for the "jet whistle," the air directed at the mouth aperture from a distance so as to produce sympathetic resonance, the composer directs the player to "move the airhole gradually away from the lips," to "remove the instrument rapidly to arms-length, and return to normal position gradually," and to "move the tip of the tongue rapidly from side to side of the mouth aperture." He also tells the player to turn the instrument inwards and outwards while maintaining a continuous recognizable pitch. The piece begins with the flute headjoint fully extended, and at one place in the score the flutist must shake the instrument. All of these actions add an extra dimension of theatricality to the performance of *Unity Capsule* (see Example 28).

"*H*" *for Wind Quintet* by that master oboist, Heinz Holliger, contains several unusual directives for producing breath effects on one or the other of the wind instruments. For example: "Press mouth against the [flute] aperture and suck air into the mouth-hole, making a 'smacking' noise." The flutist must also create an air noise by keeping the mouthpiece some distance from the lips, while the oboist is to place an empty cap on his instrument and tighten the lips as though playing on a trumpet mouthpiece.

A few composers have been unusually graphic in their instructions for wind instrument breath sounds: "Blow sharply into any tone hole [of bassoon] as if to clean it" is the way Barney Childs put it in his *Nonet*, while "Sound produced by sucking" is David Rosenboom's phraseology in *and come up dripping*. In Edward Boguslawski's *Canti* the flutist is told to produce a breath sound "by holding the instrument 1½ cm from the lower lip," while directing the air stream toward the mouthpiece, and in Larry Austin's *Changes* the solo trombonist is instructed to "blow a stream of 'whistling' air" through the instrument. In *Anatomy*, Richard Barrett directs the horn player to "breathe noisily" through the mouthpiece.

Other recent scores that require woodwind breath sounds independent of any tone production include:

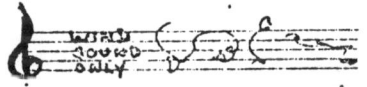

W. Albright: *Saints Preserve Us*
T. Antoniou: *Five Likes for Solo Oboe*
I. Bazelon: *Sound Dreams*
W. Benson: *The Dream Net*
E. Brown: *Available Forms 2; Times Five*
T. Bruynel: *Signs*
S. Bussotti: *Couple*
N. Castiglioni: *Consonante*
F. Cerha: *Enjambments*
S. Cervetti: *Six Sequences for Dance*
B. Childs: *Nonet*
G. Crumb: *Echoes of Time and the River*
N. T. Dao: *Tây Nguyên*

S. Hodkinson: *Fresco*
W. Holab: *Woodshedding*
J. Ibert: *Suite Symphonique*
M. Kelemen: *Entrances*
H. Lachenmann: *Dal Niente for Solo Clarinet Player*
B. Levy: *Orbs with Flute*
G. Ligeti: *Apparitions; Aventures*
R. Maros: *Eufonia No. 3*
D. Martino: *Concerto for Wind Quintet*
T. Mayuzumi: *Metamusic*
R. Meale: *Clouds now and then*
J. Mekeel: *The Shape of Silence*
F. Miroglio: *Phases; Réfractions*
P. Nørgård: *Symphony No. 2*

W. Eisma: *Non-lecture II*
D. Erb: *The Seventh Trumpet*
L. Ferrari: *Société II*
L. Foss: *Orpheus*
H. Gaber: *Voce II*
V. Globokar: *Accord*
E. Grosskopf: *Dialectics*
C. Halffter: *Lineas y puntos; Planto por las victimas de la violencia*
H-J. Hespos: *Passagen*
B. Rands: *Actions for six; Ballad 1*
R. M. Schafer: *Son of Heldenleben*
M. Subotnick: *Lamination I*
W. Szalonek: *Aarhus Music*
A. de la Vega: *Interpolation for Solo Clarinet*
O. Wilson: *Echoes for Clarinet and Tape*
B. A. Zimmermann: *Tempus loquendi*

Similar directives for the brass instruments, individually or collectively, are to be found in the following scores:

C. Alsina: *Trio 1967* (Example 32)
L. Austin: *Changes*
M. Bamert: *Inkblot*
J. Bark, F. Rabe: *Bolos*
D. Bedford: *Trona*
L. Berio: *Sequenza V*
E. Brown: *Available Forms 2; From Here*
S. Bussotti: *Torso*
G. Cacioppo: *Time on Time in Miracles*
J. Cage: *Solo for Sliding Trombone*
B. Childs: *Music for Trombone*
M. Colgrass: *As Quiet As*
G. Crumb: *Echoes of Time and the River*
N. T. Dao: *Phū-Dōng*
J. Druckman: *Animus 1* (Example 36)
D. Erb: *Concerto for Solo Percussionist; Symphony of Overtures*
L. Ferrari: *Société II*
L. Foss: *For 24 Winds*
V. Globokar: *Etude pour Folklora II*
C. Halffter: *Lineas y puntos; Planto por las victimas de la violencia*
R. Haubenstock-Ramati: *Credentials*
W. Heider: *-einander*
H. W. Henze: *Sinfonia N. 6*
S. Hodkinson: *Fresco*
M. Kelemen: *Olifant* (Example 46)
A. Lanza: *Acúfenos I*
G. Ligeti: *Aventures; Nouvelles Aventures*
R. Maros: *Eufonia No. 3*
R. Meale: *Clouds now and then*
A. Mellnäs: *Gestes sonores*
M. Mitrea-Celarianu: *Seth*
W. Ross: *Concerto for Trombone*
W. Sydeman: *Texture Studies for Orchestra*

An instrumental simulation of electronic "white noise" is requested by James Fulkerson in *Patterns III,* the solo tuba player being directed to blow air into the mouthpiece through clenched teeth. In Dao's *Phū-Dông,* on the other hand, the player is to "suck in air through the mouthpiece like a kiss"; also to blow into the bell of the instrument—the latter an awkward requirement to ask of any tuba performer. A directive in *The Rainbow Snake* of Donald Erb tells the trombonist to blow on the mouthpiece into a Harmon mute. All of the brasses in Jonathan Harvey's *Inner Light III* are to make wind sounds by moving the pistons or slides of their instruments rapidly and randomly.[2]

A trill or tremolo effect with the breath alone (but into the instrument) is the

WOODWINDS AND BRASSES 151

rough equivalent of flutter-tonguing without tone; it has been demanded in the following works:

W. Albright: *Danse Macabre*
J. Bark, F. Rabe: *Bolos*
L. Berio: *Gesti*
G. Braun: *Monologe I*
S. Bussotti: *Couple; Torso*
S. Cervetti: *Six Sequences for Dance*
A. Corghi: *Stereofonie X4*
G. Crumb: *Eleven Echoes of Autumn*
L. Ferrari: *Société II*
J. Fox: *All Things Fancy*

V. Globokar: *Discours II*
G. Ligeti: *Ten Pieces for Wind Quintet*
M. Mitrea-Celarianu: *Seth*
P. Nørgård: *Prism*
R. Reynolds: *"From Behind . . ."*
E. Schwartz: *Options I*
A. de la Vega: *Interpolation for Solo Clarinet*
D. Wilson: *Doubles*

In his composition cited, Cervetti directs the brass players to flutter-tongue into the instrument with the mouthpiece removed, an effect virtually indistinguishable from an unpitched breath tremolo.

In both *Aarhus Music* and *Les Sons*, Witold Szalonek directs the flutist to blow normally, to the opposite side of the mouthpiece, but to change the angle of airflow by turning the instrument in such a way that a full tone is not obtained. Bernard Rands asks for similar action on the flutist's part in his *Actions for six*. Werner Heider includes directions in his solo recorder *Katalog* to produce a breathy, exhalant effect, and to create the sound of rushing air on a definite pitch with perceptible but rather weak overtones.

Breath sounds may also be combined with actual instrumental tone, emphasizing the one or the other in varying degrees; see:

W. Albright: *Danse Macabre*
G. Braun: *Monologe I*
G. Crumb: *Eleven Echoes of Autumn*

V. Globokar: *Discours II*
D. Martino: *Concerto for Wind Quintet*
L. Widdoes: *From a Time of Snow*

In addition, percussive devices (key or valve clicks, or audible fingerings) may be freely mixed with unpitched air sounds, as found, for instance, in these scores:

T. Albert: *Sound Frames*
W. Albright: *Danse Macabre*
F. Cerha: *Enjambments*
H-J. Hespos: *Passagen*
B. Jolas: *Fusain*

O. Knussen: *Masks for Solo Flute*
B. Maderna: *Concerto for Oboe*
R. Moryl: *Improvisations*
R. M. Schafer: *Son of Heldenleben*
M. Subotnick: *Lamination I*

Most commonly used in the production of harmonics (see pages 55–56) the technique of overblowing has been stipulated by several composers in their wind parts to alter pitch and timbre, such as breath sounds to clear tone, or the reverse (as in the *Keime und Male* of Hespos). Overblowing has been specified to achieve a harsh and strained tonal quality (in Paul Chihara's *Branches,* for example), and to produce a shrill wind sound (Crumb's *Eleven Echoes of Autumn*).

The wind instruments are all capable of producing attacks that emphasize a strong breathy quality. In Marc Wilkinson's *Voices* the composer asks for a "soft, windy attack"; later, one articulated by the player pronouncing "the," and at still another point, a sharp attack with an exaggerated "t" sound. There are similar directives to the wind players in the *Bolos* of Jan Bark and Folke Rabe, John Cage's *Solo for Sliding Trombone,* and *Interpolation* of Aurelio de la Vega.

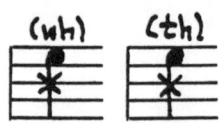

In proportionately notated music (time-notation) wind players are frequently instructed to hold a tone until their breath is exhausted. To do so produces a noticeable decay of both amplitude and frequency. See, for instance:

D. Bedford: *Music for Albion Moonlight*
A. Gilbert: *The Incredible Flute Music*
J. Heinke: *Music for Trombone and Percussion*

G. Ligeti: *Aventures*
P. Méfano: *Paraboles*
F. Miroglio: *Phases; Réfractions*
T. Takemitsu: *Eucalypts (I)*

A number of singular directives regarding wind instrument techniques and tonal quality appear in various twentieth-century scores. For instance: In *Cassandra's Dream Song,* Brian Ferneyhough tells the flutist to sound a pitch by expelling air into the instrument without tonguing, and to employ a "gasping tone" by using a very wide embouchure so that all the player's air is expelled from the lungs, resulting in more noise than pitched sound. Without explaining the technical procedure, Varèse asks the oboist in *Integrales* to produce a "shrill, pinched tone," while the clarinet is to be "hollow sounding." The player in Cage's *Solo for Clarinet* must buzz with the lips into the instrument barrel, the mouthpiece detached, while in Serocki's *Swinging Music* the clarinetist is to blow air across the barrel opening. Both the clarinet and the horn in Arnold Bax's *Second Symphony* are to be "coarsely blown." Heinz Holliger tells the bassoonist in *"H" for Wind Quintet* to tighten the lips on the instrument crook and force air out of the mouth-hole, and in *Le Joli Jeu de Fouret* of Jean-Jules Roger-Ducasse the bassoon must sound "as nasal as possible."

Still other detailed directives include the following: "Turn the flute very slowly backwards and forwards over the blowhole" appears in Alexandre Hrisanide's *Directions*. "Enclose outlet of mouthpiece with the lips and depress reed with a finger while inhaling air," and "Enclose mouthpiece and lips with palms of the hands twisted into a cone" are instructions that appear in *Improvisations sonoristiques* of Szalonek. The clarinetist in Roger Hannay's *Fantôme* is told to play with a fuzzy tone that disintegrates into a hiss of air as it slides past the instrument reed. Finally, all the brass players in *Olifant* of Milko Kelemen are directed to breathe audibly in and out but without producing any tone.

Flexible or unstable pitch is a requirement found in a number of recent scores. In Luc Ferrari's *Interrupteur* and *Société II*, for example, unstable pitch is to be produced by irregular pressure of the lips on the reed. This technique is termed "nota flessuoso" in *Proporzioni* of Franco Evangelisti, and indicated by the following symbol:

Bartolozzi refers to his related directive in the *Concertazioni per oboe* as "suono rotto" (broken sound), different timbres brought about by beats (amplitude modulation).

Mention must be made of "beat [or beating] tones," achieved either by a single wind instrument playing intervallic structures or by two instruments of similar timbre playing together. As a concrete example of the first category: in Lukas Foss's wind quintet (*Cave of the Winds*) the four woodwinds are each directed to hold certain blown pitches, gradually increasing both air and lip pressure; the result is a microtonal multiphonic whose composite tones create amplitude beats at regularly recurring intervals.

In the second symphony of Per Nørgård, amplitude beats are to be produced by two clarinets playing soft pitches a microtone apart. And as a dedicated advocate of this acoustical device, Iannis Xenakis calls for beating tones between clarinet and cello in *Charisma* and between horn and trombone in *Linaia—Agon;* in each instance the composer indicates a fluctuating number of amplitude beats per second. Thus, in these and other recent vanguard works, an acoustical phenomenon once accidentally created by faulty intonation is now an actively sought after sonic effect by our experimentally motivated composers.

A recent technical development on the wind instruments is known as "circular breathing." In the words of flutist–composer Robert Dick, this effect is accomplished by the player inflating the cheeks while playing and then using the air in the cheeks to play momentarily while air is inhaled through the nose.

MOUTHPIECE AND TUBING EFFECTS

A technical phenomenon of recent vintage, one congenital to both woodwind and brass instruments, is the production of sound or indefinite noise on the reed or mouthpiece alone, removed from the instrument. Precise pitches, however, can often be produced when a woodwind player blows on the unattached reed or a brass player on the mouthpiece alone, or else the illusion of relative pitch can be obtained through embouchure manipulation. These several effects have been specified in the following works:

M. Bamert: *Inkblot*
D. Bedford: *Trona*
E. Krenek: *Five Pieces for Trombone and Piano*

G. Ligeti: *Apparitions*
B. Rands: *Metalepsis 2*

Related to these techniques are so-called "ghost notes." These are pitches blown so softly that they are almost inaudible. As Gunther Schuller explains it, "a ghost note is sort of 'swallowed' by the player, giving it almost no air support and no projection." Examination of Schuller's *Journey into Jazz* will demonstrate this technique at work.

Various vanguard composers have asked the double-reed players to "crow" on the detached reed, producing a harsh squawk:

T. Bruynel: *Signs*
B. Childs: *Nonet*
D. Erb: *Concerto for Solo Percussionist*
R. Felciano: *Contractions*
S. Hodkinson: *Fresco*

A. Hrisanide: *A la recherche de la verticale*
D. Rosenboom: *and come up dripping*
A. de la Vega: *Exospheres for Oboe and Piano*

Actually, two kinds of sound can be obtained by this action: open, the reed held in the fingers while enclosed with the lips; muted, the other hand cupped around the reed to muffle the sound.

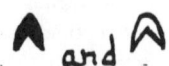

It is possible to make a transition from an unpitched squawk on the reed to a fully pitched tone by gradually pushing the staple back into the instrument while blowing; this directive to the player appears in David Cope's *Indices* for solo oboe.

Composers of experimental music also frequently direct the woodwind players to blow into the instrument after removing the mouthpiece or reed. Flutists are instructed to blow into the detached head-joint or else into the barrel itself, as required by Barney Childs in *Jack's New Bag,* Matthias Bamert in *Inkblot,* and David Bedford in *Trona.* It is also possible to play into the body of the instrument, the head-joint removed, with an oboe, clarinet, or bassoon reed, or with various brass mouthpieces. Of these various unconventional agents, however, only a clarinet or bassoon reed produces a viable sound effect.

Reed instrument players have been frequently asked to take the reeds completely out of the staple or mouthpiece and to blow directly into the tube opening, as in:

H. Holliger: *Siebengesang*
G. Ligeti: *Apparitions; Ten Pieces for Wind Quintet*
Y. Yannay: *preFIX-FIX-sufFIX*

The oboist in *Jack's New Bag* is also directed to reverse his instrument and to blow forcefully into the bell. And both Childs in his *Nonet* and William Sydeman in *Texture Studies* request the bassoonist in their works to remove the reed from the mouthpiece and to tongue into either the neck or the crook of the instrument. Other recent composers have asked that the woodwind and brass players blow forcibly (like a "phh") into the tubing, with the reed or mouthpiece out:

B. Childs: *Jack's New Bag*
M. Constant: *Winds*
A. Hrisanide: *A la recherche de la verticale*
M. Kelemen: *Entrances*
G. Ligeti: *Apparitions*

Among a number of other avant-garde scores that require mouthpiece or reed effects, independent of the instrument, we might cite:

T. Antoniou: *Five Likes for Solo Oboe*
P. D. Q. Bach: *Grand Serenade*
J. Bark, F. Rabe: *Bolos*
D. Bedford: *Gastrula; That White and Radiant Legend*
W. Benson: *The Dream Net*
A. Bloch: *Erwartung*
B. Childs: *Nonet*
G. Darvas: *Sectio Aurea*
W. Holab: *Woodshedding*
W. Kilar: *Générique*
W. Kotonski: *Oboe Concerto*
T. Marco: *Jetztzeit*
A. Mellnäs: *Aura*
S. Montague: *At the white edge of phrygia*
K. Penderecki: *Fluorescences*
Z. Rudzinski: *Contra Fidem*

M. Ellis: *Mutations*
D. Erb: *The Seventh Trumpet;*
Symphony of Overtures
R. Felciano: *Contractions*
L. Ferrari: *Société II*
C. Halffter: *Anillos*
H. W. Henze: *Sinfonia N. 6*

B. Sakač: *Struktur I*
B. Schäffer: *Scultura*
M. Subotnick: *Lamination I*
W. Szalonek: *Concertino per flauto ed orchestra da camera; Les Sons*
A. de la Vega: *Exospheres*
R. Wittinger: *Om per Orchestra*

In addition to the foregoing, several other unusual mouthpiece effects have been stipulated by vanguardists in their scores:

1. Speaking words over the flute mouthpiece ("speak-flute") while fingering certain notated pitches

G. Crumb: *Madrigals—IV*

2. Forcibly blowing a "swoosh" into the detached mouthpiece (of the horn)

S. Cervetti: *Six Sequences for Dance*
B. Childs: *Jack's New Bag*
P. Méfano: *Lignes*

3. Making a kind of "fore-sound" by blowing a broad air-stream at the mouthpiece from a short distance

W. Kilar: *Générique*

4. "Kissing" with the lips against the detached mouthpiece, which produces a sharp, non-pitched and accented sound

M. Bamert: *Inkblot* (all woodwinds)
S. Hodkinson: *Fresco*

5. Holding the oboe reed in the mouth while singing through the nose

V. Globokar: *Atemstudie für Oboe*

6. Sucking through the reverse end of the clarinet mouthpiece while pressing the reed with a finger

W. Szalonek: *Improvisations sonoristiques*

7. Enclosing the mouthpiece and mouth with the clenched fist, gradually unclenching it

W. Szalonek: *Les Sons*

WOODWINDS AND BRASSES 157

8. Making a squeaky sound by sucking with the lips on the mouthpiece

R. Aitken: *Kebyar*
L. Austin: *Changes*
B. Childs: *Music for Trombone*
D. Rosenboom: *and come up dripping*

9. Making a high-pitched whistle through the mouthpiece

J. Fulkerson: *Patterns III for Solo Tuba*

10. Whistling over the stem of the brass mouthpiece, the hand covering the other end

E. Krenek: *Five Pieces for Trombone and Piano*

11. "Buzzing" into a detached brass instrument mouthpiece, either open or closed, the latter effect achieved by cupping the hand over the mouthpiece

L. Austin: *Changes*
J. Bark, F. Rabe: *Bolos*
D. Erb: *Concerto for Solo Percussionist; The Seventh Trumpet*
S. Hodkinson: *Fresco*
A. Lanza: *Eidesis II*

12. Blowing into the horn with inverted mouthpiece

Y. Yannay: *preFIX-FIX-sufFIX*

Trombonists are sometimes directed to blow or buzz through the detached slide (Barney Childs so requests in *Jack's New Bag*). Also, they must sometimes make audible inhalant and exhalant noises with the moist lips into the mouthpiece, independent of tone production:

C. Alsina: *Consecuenza; Trio 1967*
L. Berio: *Sequenza V*
J. Druckman: *Animus I*
V. Globokar: *Discours II*
M. Stibilj: *Condensation*

In Roger Reynolds' *Blind Men,* the trombonist is asked to produce high, whistlelike sounds by using a trumpet (smaller bore) mouthpiece; in *Patterns III,* James Fulkerson requests similar sounds, but does not specify a change of mouthpiece.

Other possibilities for unconventional sound production on the trombone, the most favored of the brasses among the avant-garde, include removing either the outer slide, the tuning slide, or the F-attachment slide and blowing into the instrument, with or without mouthpiece. See, for example:

L. Austin: *Changes*
J. Cage: *Solo for Sliding Trombone*
E. Krenek: *Five Pieces for Trombone and Piano*

An intriguing "echo" effect can be obtained by taking out the F-attachment, blowing a pitch and, at the same time, flipping on the F-attachment lever; the result is a double sound—from the bell and from the open tube at the rear of the instrument. This device appears in the Krenek work cited above.

Mention has been made of certain woodwind and brass effects borrowed from jazz and popular music techniques, such as "ghost notes," the "growl," and "rips," as well as lip glissandi. Other jazz-based techniques appropriated by today's serious composers include the following:

1. "Buzz," produced by the lips, an effect without pitch

J. Bark, F. Rabe: *Bolos*

2. "Doink," or "doit"—a short glissando up from the attacked pitch

M. Colgrass: *As Quiet As*

3. "Screech," "shriek," "squeak," "squeal"—all are violent unpitched sounds

S. Hodkinson: *Interplay*
D. Reck: *Blues and Screamer*

E. Schwartz: *Essays for Trumpet and Trombone; Rip*
M. Subotnick: *Serenade No. 3*

4. "Smear"—a short slide into the next note

M. Gould: *Jekyll and Hyde Variations*
E. Schwartz: *Essays for Trumpet and Trombone*

5. "Wah-wah"—obtained by rapidly opening and closing the bell of brass instruments with the hand

J. Bark, F. Rabe: *Bolos*
R. L. Finney: *Divertissement*

A. Paccagnini: *Musica da camera*
N. Sheriff: *"Destination 5'"*

MULTIPHONICS

Of all the newer techniques applicable to the wind instruments, none figure more prominently in the scores of the avant-garde than multiphonics. The result of certain combinations of embouchure, unusual fingerings, and auxiliary keys or valves, multiphonics create sounds that extend from a simple interval of two pitches to complex chords of four, five, or six notes.[3] Thus, instruments that have long been considered as strictly unisonal have been liberated to the extent that they can now produce harmonic structures, though admittedly the individual tones vary considerably in amplitude and timbre, not to say in certainty of production.

Multiphonic chords are composed, in reality, of a blown fundamental plus certain harmonics of theoretically equal amplitude. Such structures can be completely homogeneous in timbre, but they may be heterogeneous as well, each note in the structure having a subtly different coloring. These chords result from fingering patterns that in principle provide several tube-lengths on which to produce composite tones. Double harmonics, as well as microtonal inflections, can be incorporated into multiphonic chords, and multiple trills can often be

WOODWINDS AND BRASSES

created between two such multipitched structures. Parenthetically, it may be noted that all varieties of tonguing, including flutter-tongue, may be applied to most multiphonics, though usually at a low level of intensity. No multiphonic structures, however, can utilize vibrato, as the air flow must be stable to produce such chords.

All of the standard woodwinds can produce multiphonics, though the complexity of the structures, the ease with which they are produced, and the relative quality of sound vary considerably from instrument to instrument. The majority of the examples found in recent scores relate to the four regulars—flute, oboe, clarinet, and bassoon. Fewer instances of multiphonic structures for piccolo, alto flute, English horn, bass clarinet (see Henze's *Heliogabalus Imperator*), saxophone, and contrabassoon are to be located in new compositions; this imbalance may in time change as the technique itself is more thoroughly developed and refined for all the instruments of the section.

The concept of multiphonics also includes sung and hummed pitches superimposed on blown tones. That is, the wind player is asked to sing or hum either the same pitch he is blowing or a different note, thus creating a simple two-voiced polyphony with two distinct timbres. The brass instruments as well as the woodwinds are capable of utilizing this technique; indeed, multiphonics for the brasses are limited to this type of multiple-tone production and thus to two-note structures only. Owing to the basic construction and the sound-producing principle of the instruments, the brasses cannot create the more complex sonorities generally available to the woodwinds. Although a "difference tone" is theoretically present when a blown brass note is coupled with a sung or hummed pitch a tenth higher, it is sometimes so faint as to be almost inaudible.

A composer may direct in his score that either the vocalizations or the blown tones gain the ascendant; that is, the player may gradually stop sounding various pitches and end by only singing or humming, or he may accomplish the direct reverse. Either or both of these stipulations are to be found in:

L. Berio: *Gesti*
A. Gilbert: *The Incredible Flute Music*
V. Globokar: *Discours II*

B. Jolas: *Fusain*
J. Mekeel: *The Shape of Silence*

The sung or hummed pitch may also waver above or below a lipped pitch after beginning in unison, or it may contract into a unison after commencing at a certain interval from the blown pitch (as in David Cope's *Indices* and James Heinke's *Music for Trombone and Percussion*). See also David Reck's *Five Studies for Tuba Alone* (Example 37).

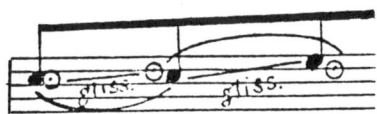

In Ferneyhough's *Cassandra's Dream Song* the flutist sings the same pitch as fingered, but by varying the breath is able to produce distinct beats.

The problem of accurately notating multiphonics is twofold: first, the composer must know what structures are possible on the various wind instruments and, second, he must know how to indicate clearly the required fingering patterns. Generally speaking, these notations should conform to the diagrams shown in Examples 2 and 34, included either in prefatory notes to the composition or else placed above or below the staff at the appropriate moments.

Curiously, multiphonic chords for various of the woodwinds in Harrison Birtwistle's *Verses for Ensemble* are notated on three staves each. The reason—and necessity—for this visual complexity is not clear.

Additional technical expertise, both as to possible structures and to their notations, is available in the following reference sources:[4]

Bruno Bartolozzi: *New Sounds for Woodwind*
Robert Dick: *The Other Flute*
John Heiss: *Some Multiple Sonorities for Flute, Oboe, Clarinet, and Bassoon*

Thomas Howell: *The Avant-Garde Flute*
James Pellerite: *A Modern Guide to Fingerings for the Flute*
Philip Rehfeldt: *New Directions for Clarinet*

There is one further problem for the notator of multiphonics that include hummed or sung pitches, albeit a minor one: to be realistic, two vocal pitches ought to be indicated, one for a high (or female) voice and another at the lower octave for a low (male) voice. This is no token gesture to Women's Liberation but is a matter of compositional accuracy; the register relationship of the vocal to the blown tones will naturally vary according to the gender of the performer.

Among the innumerable recent compositions that feature multiphonics, in addition to those previously mentioned, are included:

Piccolo, flute, and/or alto flute

L. Berio: *Sequenza I*
T. Bruynel: *Signs*
Chou Wen-chung: *Cursive*
K. Gaburo: *Two*
J. Heiss: *Four Movements for Three Flutes*
B. Levy: *Orbs with Flute*
G. Ligeti: *Aventures*
C. Polin: *The Death of Procris; O, Aderyn Pur*

R. Reynolds: *Quick are the Mouths of Earth; Traces*
R. Smith Brindle: *Andromeda M. 31*
W. Szalonek: *Proporzioni II*
T. Takemitsu: *Voice*
L. Widdoes: *From a Time of Snow*
B. A. Zimmermann: *Tempus loquendi*

Recorder

W. Heider: *Katalog*

WOODWINDS AND BRASSES

Oboe and/or English horn

T. Albert: *Sound Frames*
G. Amy: *Jeux*
T. Antoniou: *Five Likes for Solo Oboe*
B. Bartolozzi: *Concertazioni per Oboe*
L. Berio: *Sequenza VII*
J. Casken: *Music for the Crabbing Sun*
E. Denisov: *Romantische Musik*
L. Foss: *Orpheus*
V. Globokar: *Discours III*
T. de Kruyf: *Mosaico*
W. Lutoslawski: *Concerto for Oboe, Harp and Chamber Orchestra*
K. Penderecki: *Capriccio per Oboe*
G. Read: *Phantasmagoria*
D. Rosenboom: *and come up dripping*
T. Takemitsu: *Eucalypts II*

Clarinet and/or bass clarinet

R. Aitken: *Kebyar*
T. Antoniou: *Three Likes for Clarinet*
J. Fox: *All Things Fancy*
A. Gilbert: *Spell Respell*
W. Holab: *Woodshedding*
P. Maxwell Davies: *Eight Songs for a Mad King*
R. Reynolds: *I/O: A Ritual*
T. Takemitsu: *Waves*
A. de la Vega: *Interpolation for Solo Clarinet*

Bassoon and/or contrabassoon

Y. Yannay: *preFIX-FIX-sufFIX*

Saxophone

W. Benson: *The Dream Net*
W. Duckworth: *Reel Music*
C. Polin: *O, Aderyn Pur*

Flute and oboe

T. Takemitsu: *Eucalypts (I)*

Clarinet and bassoon

D. Wilson: *Doubles*

Flute, oboe and clarinet

S. Montague: *At the white edge of phrygia*

Flute, clarinet and bassoon

B. Bartolozzi: *Concertazioni a quattro; Trés Recuerdos del cielo*
L. Foss: *Cave of the Winds*

Oboe, clarinet and bassoon

D. Erb: *Symphony of Overtures*
H. W. Henze: *Heliogabalus Imperator*
W. Szalonek: *Aarhus Music* (Example 35)

Flute, oboe, clarinet and bassoon

B. Bartolozzi: *Collage* (Example 34)
C. Halffter: *Tiento*

Example 34
Bruno Bartolozzi: from *Collage* **(p. 3)**

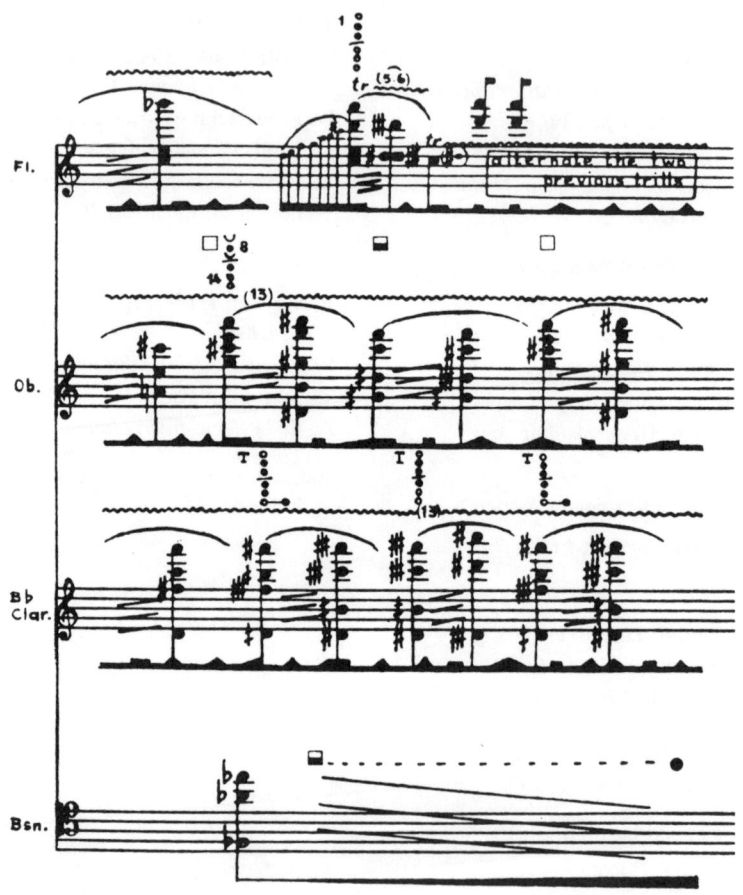

© Copyright 1967 Oxford University Press, London. By permission.

Works calling for brass instrument multiphonics, limited to simultaneous vocalized and blown pitches, include:

Horn

G. Cacioppo: *Time on Time in Miracles*

G. Ligeti: *Aventures; Nouvelles Aventures*

K. Stockhausen: *Adieu für Wolfgang Sebastian Meyer*

Y. Yannay: *preFIX-FIX-sufFIX*

Trumpet

B. Childs: *Nonet*

Example 35
Witold Szalonek: from *Aarhus Music* (p. 7)

© Copyright 1971 by Seesaw Music Corp., New York. Reproduced by permission.

Trombone

R. Aitken: *Kebyar*
C. Alsina: *Consequenza; Trio 1967*
L. Austin: *Changes*
J. Bark, F. Rabe: *Bolos*
L. Berio: *Sequenza V*
R. du Bois: *Music for a Sliding Trombone*
G. Cacioppo: *Time on Time in Miracles*
B. Childs: *Music for Trombone*
J. Druckman: *Animus 1* (Example 36)
R. Erickson: *Ricercar à 5*
J. Fulkerson: *Patterns III for Solo Tuba*

V. Globokar: *Accord; Fluide*
J. Heinke: *Music for Trombone and Percussion*
A. Imbrie: *Three Sketches for Trombone and Piano*
E. Krenek: *Five Pieces for Trombone and Piano*
K. Kroeger: *Toccata for Clarinet, Trombone and Percussion*
B. Rands: *Ballad 1*
E. Schwartz: *Options I; Rip*

Tuba

C. Polin: *The Death of Procris*
D. Reck: *Five Studies for Tuba Alone* (Example 37)

VOCALIZATIONS

Vocal effects other than singing and humming—speaking, whispering, laughing, enunciating vowels and consonants, and the like, and combined with the production of specific pitches—are rapidly becoming equally standard multiphonic procedures. In his *Music for Trombone,* for instance, Barney Childs directs the player to "mutter, talk, yell—all manner of rhythmically irregular violent vocal sounds while playing a sustained pitch." And not to be outdone, Robert Erickson in *Ricercar à 5* tells the trombonist to "bellow in imitation of cows" while playing. Equally theatrical is Donald Erb's directive in *The Seventh Trumpet:* "Almost all the wind players shout and scream angry things through their instruments. This gradually diminishes to a mutter, then to a whisper." Less theatrical, perhaps, the hornist in Richard Barrett's *Anatomy* must merely growl into his instrument while playing, as well as cough audibly.

The following list is a sampling of recent compositions that call for such vocalizations from wind players:

W. Albright: *Danse Macabre*
M. Bamert: *Inkblot*
L. Berio: *Sequenza V*
E. Brown: *Available Forms 2; Hodograph I*
P. Chihara: *Willow, Willow*
B. Childs: *Jack's New Bag; Nonet*
G. Crumb: *Echoes of Time and the River*

J. Druckman: *Animus 1* (Example 36)
H. Gaber: *Voce II*
V. Globokar: *Accord; Discours II*
W. Heider: *-einander, Katalog*
J. Heinke: *Music for Trombone and Percussion*
H-J. Hespos: *Passagen*
S. Hodkinson: *Interplay*
M. Kagel: *Anagrama*

WOODWINDS AND BRASSES

Example 36
Jacob Druckman: from *Animus 1* (p. 5)

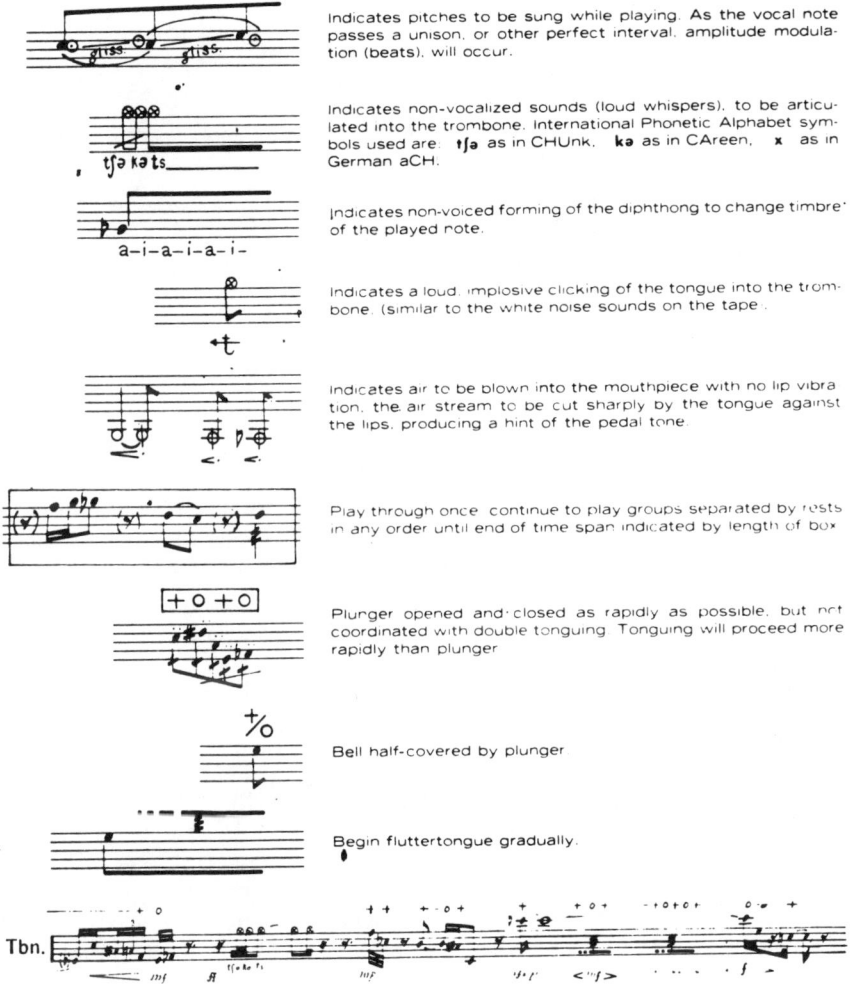

© Copyright 1967 by MCA Music, a Division of MCA, Inc. Reprinted by permission of Boosey & Hawkes, Inc., Sole Agent.

G. Ligeti: *Aventures; Nouvelles Aventures*
J. Mekeel: *The Shape of Silence*
M. Mitrea-Celarianu: *Seth*
B. Rands: *Ballad 1*
R. Reynolds: *Ambages; Blind Men*
E. Schwartz: *Rip*

W. Szalonek: *Aarhus Music*
T. Takemitsu: *Green; Voice*
E. Varèse: *Ameriques*
A. de la Vega: *Interpolation for Solo Clarinet*
R. Wittinger: *Om per orchestra*

Example 37
David Reck: from *Five Studies for Tuba Alone* (p. 6)

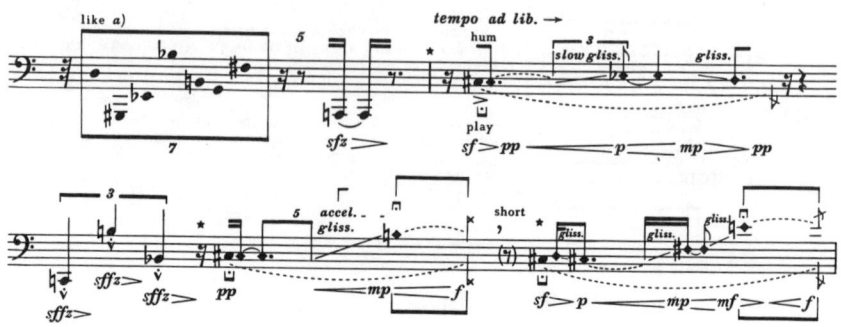

* hold c♯ while humming ♦ notes

© 1968 by C. F. Peters Corporation, New York. Used by permission.

Nonvocalized sounds (mutterings, barks, hisses, grunts, yelps, coughs, buzzes, groans, and assorted squawks) may be combined with fingering pitches on both woodwind and brass instruments; they may also be articulated through the instrument without fingering specific pitches. Among a number of recent works calling for these effects one might mention:

C. Alsina: *Trio 1967*
J. Bark, F. Rabe: *Bolos*
W. Benson: *The Dream Net*
J. Cage: *Solo for Sliding Trombone*
G. Crumb: *Echoes of Time and the River*
J. Druckman: *Animus 1* (Example 36)
D. Erb: *Concerto for Solo Percussionist*
R. Erickson: *General Speech*

V. Globokar: *Accord; Discours II*
G. Heussenstamm: *Poikilos*
E. Krenek: *Five Pieces for Trombone and Piano*
B. Rands: *Ballad 1*
D. Reck: *Blues and Screamer*
W. Szalonek: *Aarhus Music*

Speech sounds or other vocalizations, including singing and humming, and noises may be directed into the mouthpiece alone, taken from the instrument. These requirements may be found in the following scores:

J. Bark, F. Rabe: *Bolos*
L. Berio: *Sequenza V*
P. Chihara: *Willow, Willow*
J. Druckman: *Animus 1* (Example 36)
J. Fulkerson: *Patterns III for Solo Tuba*

V. Globokar: *Accord*
M. Mitrea-Celarianu: *Seth*
D. Reck: *Five Studies for Tuba Alone*
R. Wittinger: *Om per Orchestra*

MISCELLANEOUS EFFECTS

Several recent wind-instrument effects capitalize on the principle of sympathetic vibration: one is the "Duffalo effect," invented by Richard Duffalo, an original member of Lukas Foss's improvisation group. The device, which Foss first used in *Echoi,* consists of the clarinetist's gently moving the bell of his instrument over the head of one timpano while blowing specific pitches, the angle and speed of movement *ad libitum.* The drumhead acts as a resonator, picking up the vibrations of the clarinet sound and subtly altering its pitch and timbre as the instrument bell moves freely over the membrane. The identical action is required of a clarinetist in Christopher Rouse's *Rotae Passiones* and of the solo trombonist in *Dialogues* of Dennis Good.

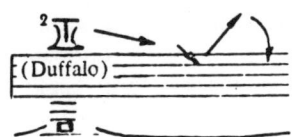

A related sonic effect is obtained by a wind player's directing his playing into the interior of a grand piano, the sustaining pedal held down by the pianist, or—as in the case of David Cope's solo oboe *Indices*—depressed by mechanical means, such as a heavy brick. Other works that call for this effect are:

W. Albright: *Seven Deadly Sins*
D. Bedford: *Music for Albion Moonlight*
W. Bolcom: *Session 3*
G. Crumb: *Eleven Echoes of Autumn*
R. L. Finney: *Divertissement*
L. Foss: *Echoi*
R. Hannay: *Fantôme*

G. Levinson: *Trio for Clarinet, Violoncello and Piano*
T. Marco: *Jetztzeit*
P. Patterson: *Rebecca*
W. Szalonek: *Improvisations sonoristiques; Mutanza per orchestra*

This device is most feasible, of course, for the flute and oboe family members and for the clarinet; it would be more difficult, not to say impractical, for bass clarinet, saxophone, bassoon, and contrabassoon.

Singly or in ensemble, the brasses have also been directed to blow pitches into the interior of the piano—a device widely favored at one time in the big jazz bands. The following vanguard works require this procedure:

A. Imbrie: *Three Sketches for Trombone and Piano*
E. Krenek: *Five Pieces for Trombone and Piano*

E. Schwartz: *Music for Napoleon and Beethoven* (Example 31); *Options I*
I. Xenakis: *Eonta*

The hornist in Takemitsu's *Waves* is to direct his playing into various of the percussion instruments to achieve unusual resonances. Similar unorthodox effects might be created by certain of the woodwind and brass instruments—oboe, clarinet, and trumpet, for instance—playing with the bell of the instrument over a tub of water, even with the bell submerged. One awaits the results of such an experiment with more than casual interest.

Raising the bell of a brass instrument on high to achieve a measure of added volume is not, of course, a new device in orchestration. In Henze's virtuoso *Heliogabalus Imperator,* however, the four trumpeters are directed to gradually raise their instrument bells while sustaining a high pitch. The result, visual as well as acoustic, can be described as a modified version of the "Doppler effect" (see page 136). Less common for the woodwind instruments than for the brasses, bells up have nevertheless been stipulated in the following twentieth-century works (but excluding the several instances in the Mahler symphonies):

- G. Amy: *Jeux pour (là 4) hautbois* (oboe)
- A. Berg: *Drei Orchesterstücke* (oboes and clarinets)
- A. Casella: *Le Couvent sur l'eau* (same)
- P. Lazăr: *Le Ring* (same)
- C. Rouse: *The Infernal Machine* (same)
- P. Lazăr: *Tziganes* (clarinet and saxophone)
- R. Stephan: *Musik für Orchester* (oboes, English horn and clarinets)

HYBRID AND MODIFIED INSTRUMENTS

During the present century no patently new instruments have been added to the existing families of the woodwinds and the brasses. To counterbalance this lack of new instrumental sound resources, today's orchestrators are experimenting with hybrid or altered standard instruments. Attaching a woodwind reed to a brass instrument tubing, or using a brass mouthpiece on a woodwind barrel, are two ways of creating "new" instruments. Also, a certain amount of intra-choir exchange of sound-producing apparatus may take place. For example: the flute tubing (with headjoint removed) may be played upon with an oboe, clarinet, or bassoon reed; the oboe or English horn may substitute a bassoon reed for their customary equipment (as called for in Christopher Rouse's *Mitternachtlieder*), while a bassoonist may produce his sounds with an oboe reed.

Likewise, the different brass members may exchange mouthpieces, the horn functioning with a trombone mouthpiece, for instance, or a trumpet using a tuba mouthpiece. Obviously, the utilization of a large-bore mouthpiece on a relatively small tubing, or a small-bore mouthpiece on an instrument having a larger tubing, can present problems of embouchure. In his *Hornpipe,* Gordon Mumma directs the hornist to play with an oboe reed; the resulting hybrid instrument he calls a "cybersonic horn." The trombone player in *Olifant* of Kelemen also uses an oboe reed, in this case to simulate the sound of a Turkish *zurla*. In Dennis Smalley's *Gradual for Tape and Solo Clarinet* either a clarinet or a saxophone reed substitutes for the normal trombone mouthpiece in the tape part; the composer terms this hybrid a "tromaphone." Quite recently a modified trumpet having three bells, seven valves, and a trombone slide attached to one of the bells, was designed to produce a cross between a trumpet and a trombone, called a "mutantrumpet" by its inventor, Ben Neill. Even more exotic is the piece of ordinary garden hose played with a trombone mouthpiece in Pauline Oliveros's *Theatre Piece for Trombone Player and Tape.*

Although the sonic results of all of these experimentations are intriguing and, to a considerable extent, completely viable, there is no uniformity in quality of sound or predictable new timbre so produced. The interested composer is urged to probe further in the area of hybrid and modified instruments, ideally in collaboration with experienced and highly capable performers. One recent example: the renowned P. D. Q. Bach, together with a certain Professor Peter Schickele, constructed an instrument they call a "slide windbreaker." This is a collection of nesting cardboard tubes that is played like a trombone. Other than its appearance in the *"Erotica" Variations,* this "instrument" has evidently not been utilized by any other composers—to the obvious benefit of contemporary music.

Bruno Bartolozzi has stated (in *New Sounds for Woodwind*) a truism that bears repetition: "The evolution of instrumental music has always been brought about by reciprocal collaboration between composers and performers. . . . That composers and performers have sometimes in the past been one and the same person does not alter the problem in the least. . . . The fact remains that true instrumental conquests have never been the fruit of abstract conceptions, but of toilsome direct experience." This statement indubitably applies to the totality of techniques discussed throughout this book, whether they are of traditional lineage or are manifestly new in concept. There is no reason to believe that the historic process will change in the years to come.

NOTES

1. *New Sounds for Woodwind.*
2. Lacking a wind machine, deemed essential for a scheduled performance of his *Sinfonia Antarctica,* Vaughan Williams fortuitously discovered an effective alternative: he had the hornists whistle through their instruments to create a convincing wind sound.
3. According to Robert Dick every known flute fingering can produce at least one multiple sonority, and more commonly from four to six structures. At least 1,000 flute multiphonics have so far been catalogued.
4. Refer to Bibliography for details concerning these sources.

10

PERCUSSION

TUNING OF UNPITCHED INSTRUMENTS

Until the present era of intense exploration of new instrumental techniques, specific pitches on the membranophones were limited to timpani and to especially tuned tom-toms and bongos. More recently, however, experimental composers have been intrigued with the possibility of altering the tone of a nonpitched drum while striking it. This is accomplished by exerting pressure on the skin with the hand, fingers, or elbow, depending upon the size of the drumhead. The pressure increases the tension of the stretched membrane or plastic surface and thus raises the normal pitch of the drum. A rising scale of pitches can be obtained by a slow and progressively heavier pressure exerted on the drumhead; a descending scale can be achieved by beginning with heavy pressure and then gradually relaxing it.

Recent scores that require this new percussion technique include:

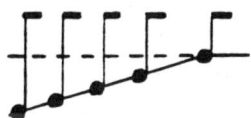

G. Crumb: *Echoes of Time and the River*
H. Farberman: *Alea*
S. Hodkinson: *Fresco*
K. Penderecki: *Fluorescences*

R. Reynolds: *Quick are the Mouths of Earth*
G. Rochberg: *Tableaux*
G. Schuller: *Contours; Spectra*
W. Szalonek: *Concertino per flauto*

Relative pitches in ascending or descending order can also be obtained from an array of membrane and wood instruments, graded in size and position. Thus, a rising "scale" might be suggested by striking in turn the following sequence of instruments: bass drums (large, small), tom-toms (low, medium, high), tenor drum, temple-blocks (set of five, from low to high), snare drum with snares off, woodblocks (low, medium, high), claves, and—finally—slapstick. Striking these instruments in reverse order would, of course, simulate a series of descending pitches.

Until recent years it did not seemingly occur to orchestrators that the bass drum might be "tuned" by tightening or slackening the drumhead, usually before rather than during actual playing on the instrument; see, for example, *Siebengesang* of Heinz Holliger and *Tenebrae* of Klaus Huber. Presumably, the two heads of the bass drum could be tuned differently and struck simultaneously with two beaters. The latter specification does occur, of course, in several twentieth-century scores (including Harrison Birtwistle's *Nomos* and my own *Los Dioses Aztecas*), but without specifying different tunings.

Just as a series of relative pitches can be suggested by the tones elicited from various-sized drums, so high, medium, and low pitches may be suggested by a seried group of hung cymbals, gongs, and other metallic instruments, scaled from large to small. A descending order of pitches, for instance, could be approximated by striking the following sequence of metal instruments: small triangle, crotale, large triangle, suspended cymbals (three or more, arranged from high to low), high gong, deep tam-tam. Other analogous groups can easily be formulated, utilizing only the unpitched percussion, to suggest graduated scales of indefinite but relative pitch.

There are still other ways by which the metallic percussion can be made to create the illusion of changing tessitura. One method is to immerse the instrument in a tub of water after striking it; aptly termed "water gongs," they are required in:

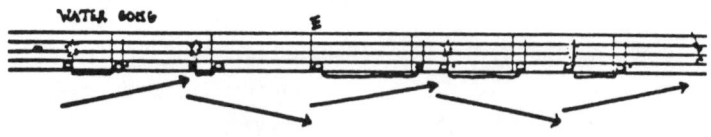

J. Cage: *First Construction (in Metal)*
J. Cage, L. Harrison: *Double Music*
G. Crumb: *Echoes of Time and the River*
F. Evangelisti: *Spazio a 5*

P. Méfano: *Lignes*
J. Schwantner: *In Aeternum II; Magabunda*
J. Yuasa: *Scenes from Bashô*

These are merely ordinary Chinese gongs, suspended by a cord, which the player slowly lowers into a tub of water after, or while, striking with various stipulated beaters. When the vibrating gong is immersed, the pitch is depressed slightly; when the gong is lifted out of the water, the pitch appears to rise somewhat.

A pitch change can also be simulated by applying a metal object (a thin rod, a coin, a wirebrush, and the like) to the vibrating rim of suspended cymbal, gong, or tam-tam—an effect requisitioned in:

G. Crumb: *Echoes of Time and the River*
L. Foss: *Elytres*

K. Penderecki: *Dimensions of Time and Silence*
G. Read: *Haiku Seasons*

NEW AREAS OF STRIKING

Twentieth-century scores are customarily very precise about indicating the area on which a percussionist should strike a membrane or metallic instrument. On occasion one finds directions to hit the frame, shell, or casing of these various instruments instead of the normal surface. On timpani, for instance, the player may be required to strike the kettle (or bowl) with regular timpani mallets or other objects, or to hit the metal rim surrounding the drumhead. On old-fashioned, hand-tuned drums he could also strike the tuning screws. The following works contain one or the other of these requirements:

M. Colgrass: *As Quiet As*
D. Erb: *Concerto for Solo Percussionist; Symphony of Overtures*
F. Evangelisti: *Ordini*
R. L. Finney: *Three Studies in Fours*
M. Gielen: *Musica*
T. Harsanyi: *La joie de vivre*
S. Hodkinson: *Fresco*
M. Kagel: *Sonant*
W. Kotonski: *Musica per fiati e timpani*
L. Kupkovič: *Das Fleisch des Kreuzes*

G. Ligeti: *Apparitions*
B. Martinu: *Symphony No. 4*
G. Read: *Diabolic Dialogue; Los Dioses Aztecas*
D. Reck: *Blues and Screamer*
H. Sauget: *La Rencontre*
W. Szalonek: *Geständnisse*
H. Villa-Lobos: *Danses Africaines*
W. Walton: *Façade*
B. A. Zimmermann: *Canto di speranza*

The metal rims and the wood or metal casings of the smaller drums—snare, tenor, bongos, tom-toms, and so on—as well as of the larger bass drum, can all be struck in some manner. The sounds will vary according to the size of the drum, the part of the casing hit, and the agent used. An impressive variety of objects have been designated by vanguard orchestrators for striking the outsides of the various drums: the wood end of a regular mallet, metal rods, wire-brushes, crotale, cymbal, clave, maraca, and other equally exotic agents of attack. These specifications may be observed in the following scores:

S. Bussotti: *Memoria*
D. Erb: *The Seventh Trumpet; Symphony of Overtures*

J. Moross: *Paeans*
K. Penderecki: *Dimensions of Time and Silence; Fluorescences*

L. Ferrari: *Société II*
G. Heussenstamm: *Poikilos*
M. Kagel: *Anagrama; Sonant*
S. Montague: *At the white edge of phrygia*

G. Read: *Los Dioses Aztecas*
S. Revueltas: *Sensemayá*
K. Serocki: *Continuum; Episodes*
E. Varèse: *Intégrales*

On occasion the metal frame or the resonators under the plates of vibraphone, marimba, or xylophone have been designated for percussive attack (non-glissando), either with regular mallets or the wood end of a stick (see *Scultura* of Boguslaw Schäffer, for example).

UNUSUAL AGENTS OF ATTACK

Directions to percussionists for employing different kinds of mallets and beaters are as common in contemporary scores as the designations of surface area to be struck; hence they need no further explication here. Even the mallet symbology has achieved a measure of concurrence:

♩ = hard sticks,   ♩ = soft sticks,   ✝ = wire brushes

Vanguard orchestrators are notably partial to the use of the player's fingertips and nails in creating delicate sounds on membranophones and idiophones alike. Somewhat more robust sounds are achieved, of course, by the use of the flat hands or the knuckles on the drum surfaces. The following are some of the stipulations to be found in recent compositions:

1. Tap, roll, or strike on the drum surface with the fingertips

T. Baird: *Etiuda*
S. Bussotti: *Mit einem gewissen sprechenden Ausdruck*
M. Colgrass: *As Quiet As; Six Allegro Duets*
G. Crumb: *Echoes of Time and the River*
H. Farberman: *Alea*
R. L. Finney: *Three Pieces*
L. Foss: *Fragments of Archilochos*
O. Henry: *Do Not Pass Go*
G. Heussenstamm: *Seventeen Impressions*
P. Hindemith: *Konzert für Violoncello und Orchester*

M. Kagel: *Sonant*
W. Kotonski: *Musica per fiati e timpani*
D. Martino: *Piano Concerto*
L. de Pablo: *Reciproco*
B. Rands: *Canti lunatici*
G. Read: *Diabolic Dialogue; Los Dioses Aztecas*
R. Smith Brindle: *Auriga*
M. Stibilj: *Condensation*
W. Sydeman: *Study for Orchestra No. III; Trio for Flute, Double Bass and Percussion*

2. Same, with the flat hand

D. Burge: *Sources III*
S. Bussotti: *Mit einem gewissen sprechenden Ausdruck*
E. Carter: *Eight Pieces for Four Timpani*
R. L. Finney: *Concerto for Percussion; Three Studies in Fours*

O. Henry: *Do Not Pass Go*
W. Kotonski: *Musica per fiati e timpani*
M. Mestres-Quadreny: *Tramesa a Tapies*
W. Sydeman: *Trio for Flute, Double Bass and Percussion*

3. Same, with the knuckles

L. de Pablo: *Reciproco*
M. Stibilj: *Condensation*

4. Scratch or strike on the drumhead with the fingernails

A. Bax: *Second Symphony*
S. Cervetti: *Six Sequences for Dance*
B. Childs: *Music for Bass Drum*
M. Colgrass: *As Quiet As*
D. Erb: *Symphony of Overtures*
M. Kagel: *Anagrama; Sonant*
P. Maxwell Davies: *Eight Songs for a Mad King*
K. Penderecki: *Dimensions of Time and Silence*

B. Rands: *Actions for Six*
G. Read: *Los Dioses Aztecas*
R. Reynolds: *Quick are the Mouths of Earth*
R. M. Schafer: *Requiems for the Party-Girl*
M. Stibilj: *Condensation*

5. "Write" on the drumhead with the fingernail

M. Kagel: *Anagrama; Sonant*

6. Rub on the drumhead with the fingers

J. Druckman: *Animus 2*
C. Halffter: *Fibonaciana*
G. Read: *Los Dioses Aztecas*

7. Same, with the flat hand or the fist

H. Farberman: *Alea*
M. Kagel: *Sonant*

K. Penderecki: *Fluorescences*
M. Stibilj: *Condensation*

8. Roll, strike, or tap on the bars of the idiophones (vibraphone, marimba, etc.) with the fingertips

M. Finnissy: *As When Upon a Tranced Summer Night*
G. Read: *Haiku Seasons*
W. Sydeman: *Trio for Flute, Double Bass and Percussion*

9. Same, with the fingernails

G. Crumb: *Madrigals—I*
G. Read: *Haiku Seasons*

10. Same, with the palm or flat hand

G. Amy: *Cycle pour six percussions*
T. Antoniou: *Mikrographia für grosses Orchester*

11. Roll, strike, or tap on suspended cymbal, gong, or tam-tam with the fingertips

G. Crumb: *Echoes of Time and the River*
L. Foss: *Fragments of Archilochos*
L. de Pablo: *Reciproco*

B. Rands: *Canti lunatici*
G. Read: *Haiku Seasons*

12. Same, with the flat hand

G. Arrigo: *Thumos*
J. Druckman: *Animus 2*
R. L. Finney: *Three Studies in Fours*
V. Globokar: *Accord*
M. Kagel: *Anagrama*

D. Martino: *Piano Concerto*
M. Mestres-Quadreny: *Tramesa a Tapies*
G. Read: *Haiku Seasons; Los Dioses Aztecas*

13. Same, with the fingernails

M. Finnissy: *As When Upon a Tranced Summer Night*
L. Foss: *Time Cycle*
M. Kagel: *Anagrama*

14. Tap on a maraca with the fingers

D. Banks: *Tirade*

15. Same, with a pair of claves

M. Constant: *14 Stations*

16. Strike maraca against tambourine

A. Schindler: *Cirius and Beyond*

17. Drag triangle beater across cymbal surface, from dome to edge

Idem

In his unusual *Music for Bass Drum,* Barney Childs gives elaborate instructions for snapping or flicking the nails on the flat part of the drum tuning handle, the edge of the shell, near to the tie rod, and at the membrane node. Further specifications are to tap with the ball of the finger at the drumhead edge and on the flat part of the wooden rim; also, to roll with the fingers on both shell and skin; tap with the nails at the middle of the casing and on the drumhead, and rap with the knuckles on skin, tuning handle, and tie rod.

Essentially a conservative device, the rapid alternation of hard and soft mallets on a timpani head is nonetheless a viable sonoric technique; it is prominently displayed in *Versuche* by Dieter Schnebel.

PERCUSSION   177

Highly intriguing in sonic terms are the special sounds available to the orchestrator when timpani and other drums are struck not with standardized sticks and mallets but with such exotic objects as a clave, maraca, woodblock, triangle, tambourine, or hand cymbal, as well as with sleigh bells and chains. In actuality, these striking procedures convey a two-fold aural impression to the listener—the percussive impact of the unusual agent on the instrument membrane and the inherent sound of the object itself.

A few of the bizarre effects demanded by experimental composers include the following:

1. Play close to the timpani rims with thin triangle beaters

H. Brant: *Verticals Ascending*

2. Play on drum surface with chains (dragged across the drumhead, or dropped onto it)

H. W. Henze: *Sinfonia N. 6*

3. Same, with a plastic fly swatter

B. Childs: *Nonet*

4. "Write" name and address with tip of snare drum stick on the drumhead

B. Childs: *Jack's New Bag*

5. Press the thick end of a snare drum stick down on the drumhead and drag it across from rim to rim

G. Read: *Los Dioses Aztecas* (Example 38)

6. Rub or scrape in a rotary motion on the drumhead with a wirebrush

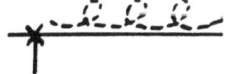

H. Badings: *Symphonische Klangfiguren*   W. Duckworth: *Gambit*
L. Bassett: *Variations for Orchestra*   J. C. Eloy: *Equivalences*
D. Bedford: *Piece for Mo*   E. Raxach: *Estrofas*
J. Cage: *Amores*   G. Read: *Los Dioses Aztecas*
S. Cervetti: *Six Sequences for Dance*

7. Same action, with a superball mallet

R. Reynolds: *"From Behind . . ."*

8. Scrape a dull knife blade across the drumhead

R. Reynolds: *Quick are the Mouths of Earth*

9. Rub the surface of the drum with a hairbrush

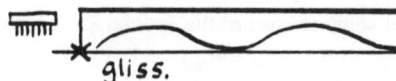

A. Mellnäs: *Aura*

10. Same, with sandpaper blocks

G. Read: *Los Dioses Aztecas*

11. Same, with a piece of aluminum paper while crushing it

C. Alsina: *Trio 1967*

12. Strike the underneath rim of a cymbal laid curved side down on a timpano head

M. Constant: *14 Stations*
W. Kotonski: *a battere* (Example 39)

13. Roll across timpani head with an inverted cymbal

C. Rouse: *Rotae Passiones*

14. Lay a cymbal, dome up, on the timpano head and tremolo on the cymbal with sticks while glissandoing with the pedal

C. Halffter: *Tiento*
S. Hodkinson: *Drawings, Set No. 9*
A. Vieru: *Clepsidra II*

15. Same action with a Japanese bowl on the timpano head

L. Foss: *Exeunt*

16. Beat on timpano membrane with maracas

L. Bernstein: *"Jeremiah" Symphony*

17. Lay Temple gongs on several timpani heads and play on them with vibraphone mallets

J. Yuasa: *Scenes from Bashô*

18. Lay the bottom bar of a triangle on the timpano head; strike the triangle while moving the drum pedal up and down

D. Erb: *The Seventh Trumpet*
C. Rouse: *Falcano Luminis*

19. Spin a silver dollar on the timpano head, making a slow glissando with the pedal at the same time

M. Ellis: *Mutations*

20. Get any wind-up mechanical toy which hops or jumps; wind it up and let it hop about on a timpano surface

B. Childs: *Jack's New Bag*

PERCUSSION   **179**

    21. Strike on head of snare drum with maracas

B. Conyngham: *Three*

    22. Stroke the surface of snare drum (snares off) with two cloths

G. Ligeti: *Aventures*

    23. Rub a rosined glove or cloth over a snare drum stick whose tip is pressed against the center of a bass drumhead

W. Russell: *Fugue for Eight Percussion Instruments*

    24. Spin a coin (silver dollar, quarter, etc.) on the drumhead (snare, tenor, tom-tom, etc.)

B. Childs: *Jack's New Bag*	M. Kagel: *Sonant*
V. Globokar: *Accord*	M. Mestres-Quadreny: *Tramesa a Tapies*

    25. Hold one clave against the bass drum membrane and strike it with another clave

G. Crumb: *Music for a Summer Evening*

    26. Lay a string of sleighbells on the flat bass drum; play normally on the drumhead

N. T. Dao: *Máy*

Dropping an object onto the surface of timpani or the other drums, as well as on the bars of the idiophones, is a device much favored today. The objects used range from coins of various sizes, small hand cymbals or crotales, steel balls or marbles, chains, cowbells, tambourine, and rubber erasers, to sticks and rods of different materials and sizes. These requirements appear in:

C. Alsina: *Trio 1967*	M. Kagel: *Sonant*
L. Ferrari: *Société II*	P. Nørgård: *Waves*
L. Foss: *Echoi*	B. Schäffer: *Scultura*
V. Globokar: *Accord*	

In Merrill Ellis's *Mutations* the timpanist is instructed to drop a tennis ball on the drumhead from a height of two feet, letting it bounce freely on the surface (and on to the floor?).

An even more drastic effect—visually and acoustically—is obtained by dropping instruments such as cymbal, cowbell, or tambourine on the floor or onto a tabletop (as in Alsina's *Trio* and Stravinsky's *Petrouchka*).

Recent and unorthodox methods of playing on the metal plates and wooden bars of the idiophones include striking them with a hand cymbal, finger crotale, coin, or other metal object:

E. Brown: *Available Forms 1*	M. Kagel: *Anagrama; Match*
L. Foss: *Echoi; Elytres*	B. Schäffer: *Scultura*

Example 38
Gardner Read: from *Los Dioses Aztecas* (p. 9)

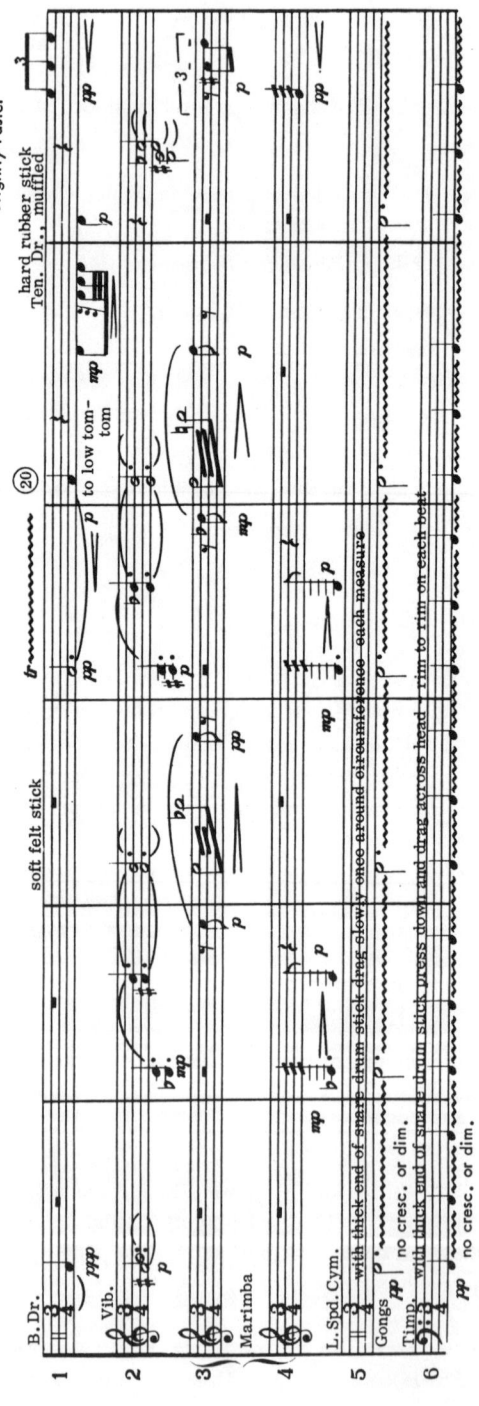

© Copyright 1969, M. M. Cole Publishing Company, 251 E. Grand Avenue, Chicago, Illinois 60611. Used by permission.

Example 39
Wlodsimierz Kotonski: from *a battere* (p. 17)

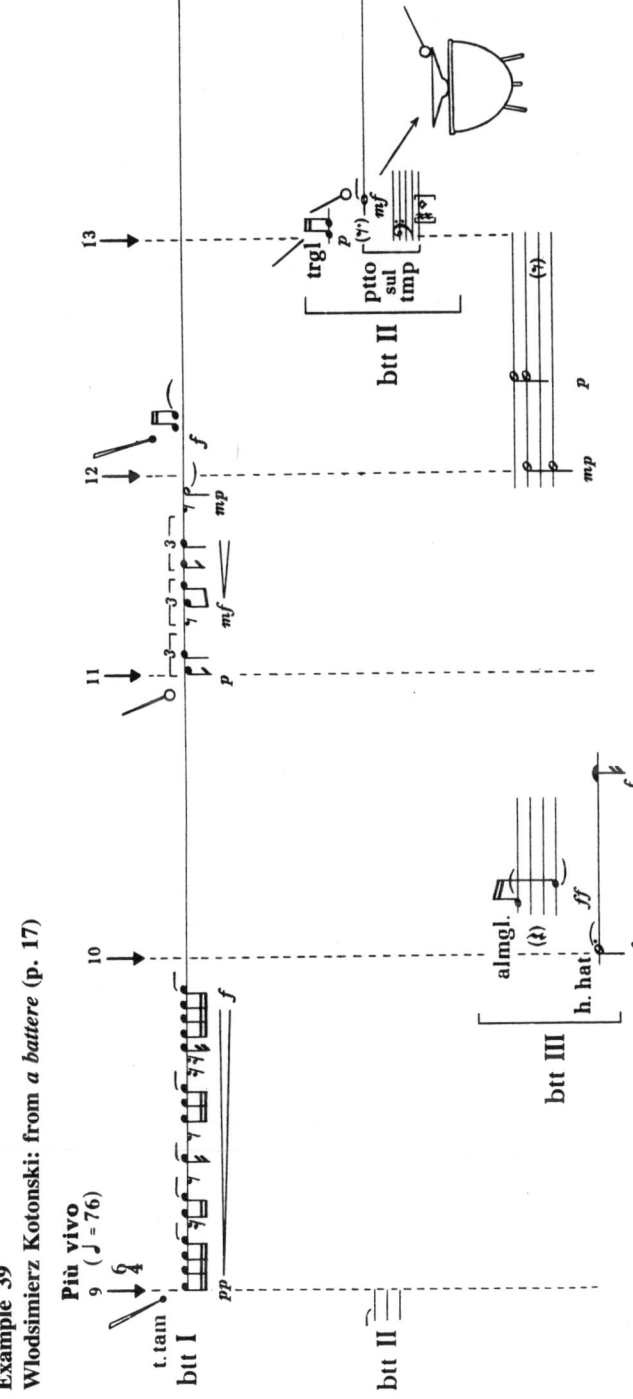

© Copyright 1968 by Moeck Verlag. Abdruck mit Genehmigung des Moeck Verlags, D-31 Celle.

Not primarily a percussive effect but one simulating the timbre of string *sul ponticello* is the directive to the marimba player in Roger Reynolds' *Islands from Archipelago: II. Autumn Island* to strike the bars "over the node." William Kraft tells the glockenspiel player in his *Suite for Percussion* to hold the mallet in a vertical position and to strike the side of the metal bar. In his *Oboe Concerto*, Kotonski asks the vibraphonist to play on the suspended tubes with several mallets. A final technique on this instrument: while tremoloing with a mallet in one hand, the player uses his other hand to adjust the motor speed in Stuart Smith's *Two Makes Three*, an effect that could be replicated by the services of a second percussionist.

An increasing number of composers of experimental music have directed the idiophone players to draw a well-rosined cello or doublebass bow across the near edge of a metal plate on vibraphone and glockenspiel or a wooden bar of xylophone or marimba. On the vibraphone this action produces a disembodied, singing tone; on the marimba it creates a breathy, almost husky sound. Standing in his normal position in front of the instrument, the player can bow only on the "white-note" (or front) plates; to bow the rear, "black-note" bars he must stand behind the instrument. It is quite possible, of course, to utilize two players, one for the natural pitches and one for the chromatic notes. Composers who have made use of this very effective technique include:

I. Anhalt: *Foci*
T. Antoniou: *Fluxus für Orchester; Parastasis II*
L. Austin: *The Maze*
I. Bazelon: *Sound Dreams*
B. Conyngham: *Mirages*
G. Crumb: *Music for a Summer Evening*
D. Erb: *Concerto for Brass and Orchestra*
S. Garant: *Phrases I*
C. Halffter: *Fibonaciana; Planto por las victimas de la violencia* (Example 40)
R. Reynolds: *"From Behind . . ."*
W. Russell: *Fugue for Eight Percussion Instruments*
C. Ung: *Spiral*
A. Woodbury: *Remembrances*
J. Yuasa: *Scenes from Bashô*

Also greatly favored by vanguardists is the sound of vibraphone or glockenspiel played with knitting needles—a delicate and highly refined percussive effect, as stipulated in Austin's *The Maze* and this writer's *Haiku Seasons*. Not quite as delicate a sound, perhaps, the vibraphone plates in the Roger Reynolds work cited above are to be tapped with a large comb.

The tubular chimes have also come in for their share of unorthodox performance techniques: for example, they have been struck on the upper edges of the tubes with a pair of claves (in *Anagrama* of Kagel), and on the actual tops of the tubes (with a regular chime mallet) in William Kraft's *Monumentum*. The chimes are to be clashed together with the player's hands or outstretched arms, as required in:

PERCUSSION   183

Example 40
Cristobal Halffter: from *Planto por las victimas de la violencia* (p. 30)

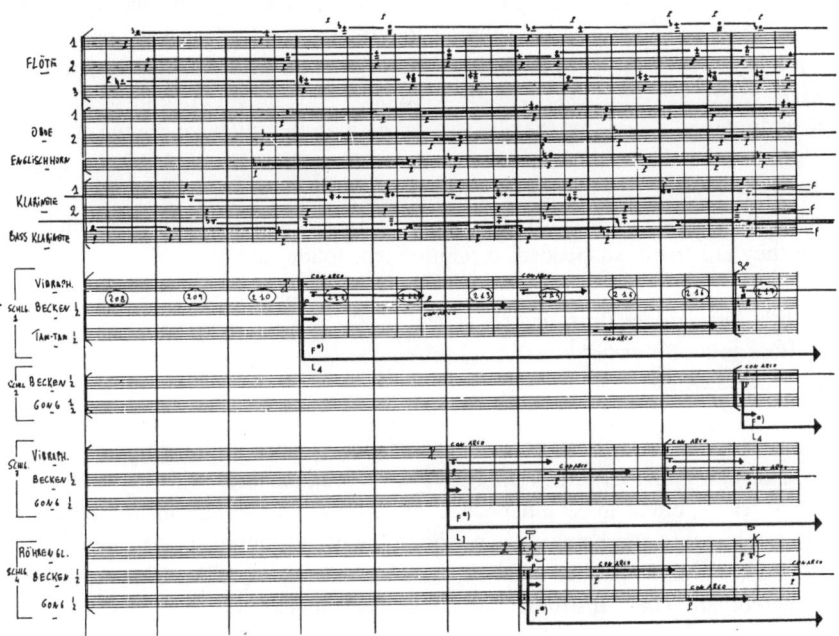

© Copyright 1971 by Universal Edition (London) Ltd., London. All rights reserved. Used by permission of European American Music Distributors Corporation, sole U.S. and Canadian agent for Universal Edition, London.

  I. Bazelon: *De-Tonations for Brass Quintet and Orchestra*
  J. Gilboa: *The Jerusalem Chagall Windows*
  M. Kagel: *Anagrama*

A further refinement of this action appears in Witold Lutoslawski's cello concerto: "Gather a few chime tubes between the hands, squeeze them firmly together to produce the sound, and release them to vibrate freely." A very delicate effect can be obtained by stroking the chime tubes with a wirebrush, as called for in Grazyna Bacewicz's *In una parte*. Also, the chimes can be stroked with a doublebass bow, an action required in the Irwin Bazelon score cited above. Several composers have asked the percussionist to blow into the tube opening of a chime, creating a refined "whoosh"; see Carlos Alsina's *Trio* and the *Chamber Piece* of Zbigniew Bujarski.

Highly welcome newcomers to the percussion section are the various wind chimes, made of bamboo, metal, or glass. Ordinarily, they are set in motion by a sweep of the flat fingers or a stick, but in *Voie* of Vinko Globokar and *Máy* of

Nguyeñ Thiên Dao the composers request the percussionist to agitate the chimes with both hands. Reginald Smith Brindle in *Orion M. 42* and Bruno Maderna in his first oboe concerto ask the player to grasp the chimes with one hand. In *The Edge of the Land* Charles Boone directs that the chimes be "smashed together" by holding them tightly with the two hands so that they do not continue to vibrate. Roger Reynolds asks that the wind chimes be blown upon in *Wedge*—a logical directive!—and that they be stroked with a ruler in *Quick are the Mouths of Earth*. More conventionally, Warren Benson requires the wind chimes in his *Helix* to be patted with the hand to produce a gentle susurration.

As with regular chimes, it is possible to bow the antique cymbals (crotales) when they are freely suspended, a requirement found in:

D. Erb: *Concerto for Brass and Orchestra*
S. Hodkinson: *November Voices*
J. Schwantner: *Elixir*

Many contemporary composers specify that drums or hanging cymbals, gongs, or tam-tams, be struck alternately or simultaneously with two different kinds of sticks, either in each hand.[1] At other times two similar instruments are to be struck, again alternately or concurrently, with two contrasting mallet types; for example, high suspended cymbal hit with a snare drum stick and low cymbal with wirebrush. These instrumentational devices appear in:

I. Dan: *The Silk Road*   R. Reynolds: *Wedge*
H. Farberman: *Alea*   K. Stockhausen: *Kreuzspiel*
G. Read: *Los Dioses Aztecas*   B. A. Zimmermann: *Photoptosis*

A certain amount of mallet and stick "borrowing" is quite common in today's scores. That is to say, some percussion instruments are played upon with beaters ordinarily employed on other instruments. The chimes, for instance, might be struck with vibraphone mallets, or the marimba bars struck with hard felt timpani sticks. The glockenspiel or vibraphone might be played upon with a triangle beater or with snare drum sticks, to cite only a few of the many possibilities existing for such mallet exchanges.

NEW METHODS OF STRIKING

An effect common to both the pitched mallet instruments and the membranophones is known as the "dead stick" technique: the mallet is not allowed to rebound from the plate or drum surface after striking, but is kept pressed down. The result is a curiously dead and muffled sound, somewhat akin to *sons étouffées* on harp or finger-muted tones on piano strings. The technique is prominently used in the following works:

PERCUSSION

P. Boulez: *Éclat*
E. Brown: *Available Forms 1; Hodograph 1*
E. Carter: *Eight Pieces for Four Timpani*
G. Crumb: *Madrigals—I*
H. El-Dabh: *Mosaic No. 1*
L. Foss: *Echoi; Time Cycle*

M. Kagel: *Anagrama; Match*
W. Kraft: *Configurations*
G. Read: *Diabolic Dialogue*
R. Reynolds: *Islands from Archipelago: II. Autumn Island*
B. Schäffer: *Music for Mi*

Certain of the percussion instruments can be struck in unorthodox positions; that is, the instrument itself can be placed unconventionally, as by turning the snare drum upside down, the snares on top (required in Kagel's *Anagrama*). With the drum in this position the player can also pluck the taut snares, *a la guitarra*, with the fingers or the nails. The tambourine may be placed on a pad and struck with sticks, with either the rim side or the flat head uppermost, a requirement appearing in my *Haiku Seasons* and *Los Dioses Aztecas*.

While rim-shots have long been staples of contemporary percussion devices, several new allied techniques have been introduced by vanguard instrumentators. One is to strike the rim and drumhead with a single stick; to accomplish this the player holds the stick at its center and strikes with a downward motion. The following works call for this specific playing technique:

L. Berio: *Sinfonia*
S. Bussotti: *Mit einem gewissen sprechenden Ausdruck*

K. Penderecki: *Anaklasis; Fluorescences*
K. Stockhausen: *Momente*
E. Varèse: *Déserts; Ecuatorial*

A variant of this technique is to lay one drumstick on the membrane and strike it with another stick; see, for example:

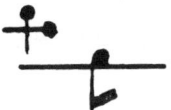

H. El-dabh: *Mosaic No. 1*
M. Kagel: *Sonant*
K. Penderecki: *Anaklasis; Fluorescences*

W. Russell: *Fugue for Eight Percussion Instruments*
K. Serocki: *Segmenti*
K. Stockhausen: *Momente*

Obviously, both of these effects are useful only at a high dynamic level. A related technique, one possible at all levels of amplitude, is to strike one snare drum stick against another, like a pair of claves; this stipulation appears in my *Los Dioses Aztecas*.

Directives for striking suspended cymbals, gongs, and tam-tams are amazingly diverse and imaginative in late twentieth-century scores. They—and all the other performance techniques catalogued here—are reliable indices of how far percussive concepts have developed since the pioneering explorations of Bartók, Milhaud, and Varèse, not to mention the most recent probings of Cage, Crumb, Kagel, and Penderecki. It would be quite literally impossible to enumerate all of the unusual directions to be found in recent scores relating to playing on the metallic percussion; those that are listed below are representative samplings, and will surely provide the orchestrator with substantial food for thought.

Striking procedures on these instruments can be unconventional in the area to be struck, the agent used for playing, or both. In the first category would fit the following instructions culled from recently published compositions:

1. Play on both surfaces of gong or tam-tam simultaneously

F. Cerha: *Relazioni fragili*
H. Farberman: *Alea*

Rarely used, but quite possible, is the device of striking the centers of both sides of gong or tam-tam with the clenched fist of one hand and a regular beater in the other.

2. Lay gong flat for striking (no resonance)

M. de Falla: *El Retablo de Maese Pedro*

3. Strike edge of suspended cymbal with a stick held at right angles to the rim

D. Bedford: *Piece for Mo*

4. Scrape the bottom surface of suspended cymbal with a metal (triangle) stick

R. Moeves: *Et Occidentem Illustra*

5. Rub the rim of suspended cymbal with a metal stick

L. Bassett: *Variations for Orchestra*
M. Ishii: *Sieben Stücke*
L. de Pablo: *Reciproco*

6. Rub the two cymbals together in a circular, irregular movement

M. Kagel: *Match für drei Spieler*
P. Méfano: *Paraboles*

7. Rub the bottom bar of a triangle with the metal beater

K. Serocki: *Niobe*

Under the second category—unorthodox agents of percussive attack on the metallic instruments—one might list:

PERCUSSION

1. Strike cymbal surface with the fingernails

S. Bussotti: *Memoria*
K. Serocki: *Continuum*

2. Draw the edge of a fingernail across the surface of suspended cymbal

K. Penderecki: *Dimensions of Time and Silence*

3. Same, with hand and a finger ring simultaneously

C. Alsina: *Trio 1967*

4. Strike suspended cymbal with the hand

S. Bussotti: *Memoria*
A. Paccagnini: *Gruppi concertanti*
K. Stockhausen: *Kontakte*
E. Varèse: *Arcana*

5. Roll or trill on suspended cymbal, triangle, cowbell, gong, or tam-tam with knitting needles

T. Antoniou: *Mikrographen für grosses Orchester*
L. Austin: *The Maze*
W. Fortner: *The Creation; Mouvements*
K. A. Hartmann: *1.Symphonie*
H. W. Henze: *4.Sinfonie*
P. Hindemith: *Konzert für Violoncello und Orchester*
G. Read: *Haiku Seasons*
E. Toch: *1st Symphony; 3rd Symphony*
G. Wilson: *Concatenations*
I. Yun: *Dimensionen*

6. Scrape surface of suspended cymbal with a coin

G. Crumb: *Ancient Voices of Children; Madrigals—IV*

7. Dangle chains on surface of iron (suspended) cymbal

H. W. Henze: *Sinfonia N. 6*

8. Strike suspended cymbal with a triangle

W. Walton: *Façade*

9. Strike suspended cymbal with back edge of a saw blade; also draw a saw blade, teeth down, across the surface or rim of suspended cymbal

W. Russell: *Three Dance Movements*

10. Rub or stroke surface of suspended cymbal with the tips of a hard rubber comb

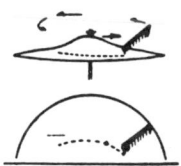

R. Reynolds: *Blind Men*
T. Takemitsu: *Asterism*

11. Strike gong surface with the fist

B. Conyngham: *Three*

12. Strike gong with a hand cymbal

W. Haupt: *Volume*

M. Kagel: *Anagrama*

13. Same, with a maraca

L. de Pablo: *Reciproco*

14. Same, with triangle beater near the edge

W. Kraft: *Suite for Percussion*

15. Press a woodblock against tam-tam; strike other surface with a clave

M. Kagel: *Anagrama*

16. Strike tam-tam with a fiberbrush, a wooden stick and a triangle beater, a knife blade and a steel spring

R. Haubenstock-Ramati: *Jeux 6 für zwei Schlagzeuger*

17. Touch the vibrating tam-tam with a triangle beater

P. Nørgård: *Waves*

18. Rub surface of gong with head of vibraphone mallet

L. Foss: *Echoi*

19. Same, with a super-ball mallet

J. Yuasa: *Scenes from Bashô*

20. Rub tam-tam with a cardboard tube to make a whistling sound

D. Burge: *Sources III*

21. Make a high-pitched squeak on the tam-tam by means of a piece of unpolished wood, which is scraped a very short distance, very hard

J. Harvey: *Persephone Dream*

22. Scrape surface of tam-tam with the four open edges of one half of a metal tea container (canister) of medium size

I. Anhalt: *Foci*

23. Stroke a glass vase (or a piece of glass) over the surface of the tam-tam

J-Y. Bosseur: *Un arraché de partout*

C. Halffter: *Fibonaciana*

24. Slide in a continual circle at the center of gong or tam-tam with a triangle beater

L. Bassett: *Designs, Images and Textures*

H. W. Henze: *Sinfonia N. 6*

A. Nordheim: *Response I*

D. Burge: *Sources III*
J. Druckman: *Dark Upon the Harp; Incenters*
E. Raxach: *Paraphrase*
G. Read: *Los Dioses Aztecas*
I. Stravinsky: *Le Sacre du Printemps*

25. Trail chains gently over the tam-tam

P. Maxwell Davies: *Vesalii Icones*

26. Tremolo on a cymbal plate [suspended] with a cello bow

A. Schönberg: *Fünf Orchestra Stücke*

27. Stroke a crotale with a cello bow

D. Erb: *Concerto for Brass and Orchestra*

28. Strike triangle with a tenpenny nail

G. Crumb: *Ancient Voices of Children*

29. Trill on triangle with a wirebrush

W. Sydeman: *Trio for Flute, Double Bass and Percussion*

30. Same, with a $1/16''$ airplane wire, long enough to be "whippy"

B. Childs: *Jack's New Bag*

Performance directives that involve both an unusual instrument area to be struck on the metal instruments and a novel agent to be utilized include the following:

1. Using the thick end of a snare drum stick, drag it slowly around the circumference of the suspended cymbal

G. Read: *Los Dioses Aztecas* (Example 38)

2. Agitate a suspended cymbal with its rim between the wires of a wirebrush

Z. Bujarski: *Kinoth*

3. Enclose (by clapping together) the rim of suspended cymbal with a slapstick

M. Kagel: *Anagrama*

4. With a circular motion rub flat side of the gong with the flat side of a triangle beater; also slide the fist over the knob

W. Kraft: *Suite for Percussion*

5. Strike rim of tam-tam with snare drum sticks

G. Crumb: *Echoes of Time and the River*
J. Harvey: *Inner Light III*

6. Scrape rim of the tam-tam with a triangle beater or a knitting needle

T. Antoniou: *Parastasis II*
D. Martino: *Notturno*

7. Slowly slide (or rub) triangle beater around outer edge of suspended cymbal, gong, or tam-tam

M. Ishii: *Aphorismen*
L. de Pablo: *Reciproco*
E. Raxach: *Estrofas*
G. Read: *Haiku Seasons*

8. Scrape the teeth of a guiro (rasper) over the rim of the tam-tam with one hand while striking the center with a stick in the other hand

F. Miroglio: *Réfractions*

9. Rub polystyrene on a rosined patch on the back of the tam-tam

J. Harvey: *Inner Light III*

10. Rub back of tam-tam (like a tambourine thumb-roll) with rubber finger-tip; also flick surface with a fingernail

R. O'Donnell: *Microtimbre I*

11. Stroke (with a vertical upwards motion) the rim of gong, tam-tam, cowbell, or hand-held cymbal with a cello or doublebass bow

W. Albright: *Danse Macabre*
C. Alsina: *Symptom*
P. Chihara: *Willow, Willow*
B. Childs: *Jack's New Bag*
G. Crumb: *Music for a Summer Evening*
L. Foss: *Exeunt*
R. Gerhard: *Concerto for Orchestra*
C. Halffter: *Noche Pasiva del Sentido; Planto por las victimas de la violencia* (Example 40)
S. Hodkinson: *Fresco*
S. Montague: *At the white edge of phrygia*
R. O'Donnell: *Microtimbre I*
K. Penderecki: *Dimensions of Time and Silence*
R. Reynolds: *Blind Men; Quick are the Mouths of Earth*
G. Rochberg: *Tableaux*
J. Schwantner: *In Aeternum (Consortium IV)*
T. Takemitsu: *Asterism*
A. Woodbury: *Remembrances*
B. A. Zimmermann: *Photoptosis*

By changing the degree of bowing pressure and the speed at which the bow is moved across the rim, a simulation of pitch change can be produced. According to Roger Reynolds, by touching the tam-tam nodes while bowing on the rim, a high and complex resonance is produced, an effect called for in his *The Promises of Darkness*.

12. Rub the edges (upper rims) of the chime bars with a metal stick

G. Self: *Warwick*

The British composer Richard Meale, in his *Clouds now and then,* directs that after the gong has been struck, the percussionist must sway to and fro the metal bar from which the gong is hung. This action is analogous to the shaking of a pair of cymbals after having clashed them together (see page 36) in that a faint but discernible oscillation of pitch can be perceived.

A final category comprises not only unusual areas and agents of percussion attack but highly unconventional "instruments" as well; a prime example is the directive in Peter Maxwell Davies' *Revelation and Fall* to rub the edge of a knife blade over a wet sheet of glass.

TREMOLI VARIANTS

In many recent scores several new tremolando effects have been applied to the pitched mallet instruments. One such device is a tremolo between two of the suspended tubes (resonators) of vibraphone or marimba, usually with a metal rod or the wood end of a mallet (see Kazimierz Serocki's *Continuum,* and *Fantasmagoria,* for example). In *Epifanie* Luciano Berio asks for a simultaneous tremolo on both the upper and lower surfaces of a marimbaphone bar—on the "white-note" row for player 1 and on the "black-note" row for player 2, who is stationed on the far side of the instrument. The actual procedure is best explained in the composer's own words: "The player should hold two very soft sticks in each hand . . . like a fork—one stick over and one under the end of the keys. The notes are to be quickly tremoloed in such a way that . . . the sticks strike alternately against the upper and lower side of the keys." There is no reason, of course, why this technique could not easily be transferred to the other idiophones.

A technique strictly limited to the vibraphone is turning the motor or fan on or off at the very moment of striking the plates, or after the plate has been struck and the tone is still sounding; see:

D. Burge: *Sources III*
G. Read: *Haiku Seasons*

Also confined to the peculiar mechanism of the vibraphone is fastening down the pedal so that any or all of the struck tones vibrate to maximum duration, while leaving the performer free to move about without hindrance (as in Sydney Hodkinson's *Fresco*).

An unorthodox tremolo action is demonstrated in Christopher Rouse's *The Infernal Machine:* the percussionist playing a maraca must hold it vertically with the handle up while rotating it with a circular motion.

IDIOPHONE CLUSTERS

It should be evident that the idiophones alone among all the percussion instruments have the capacity of producing cluster sounds. Formerly, these closely knit sonorities—indeed, all so-called "chords"—were restricted on the mallet instruments to not more than six notes, three to either hand. Only under optimum conditions (ample time for positioning the mallets in either hand and chords that were conveniently spaced) was the player able to strike more than three pitches in either hand. But with the recent invention of "cluster-sticks" (mallets shaped like a T, the stem being their handles and the top crossbar their striking areas, the latter varying between 17 and 25 cm in width), the player is able to hit from two to five plates with either hand if the pitches are in diatonic order. On glockenspiel, more than five bars can be struck simultaneously with either hand, owing to the smaller width of the metal plates. Among the new scores requiring the use of cluster-sticks are:

D. Bedford: *Piece for Mo*
D. Eberhard: *Parody*

R. Reynolds: *Quick are the Mouths of Earth*
K. Serocki: *Continuum; Fantasmagoria*

Yet other methods have been devised to produce idiophone clusters: in *Apparitions,* for instance, Ligeti asks the player to strike as many plates as possible with

Example 41
Donald Erb: from *The Seventh Trumpet* (p. 27)

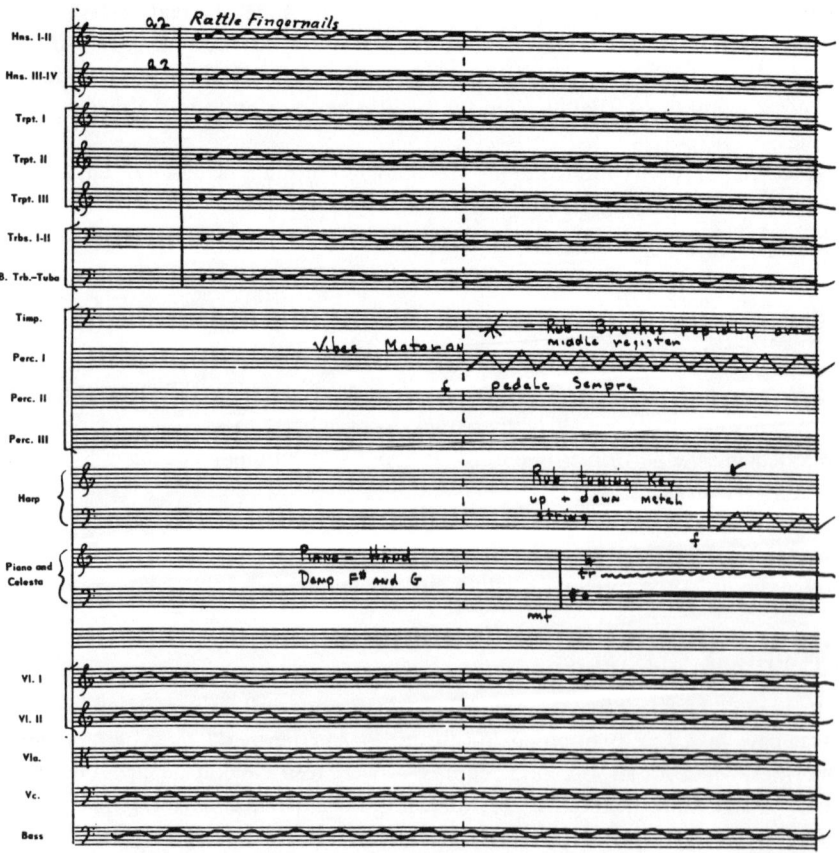

© 1972 Merion Music, Inc. Used by permission of the Publisher. Sole Representative, Theodore Presser Company.

two rulers held horizontally. In Kagel's *Anagrama,* glockenspiel clusters are to be played with a metal rod, also held horizontally, and later with a cymbal clashed on the plates. Vibraphone clusters are to be executed with triangle beaters held flat in Theodore Antoniou's *Nenikikamen,* while in *The Seventh Trumpet* (Example 41) of Donald Erb, wirebrushes are to be rubbed over the plates, creating a subdued cluster effect in spite of the requested dynamic level. A percussionist in the Kagel score just cited is instructed to strike as many contiguous chime tubes as possible with a pair of hand cymbals, moved in a circular motion—an action that is guaranteed to produce an impressive racket.

Finally, in George Crumb's *Madrigals—Book I,* the vibraphonist is directed to strike the instrument damper bar so sharply that all the plates vibrate sympathetically, creating a three-octave chromatic-cluster simulation.

Although not as yet discovered in any recent score, it is possible to "prepare" the vibraphone or glockenspiel by attaching a paper clip or similar metallic object to one or more bars, held in place with rubber bands or masking tape.

MISCELLANEOUS EFFECTS

The American and European orchestrator has by now greatly enlarged his percussive resources by frequently bringing into the section instruments indigenous to other parts of the world. From Latin America he has appropriated bongos, cabacas, chocolo, conga drums, claves, cuica, guiro, maracas, reco-reco, and timbales; from Africa he has borrowed darabukas, log and slit drums, and thumb piano; from the Far East he has imported bamboos, elephant bells, Indian hand bells, koto, sho, tablas, Thailand gongs, and Tibetan prayer stones. Not content with these exotica, however, he has also requisitioned such rarities as the following:

1. Elastic bands of various thicknesses and tension to snap; a large, thick book whose pages are to be riffled; a tightly filled cushion to be struck with a carpet-beater; a resonant piece of furniture to be struck with a cudgel; a paper bag to be inflated and exploded; a suitcase with a rough surface to be stroked with emery paper

G. Ligeti: *Aventures*

2. Sheets of paper to be torn apart; a thick carpet, suspended, to be struck with a straw rug-beater; a tin can to be smashed with a hammer; a wooden lath to be broken in two; a plastic cup to be crushed; an inflated balloon to be stroked with wet fingers; a toy tin frog which makes a loud creaking to activate; a large bottle to be smashed against an iron plate; a silk cloth to be torn apart; a metal tray filled with dishes to smash; a wooden bowl filled with marbles to rattle; paper-thin metal foils to be softly fluttered

G. Ligeti: *Nouvelles Aventures*

3. An inflated balloon to be rubbed and popped in palms of hands; an automobile horn (battery operated or on tape) to sound; two iron pipes to be struck with a third pipe; a framed piece of glass to be scratched on with the rim of a hard plastic container; a

pistol with blanks or a cap pistol to fire off; a bottle to be blown on (tuned to A220); a bulbous type bicycle horn to be honked; a police-, dog-, and slide-whistle to blow; a duck horn to sound; a transistor radio to play; a large piece of glass to be broken

A. Curran: *Home-made*

4. A saw to rub with a cello bow; a metal coil to twang; a washboard to rub; a garbage can cover to strike; a tree stump to hit with an axe; several salad bowls to strike; a large crate to smash; a bag of steel pipes to pour into a steel barrel; several door bells to ring; a player piano to pump; some toy noisemakers to sound; several music boxes to turn on

L. Austin: *The Maze*

5. A band kit; an anvil (small); several sanctus bells; a short length of scaffolding; a grater; a ratchet; a whistle; a toy clarion; a biscuit tin (filled with broken glass); some chains; a typewriter; a saucepan; two pebbles, and a blacksmith's bellows

P. Maxwell Davies: *Vesalii Icones*

This listing by no means exhausts the unusual percussive "instruments" to be encountered in the avant-garde scores of the last few years. The point is well made, nonetheless, that today anything and everything is grist for the orchestrational mill. As John Cage prophesied in 1937: "I believe that the use of noise to make music will continue and increase . . . any and all sounds that can be heard will be made available for musical purposes." No one can argue that his prediction has come to pass in ways that surely even Cage did not anticipate.

NOTE

1. An early prototype of this action appears in the finale of Mahler's seventh symphony (1908): the bass drum is struck simultaneously with a birch switch and a sponge-headed mallet.

11

HARP AND OTHER PLUCKED INSTRUMENTS

Of the specific harp effects catalogued throughout this book, most were invented, or indirectly influenced, by the Franco-American harpist and composer Carlos Salzedo. No modern instrument, not even a member of the vastly enlarged percussion family, has undergone such a metamorphosis in the twentieth century as the harp. The transformation is not in terms of the harp's construction or basic performing technique but in the vanguard orchestrators' conception of what the instrument can and should do in the milieu of experimental music. To compare the earlier harp writing of Hector Berlioz with that of the later Impressionists—Claude Debussy in *La Mer* or *Jeux,* let us say—is to understand clearly that the one composer defined the harp's physiognomy and the other its psychology. But to compare the demands made by Debussy, Ravel, or Salzedo himself with those currently operative in the scores of Bussotti, Kagel, Berio, or Bernard Rands, for example, is to hear a new definition of harp sound—no longer the delicate embodiment of grace and tonal refinement once thought to be the ultimate characteristic of the instrument, but a modern tonal agent almost totally new in terms of timbre and technical scope.

FINGERNAIL PLUCKING

Plucking the strings with the fingernails was termed "plectric sounds" by Salzedo; the technique is used in many of his works, including the *Sonata for Harp and Piano*. Played close to the soundboard, nail pluckings became "guitaric sounds"; either the one or the other of these two methods has been stipulated in their scores by the following composers:

T. Baird: *Erotyki*
J. Barraqué: *Séquence*
L. Berio: *Circles*
H. Birtwistle: *Entr'actes and Sappho Fragments*
E. Brown: *Available Forms 2*
S. Bussotti: *Fragmentations*
G. Crumb: *Madrigals—III*
L. Foss: *Fragments of Archilochos*
H. Holliger: *Glühende Rätsel*
M. Kagel: *Sonant*

M. Kelemen: *Changeant*
T. de Leeuw: *Spatial Music III*
S. Matsushita: *Fresque Sonore*
C. Polin: *Summer Settings*
B. Rands: *Formants 1; Wildtrack 1*
G. Read: *Sonoric Fantasia No. 3*
B. Schäffer: *Scultura*
K. Serocki: *Musica concertante; Segmenti*
Z. Wiszniewski: *Tre Pezzi*

The antithesis of Salzedo's "guitaric sounds" is present in R. M. Schafer's *The Crown of Ariadne:* the harpist is to softly rub up and down with one or more fingers on a single bass string.

PEDAL GLISSANDI AND TRILLS[1]

Standard glissandi variants and novel percussive devices alike, as applied to the harp, have been discussed on earlier pages, as have muting techniques and microtonal tunings. Here we deal with some remaining aspects of modern harp usage, such as unconventional manipulations of the pedals. One effect currently favored is to instruct the harpist constantly to change the pedal positions in a random order, usually in the context of a continual glissando or a chord bisbigliando; see:

L. Berio: *Chemins I; Sequenza II* (Example 6-c)
M. Kagel: *Sonant*

G. Read: *Haiku Seasons*
L. Schifrin: *Continuum for Solo Harp*
T. Takemitsu: *Eucalypts (I)*

Another technique is for the player to hold a specified pedal between two positions (flat and natural, or natural and sharp) while, or just after, the requisite string is plucked; Salzedo called this technique "metallic sounds," and it has been used by the following composers:

L. Berio: *Chemins II; Epifanie*
F. Cerha: *Relazioni fragili*
D. Eberhard: *"Especially. . ."*
D. Erb: *Concerto for Solo Percussionist; The Seventh Trumpet*
B. Jolas: *Tranche pour harpe seule*
S. Matsushita: *Fresque sonore*
F. Miroglio: *Réseaux pour harpe et orchestre*
B. Rands: *Actions for six; Formants 1*
G. Read: *Haiku Seasons*
E. Varèse: *Ameriques; Offrandes*

The same effect may also be accomplished by releasing a pedal from one of the notches so slowly that it stays in half-position (as in Ligeti's *Apparitions*). In addition, after plucking a string, the harpist may depress its pedal in such a way that the vibrating string strikes against the tuning pins, creating a distinct "buzz"; refer to:

M. Bamert: *Five Aphorisms*
L. Berio: *Chemins I*
E. Denisov: *Canon in Memory of Igor Stravinsky*
R. Felciano: *Crasis*
M. Kagel: *Sonant*
F. Miroglio: *Réseaux pour harpe et orchestre*
W. Szalonek: *Concertino per flauto ed orchestra da camera*
T. Takemitsu: *Stanza II*
B. Van Nostrand: *Ventilation Manual*

Pedal glissandi and trills are feasible new techniques and have been utilized by a number of contemporary orchestrators. To achieve the former effect, the string is first plucked and then the corresponding pedal is immediately and fully raised or depressed. To raise the pedal from the lowest to the highest notch creates a descending slide of a whole tone, while to depress it from highest to lowest notch produces an ascending whole-step glissando. Among many works calling for this technique may be cited:

A. Bancquart: *Palimpsestes*
D. Banks: *Triade*
S. Barber: *Souvenirs*
M. Kagel: *Anagrama; Sonant* (Example 13-j)
K. Kohn: *Son of Prophet Bird*

Example 42
Francis Miroglio; from *Réseaux pour harpe et orchestre* (p. 1)

© Copyright 1966 by Universal Edition (London) Ltd., London. All rights reserved. Used by permission of European American Music Distributors Corporation, sole U.S. and Canadian agent for Universal Edition, London.

L. Bassett: *Variations for Orchestra*
L. Berio: *Chemins I*
S. Bussotti: *Fragmentations*
G. Crumb: *Madrigals—IV*
D. Erb: *Concerto for Solo Percussionist*
R. Felciano: *Background Music*
L. Foss: *Elytres; Orpheus*
R. Gerhard: *Concerto for Orchestra*
S. Hodkinson: *November Voices*
K. Huber: *Des Engels anredung an die Seele*

A. Lanzi: *Quattro Pezzi per Arpa*
R. Lomon: *Dust Devils*
F. Miroglio: *Réseaux pour harpe et orchestre* (Example 42)
R. Moeves: *Et Occidentum Illustra*
B. Rands: *Aum*
G. Read: *Toccata Giocoso*
R. Romiti: *Palingenesis*
G. Schuller: *Fantasy for Solo Harp*
J. Serebrier: *Colores Mágicos*
T. Takemitsu: *Eucalypts II*
D. Welcher: *White Mares of the Moon*

The pedal trill is achieved by plucking a specified string and then moving the corresponding pedal up and down as quickly as possible and for as long as the sound persists; see:

L. Berio: *Sequenza II*
M. Kagel: *Sonant*

Y. Sadai: *Nuances*
T. Takemitsu: *Asterism*

The ultimate in pedal effects is undoubtedly Salzedo's "esoteric sounds": the player moves all the pedals in random order and as vigorously as possible but does not play on the strings. The aural result of this balletic activity is a subdued percussive rustle, though it is clear that both Berio (in *Sequenza II*) and Bussotti in his *Fragmentations* (Example 43) had a visual goal in mind as well.

HARP AND PLUCKED INSTRUMENTS

Example 43
Sylvano Bussotti: from *Fragmentations* (p. 1)

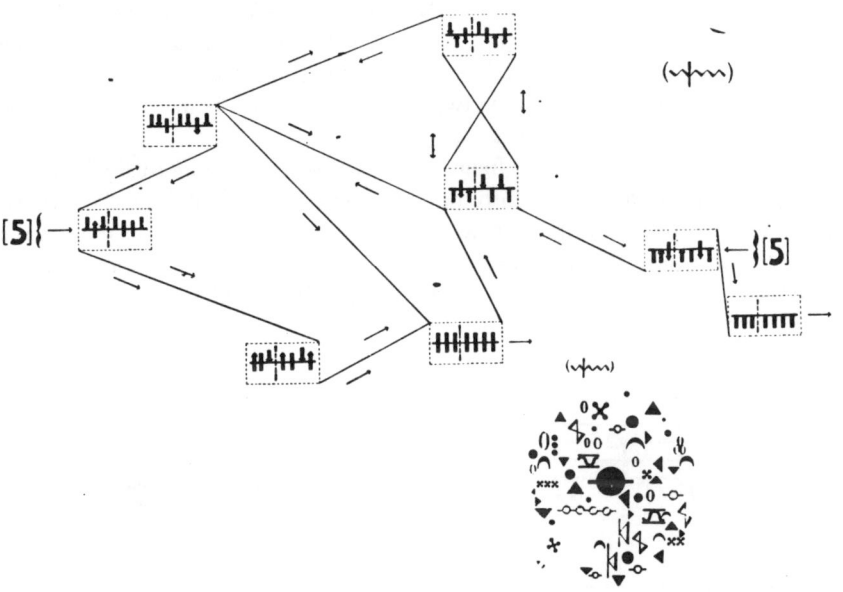

© Copyright 1968 by Aldo Bruzzichelli Editores. Sole agent, Margun Music, Inc., Newton, MA.

TUNING-KEY AND TUNING-PIN EFFECTS

In addition to inventing the tuning-key glissando, discussed on page 42, Salzedo also devised other ways of employing this necessary agent in performance. To achieve his "fluidic sounds" the harpist places the center of the tuning key against the very top of the string, which is plucked near to the soundboard. Another playing method, called "rocket-like sounds," follows the same procedure, but the tuning key is quickly slid along the string as it is plucked. A few of Salzedo's solo harp pieces utilize this device, as do Richard Felciano's *Background Music* and *Actions for six* of Bernard Rands. A closely related effect, of course, is to slide the tuning key on a bass wire string (the "fluidic glissando" described on page 42), but at the end of the slide the key is pulled abruptly from the string, plucking it with a metallic twang; see Salzedo's *Scintillation*, for example.

There are still other ways in which the tuning key may be utilized for special effects: in one, the player holds the key in his right hand, with the metal shank exerting pressure on the string which is to be plucked normally; the result is a deadening of the string's natural resonance. In addition, any string may be struck or rhythmically tapped with the key-end (as in Donald Erb's *Symphony of Overtures*), or any three or four contiguous strings can be struck with the broad wooden handle; this latter effect was called for by Salzedo in a number of his solo harp pieces. Furthermore, a plucked and still vibrating string can be lightly touched with the metal end of the tuning key, resulting in a metallic buzz; this device appears in the Erb work just cited and in Per Nørgård's *Symphony No. 2*. In his harp and orchestra *Réseaux*, Miroglio calls for a tremolo with the tuning key between two strings, while Felciano in *Crasis* tells the harpist to insert the handle of the tuning key between two strings, then pluck both strings and slide the key down to the soundboard.

The tuning pegs of the harp figure prominently in several unusual effects: for instance, harpists have frequently been instructed to play high on the strings, quite close to the metal pins, in contradistinction to the normal position in the center of the strings or the more conventional requisition of *près de la table*. Playing in this position produces a thin, brittle sound, and has been exploited in the following recent compositions:

E. Brown: *Available Forms 2*
S. Bussotti: *Fragmentations*
H. Gorecki: *Monologhi*
M. Kagel: *Sonant* (Example 13-h, p)
P. Méfano: *Paraboles*

F. Miroglio: *Réseaux pour harpe et orchestre*
B. Rands: *Formants 1*
E. Raxach: *Paraphrase*
G. Read: *Sonoric Fantasia No. 3*

And in Earle Brown's *Available Forms 2* and *Times Five*, the composer directs the harpist to play *above* the tuning pins, where pitch is indeterminate and string resonance is weak.

To effectuate Salzedo's "vibrant sounds," the left thumb presses down with rapid motions on the strings between the tuning pegs and the metal discs, while the right hand plays normally on the strings; see various of Salzedo's harp pieces, as well as Vinko Globokar's *Voie*.

While scordatura is not a common harp technique, it has been notably prescribed by Gunther Schuller in his solo harp *Fantasy*. G♮^{1} is to be tuned to g♭, while b♮^{2} is tuned to b♯, both retunings for the purpose of obtaining pitches not otherwise possible during traversal of the piece. Because of these retunings, g♮ is obtained by plucking written g♯ and b♮ by plucking notated b♭.

Finally, in *Mit einem gewissen sprechenden Ausdruck* of Bussotti, the harpist is directed to draw a metal stick heavily along the row of tuning pins, creating a violent clacking, the same effect produced in *Réseaux* of Miroglio by means of the tuning key.

GUITAR, MANDOLIN, AND BANJO TECHNIQUES

As with all stringed instruments, whether fretted or not, there is a normal playing area on the strings of the guitar, mandolin, and banjo. For a change of timbre, however, some recent composers have instructed the players of these instruments to pluck the strings in unconventional locales, such as:

1. Near to or directly on the bridge

   D. Erb: *String Trio*
   L. Foss: *Fragments of Archilochos*
   R. Gerhard: *Concerto for 8*

   C. Halffter: *Codex I*
   M. Kagel: *Sonant*
   G. Read: *Canzone di Notte*

2. Above (behind) the bridge

   D. Erb: *String Trio*
   L. Foss: *Fragments of Archilochos*

   M. Kagel: *Sonant*
   A. Mellnäs: *Tombola*

3. Beyond the nut or fingerboard

   L. Foss: *Fragments of Archilochos*
   M. Kagel: *Sonant*

The combination of sounds produced normally on the strings and at the same time close to the bridge is to be found in Goffredo Petrassi's *Suoni Notturni*, an effective amalgam of different timbres. In the *Selbstportrait* of Rodion Schtschedrin the guitarist is instructed to play "quasi Balalaika," although the composer does not explain how this is to be done.

Guitar strings are normally plucked with the fingertips, but some instrumentators have on occasion requested that they be plucked with other agents:

1. The fingernails[2]

   G. Arrigo: *Tre Occasioni*
   P. Boulez: *Le marteau sans maître*
   S. Bussotti: *Memoria*
   L. Foss: *Fragments of Archilochos*

   R. Gerhard: *Concerto for 8*
   H. W. Henze: *El Cimarrón*
   M. Kagel: *Heterophonie*
   G. Read: *Canzone di Notte*

2. A plectrum or pick

   S. Albert: *Voices Within*
   T. Antoniou: *Nemikkamen*
   A. Berg: *Drei Orchesterstücke*
   W. Heckster: *Epicycle I, II*

   H. W. Henze: *El Cimarrón; Sinfonia N.6* (Example 51)
   M. Kagel: *Sonant; Tremens*
   F. Schreker: *Prelude to a Drama*
   I. Stravinsky: *Four Russian Songs*

Contrariwise, mandolin and banjo strings are ordinarily played with special picks or plectrums. Substitute agents required in several recent scores include:

1. The fingertips
   G. Crumb: *Night of the Four Moons*
   D. Erb: *String Trio*

2. A metal rod
   G. Crumb: *Songs, Drones, and Refrains of Death* (also applied to guitar)

Although Crumb has never claimed to have invented the "bottle-neck" technique of playing on these plucked instruments, he is—at the least—the most avid practitioner of the device. "Bottle-neck" playing is accomplished by holding a glass rod lightly against the E-string (of mandolin or banjo) with the left hand; after plucking the string with a metal plectrum (a paper clip makes an excellent substitute), the player then slides the rod along the string, producing various portamento pitches. The sound is somewhat like the ondes Martenot or the Theremin, disembodied and softly wailing. For glimpses of the technique at work in a musical context refer to both the *Ancient Voices of Children* and *Night of the Four Moons* of Crumb. Instead of using a glass rod, the guitarist scrapes a string with a pick in *Concatenations* of George Wilson. In order that all six strings be sounded simultaneously in Barry Conyngham's *Three*, the player uses a cloth-covered stick.

Variants of several string instrument pizzicato effects have been requisitioned by composers for the guitar, such as the Bartók, or snap, pizzicato, called for by Theodore Antoniou in *Dialog* and by David Bedford in *You Asked for It*. The equivalent of "pizzicato effleuré" (see page 238) has been applied to the guitar in Gilbert Biberian's *Prisms II*. He terms the effect a "surface pizzicato," accomplished by the player lightly resting the left-hand fingers on the strings while plucking them with the right hand.

Like the piano, the guitar can—surprisingly—be "prepared" by various materials placed on or below the strings. In *You Asked for It,* Bedford directs that folded tracing paper be put beneath the strings close to the bridge. "The paper should be thick enough to touch and damp the strings," the composer says. Paper clips are attached to the strings in William Hellerman's *On the Edge of a Node,* and a plectrum is similarly positioned between the fourth and six strings in John Schneider's *Voyage*.

The guitar strings can also be stroked with a violin, cello, or doublebass bow, as specified in the following works:

D. Bedford: *A Horse, His Name Was Hunry Fencewaver Walkins*
H. W. Henze: *Memorias de "El Cimarrón"*
M. Kagel: *Tremens*
C. Wolff: *Electric Spring III*

In Gerhard's *Concerto for 8*, the guitar is required to be held in an unorthodox position: to enable the strings to be played with a loosely strung, well-rosined cello bow, the instrument must be laid flat on the guitarist's lap.

Example 44
Sven-David Sandström: from *Surrounded*

The contemporary guitar has also borrowed the bowed string-instrument device of scordatura; the works cited below stipulate that certain strings be raised or lowered in pitch—by quarter-tones in the Sandström score listed.

J. Antunes: *Signs for Guitar*
W. Bland: *An Homage to Picasso*
G. Crumb: *Songs, Drones, and Refrains of Death*
T. Darter: *Dual*
P. Gudmundsen-Holmgreen: *Solo for Electric Guitar*

S-D. Sandström: *Surrounded* (Example 44)
J. Schneider: *Voyage*
H. Shimoyama: *Dialogo No. 2*
R. Smith Brindle: *Do Not Go Gentle; Concerto "de Angelis"*

A novel device, the "vibrato bar," is attached to the instrument bridge in David Bedford's *18 Bricks Left on April 21,* which raises or lowers pitches without the player having to use his left hand. The device is only feasible on the electric guitar, which is customarily played with a plectrum. This modification of the instrument can also be played effectively with a cello or doublebass bow since the pickup clearly registers all sounds produced on the strings.

As the guitar is an extremely versatile instrument, it is certain that additional novel effects and techniques will be invented and exploited by composers in the years to come.

NOTES

1. The composer is referred to Ruth Inglefield's *Writing for the Pedal Harp* for a detailed explanation of contemporary harp techniques.
2. In his authoritative book on modern guitar techniques, John Schneider lists an amazing array of notational symbols for fingernail effects on the guitar, all invented by Alvaro Company in his pioneering treatise, *Las Seis Cuerdas.*

12

KEYBOARD INSTRUMENTS

One can confidently assert that with the single exception of the harp, no modern instrument favored by the musical avant-garde has been so radically altered in conception as the piano. The techniques presently applied to this instrument are poles removed from conventional keyboard methodology. It is not that the piano has become even more solidly entrenched as a percussive instrument, but rather that today's experimental composers have a new awareness of its tone-color potential. No longer is the piano considered to be monochromatic; neither does it function exclusively in a melodic/harmonic manner as it did up to the mid-point of the present century. Now, after intense experimentation by the vanguard, it has emerged as a hybrid instrument, combining elements of both tuned and unpitched percussion with certain tonal characteristics of harp and harpsichord. In this metamorphosis of the piano the deciding factor is the composer's concept of the interior areas, with less emphasis on the exterior keys. Indeed, the piano has become an instrument whose sound-producing mechanism is plucked rather than struck; the primary locale of playing has thus been transferred from the outside to the inside of the frame.

This conceptual transformation of the piano has not affected the other keyboard instruments. Because the harpsichord is a keyed instrument whose strings are plucked with quills rather than struck with felted hammers—not to mention its more delicate physique—the effects now feasible and common on the piano cannot, with few exceptions, be automatically transferred to the harpsichord's inner mechanism. And owing to their basic construction, neither the organ nor the celesta can be played upon in their interiors; any effects to be produced on these two instruments must perforce take place on their keys or on their frames.

PIANO AND HARPSICHORD CLUSTERS

As we are concerned on these pages more with the basic timbral nature of recent pianistic devices than with their strict chronological development, the initial techniques to be discussed involve unorthodox ways of using the keys of the piano and harpsichord. Roughly graded from a more or less traditional to an experimental conception of the existing keyboard, the techniques catalogued clearly indicate the extent of the avant-gardists' search for new and viable instrumental sound effects.

Any compendium of modern instrumentational devices must include the tone-cluster, even though it is now so ubiquitous as to be a cliché. The name of Henry Cowell is most closely associated with this technique, first used in his 1912 *The Tides of Mauannaum*. Tone clusters, however, had been used by Charles Ives, notably in the *"Concord" Sonata,* some years before Cowell's independent exploitation of this tonal device.

In their most limited form tone-clusters are produced by the bunched fingers or the flat hand on the keys; in their more extended versions they are played with the forearm (stipulated in Cowell's *Piano Concerto* of 1929) or with the elbow, as designated by Roger Reynolds in *Fantasy for Pianist*. Clusters can also be executed with a mechanical contrivance such as a wooden board (as in the *"Concord" Sonata*). Recent variant forms of cluster playing include rolled or glissando clusters, the tones of the structure being progressively added to or subtracted from by the action of the flat hand or full arm. Far too many contemporary works have used this device to warrant listing here, but those given below may be considered representative:

J. Bahk: *Mark*
J. Beckwith: *Circle with Tangents*
D. Burge: *A Song of Sixpence*
S. Bussotti: *Couple*
J. Cage: *Concert for Piano and Orchestra*
C. Cardew: *Three Winter Potatoes*
N. Castiglioni: *Cangianti per pianoforte*
H. Cowell: *Piano Concerto*
R. Gerhard: *Epithalamium*
A. Gilbert: *Sonata No. 2*

R. Haubenstock-Ramati: *Chants et prismes; Petite musique de nuit*
H. W. Henze: *Sinfonia N. 6*
M. Kagel: *Anagrama; Heterophonie*
M. Kelemen: *Dessins commentes*
A. Lanza: *Plectros I, II*
S. Lunetta: *Piano Music* (Example 45)
R. Reynolds: *Blind Men; Quick are the Mouths of Earth*
K. Stockhausen: *Gruppen für drei Orchester; Klavierstück X*

In Karlheinz Stockhausen's piano piece, cited above, the composer states that in playing cluster glissandi the pianist might wear woolen gloves with the fingers cut away—presumably in consideration of the player's fingers rather than obtaining any sonic nuances.

Clusters produced by striking the keys with the clenched fist were first requisi-

Example 45
Stanley Lunetta: from *Piano Music* (p. 66)

a.

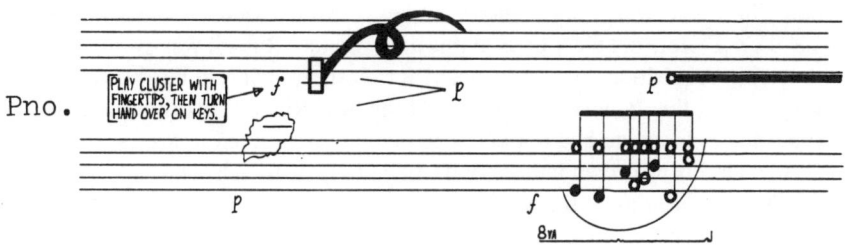

b.

© Copyright 1967, SOURCE, Vol. 1, No. 2, July, 1967. Used by permission.

tioned by Cowell in such works as his 1914 *Advertisement* and, most notably, in the *Piano Concerto* of the 20's. More recent composers who have also required this performance procedure from their pianists, solo and ensemble, include:

G. Bacewicz: *Second Cello Concerto*
D. Banks: *Horn Concerto*
E. Brown: *Hodograph I*
N. T. Dao: *Tây Nguyên*
H. W. Henze: *Sinfonia N. 6*
M. Kagel: *Transición II*
M. Ohana: *Sorôn-Ngô*

K. Penderecki: *Strophes*
R. Reynolds: *Fantasy for Pianist*
E. Schwartz: *Soliloquies*
K. Stockhausen: *Klavierstück X*
C. Surinach: *Symphonic Variations*
A. de la Vega: *Antinomies for Piano*

In his piano piece called *Joc*, Xavier Benguerel calls for black and white key-clusters to be played with two pieces of wood, each about 50 cm in length. In my own *Haiku Seasons* the pianist is directed to hold down the lowest two octaves of white and black keys with two 15-inch rulers, while a percussionist plays on the corresponding strings with mallets. Similarly, in Maurice Ohana's *Sorôn-Ngô* several felt-backed rulers are required for holding down various cluster formations.

William Russell in his *Three Dance Movements* has the pianist depress the entire chromatic scale—all eighty-eight keys—with a wooden board measuring 4' × 4" × 1". It is not clear to us at this time whether Russell was aware of Ives's pioneering requisition of a 14¾" board for cluster playing in the *"Hawthorne"* movement of the *"Concord" Sonata*. At the time Russell's work was published (1936) the Ives sonata had not yet been publicly performed in the United States and was largely unknown outside of a small group of friends who had subscribed to the private printing of the work in 1921. It is doubtful that Russell belonged to this group; hence his early use of a keyboard cluster-board is a fortuitous coincidence. But such mechanical contrivances aside, however, perhaps the ultimate in keyboard cluster effects—visually at the very least—is the directive to the pianist in both Theodore Lucas's *Aberrations No. VII* and Alvin Lucier's *Action Music* to sit emphatically on as much of the keyboard as possible.

KEY ATTACKS

Modern variants of traditional piano keyboard attack include the following actions:

1. Pluck the key ("plucked accent") instead of striking it, simulating pizzicato

K. Korte: *Concerto Mutabile*

2. Strike key forcefully, staccato, and immediately depress it silently

S. Bussotti: *Pour Clavier*   K. Stockhausen: *Klavierstücke*
M. Kagel: *Transición II*   B. A. Zimmermann: *Perspektiven*
H. Pousseur: *Mobile; Rimes*

3. Strike the key normally, then raise it (by releasing finger pressure) and depress it again silently before the sound is more than half-dampened

A. Gilbert: *Sonata No. 2*
R. Reynolds: *Mosaic*

4. Vibrate the key with the finger after striking it (without causing the hammer to hit the string again)

M. Kagel: *Metapiece (Mimetics)*

5. Trill on two adjacent black keys with the knuckles

R. Reynolds: *Blind Men*

6. As a key is pressed down with one hand, strike the palm simultaneously with the free hand

M. Kagel: *Metapiece (Mimetics)*

7. Rapidly wriggle the fingers over the keys; silently jiggle the keys

S. Lunetta: *Piano Music* (Example 45)

L. Moss: *Omaggio*

8. Lightly strike key with flesh of finger (or with nail) without causing hammer to hit the string

S. Bussotti: *Pour Clavier*

M. Kagel: *Improvisation ajoutée; Transición II*

B. Rands: *Espressione IV*

9. Rub with the fingernails on the keys (without depressing them) with a constant and uniform movement, as fast as possible

N. Castiglioni: *Consonante*

10. Depress key and strike it with a finger-ring

M. Kagel: *Transición II*

11. Play on the keys with a heavy wool sock on the left hand

R. Reynolds: *The Promises of Darkness*

12. Drop a heavy wood stick onto the keys

X. Benguerel: *Joc*

A number of composers have borrowed ideas from avant-garde organ techniques and have devised methods of keeping certain preselected piano keys depressed. For example, in *Three Winter Potatoes* Cornelius Cardew directs the pianist to insert a wedge in the crack between two white keys, one of which is depressed; a folded piece of paper or cardboard makes a satisfactory wedge. In Books 3 and 4 of his *Etudes Australes,* Cage specifies that certain keys are to be held down with rubber wedges, while in William Duckworth's *The Time Curve Preludes: Book One,* seven of the piano keys are depressed by means of lead weights. David Bedford, in *Music for Albion Moonlight,* asks for lead weights to be silently placed on certain keys to keep them down while the pianist's two hands are busy elsewhere. These devices, of course, are designed to take the place of the middle pedal in the upper keyboard area where the pedal does not function.

PEDAL EFFECTS

Aside from percussive effects with and on the three piano pedals (see page 88), many current piano works indicate varying foot pressures on the sustaining pedal: ½, ¼, ¾, or other fractional manipulations. These requirements are seen frequently in the eleven *Klavierstücke* of Stockhausen, for instance, and in Boulez's third piano sonata and *Structures* for two pianos, among a long list of contemporary works. The use of a fluctuating (fluttering, oscillating) pedal is also a common stipulation, the player moving the pedal at different speeds and with constantly differing pressures, as in:

G. Amy: *Cahiers d'epigrammes*   M. Kelemen: *Dessins commentes*
W. Bolcom: *Duets for Quintet*   D. Lumsdaine: *Kelly Ground*
M. Finnissy: *Song 9*   G. Rochberg: *Tableaux*

In George Crumb's *Five Pieces for Piano* the performer must strike the key forcefully, then immediately depress the damper pedal sharply; this results in a faintly audible echo of the pitch. Edward Boguslawski in his *Intonations* calls for a somewhat similar echo effect, which is achieved by a voiceless pressing down of the damper pedal.

There is an intriguing instruction to the pianist in Jacob Druckman's *Windows*—to tap the strings with the dampers by means of a fast upward motion of the pedal; the sound is then prolonged by immediately depressing the pedal.

Kagel, in *Metapiece (Mimetics),* requires the pianist to release the sustaining pedal slowly enough that the sound of the dampers springing back can be heard, a subtle percussive addendum to the sound produced on the strings.

In Ligeti's theatrical *Nouvelles Aventures* the pianist must fasten down the sustaining pedal at one point with a wooden wedge. He does so because he is required to play in the interior with clothes brushes in either hand, standing at the left side of the instrument. Lacking a wedge, the pianist can naturally call on the services of an assistant to operate the pedal. Two other vanguard works also require the use of a pedal wedge: Istvan Anhalt's *Foci* utilizes it briefly, while in Elliott Schwartz's *Options I* it functions throughout the piece.

INTERIOR DEVICES

Some piano interior effects have already been catalogued, in particular those that are primarily percussive in nature (see pages 80–87). Normally, of course, the piano strings are set in vibration by key and hammer action or by striking, plucking, or rubbing with extraneous agents—fingers, fingernails, mallets, and the like. In addition, a finger may lightly touch a string and then lift off with a sliding motion (as in Christian Wolff's *Duet I*), or may press down on a string and then release the pressure suddenly; both actions will cause the string to vibrate faintly.

What must surely be the most unusual method of setting the strings in vibration was devised by Ligeti in his *Apparitions*: the player strokes the strings with two cloths. In *Traces,* Roger Reynolds has the pianist produce shrill, ringing sounds by pressing down a plastic ruler lengthwise on the strings of the highest section and sliding it to the back.

KEYBOARD INSTRUMENTS

Many contemporary composers effectively simulate harp and harpsichord tone-color on the piano by directing performers to pluck the strings with the fingernail. In addition to such percussive pluckings, already discussed (pages 77–80), certain instrumentators have requested a "metallic vibrato": the fingernail (or a paper clip) is very lightly placed against a vibrating string, creating a delicate buzzing sound. George Crumb calls for this device in his *Five Pieces for Piano* and in *Vox Balaenae*. Also, a string may be plucked with the player's nail, which is immediately turned over so as to cut off the sound with a brief metallic click, an effect called for in Wolff's *Duet I*. Leslie Bassett has the pianist in *Designs, Images and Textures* depress a certain key with the left hand while plucking the string with a right-hand fingernail. In his *Mixed Quintet* Vincent Luti tells the pianist to jiggle the fingernails of the left hand across the interior strings.

As a substitute for fingernail plucking, a plectrum (or ordinary paper clip) is highly effective, as specified by the Asian composer Tôn-thât Tiet in his exotic score, *Ngũ Hành II*. Milko Kelemen directs the pianist in *Olifant* (Example 46) not only to pluck a designated string with a plectrum but also to hold a triangle beater against the vibrating string, an action likewise required in Szalonek's *Les Sons*. In her *Spirals* Ann Silsbee directs the pianist to dangle an elongated paper clip over a vibrating string, this taped to a coathanger wire about a foot in length.

In *Plectros I*, Alcides Lanza asks the pianist to raise a low, wound string with two fingers, let it twang audibly, then touch the still-vibrating string with a fingernail or a plectrum. A somewhat similar directive occurs in Donald Erb's *Concerto for Solo Percussionist:* the player is to pull up the lowest A-string, let it

Example 46
Milko Kelemen: from *Olifant* (p. 48)

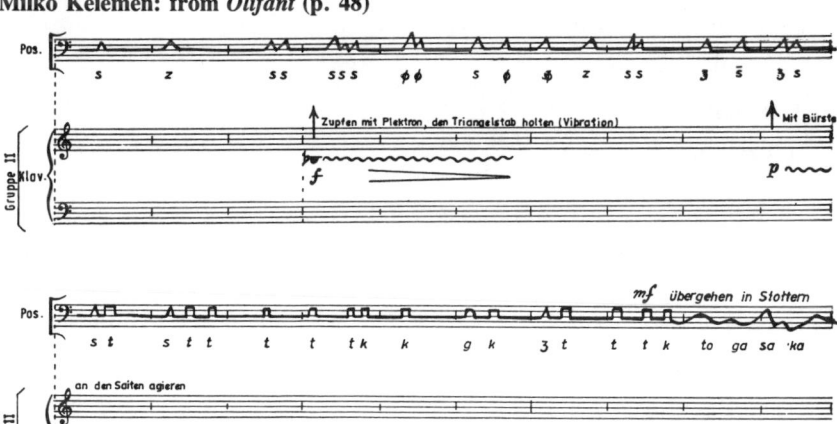

© 1974 by Henry Litolff's Verlag, Frankfurt. Used by permission of C. F. Peters Corporation, New York.

twang, and lay the metal tip of a pencil against it. On the other hand, Francis Miroglio requires his pianist in *Réfractions* to pinch together two low strings and let them clash one against the other, the damper pedal depressed.

A vibrating string, whether activated by key and hammer or by interior plucking, can also be lightly touched with some agent, such as a metal rod (triangle beater):

D. Erb: *Symphony of Overtures*
S. Lunetta: *Piano Music*
W. Szalonek: *Les Sons; Proporzioni II*

Furthermore, a group of contiguous vibrating strings can have a stick, dowel, metal bar, or other similar object laid across them; this action not only abruptly muffles the sound but adds a simultaneous percussive impact; see:

B. Childs: *Nonet*
A. Hrisanide: *Volumes*
W. Szalonek: *Les Sons*

Various cluster effects can be created by vibrating, agitating, or rubbing some object on a group of piano strings—best achieved on the wound strings in section one (far left). The listing that follows demonstrates the ingenuity of some composers in their search for interesting new sounds:

1. A wirebrush and a piece of wood

I. Anhalt: *Foci* (Example 20)

2. A cymbal, a tambourine, and a metal rod

L. Ferrari: *Société II*

3. A small metal rod

G. Bacewicz: *In una parte*

4. A fiberbrush

R. Haubenstock-Ramati: *Jeux 6 für zwei schlagzeuger*

5. Two large clothes brushes

G. Ligeti: *Nouvelles Aventures*

6. Bamboo sticks

H-U. Englemann: *Cadenza*

In his *Music for Albion Moonlight,* David Bedford calls for interior clusters on the strings to be played with a T-shaped cluster stick, very similar to that used on the percussion idiophones (see page 191).

KEYBOARD INSTRUMENTS 213

Other miscellaneous effects that involve actions within the piano interior include:

1. Stop string with fingers at varying places and with varying pressures so as to produce gong-like sounds

J. Harvey: *Inner Light III*

2. Hold a stiff piece of sandpaper against a string so that the hammer of an adjacent key hits the paper against the string

B. Childs: *Jack's New Bag*

3. Push a steel spring along the strings

R. Haubenstock-Ramati: *Jeux 6 für zwei schlagzeuger*

4. Place glass or metal balls on the strings and lightly push them

Idem

5. Rake mallets up and down the lowest strings

D. Erb: *The Rainbow Snake*

6. Slide a glass ashtray laterally across the strings

D. Eberhard: *Parody*

7. Stand several milk bottles (or glass tumblers) on the strings of one section and push them with the hand so that they wobble on the strings

D. Bedford: *Come in here child; Piano Piece 2*

8. Use a piece of rosin and one of foam plastic to simulate "white noise"

M. Shinohara: *Relations*

9. Sing, yell, speak, etc., into the piano interior with the sustaining pedal held down so that the voice is resonated by the sympathetic vibration of all the strings

B. Childs: *Jack's New Bag*
L. Ferrari: *Société II*
E. Schwartz: *Music for Napoleon and Beethoven* (Example 31)

ORGAN CLUSTERS AND KEYBOARD EFFECTS

Owing to its special construction with multiple keyboards, the organ lends itself most effectively to what might be called "transferred" clusters: the player's hand extends up from the lowest to the next higher manual, transferring the cluster formation from one to the other; or else his full arm presses down progressively on all the available manuals, in a perpendicular manner, to build up a complex sonority manual by manual. The timbres of clusters rolled in this fashion may alter progressively by means of varying registrations on the different keyboards. The organ works of Albright, Darasse, Kagel, and Ligeti, in particular, offer prime examples of this new technique.

Rolled, or glissando, clusters can be achieved on a single manual even more efficiently than on piano, celesta, or harpsichord; this is because even the slightest pressure on the organ keys makes them speak, whereas on the other instruments a weak finger pressure results in some key mechanisms not sounding the pitches.

Ordinarily, rolled and glissando clusters would be accomplished by using the flat hand, but in William Bolcom's virtuosic *Black Host* and *Hydraulis* they are to be played with the clenched fist sliding across the keys, an action also stipulated by Xavier Darasse in *Organum I*, by Alan Stout in *Study in Densities and Durations*, and by this writer in *Sonoric Fantasia No. 4*.

Among a number of recent works, some for organ alone and some for the instrument used in ensemble, requiring the specialized technique of rolled and glissando clusters, one might list:

D. Acker: *Myriaden I*
W. Albright: *Organbook II; Pneuma*
G. Cacioppo: *Holy Ghost Vacuum*
J. Druckman: *Windows*
L. Foss: *Baroque Variations*
H. W. Henze: *Sinfonia N. 6*

K. Huber: *Tenebrae*
W. Jacob: *Da Pacem*
M. Kagel: *Improvisation ajoutée*
G. Ligeti: *Volumina* (Example 47)
R. Perera: *Reverberations*

Also dependent upon the unique physical properties of the pipe or electronic organ are sustained clusters of long duration. Massed tones of diatonic or chromatic construction can be held ad infinitum by the player's hands or arms pressed down on the keys. To enable the organist to utilize clusters but at the same time to free his two hands for other matters, a "cluster rake" has been recently invented. This mechanical device is a 9" board which is placed over the keys; felt-tipped knobs, spaced off on its under surface, hold down the selected keys required in the cluster. Its use makes it possible to sustain a cluster on one manual while occupying both hands on a different keyboard. Though not specified by Mauricio Kagel in his *Improvisation ajoutée*, the cluster rake is a necessity on several of its pages.

Contemporary organists also have at their disposal a newly designed cluster weight-board, a somewhat different version of the cluster rake. This device is a heavy wooden board that fits over the entire keyboard with a perforation in it over every key, black and white; lead weights are inserted in the perforations to hold down certain keys, whether contiguous or not; see:

M. Kagel: *Improvisation ajoutée*
A. Mellnäs: *Fixations*
J. W. Morthenson: *Eternes; Pour Madame Bovary*

Example 47
György Ligeti: from *Volumina* (p. 10)

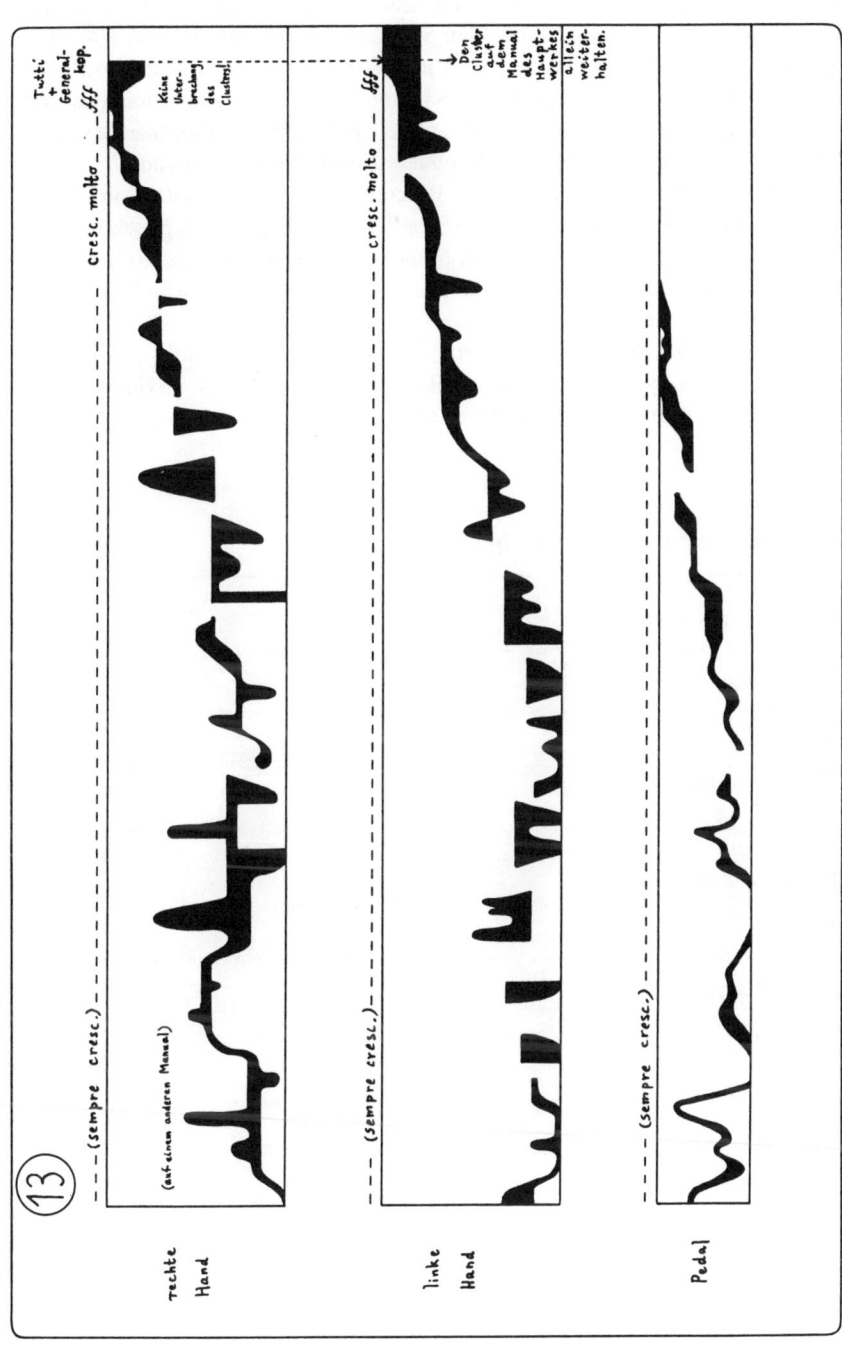

© Copyright 1973 by Henry Litolff's Verlag. Sole selling agents C. F. Peters Corporation. Reprinted by permission of the publisher.

Other works requiring the use of cluster-boards on the manuals or pedals include Schwantner's *In Aeternum II* and Alan Stout's *Study in Densities and Durations* (put in place by the organist's assistant). In *Gmeeorh* of Xenakis the boards are laid on both the manuals and the pedals by the soloist's two assistants. The work ends with a rhythmical pressing down and releasing of the cluster-boards so as to create, in the composer's words, "a tidal wave of onsets [of sound]."

Instead of a wooden cluster-board, Bolcom substituted a plastic yardstick in *Hydraulis* (Example 48). If this object is sufficiently flexible, the player can vary the pressure on the manual over a part of the total compass. This action, it should be noted, works only on a tracker or double-action keyboard, which allows for gradations of intensity.

Lacking either a cluster rake or weight-board, organists can hold down certain preselected keys by inserting thin pencil tips between the keys; obviously, sufficient time must be allowed the player to accomplish this action (as in Niccolo

Example 48
William Bolcom: from *Hydraulis* (p. 20)

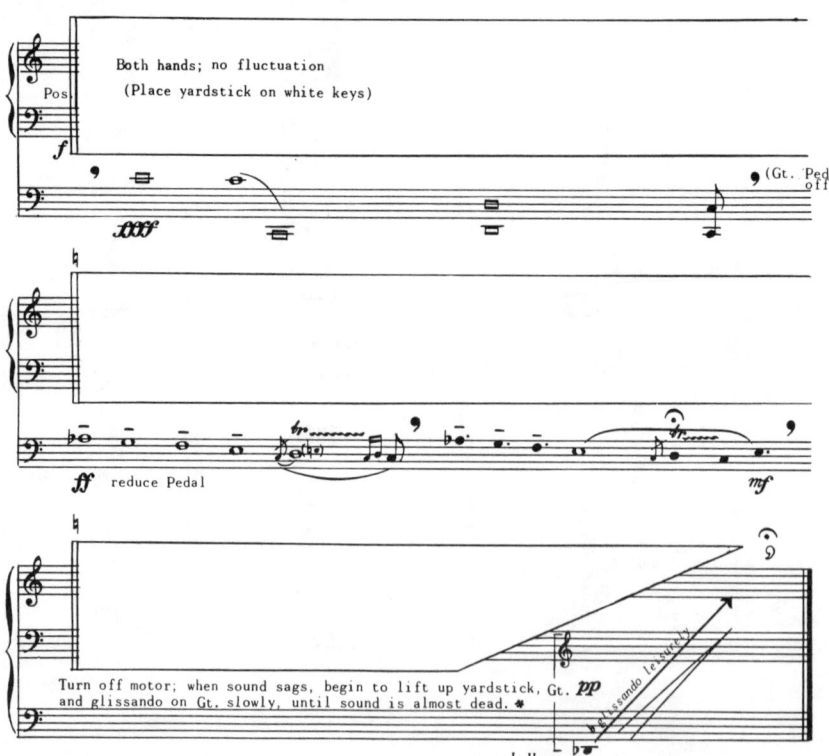

© Copyright 1976 by Edward B. Marks Music Company. International Copyright Secured. All rights reserved. Used by permission.

Castiglioni's *Sinfonie guerriere e amorose*), or else the preparation may be done by an assistant (see William Albright's *Organbook II,* for example).

A more limited employment of individual key cluster-weights appears in Albright's *Organbook II,* Daniel Pinkham's *When the Morning Stars Sang Together,* and my own *Galactic Novae.* As surrogate for either a cluster-board or key weights, clusters are designated to be played with the full arm of the player laid across the keyboard; such a requirement is to be found in Helmut Eder's *Vox Media* and Jan Morthenson's *Farewell.*

A unique manner of playing cluster tremoli, on a single manual or between two keyboards, is exploited in Xavier Darasse's *Organum I:* aptly and picturesquely called a "karate tremolo," the action calls for the two hands to be held upright, thumbs raised, the edges of the hands literally chopping on the keyboards. Visually, the technique provides an added element of theatricality to any performance.

An unconventional keyboard effect, strictly limited to pipe organs having old-fashioned tracker action, requires the keys to be depressed partially rather than fully. This action results in the gradual emergence of sound, rather like depressing the keys of a parlor organ (harmonium) and then slowly beginning to pump the pedal. Arne Mellnäs specified this effect in his *Fixations.*

REGISTRATION DEVICES

Ordinarily, organ registrations are either preset or are changed during playing in carefully designated sequences or patterns. An outstanding example of patterned registration changes occurs in the *Organum I* of Darasse: one hand sustains a cluster-chord on a stipulated manual while the other alternately adds and cancels certain stops according to a very precise rhythmic sequence shown on a supplementary staff.

An increasing number of avant-garde composers of organ music are requesting random and unpatterned registrational changes, with the selection of individual stops on any one manual or on the pedal keyboard left solely to chance or to the inspiration of the moment. Consult the following works:

W. Albright: *Organbook I; Pneuma*
W. Bolcom: *Black Host*
N. Castiglioni: *Sinfonia guerriere e amorose*
R. Felciano: *Ekagrata; Glossolalia*
A. Janson: *Canon*

M. Kagel: *Improvisation ajoutée*
G. Ligeti: *Volumina*
R. Perera: *Reverberations*
A. Stout: *Study in Densities and Durations*

The organist himself is customarily responsible for changing registrations, whether planned or random, but several recent works for organ require the services of assistants to handle the changes of stops and couplers while both hands of the player are engaged on the manuals, as in:

W. Albright: *Organbook II; Pneuma*
X. Darasse: *Organum I*
L. Foss: *Etudes for Organ*
M. Kagel: *Improvisation ajoutée*
A. Mellnäs: *Fixations*

Restricted to the draw-stop type of console is Alfred Janson's directive in *Canon* to pull the stops out gradually; this action causes the individual stops to be activated with a little spurt of sound, an effect also prominent in Albright's *Organbook II*.

MISCELLANEOUS EFFECTS

Either the organist or an assistant can create a "coupler tremolo"; this is accomplished by rapidly moving one of the 16', 8', 4', or 2' manual or pedal couplers off and on while sound is being produced on the affected keyboard or on the pedals. The result is a continual adding and canceling of unison, octave, and double-octave registration from other manuals. This action is most easily handled on an instrument with coupler tabs; they have merely to be flicked up or down rather than pulled out and pushed in, as required by old-fashioned stopknobs. *Fixations* of Arne Mellnäs is a work that makes extensive use of this technique, as does my *Sonoric Fantasia No. 4*.

Assistants are also occasionally called upon to play on manuals or pedals while the organist's two hands and feet are occupied, a performance requirement appearing in Darasse's *Organum I*.

Another novel organ technique, one that affects dynamics, is rapidly opening and closing the swell or choir shades; this action on the performer's part obviously requires that one foot is free to operate the requisite shutter pedals. As the swell and choir pedals are usually next to each other, they may be opened or closed simultaneously with one foot. Albright's *Organbook II* provides excellent examples of this idiomatic technique.

A final device, and one mechanically limited to electrically activated instruments, is the switching on or off of the motor while the manual keys and/or pedals are depressed. In the first instance the sound comes on with a sudden explosive spurt; in the second it fades away slowly as the wind is emptied from the pipes. Composers who have relied on this unique idiomatic effect include:

W. Albright: *Pneuma*
C. Cardew: *The Great Learning, Paragraph 1*
W. Jacob: *Da Pacem*
A. Janson: *Canon*
G. Ligeti: *Volumina*
A. Mellnäs: *Fixations*
J. W. Morthenson: *Eternes; Pour Madame Bovary*
K. Penderecki: *St. Luke Passion*
G. Read: *Sonoric Fantasia No. 4*
I. Yun: *Dimensionen*

In an article on new concepts of organ technique, Leonard Raver (see Bibliography) suggests experimentation with revoicing various of the organ pipes as well as making adjustments in the wind pressure. Both procedures, he says, "could radically alter and expand the sounds we now expect to hear from the organ." To date, however, no instances of either experimentation have come to light in the recent organ works surveyed.

Other than amplification, percussive blows on the instrument frame, and various tone-cluster techniques—all of which have been discussed—there is little else in the way of special effects that can be applied idiomatically to either the celesta or the harpsichord. Consequently, the score-reader will find few examples of these two instruments used in unorthodox ways.

ACCORDION TECHNIQUES

The free-bass accordion is a much neglected, not to say a much misunderstood and underestimated, modern instrument. In essence a miniaturized and portable reed organ, it is capable of impressive sustaining power and richness of tone and possesses a wide and flexible dynamic range. Furthermore, the free-bass accordion can produce a number of sonic effects that clearly ought to endear it to innovative composers and orchestrators. For example: in addition to chromatic manual and diminished-seventh chord button keyboard glissandi (described on page 51) and a number of unique percussive effects (see page 91), the accordion can create perceptible timbre changes when the registration switches are depressed while the manual keys are held down. Amplitude vibratos of different speeds and intensities can be produced by shaking the instrument with the hand or body while playing, and sustained pitches can be tremoloed by rapid agitation of the bellows, known to players as a "bellows shake."

The several works listed below will repay study as to the idiomatic uses of the new accordion techniques and their specialized notations:

S. Dolin: *Sonata for Accordian*
T. Lundquist: *Metamorphoses; Partita Piccola*
O. Schmidt: *Toccata No. 1 for Accordian*

MODIFIED KEYBOARD INSTRUMENTS

In recent years several unusual developments have taken place in the design of certain keyboard instruments. One is the invention of the French concert pianist, Monique de la Bruchollerie, who designed a curved, or crescent-shaped, piano keyboard that has five extra notes at the bottom and ten extra keys at the top. The inventor also proposed constructing the loud and damper pedals as curved bars extending the entire length of the keyboard, thus making it easier for the player to manipulate them during performance. In addition, plans were made to incorporate an electronic system whereby one could create intervals and chords up to twelve notes by striking only one key. It is presently not known if this unorthodox instrument is actually extant or still exists only in theory.

Another proposed modified keyboard is called the "Carmi-chord," after its inventor, the Israeli musician Avner Carmi. This is an ordinary upright piano with an altered soundboard, designed to produce a timbral cross between the piano and the harpsichord. Its appearance in any recent work is likewise an unknown.

Yet one more modified acoustic piano is the newly-invented Yamaha Midi-Grand, an instrument intended to overcome the inherent inability of the standard model to prolong a tone to the same degree as can an organ. Various tone generators linked to the instrument make this possible. Unlike the two previously mentioned inventions, this instrument has had a number of new compositions specifically written for it by today's composers.

It can be maintained without argument that the prepared piano of John Cage and other contemporaries constitutes a hybrid keyboard instrument (see previous discussion on page 26). As the prepared piano sound is a close simulation of the Indonesian gamelan, Richard Bunger has suggested that a prepared piano be called a "Klaviergamelan." But whatever one chooses to call it, unlike the recent modifications just discussed, the prepared piano has firmly established itself as a highly viable component of experimental twentieth-century music.

Serious contemporary composers, on the other hand, will have little if any use for certain newly manufactured electronic keyboards—the Yamaha Disklavier or the "Cairo" keyboard, for instance—which are designed solely for the convenience of amateurs. Capable of simulating any number of legitimate instrumental timbres, plus such esoterica as bird calls, sirens, and approximations of dripping water, these electronic contrivances offer little incentive to the creative composer of our time.

It also does not lie within the scope of this survey to describe or evaluate the plethora of homemade and highly personalized instruments constructed and used by amateurs. As none of these have entered into the mainstream of today's serious music, there is little point in describing any of them. In the years to come it is possible that some—perhaps even many—will evolve sufficiently to become viable additions to the arsenal of conventional instruments familiar to all composers. As always, time will provide the ultimate answer.

13

STRINGS

New string techniques cover a wide variety of procedures, from variants of traditional bowing and fingering patterns, pizzicato, and *sul ponticello,* to current experimentation with hybrid instruments. Though it cannot be maintained that the strings now occupy the same exalted position in the hierarchy of instruments they enjoyed in previous periods, they have by no means been relegated to positions of inferiority in the aggregate of sound-producers available to the contemporary composer. The vanguardist may not use his strings as lyric members of his ensembles, but he cannot yet do without them—as the following pages will corroborate.

BOWING DEVICES

Experimental scores of the past several decades have displayed new and patently radical methods of employing the bow to produce string tone. The procedures discussed below, however, all have direct antecedents in past practice. The "newness" is more a question of degree than of substance, as there are, after all, only so many ways in which a bow can be held by the hand, moved with the arm, and pressed against a string.

A tight and nonrhythmicized bow-tremolo is perhaps the most prevalent among the newer bowing techniques. It has been requisitioned by far too many recent orchestrators to cite each score individually, but a glance at almost any one of Krzysztof Penderecki's orchestral scores will show an extensive use of the device. Parenthetically, this composer's notation, given below, is the clearest and most concise of all the many symbols devised and currently used:

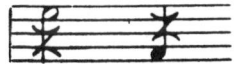

An equally ubiquitous score directive today tells the players to change bow direction at will on sustained notes of long duration. In other words, uniform down-bows and up-bows are to be avoided as much as possible, thus nullifying simultaneous accent.

In the remaining contemporary bowing variants to be catalogued, the player must accomplish a number of unusual actions, such as: exert exaggerated force on the string by pressing the bow so heavily, with a twisting, grinding motion, that no precise tone but only a strident, creaking, or rasping noise is heard. This stipulation may be seen in the following works:

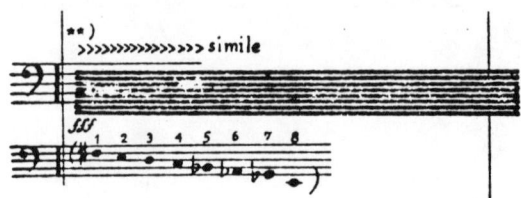

R. Barrett: *Anatomy*
D. Bedford: *Five for String Quartet*
W. Benson: *The Dream Net*
M. von Biel: *1.Quartett*
G. Cacioppo: *Time on Time in Miracles*
J. Casken: *Music for a Tawny-Gold Day*
A. Corghi: *Stereofonie X4*
G. Crumb: *Echoes of Time and the River*
J. Deak: *Color Studies for Contrabass* (Example 49)
J. Dillon: *Uberschreiten*
J. Druckman: *Incenters; String Quartet No. 2*
D. Erb: *Concerto for Solo Percussionist; String Trio*
L. Foss: *Orpheus*
V. Globokar: *Accord*
H. Gorecki: *Canti strumentali; Elementi*
C. Halffter: *Fibonaciana*
J. Harvey: *Persephone Dream*
R. Haubenstock-Ramati: *Multiple 5*
W. Heider: *Plaket*

H-J. Hespos: *Pasagen*
G. Heussenstamm: *Pentalogue*
J. M. Horvath: *Redundanz 2*
K. Huber: *Tenebrae*
M. Ishii: *Aphorismen*
M. Kagel: *Match; Sonant*
R. Kayn: *Galaxis*
M. Kelemen: *Abecedarium*
A. Lanza: *Eidesis II*
H. U. Lehmann: *Sonata "da chiesa"*
G. Ligeti: *Nouvelles Aventures*
F. Miroglio: *Réfractions; Tremplins*
P. Nørgård: *Symphony No. 2*
K. Penderecki: *Capriccio for Violin; De Natura Sonoris (I)*
R. Reynolds: *The Promises of Darkness; Quick are the Mouths of Earth*
G. Rochberg: *Tableaux*
W. Szalonek: *1+1+1+1; Les Sons*
K. E. Welin: *Nr. 3-1961*
Y. Yannay: *preFIX-FIX-sufFIX*

An interesting variant of this technique is the directive in Jack Fortner's *Quartet:* gradually raise the left-hand fingers from the strings to a position that would ordinarily produce a harmonic; at the same time, increase the bowing pressure so that recognizable pitches disintegrate into a grinding noise. On the other hand, Lejaren Hiller directs the string players in his fifth quartet to "produce a rasping grating noise by slowly dragging the bow across the strings while

Example 49
Jon Deak: from *Color Studies for Contrabass* (p. 2)

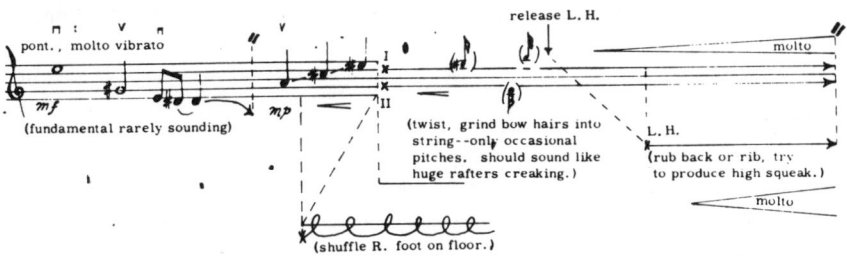

© Copyright MEDIA PRESS, 1969. All rights reserved. Used by permission. Media Press Box 895, Champaign, Illinois, 61820.

at the same time damping the string by pressing down on it to suppress its vibrations." And in *Charisma,* Xenakis directs the cellist to "grind on the bridge with the bow," which produces a "brutal" sound according to the composer, a description one is not inclined to question. A further variant of this action instructs the player to press down on the strings with the left hand, moving the fingers up and down. At the same time, as Tison Street puts it in his *String Quartet 1972,* "the bow is made to come down on the strings in a staccato stroke so heavy that instead of notes one hears merely a 'crunch' sound."

Other twentieth-century bowing techniques require the player to:

1. Use a rebounding bow-stroke in which pairs of notes are taken in rapid alternate up- and down-bows; known to string players as "feather bowing" or "drum stroke bowing," this technique is actually a species of ricochet (*jeté, saltando*)

B. Rands: *Étendre*
I. Stravinsky: *Le Sacre du Printemps* (see Violin I, No. 24–28)

2. Barely touch the bow-tip to the string in a sort of "lifting off" motion

W. Sydeman: *Texture Studies for Orchestra*

3. Bounce the bow on the string, at the same time keeping the bow-hair tight and elastic by pressing it at the nut with the thumb

W. Szalonek: *Concertino per flauto ed orchestra da camera; Les Sons*

4. Bounce the tip of the bow along the length of a string, a left-hand finger lightly dampening the string near the nut as though producing a harmonic. On violin and viola the bow direction is from near the bridge to close to the finger on the string; on cello (and doublebass) it is from the end of the fingerboard (below the left-hand fingers) toward the bridge

M. Powell: *Filigree Setting* (Example 23, Violin I)

5. "Scratch" the string, using up-bow at the frog, with maximum pressure. Ordinarily, up-bow is taken at the middle or the tip of the bow, where the player has

maximum control of his arm movement. To request up-bow starting at the frog gives little room in which to maneuver and creates problems of bow control, but the rough and strained quality inherent in this manner of attacking the string is precisely what the avant-gardists want

S. Hodkinson: *Fresco*
K. Huber: *Tenebrae*

6. Stifle a note by stopping the bow "dead" on the string, while at the same time pressing a finger down on an adjacent pitch on the same string; this technique was invented by Howard Colf, cellist in Lukas Foss's improvisation ensemble, and used in

J. Druckman: *Incenters; String Quartet No. 2*
R. Felciano: *Crasis*

L. Foss: *Echoi; Time Cycle*
W. Sydeman: *Projections I*

7. Scrape, scratch, or glide the bow lengthwise (vertically) along the string

W. Albright: *Danse Macabre*
N. Castiglioni: *Eine kleine Weihnachtsmusik*
A. Curran: *Home-made*
J. Deak: *Color Studies for Contrabass*

L. Hiller: *String Quartet No. 5*
A. Hrisanide: *Volumes*
M. Kelemen: *Abecedarium*
A. Mellnäs: *Aura*
F. Miroglio: *Projections; Réfractions*

8. Begin a down-bow at the normal distance from the bridge, gradually sliding to and over the fingerboard as the bow-stroke approaches the tip; the player then quickly and lightly returns to the bridge area with an up-bow stroke. This technique, called "circular bowing," is more feasible on cello and doublebass than on violin and viola, owing to greater string length

STRINGS

M. von Biel: *1. Quartett*
P. Chihara: *Logs; Sequoia for String Quartet and Tape*
J. Deak: *Color Studies for Contrabass*
A. Silsbee: *Spirals*

9. Attack the string up-bow, the bow then moving down, rather than across, the string until the frog is reached, then returning up the string with a rapid down-bow motion; termed "eliptical bowing," the effect is possible only on cello and doublebass

J. Deak: *Color Studies for Contrabass*

10. Bow on the string(s) with a rotating movement

F. Miroglio: *Projections; Réfractions*

11. Bow *col legno tratto* so that an almost inaudible "whispering" scrape is heard

N. Castiglioni: *Eine kleine Weihnachtsmusik*
A. Curran: *Home-made*
A. Mellnäs: *Aura*
P. Nørgård: *Symphony No. 2*

12. Cover strings gently with the left hand; draw bow close to the hand, producing a wooden sound

C. Halffter: *Pourquoi für Streicher*

13. Bow as close as possible to the left-hand fingers on the string(s), but on the normal side of the fingers

L. Bassett: *Music for Cello and Piano*
M. Kagel: *Match für drei Spieler*

14. Bow *behind* the left-hand fingers stopping the strings (on violin or viola), or *above* the fingers on cello and doublebass

S. Cervetti: *Zinctum*
G. Crumb: *Eleven Echoes of Autumn; Songs, Drones, and Refrains of Death*
J. Deak: *Color Studies for Contrabass*
J. Fortner: *Quartet*
B. Rands: *Étendre*

15. Stop the E' with just room enough for the bow between the fingers and the bridge

D. Erb: *Concerto for Solo Percussionist*

16. Bow between the tuning pegs and the fingerboard (very near to the nut)

S. Cervetti: *Zinctum*

17. Bow near the tuning pegs, on the "wrong" side of the left-hand fingers, the instrument (violin and viola) held like a viol and the bow also held in the manner of playing viols

G. Crumb: *Black Angels*

18. Bow *underneath* the strings, just in front of the bridge;[1] this is most feasible, of course, on cello or doublebass

B. Childs: *Jack's New Bag; Nonet*
P. Méfano: *Lignes*
K. Penderecki: *Capriccio per Siegfried Palm*
W. Peterson: *Trialogue*

P. Phillips: *Sonata for String Bass*
G. Read: *Diabolic Dialogue*
R. Roxbury: *Aria for Cello and Piano*
G. Schuller: *Sonata Serenata*

19. Play with the bow-hairs quite slack, which produces a rather pale and tenuous tone

G. Crumb: *Eleven Echoes of Autumn*

20. Draw bow across the strings without producing any sound

C. Halffter: *Pourquoi für Streicher*

21. Strike or tap with the bow-hair on the string(s) behind the bridge

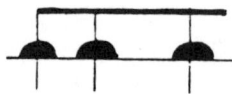

L. Berio: *Epifanie*
S. Cervetti: *Zinctum* (Example 52)
P. Chihara: *Driftwood*
R. Gerhard: *Epithalamium*
A. Ginastera: *Bomarzo Cantata*
L. Harrison: *Suite for Symphonic Strings*
K. Huber: *Tenebrae*
K. Husa: *String Quartet No. 3* (Example 3)

A. Lanza: *Cuarteto V para cuerdas*
S. Matsushita: *Fresque sonore*
A. Mellnäs: *Per caso*
K. M-Nazar: *Variazioni concertanti*
K. Penderecki: *Fluorescences; Quartetto per archi No. 2*
A. de la Vega: *Segments for Violin and Piano; Structures for Piano and String Quartet*

22. Bow on the body of the instrument (edge of the fingerboard, the belly, or side), producing a faint, breathlike sound

C. Alsina: *Trio 1967* (Example 32)
V. Globokar: *Accord*
C. Halffter: *Fibonaciana*
K. Penderecki: *Fluorescences*

R. M. Schafer: *Requiems for the Party-Girl*
W. Sydeman: *Texture Studies*
I. Xenakis: *Eridanos*

23. Bow on the tailpiece; on the cello and doublebass this produces a low groaning noise

M. von Biel: *1. Quartett*
E. Bujarski: *Kinoth*
B. Conyngham: *String Quartet*
G. Darvas: *Sectio Aurea*
J. Deak: *Color Studies for Contrabass*
R. L. Finney: *Percussion Concerto*
R. Gerhard: *Concerto for 8*

V. Globokar: *Accord*
G. Heussenstamm: *Pentalogue*
M. Ishii: *Aphorismen*
P. Oliveros: *Trio*
K. Penderecki: *Capriccio per Siegfried Palm; Threne*
W. Szalonek: *Les Sons*

24. Bow on the string behind the tailpiece, which produces a very shrill and penetrating tone

F. Miroglio: *Réfractions*

25. Bow on the top or side of the mute, which is placed in the normal position over the bridge

V. Globokar: *Accord*
C. Halffter: *Fibonaciana; Pourquoi für Streicher*
T. Marco: *Quasi un Requiem*

In her *Viola Concerto,* Thea Musgrave directs the orchestral string players to change bow direction randomly, as well as to quickly alternate down and up bows on a held note, but not as a measured tremolo. Another curious directive: Michael von Biel in his first string quartet has the cellist place a doublebass mute on the strings between the bridge and the end of the fingerboard, and must alternate playing on the upper and the lower part of the strings.

Although no instances of its use have been so far unearthed, it is possible on the violin and viola to bow in the peg box of the middle two strings, creating a soft, high, indeterminate pitch.

One final bowing action: it is possible to bow on the floor-peg of either the cello or the doublebass, an effect called for in Kelemen's *Abecedarium.*

It does not seem possible that further bowing variants will—or can—be devised by our avant-garde instrumentators, yet one would be rash, indeed, to make any firm prophecy. Tomorrow's new scores will doubtless handsomely repudiate even this momentary questioning.

SUL PONTICELLO VARIANTS

Until about the end of the first quarter of the present century, composers utilized only one basic form of *sul ponticello.* Today there are several variant methods of employing this useful device, such as playing on the bridge itself, or on the short length of string between the bridge and the tailpiece. Each method produces a perceptible difference in timbre. When the bow is kept as close to the bridge as possible, without actually touching it, the resultant tone is dead and nasal. Although this is the manner in which authentic *sul ponticello* should be played, few players observe it without special directives such as one finds in

Klaus Huber's *Alveare vernat* and in the *Filigree Setting* and *Two Prayer Settings* of Mel Powell. Quite frequently the stipulation is coupled with a request to play nonvibrato, which further enhances the disembodied color of *sul ponticello*. William Sydeman is very specific in his *For Double Bass Alone* in designating the precise distance from the bridge the player must bow—at least one-half to one inch.

Playing directly over the bridge (on the string) results in a buzzing sound rather than any identifiable pitch. Some of the composers who have asked for this effect include:

B. Bartolozzi: *Quartetto per archi*
D. Bedford: *Five for String Quintet; That White and Radiant Legend*
L. Berio: *Sincronie*
M. von Biel: *1. Quartett*
A. Boucourechliev: *Archipel II*
S. Cervetti: *Zinctum* (Example 52)
G. Darvas: *Sectio Aurea*
J. Deak: *Color Studies for Contrabass*
V. Globokar: *Accord*
H-J. Hespos: *Passagen*
A. Hrisanide: *Volumes*
M. Kagel: *Match für drei Spieler*

R. Kayn: *Galaxis*
W. Kilar: *Riff 62*
M. Kopelent: *3. Quartetto*
A. Lanza: *Cuarteto V para cuerdas*
B. J. Layton: *Divertimento*
G. Ligeti: *Aventures; Cello Concerto*
T. Musgrave: *Viola Concerto*
K. Penderecki: *Fluorescences*
R. Reynolds: *Quick are the Mouths of Earth*
W. Sydeman: *Projections I*
E. Valcarcel: *Dicotomia III*

Playing near to the bridge, violins and violas in Benjamin Britten's *Les Illuminations* are to create "a fanfare-like effect, simulating trumpets." Whether the massed strings in *Les petits métiers* of Manuel Rosenthal are to employ *sul ponticello* in order to sound "like an accordion" is not stipulated by the composer.

A few composers have also directed their string players to strike the strings directly over the bridge with the heel of the bow, producing a rough and rasping noise:

B. Bartolozzi: *Quartetto per archi*
S. Cervetti: *Zinctum* (Example 52)
J. Harvey: *Inner Light III*

A. Lanza: *Cuarteto V para cuerdas*
T. Takemitsu: *Waves*

It is possible, although rather awkward, to bow on the bridge of the cello or doublebass without touching the strings, accomplished by the player's holding the bow parallel to the strings (requested in Roger Reynolds' *Quick are the Mouths of Earth*). On all the string members the players may bow on the side of the bridge; on violin and viola this manner of bowing creates a faint hissing, while on cello and doublebass it produces a kind of high-pitched groan. Refer to:

STRINGS

M. von Biel: *1. Quartett*
D. Cope: *Angel's Camp II* (Example 50)
J. Deak: *Color Studies for Contrabass: Surrealist Studies*
M. Kelemen: *Olifant*
M. Mitrea-Celarianu: *Seth*
K. Penderecki: *The Devils of Loudun; Polymorphia*
B. Rands: *Memo 1* (Example 30)
K. Stockhausen: *Mixtur*

Example 50
David Cope: from *Angel's Camp II* (p. 6)

© Copyright 1971 by Seesaw Music Corp., New York. Reproduced by permission.

Playing with the bow-hair on the strings behind the bridge has become one of the most ubiquitous bowing requirements to be found in current vanguard scores. No precise pitch is obtainable, of course, on the very short length of string in that area, but only an indefinite squeaking sound. The glassy edge to the sounds normally associated with *sul ponticello* are thus even further magnified. A casual perusal of almost any score of the Polish avant-gardists, in particular those of Penderecki, will amply illustrate the technique.

A commonly utilized facet of this new instrumental procedure is to arpeggiate the bow across the four strings (or over only two or three) between the bridge and tailpiece, creating a rustling metallic susurration, as in Hans Werner Henze's *Sinfonia N. 6* (Example 51). Although Penderecki must be accorded credit for inventing the following pictorial and highly pragmatic notation:

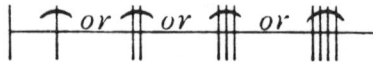

the device is used almost excessively in various of his scores. One should be well aware that this unique technique can rather easily wear out its welcome.

There is little room to maneuver the bow on the strings behind the bridge, yet Michael von Biel in his first string quartet specifies that the player's bow should operate closer to the tailpiece in one instance and nearer to the bridge in another. On cello and doublebass, of course, the player has considerably more string length back of the bridge and thus is able to make a greater distinction between keeping the bow close to the bridge area or to the tailpiece itself.

A further refinement of beyond-the-bridge playing is stipulated in Sydney Hodkinson's orchestral *Fresco:* the bow is to be gradually moved from close to or actually atop the bridge proper to behind it. The reverse effect is also feasible, the bow moving from near the tailpiece to or beyond the bridge on the fingerboard side; so far this stipulation has eluded discovery in any contemporary score.

Curious directives are almost commonplace in avant-garde works, but one of the most intriguing appears in the Israeli composer Yizhak Sadai's *Nuances:* the violins are told to play behind the bridge with a pocket comb—an effect that is quite impossible to describe.

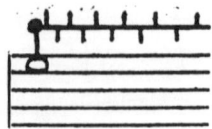

Directly related to these *sul ponticello* refinements just described are the techniques of bouncing the bow, *saltato,* or *jeté,* from over the fingerboard

STRINGS   231

Example 51
Hans Werner Henze: from *Sinfonia N. 6* **(p. 81)**

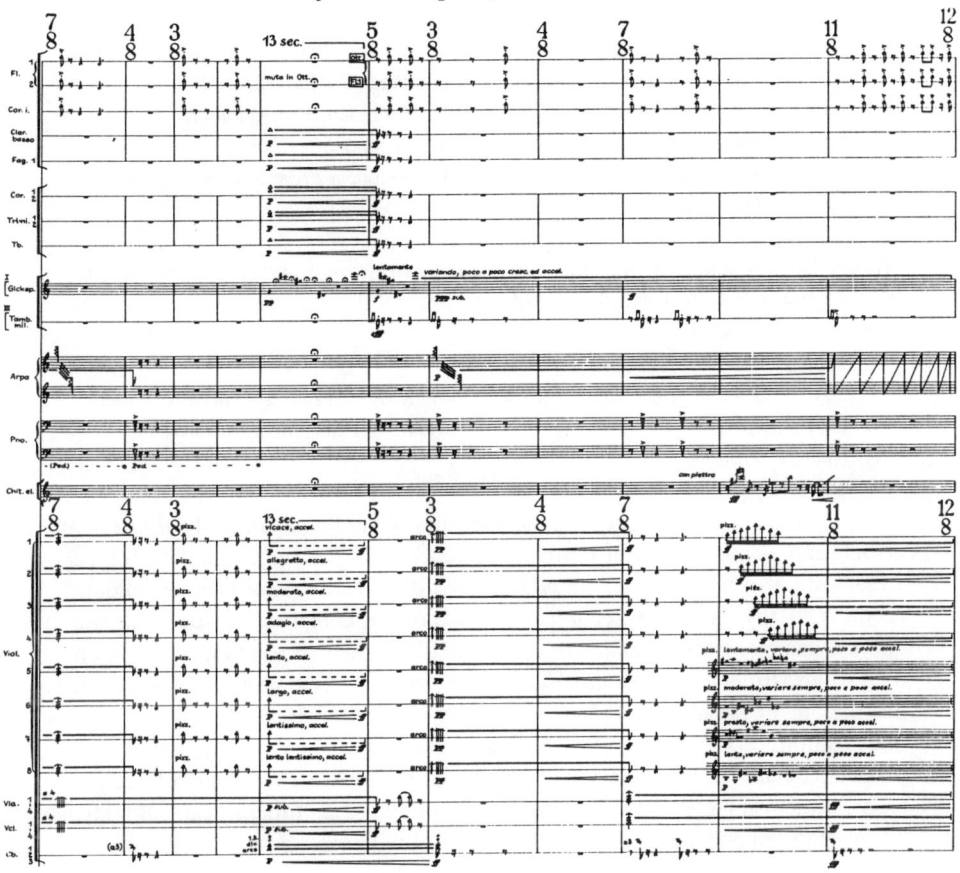

© B. Schott's Soehne, Mainz, 1970. All rights reserved. Used by permission of European American Music Distributors Corporation, sole U.S. and Canadian agent for B. Schott's Soehne.

toward or literally over the bridge, or in the reverse direction, from bridge to fingerboard. Some of the recent works requesting these allied techniques include:

I. Anhalt: *Foci* (Example 20)
L. Berio: *Sincronie*
B. Childs: *Nonet*
M. Colgrass: *As Quiet As*
J. Druckman: *Incenters; String Quartet No. 2*
M. Kopelent: *3. Quartetto*
R. Reynolds: *Quick are the Mouths of Earth*

Also the bow can be made to move slowly, often in tremolo, from the bridge area to over the fingerboard, close to the left-hand fingers on the strings; see:

L. Bassett: *Music for Cello and Piano*
E. Brown: *Available Forms 2; String Quartet*
L. Foss: *Elytres*
R. Haubenstock-Ramati: *Séquences*
M. Kagel: *Heterophonie*

G. Ligeti: *Aventures; Cello Concerto*
G. Read: *Symphony No. 3*
W. Sydeman: *Projections I*
V. Wagenheim: *Klangspiel I*
L. Widdoes: *From a Time of Snow*

The reverse procedure—moving with the bow from high on the fingerboard, or from normal position, toward the bridge or beyond it—is equally feasible and as frequently requested:

J. Cage: *26'1.1499" for a String Player*
D. Erb: *Basspiece*
R. Hannay: *Fantôme*

M. Kagel: *Sexteto de cuerdas; Sonant*
R. M. Schafer: *String Quartet*

Rapid-fire alternations between the extremes of *sul ponticello* and *sul tasto*—or between string attacks in normal position and in the fingerboard or bridge areas—are also feasible, though admittedly difficult of control. The technique, needless to say, is highly regarded by our present composers. This coloristic concept has also been extended to comprise all manners of sound production on the various stringed instruments. Hence, one frequently finds notational or verbal instructions to the player to alternate rapidly between arco techniques—in normal position, on the bridge, over the fingerboard, in harmonics, and so on—and pizzicato (snap, behind the bridge, with the nail, glissandi, and the like) and *col legno,* either on the strings, the tailpiece, or other areas of the instrument body. These requirements are well illustrated in the following works:

E. Brown: *String Quartet*
D. Erb: *Concerto for Brass and Orchestra*
S. Fisher: *Concert Piece*
H. Lazarof: *Koncordia for String Orchestra*

D. Martino: *Cinque Frammenti; Triple Concerto*
B. Rands: *Wildtrack 1*
T. Takemitsu: *Green*

In Rand's *Memo 1* for solo doublebass (Example 30), the composer has included a pictogram of the instrument bridge on which the constantly changing position of the bow is shown.

An exaggerated *sul ponticello* action in which the player presses the bowhair against the mute in its usual position atop the bridge is a technical feature of Jacob Druckman's second string quartet. Not only is the timbre drastically altered by this action but the pitch is obscured as well.

FINGERING EFFECTS

To make a virtue out of a necessity is a maxim that often applies to avant-garde instrumentational experimentation. A clear case in point is the utilization of string instrument fingering action without the customary accompanying bow-strokes. In other words, the player is asked to finger audibly a series of notated pitches (or to follow the contour of a sequence of approximate pitches suggested by a series of note-stems minus note-heads). In either case, the bow is not brought into play on the strings. The aural result of this action is a faint and delicate rustling, a percussive quality both illusive and provocative. A great many composers have requested this technique, among them the following:

W. Albright: *Danse Macabre*
T. Antoniou: *Jeux for Cello and Strings*
D. Bedford: *Five for String Quintet;*
  That White and Radiant Legend
A. Boucourechliev: *Archipel II*
F. Cerha: *Relazioni fragili*
B. Childs: *Nonet*
G. Crumb: *Madrigals—I*
M. Davidovsky: *Synchronisms No. 3*
A. Dobrowolski: *Musik für Streichen
  und 4 Bläsergruppen*
J. Fortner: *Quartet*
L. Foss: *Baroque Variations; Echoi*
S. Hodkinson: *Fresco*
A. Hrisanide: *Volumes*

M. Kagel: *Match; Sonant*
E. Karkoschka: *Quattrologe*
M. Kelemen: *Changeant; Surprise*
G. Ligeti: *Apparitions; Ramifications
  for Double String Orchestra*
F. Miroglio: *Tremplins*
K. Penderecki: *Capriccio per Siegfried
  Palm; Emanationen*
G. Read: *Villon*
D. Reck: *Blues and Screamer*
R. Reynolds: *Quick are the Mouths of
  Earth: Shadowed Narrative*
W. Sydeman: *Texture Studies*
G. B. Wilson: *Concatenations*
I. Yun: *String Quartet No. 3*

Equally effective in sound is an audible roll or tremolo on one string with two left-hand fingers, as in:

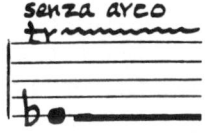

N. Castiglioni: *A Solemn Music II*
A. Hrisanide: *Volumes*
M. Kupferman: *Infinities 24*

E. Kurtz: *Improvisation for Contrabass*
K. Penderecki: *Quartetto per archi*
B. Schäffer: *Scultura; String Quartet*

In Charles Whittenberg's *Conversations for Solo Doublebass,* the composer specifies a finger-roll on an open string gradually going into a fingered pitch: two fingers alternately trill on the string while a third finger slowly presses down on it.

A drumlike roll using from two to four fingers on two adjacent strings is most feasible on the larger stringed instruments, cello and doublebass, as, for instance, in:

G. Crumb: *Madrigals—I*
B. A. Zimmermann: *Sonate für Cello Solo*

Loud fingering action can also be combined with certain bowing procedures: in *Blues and Screamer,* for example, David Reck stipulates that the bow be used very lightly, producing a barely audible tone while at the same time the left-hand fingers strongly finger the designated pitches. A more delicately articulated fingering, coupled with very light bowing pressure, is several times requested by Boguslaw Schäffer in his *Two Pieces* for violin and piano. Trilling on two strings with a heavy, hammering finger action is stipulated by Penderecki in *Emanationen.*

Another ramification of this technique is to gradually stop the bow action but continue the perceptible fingerings of the notated pitches (as in Ligeti's cello concerto). Ordinarily, the fingertips are used for audible fingerings, but the nails may also be specified. In György Ligeti's *Aventures,* for example, the composer instructs the solo doublebass player: "With the fingernails travel delicately, very slowly and aperiodically along the strings."

A finger-roll is combined with *sul ponticello* bowing on the same string in Barry Brosch's *Prolations,* and in *Valentine* of Jacob Druckman the solo bassist is asked to bring a finger down on an open string so hard that the string resonates.

In Szalonek's curiously titled *1+1+1+1* (a string quartet), a trilling finger is to drop heavily on the bow, creating a sudden grating sound. The composer also directs the player to press on the string lightly as though to produce a harmonic, but is to carefully avoid touching the string nodes. Two additional fingering actions: a distorted sound requested by Ann Silsbee in her *Spirals* is achieved by a progressively wide vibrato and varying finger pressure, from heavy to light, on the string. The solo cellist in Antoniou's *Jeux for Cello and Strings* is asked at one point to finger loosely on the string, producing a soft quasi-harmonic effect.

Several unorthodox fingering actions are featured in Luciano Berio's virtuoso *Sequenza VI* for solo viola (and related *Chemins II*). For example: the fingers are to be shifted randomly in both a wide and a minimal distance from the necessary position to sound a given four-note structure, creating a highly unstable frequency situation. For wide shiftings the finger-slides must, of course, be in the same direction on the four strings; for minute shiftings the slides may actually be in contrary motion. A further directive in Berio's score is to alternate as quickly as possible the normal and the harmonic positions of the fingers on all four strings; that is, to press down firmly with the fingers and then to raise them so that they only lightly touch on the strings, as at a harmonic node.

Other unorthodox fingering effects include the directive in Josef Horvath's *Redundanz 2:* "Place the finger lightly on the string, as when playing a harmonic. The noise predominates, so that the fingerings need not necessarily be entirely precise." Ligeti tells his string players in *Apparitions* not to put the finger all the way down on the string, and to draw the bow without any pressure. Michael von Biel says to lightly touch the strings with the fingers (in his first string quartet) while slowly rotating the bow over the four strings.

In *The Seventh Trumpet,* Donald Erb directs the string players to finger with the left hand between the fingerboard and the bridge while plucking the strings over the fingerboard—a reversal of the normal relative positions of left- and right-hand fingers.

A rather elaborate set of directions to string players occurs in Roman Haubenstock-Ramati's *Multiple 5:* the fingers are to be held closely together on two, three, or four strings, with two, three, or four fingers, and the opposite— the fingers held quite far apart, but not producing multiple stops in either instance. The sonic result is a vague tonal haze in which no specific pitches predominate.

PIZZICATO VARIANTS

Pizzicato was the first of a long historical succession of unorthodox techniques applied to bowed stringed instruments. From its first appearance in Claudio Monteverdi's *Il Combattimento di Tancredi e Clorinda* of 1607, however, up to the closing years of the nineteenth century, pizzicato was basically a one-dimensional device. That is to say, pizzicato meant simply to pluck the string with the tip of the right-hand index finger. Pizzicato with the left hand, which was introduced into solo literature for the strings in the seventeenth century, enabled the player concurrently to pluck and bow the strings. Pizzicato on natural harmonics, extensively used in late nineteenth-century orchestration by such composers as Rimsky Korsakov, Mahler, and Debussy, for example, was only an extension of the basic technique and did not radically alter the generic timbre of pizzicato.

As the late Romantic instrumentators became more and more preoccupied with instrumental tone color and unusual sonorities, pizzicato gradually acquired certain notable variant forms, both in manner of production and in resultant sound. Thus such effects as are listed below were common coinage among orchestrators during the earliest years of the present century:

1. Pizzicato tremolando (or "banjo" pizzicato), the strings rapidly strummed with the forefinger (or several fingers) of the right hand, as in Sir Edward Elgar's *Violin*

Concerto, for instance. Contemporary examples would include almost any composition of Alan Hovhaness using the strings, and refer also to

J. Beckworth: *Circle with Tangents*
D. Erb: *Concerto for Brass and Orchestra*
R. Erickson: *Ricercar à 3*
J. Harvey: *Inner Light III*

E. Karkoschka: *Quattrologe*
B. Kolb: *Trobar Clus*
A. Silsbee: *Spirals*
B. A. Zimmermann: *Intercommunicazione*

2. "Reverse" pizzicato, the four strings plucked in the direction opposite to that normally employed (i.e., down for violin and viola, up for cello and doublebass)
3. "Guitar" or "brush" pizzicato (or pizzicato arpeggiato), the strings gently stroked with the thumb or several fingers; recent examples include

B. Bartolozzi: *Quartetto per archi*
B. Conyngham: *String Quartet*
G. Crumb: *Three Madrigals*
J. Deak: *Color Studies for Contrabass*
H. Dianda: *Estructuras*
G. Heussenstamm: *Pentalogue*
T. Marco: *Quasi un Requiem*
G. Perle: *Monody II for Solo Double Bass*

H. Pousseur: *Ode pour quatuor à cordes*
B. Rands: *Memo 1*
W. Szalonek: *1+1+1+1*
C. Whittenberg: *Conversations for Solo Doublebass*
I. Xenakis: *Nomos*

4. Pizzicato glissando, the string(s) plucked and then the left hand sliding quickly along the string, as in Stravinsky's *Renard* and numerous scores of Bartók; current examples are almost astronomical in number
5. "Pinch" pizzicato, the string plucked with two fingers rather than only one; early examples may be found in a number of Stravinsky scores, such as the *Concertino for String Quartet* and *Ragtime*, also in Bartók's *First Rhapsody* and the *Kammersymphonie I* of Schönberg. More recent usages include

J. Deak: *Color Studies for Contrabass*
G. Ligeti: *Aventures*
S. Matsushita: *Fresque sonore*

W. Szalonek: *Concertino per flauto; Les Sons*
R. Wittinger: *Construzioni*

6. Pizzicato over the fingerboard close to the left-hand fingers

A. Berg: *Lulu Suite*

7. "Snap" or "slap" pizzicato, à la Bartók, evidently first used in the Scherzo movement of Mahler's seventh symphony; it is now too common to warrant individual citations of current works

By the mid-point of the present century pizzicato effects had further proliferated; to the standardized variants just listed we must now add the following:

1. "Plectrum" pizzicato, the string plucked with a guitar, mandolin, or banjo pick

D. Bedford: *A Horse, His Name Was Hunry Fencewaver Walkins*
B. Childs: *Mr. T., His Fancy*
G. Crumb: *Night of the Four Moons*
F. Evangelisti: *Aleatorio*

W. Haupt: *CSS1 (Cellosolosonate)*
L. Hiller: *String Quartet No. 5*
M. Kelemen: *Changeant*
W. Kilar: *Dipthongos*
W. Szalonek: *Les Sons; Proporzioni II*

2. Pizzicato "al mandolino," a variant of the above; the instrument (violin or viola only) is held like a mandolin and the strings are strummed rapidly with a plectrum

B. Childs: *Nonet*
G. Crumb: *Eleven Echoes of Autumn*
H. Pousseur: *Ode pour quatuor à cordes*

B. Rands: *Étendre; Wildtrack 1*
W. Sydeman: *Texture Studies for Orchestra*

3. Pizzicato with a nail-file, another variant of the "plectrum pizzicato," and designated in Frank Beyer's *Versi*

The fingernails are sometimes designated as a substitute for a pick. A tremolando on a single string of either cello or doublebass can be likewise effectuated with a plectrum or the nails.

T. Antoniou: *Mikrographien für grosses Orchester*
C. Whittenberg: *Conversations for Solo Doublebass*

4. "Nut" pizzicato, the string lightly plucked not with the finger but with the nut of the bow, with a lifting motion, creating a delicate click; requested by Sergio Cervetti in his *Zinctum* (Example 52)
5. "Bisbigliando" pizzicato, the four fingers of the right hand rapidly and alternately plucking a single string; the delicate drumming sound so produced was requisitioned by Bernd Alois Zimmermann in his solo cello sonata
6. "Pulled" pizzicato, a variant of snap pizzicato on cello and doublebass; the lowest string is pulled to the side of the fingerboard as it is plucked, rebounding against the fingerboard when it is released (see Jacob Druckman's *Valentine*)
7. "Hammer on" pizzicato, an open string being plucked and the note a semitone higher immediately and forcefully fingered, thus abruptly stifling the string's vibration

B. Childs: *Mr. T., His Fancy*
T. Frederickson: *Music for Five Instruments*

8. Pizzicato "effleuré," the left-hand finger placed lightly on the string as it is plucked so that an indefinite rather than a precise pitch is produced

F. Cerha: *Enjambments; Formation et Solution*
D. Cope: *Paradigm*
G. Ligeti: *Apparitions*

W. Rudzinski: *Pictures from the Holy-Cross Mountains*
I. Yun: *Colloides sonores*

9. "Muffled" pizzicato, the outer edge of the right hand pressing down on the string(s) near the bridge as the fingers pluck the string(s), giving the pizzicato a very dull and dry sound

G. Heussenstamm: *Pentalogue*
W. Kotonski: *Pour quatre*

10. "Silent" pizzicato, the string actually not plucked but lightly knocked or flicked with the right-hand index finger so that a very soft and delicate click is heard; this was requested in *Dicotomia III* of Edgar Valcarcel
11. "Touch" pizzicato, the right hand pressing down on the string as the left hand plucks it, then abruptly releasing the finger

Although the "nail" pizzicato is no longer novel, having been used by Bartók as early as 1936 (in the *Music for Strings, Percussion and Celesta*), it is more prevalent in current scores than most of the other variant forms of pizzicato previously listed. Furthermore, there are at least eight different ways in which nail pizzicati may be utilized:

1. The string is plucked with an upward motion of the right-hand second fingernail, the most common method of employing the technique

STRINGS 239

B. Bartók: *Music for Strings, Percussion and Celesta*
M. Ishii: *Aphorismen*
M. Kagel: *Sonant*
R. Kayn: *Galaxis*

2. The string is plucked with the nail quite close to the bridge, which imparts an even greater metallic and brittle quality to the sound

J. M. Horvath: *Redundanz 2*
W. Sydeman: *Study for Orchestra No. III*
B. A. Zimmermann: *Intercommunicazione*

3. The upper nail surface is placed underneath the string, which is then plucked with a rapid upward motion of the finger; consult the *Five Pieces from Mikrokosmos* of Bartók, arranged by Tibor Serly

4. The string is plucked in a normal manner but is allowed to vibrate against the fingernail of the plucking finger; termed "buzz" pizzicato, the device has been used by

E. Brown: *Music for Cello and Piano*
E. Carter: *String Quartet No. 2*
F. Cerha: *Enjambments; Formation et Solution*
H-J. Hespos: *Passagen*
M. Kagel: *Sonant*
M. Kelemen: *Changeant*
G. Ligeti: *Apparitions*
P. Oliveros: *Trio*
B. Rands: *Memo 1*
D. Schnebel: *Versuche*
A. Silsbee: *Spirals*
I. Xenakis: *ST/4-1–080262*

5. After the string is normally plucked, the right-hand finger is turned over and slowly removed from the string so that the nail surface buzzes against the vibrating string (see Mauricio Kagel's *Sonant*)

6. The left-hand fingernail is placed lightly on the string to be plucked, just barely touching it, so that the plucked string will vibrate against the nail tip

F. Cerha: *Enjambments; Formation et Solution*
G. Ligeti: *Apparitions*
D. Martino: *Fantasy-Variations*

7. The string is plucked normally and then the left-hand fingernail lightly touches the already vibrating string

J. Druckman: *Valentine*
I. Xenakis: *ST/4-1, 080262*

8. The string is tightened by pulling it with the right-hand fingernail while at the same time the left hand plucks the string

I. Yun: *Dimensionen*

The foregoing list by no means exhausts the diversities of pizzicato to be found in recent scores of an experimental nature. Among the remaining specialized pizzicato effects are the following:

1. Normal pizzicato behind the bridge, which produces a dull and relatively unpitched sound; almost any string composition by Kagel, Ligeti, Penderecki, or Serocki, for example, will provide ample demonstration of this technique
2. Pizzicato behind the bridge, the left hand damping the strings

B. Ferneyhough: *Sonatas for String Quartet*
A. Gilbert: *Brighton Piece*

3. Pizzicato over the bridge with the bow nut

S. Cervetti: *Zinctum* (Example 52)

4. Pizzicato behind the bridge with the fingernail (see, for instance, R. M. Schafer's *String Quartet*); in Donald Erb's *Concerto for Solo Percussionist* the players of the lower-pitched strings are asked to stroke rapidly on the strings beyond the bridge with the nails
5. Pizzicato behind the bridge with a guitar pick

D. Cope: *Angel's Camp II* (Example 50)
L. Harrison: *Suite for Symphonic Strings*

6. Pizzicato with the left-hand finger lightly touching the string, like a half-harmonic, but *not* at a harmonic node

F. Cerha: *Enjambments; Formation et Solution*
G. Ligeti: *Apparitions*
I. Yun: *Colloides sonores*

7. Left-hand pizzicato and arco on the same string simultaneously

B. Conyngham: *Ice Carving; Three*   W. Kotonski: *Midsummer*
H. Dianda: *Estructuras*   A. Lanza: *Cuarteto V; Eidesis II*
E. Ghent: *Helices*   D. Reck: *Blues and Screamer*
K. Husa: *String Quartet No. 3*   H. Saeverud: *Peer Gynt*
  (Example 3)   J. Schwantner: *Elixir*

8. Left-hand pizzicato tremolando, quasi "a chitarra"

B. Maderna: *Quartetto per archi in due tempi*

9. Left-hand pizzicato, the finger slapped on the string

B. Rands: *Memo 1* (Example 30)

Example 52
Sergio Cervetti: from *Zinctum* (p. 13)

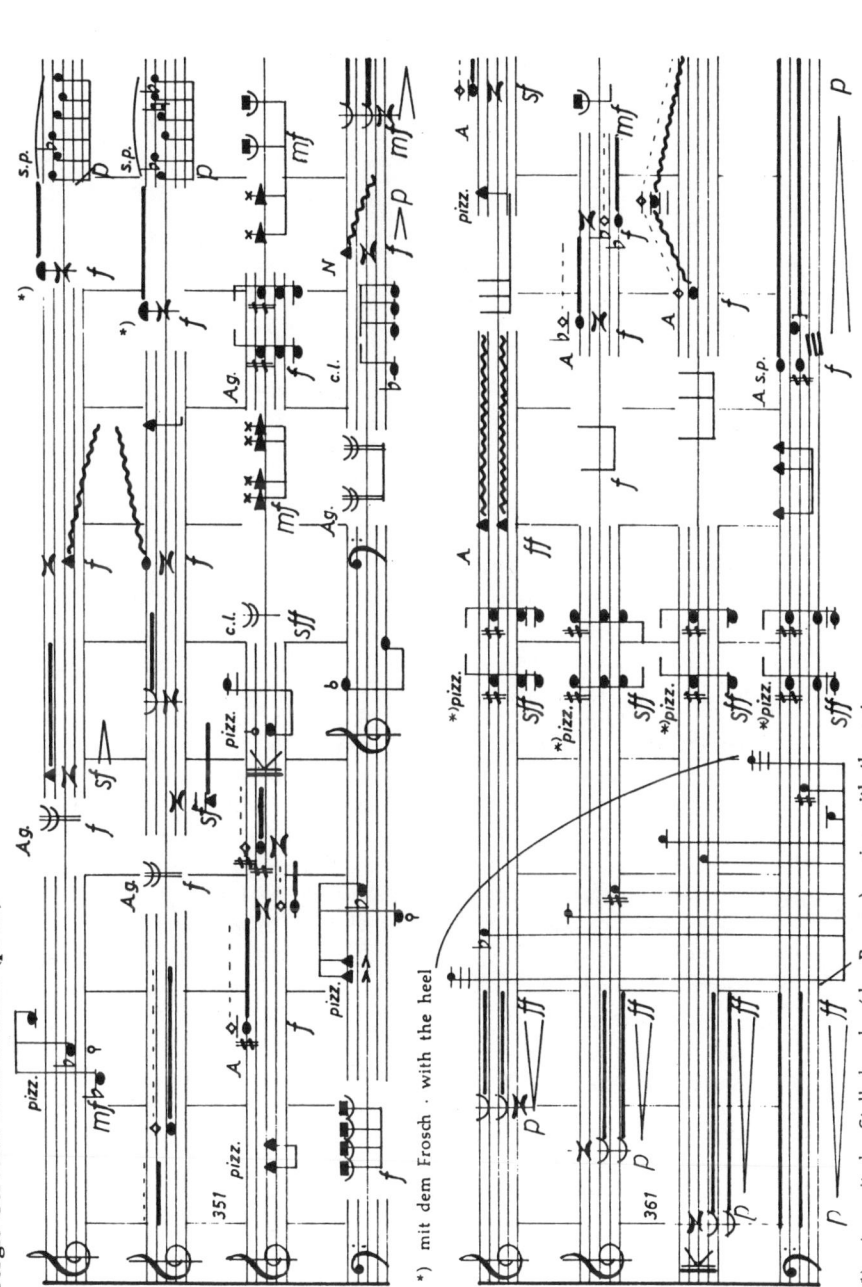

*) pizz. mit der Stellschraube (des Bogens) · pizz. with the nut
*) mit dem Frosch · with the heel

© Copyright 1969 by Moeck Verlag. Abdruck mit Genehmigung des Moeck Verlags, D-31 Celle.

10. Pizzicato rapidly alternating with arco on a single pitch, quasi-tremolo

D. Bedford: *Trona*

11. Left-hand pizzicato and *col legno* simultaneously

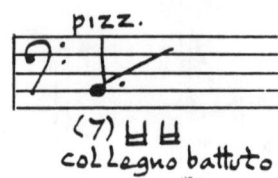

L. Berio: *Sequenza VI*
S. Cervetti: *Zinctum*

M. Kagel: *Match für drei Spieler*
P. Phillips: *Sonata for String Bass*

12. A slow and measured arpeggiated pizzicato in which the right-hand finger stretches each string before releasing it, similar to the "pulled" pizzicato described on page 240; this manner of plucking was utilized by Henri Pousseur in his *Ode pour quatuor à cordes*

13. Dampen the string by pressing down on it with the left-hand finger, then snap the string forcefully, à la Bartók

K. Huber: *Alveare vernat*
G. Ligeti: *Apparitions*
M. Mamiya: *String Quartet No. 1*

14. Pizzicato like guitar harmonics; the left-hand finger is lifted off the string immediately after the string is plucked, causing the tone to ring in a clear manner; see *Eleven Echoes of Autumn* and *Echoes of Time and the River* by George Crumb as well as Bertram Turetzky's *Poems, Portraits, Ballades and Blues*

15. "Bottle-neck" pizzicato, the string plucked with a plectrum or paper clip while the left hand holds a small glass rod which is slid along the string to produce a series of portamento pitches (called for in the Crumb works listed above)

16. Pizzicato on various specified parts of the string, ranging from near the pegs or nut to close to or beyond the bridge

L. Ferrari: *Société II* (Example 53)
G. Heussenstamm: *Pentalogue*
M. Kelemen: *Abecedarium*

17. Pizzicato on the strings (of doublebass) *above* the left-hand fingers on the fingerboard; requested in *Memo 1* by Bernard Rands

18. Pizzicato on the string area in the peg-box (of doublebass)

J. Deak: *Surrealist Studies*

19. Gradually pluck string (of doublebass) closer to the left-hand finger until right next to it

A. Russell: *Proteus*

Example 53
Luc Ferrari: from *Société II* (p. 6)

© Copyright 1968 by Moeck Verlag. Abdruck mit Genehmigung des Moeck Verlags, D-31 Celle.

A technical rather than a timbral variant of pizzicato is the directive in Strauss's opera *Elektra* to alternate the fingers of the right hand when playing triplet figures.

Not a pizzicato variant, yet an effect that depends on the fingernail, is the directive in *Match* (for cello) of Kagel to place a nail next to or underneath the string to be played arco, so that a jangling noise is heard. And in Sergio Cervetti's *Six Sequences,* the cellist is instructed to place his left-hand thumbnail on the string near to the bridge while playing arco, which produces the same general effect.

MISCELLANEOUS EFFECTS

A compositional rather than a strictly idiomatic technique is the prevalent use of massed string clusters, yet significant enough in contemporary orchestration to warrant inclusion here. Sustained clusters are generally indicated as shown at the left below, each pitch assumed by one player in the section. As devised by Penderecki, the notation at the right calls for each player to trill on his designated pitch:

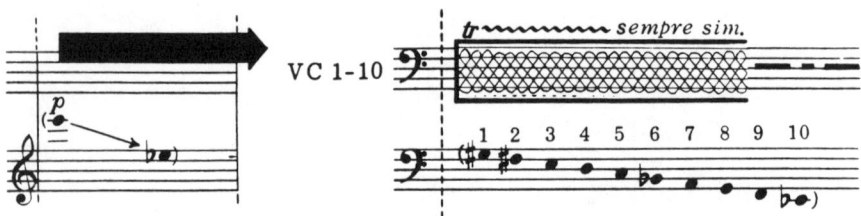

A technique limited to the larger instruments—cello and doublebass—and known to players as the "tambourine rub" is accomplished by the player's pressing his thumb hard against the front of the instrument (the belly) and rubbing it to produce a coarse frictional sound (see G. Heussenstamm: *Pentalogue*). A similar effect is achieved in Allan Strange's *Palace:* the right-hand thumb rubs the back of the instrument as the left hand plays with the bow on the open strings. The string player in Szalonek's *1+1+1+1* is to rub some part of the instrument body with his rosined palm, while in Jon Deak's *Color Studies for Contrabass* the player rubs the back or the rib of the instrument to produce a high squeak.

David Ernst's *Rounds* displays an unusual directive: insert a small piece of paper between the viola strings, which results in a pinched and buzzing noise when the strings are activated. In his *The Dream Net,* Warren Benson tells the string quartet members to attach a piece of rough watercolor paper to their sleeves (to the trouser leg of the cellist) and to strike the strings with the paper.

Finally, just as the wind and brass instruments have utilized the principle of sympathetic vibration by directing their tones into the interior of a grand piano (see page 167), so have the strings (violin and viola only) occasionally capitalized on this available modern resource (Penderecki's *Miniatures* for violin and piano, for example). More suited to chamber music than to symphonic requirements, this effect is auditory and visual in almost equal proportions, an occurrence notably capitalized on by Jani Christou in his *Praxis for 12*.

HYBRID INSTRUMENTS

Although major improvements in construction and minor refinements in detail have been applied to nearly all of the woodwind and brass instruments during the present and last centuries, the strings—individually and collectively—have undergone no such development. Quite recently, however, there have been attempts, motivated scientifically as well as musically, to redesign the family of bowed string instruments. In so doing, the aim has been to produce a more homogeneous sound from bottom to top of the total string gamut and to create a far greater dynamic range than now exists among massed violins, violas, violoncellos, and doublebasses.

The traditional format of the symphonic string section has long demonstrated a wide discrepancy between the timbres of doublebass and of violin. Furthermore, despite its size and the length of its strings in relation to the violin, the doublebass does not produce a correlated increase in amplitude. It is primarily to rectify these tonal and dynamic discrepancies that the Catgut Acoustical Society of America has recently fostered the development of eight new instruments, scaled to basic violin design and to its general tonal characteristics. Thus, the new family of stringed instruments is capable of creating a timbral and dynamic consistency between all its members, a not inconsiderable achievement.

Whether these conditions are considered as musical virtues by all composers is debatable. The criteria of certain artistic philosophies currently in high favor do not regard tonal homogeneity and dynamic equality as desirable goals. Other, and equally viable viewpoints, however, will look upon these conditions as distinct musical advantages. At any rate, whatever the philosophical point of view, new and demonstrably useful string instruments are now a reality and are available, even if in a severely limited way, to orchestrators interested in enlarging their string instrument resources.

NOTE

1. Bertram Turetzky refers to this specialized technique as "reverse bowing"; inasmuch as the identical term is applied to the technique of using up-bow on accented beats and down-bow on weak beats ($\vee\sqcap$ rather than $\sqcap\vee$), Turetzky's terminology may cause unnecessary confusion.

CODA

It is unlikely that the current widespread, almost frenetic, experimentation with instrumental devices and sonoric effects will soon slacken in pace. There will inevitably be further refinements of existing techniques, whether recently devised or long in common use. Additional multiphonic structures for the woodwinds, for instance, will be discovered; new percussive effects on brass, keyboard, and stringed instruments will be exploited; other bizarre instruments will be introduced into the percussion section of the orchestra; newly designed or hybrid instruments will take their place in the existing instrumental families in the avant-garde scores of the years just ahead. For the twentieth century has been—and will continue to be—a time when composers of all stylistic persuasions are augmenting their sound resources, humanly performed or electronically generated.

In the future, there may well be a more equalized application of new techniques among all the instrumental choirs. At the moment, some instruments (the piano, for instance) have been perhaps overexploited in the application of new and unorthodox effects; others (the horn, for one) have not been as intensely explored. Some vanguardists may come to realize that many novel devices are simply not worth the effort involved in producing them. Either the timbre distinctions created by the unusual techniques are so minute as to be virtually imperceptible, or they are so inordinately difficult and physically awkward to produce that they cannot really be regarded as compositionally legitimate.

One cannot, of course, confidently predict where the search for novel instrumental and vocal effect will ultimately lead today's composers and orchestrators, but one can hope that the present more limited focus on external means will eventually grow into a wider vision of expressive ends. Meanwhile, the search for new devices, new notations, new sounds, new techniques will continue, as it must.

BIBLIOGRAPHY

Bartolozzi, Bruno. *New Sounds for Woodwind*. London: Oxford University Press, 1967.
Blades, James. *Percussion Instruments and their History* (Chapter 15: *Techniques of Contemporary Percussion;* Chapter 16: *Composers' Use of Modern Percussion*). New York: Frederick A. Praeger, Publishers, 1970.
Brant, Henry. "Space as an Essential Aspect of Musical Composition," in *Contemporary Composers on Contemporary Music,* edited by Barney Childs and Elliott Schwartz. New York: Holt, Rinehart and Winston, 1967.
Brooks, William. "Instrumental and Vocal Resources," in *Dictionary of Contemporary Music,* edited by John Vinton. New York: E. P. Dutton & Co., Inc., 1974.
Bunger, Richard. *The Well-Prepared Piano*. Colorado Springs: Colorado College Music Press, 1973.
Cope, David. *New Directions in Music*. Dubuque: Wm. C. Brown Company Publishers, 1971.
Dempster, Stuart. *The Modern Trombone: A Definition of Its Idiom*. Berkeley: University of California Press, 1979.
Dick, Robert. *The Other Flute: A Performance Manual of Contemporary Techniques,* 2nd ed. New York: Multiple Breath Music Co., 1989.
Gilardino, Angelo. *Manuale di Chitarra per Compositori non Chitarristi*. Ancona, Italy: Edizioni Berben, 1989.
Heiss, John C. "For the Flute: A List of Double-Stops, Triple-Stops, Quadruple-Stops and Shakes." Princeton: *Perspectives of New Music,* Vol. 5, No. 1, 1966.
———. "Some Multiple Sonorities for Flute, Oboe, Clarinet, and Bassoon." Princeton: *Perspectives of New Music,* Vol. 7, No. 1, 1968.
———. "The Flute: New Sounds." Princeton: *Perspectives of New Music,* Vol. 11, No. 1, 1972.
Howell, Thomas. *The Avant-Garde Flute*. Berkeley: University of California Press, 1974.
Inglefield, Ruth K. and Lou Anne Neill. *Writing for the Pedal Harp: A Standard Manual for Composers and Harpists*. Berkeley: University of California Press, 1983.
Mas, J. L. *Sonorities nouvelles pour guitares*. Paris: Jean-Marie Mourat, 1989.
Nyman, Michael. *Experimental Music*. New York: Schirmer Books, 1974.
Pellerite, James J. *A Modern Guide to Fingerings for the Flute*. Bloomington: Zalo Publications, 1972.
Post, Nora. "Multiphonics for the Oboe." Amsterdam: *Interface,* No. 10/2, 1981.
———. "Monophonic Sound Resources for the Oboe." Amsterdam: *Interface,* No. 11, 1982.
Raver, Leonard. "Organism." New York: *Music Journal,* February, 1976.
Read, Gardner. *Music Notation: A Manual of Modern Practice*. New York: Crescendo, 1969.

———. *Thesaurus of Orchestral Devices*. Westport: Greenwood Press, Inc., 1969 (New York: Pitman Publishing Co., 1953).

———. *20th-Century Microtonal Notation*. Westport: Greenwood Press, 1990.

Rehfeldt, Phillip. *New Directions for Clarinet*. Berkeley: University of California Press, 1977.

Salzedo, Carlos. *Modern Study of the Harp*. New York: G. Schirmer, Inc., 1921.

Schneider, John. *The Contemporary Guitar*. Berkeley: University of California Press, 1985.

Smith, William O. "Contemporary Clarinet Sonorities." Elkhart: *Selmer Bandwagon*, Fall, 1972.

Smith Brindle, Reginald. *Contemporary Percussion*. London: Oxford University Press, 1970.

———. *The New Music,* Chapter 15. London: Oxford University Press, 1975.

Stokes, Sheridon and Richard Condon. *Special Effects for Flute*. Culver City: Trio Associates, 1970.

Stone, Kurt. "The Piano and the Avant-Garde." New York: *The Piano Quarterly*, No. 52, 1965.

Teal, Larry. *The Art of Saxophone Playing*. Evanston: Summy-Birchard Company, 1963.

Turetzky, Bertram. "The Bass as a Drum." Cleveland: *The Composer*, Vol. 1, No. 2, 1969.

———. "A Technique of Contemporary Writing for the Contrabass." Cleveland: *The Composer*, Vol. 1, No. 3, 1969.

———. *The Contemporary Contrabass*. Berkeley: University of California Press, 1974.

Various Authors. "New Directions in Instrumental Music." Evanston: *The Instrumentalist*, Vol. XXVIII, No. 10, 1974.

Verkoeyen, Jos. "String-Players and New Music." Amsterdam: *Sonorum Speculum*, No. 45, 1970.

INDEX OF INSTRUMENTAL REFERENCE

WOODWINDS

Flute/Alto flute/Piccolo, 5–7, 15, 31, 33, 55, 56, 63–66, 112–14, 121, 122, 130, 133, 135, 137, 138, 143–68
Oboe/English horn, 7–9, 16, 31, 56, 57, 63–66, 112–14, 122, 130, 133, 135, 137, 138, 144–68
Clarinet/Bass clarinet/Contrabass clarinet, 7–9, 15, 16, 31, 56, 63–66, 112, 114, 123, 130, 133, 135, 136, 138, 143–68
Bassoon/Contrabassoon, 7, 9, 16, 31, 56, 63–66, 114, 123, 130, 133, 135, 148–68
Recorder, 113, 122, 145, 151, 160
Saxophone, 9, 16, 56, 114, 123, 136, 146, 159, 161, 167, 168

BRASSES

Horn, 9, 10, 17–20, 31, 35, 36, 63–69, 114, 116, 130, 133–35, 137, 139, 147–68
Trumpet/Cornet, 9, 10, 17–20, 31, 35, 63–69, 114, 131, 133–35, 137, 139, 147–68
Trombone, 9, 10, 17–20, 31, 63–69, 116, 130, 133–36, 138, 145, 147–68
Tuba, 10, 35, 36, 63–69, 116, 134, 135, 147, 150–68

PERCUSSION

Timpani, 20, 57, 131, 167, 173–78
Idiophones, 21, 22, 31, 36, 37, 39, 57, 58, 123, 124, 131, 136–40, 167, 172–93
Membranophones, 21, 22, 39, 131, 136–40, 171–93

PLUCKED INSTRUMENTS

Harp, 10, 22–25, 39–45, 58, 69–76, 116, 117, 124, 135, 136, 138, 184, 195–200
Guitar, 10, 11, 25, 76, 77, 117, 123–25, 138, 139, 201–3, 240, 242
Mandolin/Banjo, 10, 31, 45, 76, 117, 201, 202, 235

KEYBOARD INSTRUMENTS

Piano, 25–29, 45–50, 58, 59, 77–91, 117, 118, 125, 126, 130, 131, 136–39, 167, 184, 194, 202, 205–13, 219, 220, 244
Harpsichord, 25, 31, 50, 125, 139, 205, 211
Organ/Harmonium, 31, 50, 51, 118, 123, 139, 205, 213–19
Celesta, 50, 205
Accordion, 51, 91, 219

STRINGS

Violin, 11, 29, 32, 51–54, 59–61, 91–107, 118–20, 126–28, 130, 131, 136, 139, 140, 221–45
Viola, 11, 29, 32, 51–54, 59–61, 91–107, 118–20, 126–28, 130, 136, 139, 140, 221–45
Violoncello, 12–14, 30, 32, 51–54, 59–61, 91–107, 118–20, 126–28, 130, 136, 139, 140, 153, 221–45
Doublebass, 11–13, 30–32, 51–54, 59–61, 91–107, 118–20, 126, 128, 135, 136, 221–45

INDEX OF COMPOSERS AND WORKS

Acker, Dieter: *Myriaden I* (GER), 214
Aitken, Robert: *Kebyar* (SAL), 61, 67, 69, 99, 101, 133, 135, 143, 145, 146, 148, 157, 161, 164
Albert, Stephen: *Cathedral Music* (CF), 122, 124–26; *Voices Within* (CF), 18, 20
Albert, Thomas: *Sound Frames* (MP), 68, 152, 161
Albright, William, 214; *Danse Macabre* (BOW), 7, 13, 46, 49, 50, 52, 64, 78, 87, 88, 90, 101, 113, 136, 137, 151, 152, 164, 190, 224, 233; *Organbook I; II* (JJ), 51, 214, 217, 218; *Pianoagogo* (JJ), 26; *Pneuma* (EV), 214, 217, 218; *Saints Preserve Us* (CFP), 149; *Seven Deadly Sins* (CFP), 50, 88, 167
Alemann, Eduardo Armando: *Spectra for 4 Recorders* (PAU), 145, 146
Alsina, Carlos Roque: *Consecuenza* (B&B), 135, 145, 157, 164; *Symptom für Orchester* (B&B), 190; *Trio 1967* (B&B), 68, 95, 96, 100–102, 133, 135, 137, 150, 157, 164, 166, 179, 183, 187, 226
Amlin, Martin: *The Black Riders* (SEE), 124
Amram, David: *Quintet for Winds* (CFP), 64
Amy, Gilbert: *Cahiers d'épigrammes* (HEUG), 210; *Cycle pour six percussions* (HEUG), 176; *5/16 pour flûte solo* (BIL), 55, 133; *Jeux pour (là 4) hautbois* (UE), 56, 146, 161, 168; *Trajectoires* (HEUG), 24, 71

Andriessen, Louis: *Hoe het is* (DON), 122
Anhalt, István: *Foci* (BMIC), 46, 47, 50, 80, 82–84, 98, 125, 130, 131, 137, 139, 182, 188, 210, 212, 231
Antoniou, Theodore: *Chorochronos I; II* (BAR), 134; *Dialog für Flöte und Gitarre* (EMOD), 202; *Five Likes for Solo Oboe* (BAR), 56, 113, 146, 149, 155, 161; *Fluxus für Orchester* (BAR), 182; *Fluxus I* (BAR), 81; *Jeux for Cello and Strings* (BAR), 233, 234; *Lyrics* (BAR), 28; *Mikrographien für grosses Orchester* (BAR), 187, 237; *Nenikikamen* (BAR), 80, 193, 201; *Parastasis II* (BAR), 12, 182, 189; *Three Likes for Solo Clarinet* (BAR), 7, 161; *Violinkonzert* (BAR), 42
Antunes, Jorge de Freitas, *Signs for Guitar* (ZIM), 203
Apfelbaum, Peter, *Lanterns and Cathedrals* (MS), 140
Arrigo, Girolamo: *Infrarosso* (BRUZ), 72, 96; *Thumos* (HEUG), 176; *Tre Occasioni* (HEUG), 77, 201
Ashley, Robert: *Describing the Motions of Large Real Bodies* (EX), 127; *Maneuvers for Small Hands* (MS), 88
Austin, Larry: *Accidents* (CPE), 26; *Changes: Open Style* (CPE), 68, 69, 116, 145, 149, 150, 157, 164; *Current for Clarinet and Piano* (CPE), 114; *The Maze* (SOU), 36, 37, 125, 131, 182, 187, 194

Babbitt, Milton, *String Quartet No. 4* (CFP), 97

Bacewicz, Grazyna: *In una parta* (PWM), 94, 183, 212; *Second Concerto for Cello and Orchestra* (PWM), 207
Bach, P.D.Q.: *"Erotica" Variations* (TP), 136, 169; *Grand Serenade for an Awful Lot of Winds and Percussion* (TP), 20, 155
Badings, Henk: *Praeludium en fuga* (DON), 118; *Symphonic Scherzo* (DON), 20; *Symphonische Klangfiguren* (DON), 177
Bahk, Junsang, *Mark* (CFP), 206
Baird, Tadeusz: *Erotyki* (PWM), 196; *Espressioni varianti* (PWM), 44, 104; *Etudia* (PWM), 174; *Exhortation* (PWM), 37, 44
Ballif, Claude, *Voyage de mon oreille* (B&B), 16
Bamert, Matthias: *5 Aphorisms* (SEE), 197; *Inkblot* (GS), 69, 150, 154–56, 164; *Introduction and Tarantella* (GS), 85, 138; *Woodwind Quintet* (GS), 143
Bancquart, Alain: *Ecorces III* (JJ), 101, 102; *Palimpsestes* (JJ), 116, 197
Banks, Don: *Assemblies* (SCHL), 46, 78, 80; *Horn Concerto* (SCHL), 17, 207; *Tirade* (SCHL), 44, 72, 87, 176, 197
Barber, Samuel: *Souvenirs* (GS), 41, 56, 197
Bargielski, Zbigniew: *Parades for Orchestra* (PWM), 26
Bark, Jan/Rabe, Folke: *Bolos* (WH), 35, 64, 67, 69, 133, 144, 150–52, 155, 157, 158, 164, 166
Barraqué, Jean: . . . *au delà au hasard* (BRUZ), 144; *Chant après chant* (BRUZ), 37; *Séquence* (BRUZ), 196
Barrett, Richard, 9; *Anatomy* (UN), 5, 7, 8, 18, 21, 36, 61, 63, 134, 149, 164, 222
Barth, Hans, 117; *Piano Concerto* (MS), 120; *Piano Quintet* (MS), 120
Bartók, Béla, 36, 51, 118, 186, 236; *Concerto for Orchestra* (B&H), 44; *Deux Portraits* (B&H), 22; *First Rhapsody for Violin and Orchestra* (B&H), 236; *Music for Strings, Percussion and Celesta* (PHIL), 238, 239; *String Quartets Nos. 1–6* (B&H), 51
Bartók, Béla/Serly, Tibor, *Five Pieces from "Mikrokosmos"* (B&H), 239
Bartolozzi, Bruno, 112, 145, 147, 160, 169; *Collage* (OUP), 9, 146, 161; *Concertazioni a quattro* (ZER), 161; *Concertazioni per oboe* (ZER), 57, 76, 113, 146, 153, 161; *Quartetto per archi* (BRUZ), 228, 236; *Trés recuerdos del cielo* (ZER), 161
Bassett, Leslie: *Designs, Images and Textures* (CFP), 48, 188, 211; *Music for Saxophone and Piano* (CFP), 146; *Music for Violoncello and Piano* (CFP), 225, 232; *Variations for Orchestra* (CFP), 177, 186, 198
Bax, Sir Arnold: *First Symphony* (CHAP), 11, 12; *Second Symphony* (CHAP), 175
Bazelon, Irwin: *De-Tonations for Brass Quintet and Orchestra* (NOV), 17, 98, 183; *Sound Dreams* (NOV), 33, 125, 149, 182
Becker, Gunther: *Diaglyphen* (UE), 96, 97, 101; *Moirologhi* (UE), 40, 73, 75
Beckwith, John: *Circle with Tangents* (BMIC), 206, 236
Bedford, David: *A Horse, His Name Was Hunry Fencewaver Walkins* (UE), 202, 237; *Brighton Piece* (UE), 138; *Come in here child* (UE), 48, 125, 213; *Bricks Left on April 21* (UE), 203; *Five for String Quintet* (UE), 52, 101, 222, 228, 233; *Gastrula* (UE), 67, 69, 100, 155; *Music for Albion Moonlight* (UE), 33, 52, 65, 87, 88, 95, 101, 133, 134, 152, 167, 209, 212; *Pentomino* (UE), 17, 130; *Piano Piece 2* (UE), 26, 28; *Piece for Mo* (UE), 20, 22, 51, 95–97, 177, 186, 192; *That White and Radiant Legend* (UE), 52, 98, 103, 119, 155, 228, 233; *Trona* (UE), 19, 67, 69, 150, 154, 155, 242; *You Asked for It* (UE), 76, 202
Beerman, Burton: *Polygraph VI* (MS), 42, 117, 124, 130, 134

INDEX OF COMPOSERS AND WORKS 255

Behrend, Siegfried: *Movimenti für Gitarre* (UE), 45
Benguerel, Xavier: *Joc for Chamber Ensemble* (MV), 207, 209; *Konzert für Gitarre und Orchester* (MV), 139
Bennett, Richard Rodney: *Commedia I* (UE), 7
Benson, Warren: *The Dream Net* (TP), 133, 149, 155, 161, 166, 222, 244; *Helix* (CF), 18, 133, 184; *Star Edge* (CF), 18
Benvenuti, Arrigo: *Polymerie* (BRUZ), 65
Berg, Alban, 3, 118; *Chamber Concerto* (UE), 7; *Drei Orchesterstücke* (UE), 168, 201; *Lulu Suite* (UE), 237; *String Quartet* (UE), 92; *Wozzeck* (UE), 10, 13
Bergsma, William: *Blatant Hypotheses for Trombone and Percussion* (GAL), 18
Berio, Luciano: *Chamber Music* (ZER), 42; *Chemins I; II* (UE), 24, 39, 42, 45, 53, 70, 71, 73, 196–98, 234, 235; *Circles* (UE), 23, 37, 73, 134, 196; *Epifanie* (UE), 19, 94, 130, 191, 197, 226; *Gesti* (UE), 144, 151, 159; *Nones* (UE), 124; *Sequenza I, II, V, VII* (UE), 19, 22–24, 39–42, 45, 56, 65, 67, 70, 75, 113, 146, 150, 157, 160, 161, 164, 166, 196, 198, 234, 242; *Sincronie* (UE), 228, 231; *Sinfonia* (UE), 19, 101, 147, 185
Berlioz, Hector, 30, 195
Bernstein, Leonard: *"Jeremiah" Symphony* (HAR), 178
Beyer, Frank Michael: *Versi für Streichorchester* (BRH), 237
Biberian, Gilbert: *Prisms II* (MS), 76, 202
Biel, Michael von: *1. Quartett* (UE), 30, 222, 225, 227–30, 235
Birtwistle, Harrison: *Entr'actes and Sappho Fragments* (UE), 117, 196; *Nomos* (UE), 22, 122, 123, 172; *Verses for Ensembles* (UE), 130, 131, 137, 160
Blackwood, Easley, 109

Bland, William: *An Hommage to Picasso* (MS), 203
Blatter, Alfred: *A Study of Time and Space* (MED), 100
Bloch, Augustyn: *Dialoghi* (PWM), 76; *Erwartung* (PWM), 145, 155; *Gilgamesz* (PWM), 126
Bloch, Ernest, 118
Blomdahl, Karl-Birger: *Forma Ferritonans* (SCHM), 20
Boesmans, Philippe: *Correlations* (JJ), 137
Boguslawski, Edward: *Apokalypsis* (PWM), 46; *Canti* (PWM), 149; *Intonations* (ZAI), 210
Bois, Rob du: *Music for Sliding Trombone* (DON), 145, 164; *Pour faire chanter la polonaise* (DON), 78, 82, 87
Bolcom, William: *Black Host* (JJ), 214, 217; *Duets for Quintet* (BOW), 130, 131, 210; *Hydraulis for Organ* (EBM), 214, 216; *Session 3* (MER), 167
Boone, Charles: *The Edge of the Land* (SAL), 184
Booren, Jo van de: *Chanson du Printemps* (DON), 146
Borup-Jorgensen, Axel: *Nordisk Sommerpastorale* (SAM), 72
Bosseur, Jean-Yves: *Un arraché de partout* (JJ), 188
Boucourechliev, André: *Anarchipel and Archipel 5* (UE), 124, 126; *Archipel II* (UE), 228, 233
Boulez, Pierre: *Eclat* (UE), 16, 18, 185; *Le marteau sans maître* (UE), 20, 21; *Le soleil des eaux* (HEUG), 23; *Sonatine pour flûte et piano* (AMPH), 5; *Structures (I)* (UE), 210; *Troisième sonata pour piano, Formant 2* (UE), 210
Boziwick, George: *Red Skies at Night* (MS), 118
Brant, Henry: *Antiphony One* (CF), 32; *Verticals Ascending* (MCA), 177; *Voyage Four* (MS), 32
Braun, Gerhard: *Monologe I* (HAN), 146, 151

Britten, Benjamin, 3: *Les Illuminations* (B&H), 228
Brosch, Barry: *Prolations for Solo Cello* (MP), 97, 234
Brown, Earle: *Available Forms 1; 2* (AMP), 17, 37, 64, 75, 116, 149, 150, 164, 179, 185, 196, 200, 232; *Corroboree* (UE), 49, 80; *From Here* (UE), 26, 64, 124, 150; *Hodograph I* (AMP), 25, 78, 164, 185, 207; *Music for Cello and Piano* (AMP), 25, 78, 82, 239; *String Quartet* (UE), 29, 94, 232; *Times Five* (UE), 42, 149, 200
Bruchollerie, Monique de la, 219
Bruins, Theo: *Sei Studie* (DON), 78
Bruynel, Ton: *Signs for Woodwind Quintet* (DON), 149, 154, 160
Budd, Harold: *III for Double Ensemble* (CPE), 69
Bujarski, Zbigniew: *Chamber Piece* (PWM), 49, 70, 113, 183; *Contraria* (PWM), 66; *Kinoth* (PWM), 46, 48, 49, 78, 82, 85, 97, 189, 227
Bunger, Richard, 220
Burge, David: *Aeolian Music* (BOW), 25, 26, 46, 48, 81, 87, 88, 90, 100, 101, 104; *A Song of Sixpence* (AB), 134, 206; *Sources III* (AB), 31, 130, 134, 136, 137, 175, 188, 189, 191
Burt, George J.: *Exit Music for 12 Players* (MS), 103, 106, 134
Bussotti, Sylvano: *Couple* (UE), 25, 45, 46, 48, 65, 78, 87–89, 113, 149, 151, 206; *Five Piano Pieces for David Tudor* (UE), 78, 80, 87, 91; *Fragmentations* (BRUZ), 24, 40, 42, 70, 71, 73–75, 116, 196, 198, 200; *Il Nudo* (MV), 25, 48, 58, 78, 80, 81, 88, 90, 94, 96, 100; *Memoria* (BRUZ), 24, 42, 58, 70, 80, 173, 187, 201; *Mit einem gewissen sprechenden Ausdruck* (MV), 45, 52, 71, 75, 81, 88, 90, 96, 174, 175, 185, 200; *Phrase à Trois* (UE), 96; *Pour Clavier* (MV), 45, 209; *Torso* (MV), 150, 151

Cacioppo, George: *Holy Ghost Vacuum or America Faints* (BMIC), 214; *Time on Time in Miracles* (BMIC), 58, 150, 162, 164, 222
Cage, John, 186, 194, 220; *Amores* (CFP), 26, 177; *Cartridge Music* (CFP), 125; *Concert for Piano and Orchestra* (CFP), 25, 206; *Etudes Australes* (CFP), 209; *First Construction (In Metal)* (CFP), 20, 22, 46, 49, 59, 172; *Imaginary Landscape No. 1* (CFP), 49; *Music of Changes I - IV* (CFP), 88; *Pastorale for Piano Solo* (CFP), 26, 78; *Solo for Clarinet in B♭* (CFP), 152; *Solo for Sliding Trombone* (CFP), 67, 150, 152, 157, 166; *26'1.1499" for a String Player* (CFP), 232; *Variations IV* (CFP), 130; *The Wonderful Widow of Eighteen Springs* (CFP), 87
Cage, John/Harrison, Lou: *Double Music* (CFP), 172
Cage, John/Hiller, Lejaren: *Hpschd* (CFP), 125, 126
Caravan, Ronald: *Excursions for "A" Clarinet* (SEE), 146
Cardew, Cornelius: *The Great Learning, Paragraph 1* (CPE), 218; *Three Winter Potatoes* (UE), 206, 209
Carmi, Avner, 220
Carrillo, Julián, 118; *Balbuceos* (MS), 109; *Preludio a Colón* (JJ), 120; *Sonata in Quarter-Tones for Solo Guitar* (MS), 117
Carter, Elliott: *8 Etudes and a Fantasy* (AMP), 144; *Eight Pieces for Four Timpani* (AMP), 20, 57, 175, 185; *Sonata for Flute, Oboe, Cello and Harpsichord* (AMP), 146; *String Quartet No. 2* (AMP), 239
Casella, Alfredo: *Le couvent sur l'eau* (RIC), 168
Casken, John: *Music for a Tawny-Gold Day* (SCHL), 222; *Music for the Crabbing Sun* (SCHL), 33, 51, 52, 64, 81, 161
Castiglioni, Niccolo: *Alef* (AVV), 56, 146; *Cangianti per pianoforte* (ZER), 206; *Consonante* (AVV), 45, 91, 149, 209; *Eine kleine Weihnachtsmusik*

INDEX OF COMPOSERS AND WORKS

(ZER), 224, 225; *Sequenze* (ZER), 58; *Sinfonie guerriere e amorose* (AVV), 217; *A Solemn Music II* (AVV), 21, 45, 233

Cerha, Friedrich: *Enjambments* (UE), 64, 65, 69, 96, 101, 104, 149, 152, 238–40; *Formation et solution* (EMOD), 25, 46, 58, 80, 238–40; *Relazioni fragili* (EMOD), 69, 186, 197, 233; *Spiegel II* (UE), 26

Cervetti, Sergio: *Five Episodes* (MV), 25; *Raga II* (MV), 123; *Six Sequences for Dance* (MV), 25, 49, 96, 97, 100, 101, 144, 149, 151, 156, 175, 177, 244; *Zinctum for String Quartet* (MV), 92, 96, 100, 101, 103, 104, 119, 225, 226, 228, 238, 240, 242

Chihara, Paul: *Branches* (CFP), 7, 65, 152; *Ceremony I, II* (CFP), 61, 104, 122, 126; *Driftwood* (CFP), 101, 226; *Logs* (CFP), 61, 102, 104, 126, 225; *Sequoia for String Quartet and Tape* (CFP), 225; *Willow, Willow* (CFP), 55, 64, 122, 123, 164, 166, 190

Childs, Barney: *Four Inventions* (TR), 113; *Jack's New Bag* (SOU), 25, 26, 28, 36, 47, 58, 61, 67–69, 80, 84, 87, 88, 90, 100, 116, 134, 155–57, 164, 177–79, 189, 190, 226; *Mr. T., His Fancy* (MS), 99, 103, 104, 134, 237, 238; *Music for Bass Drum* (BMIC), 175, 176; *Music for Singer* (BMIC), 28, 46; *Music for Trombone and Piano* (CPE), 68, 69, 87, 150, 157, 164; *Music for Two Flute Players* (MER), 5; *Nonet* (CPE), 7, 10, 28, 36, 46, 61, 65, 67, 68, 80, 94, 100, 103, 106, 133–36, 145, 149, 154, 155, 162, 164, 177, 212, 226, 231, 233, 237; *Trio for Clarinet, Cello and Piano* (BAS), 114

Chou Wen-chung: *Cursive for Flute and Piano* (CFP), 33, 78, 80, 113, 145, 146, 160; *Pien* (CFP), 33, 145; *Yu Ko* (CFP), 85

Christou, Jani: *Enantiodromia* (CPE), 88, 124, 130, 134; *Praxis for 12* (CHES), 245

Claoué, Yves: *Mutations* (JJ), 101
Colf, Howard, 224
Colgrass, Michael: *As Quiet As* (MCA), 18, 20, 29, 36, 59, 92, 113, 150, 158, 173–75, 231; *Déjà Vu* (CF), 41; *Rhapsodic Fantasy* (MCA), 92; *Six Allegro Duets for Percussion* (LG), 174
Company, Alvaro: *Las Seis Cuerdas* (ZER), 203
Constant, Marius: *Candide* (SAL), 124, 126; *Quatorze Stations* (SAL), 124, 125, 176, 178; *Winds* (SAL), 65, 69, 137, 155
Conyngham, Barry: *Ice Carving* (UEA), 95, 124, 126, 240; *Mirages* (UEA), 7, 116, 182; *String Quartet* (UEA), 227, 236; *Three* (UEA), 106, 179, 188, 202, 240
Cope, David: *Angel's Camp II* (SEE), 96, 105, 134, 136, 229, 240; *Cedar Breaks* (SEE), 136; *Iceberg Meadow* (CAP), 49, 83; *Indices for Solo Oboe* (CAP), 46, 90, 133, 137, 155, 167; *Paradigm* (CF), 238; *Parallax for Piano* (CAP), 26, 28, 58, 85, 90; *Spirals* (CAP), 67
Cordero, Roque: *Cello Sonata* (PS), 78
Corghi, Azio: *Stereofonie X4* (RIC), 151, 222
Couper, Mildred: *Dirge for Two Pianos* (NME), 118
Cowell, Henry: *Piano Concerto* (SEN), 206, 207; *Piano Music* (AMP), 46, 48, 49, 78, 207; *Set of Five* (NME), 22; *The Tides of Mauannaun* (AMP), 206
Cowie, Edward: *Clarinet Concerto* (CHES), 8
Crumb, George: *Ancient Voices of Children* (CFP), 24, 44, 46, 58, 59, 75, 113, 117, 187, 189, 202; *Apparition* (CFP), 125; *Black Angels* (CFP), 61, 98, 101, 127, 135, 139, 226; *Celestial Mechanics* (CFP), 139; *Echoes of Time and the River* (B/M), 25, 26, 28, 31, 36, 37, 46, 48, 71, 72, 81, 82, 87, 88, 101, 114, 130, 131, 133, 134, 149, 150, 164, 166, 171–74, 176, 189, 222, 242; *Eleven Echoes of Au-*

Crumb (*continued*)
  tumn (CFP), 25, 26, 48, 50, 58, 59, 78, 90, 113, 114, 133, 134, 147, 151, 152, 167, 225, 226, 237, 242; *Five Pieces for Piano* (CFP), 78, 210, 211; *A Little Suite for Christmas, A.D. 1979* (CFP), 25; *Madrigals—Books I–IV* (CFP), 44, 58, 61, 75, 99, 100, 103, 119, 135, 138, 156, 175, 185, 187, 193, 196, 198, 233, 234, 236; *Makrokosmos - Vol. I; II* (CFP), 26, 46, 48, 80, 85, 90, 125; *Music for a Summer Evening* (CFP), 28, 84, 90, 179, 182, 190; *Night of the Four Moons* (CFP), 6, 31, 64, 76, 103, 113, 126, 201, 202, 237; *Night Music I;II* (MIL), 28, 37, 48, 78, 80–84, 87–90, 100, 103; *Songs, Drones and Refrains of Death* (CFP), 11, 124–26, 134, 136, 138, 202, 203, 225; *Vox Balaenae* (CFP), 54, 59, 125, 126, 138, 211
Curran, Alvin: *Home-made* (SOU), 96, 97, 101, 104, 194, 224

Dahl, Ingolf: *Five Duets for Clarinets* (BOON), 114
Dan, Ikuma: *The Silk Road* (ONT), 184
Dao, Nguyen Thien: *Máy* (SAL), 21, 179, 183; *Phū-Dông* (SAL), 135, 150; *Tây Nguyên* (SAL), 49, 82, 84, 85, 143, 149, 207
Darasse, Xavier: *Organum I* (SAL), 214, 217, 218
Darter, Tim: *Dual* (MS), 11, 203
Darvas, Gabor: *Sectio Aurea* (EMUS), 101, 155, 227, 228
Davidovsky, Mario: *Inflections* (EBM), 78; *Synchronisms Nos. 1–4* (MMX), 64, 92, 94, 96, 97, 100, 102, 103, 233
Deak, Jon: *Color Studies for Contrabass* (MP), 104, 119, 135, 136, 222, 224, 225, 227–29, 236, 244; *Surrealist Studies* (MP), 229, 242
Debussy, Claude, 235; *Jeux* (DUR), 195; *La Mer* (DUR), 195

Delannoy, Marcel: *Grand Suite de "La Pantoufle de Vair"* (ESCH), 27
Del Tredici, David: *Pop-Pourri* (B&H), 123, 124
Delvincourt, Claude: *Pamir* (DUR), 16
Dempster, Stuart: *Didjeridervish* (MS), 136
Denisov, Edison: *Canon in Memory of Igor Stravinsky* (UE), 197; *Crescendo e Diminuendo* (UE), 100; *Romantische Musik* (UE), 42, 147, 161
Dianda, Hilda: *Estructuras I–III* (PAU), 80, 81, 236, 240
Dick, Robert, 33, 154, 160
Dillon, James: *Überschreiten* (CFP), 146, 147, 222
Dobrowolski, Andrzej: *Musik für Streichen und 4 Bläsergruppen* (PWM), 233
Dolin, Samuel: *Sonata for Accordion* (WAT), 219
Doppler, Christian Johann, 136, 137, 168
Druckman, Jacob: *Animus 1; 2* (MCA), 35, 64, 92, 143, 147, 150, 157, 164, 166, 176; *Dark Upon the Harp* (NME), 144, 189; *Incenters* (MCA), 94, 95, 100, 101, 119, 189, 222, 224, 231; *String Quartet No. 2* (MCA), 92, 222, 224, 231; *Valentine for Solo Contrabass* (MCA), 59, 61, 95, 98–100, 234, 238, 239; *Windows* (MCA), 19, 20, 22, 42, 210, 214
Duckworth, William: *Gambit* (MP), 177; *The Time Curve Preludes: Book One, Two* (HEN), 209
Durkó, Zsolt: *Iconography No. 2* (B&H), 138; *Serenata* (EMUS), 73

Eaton, John, 109: *Microtonal Fantasy* (MS), 118
Ebenhöh, Horst: *4 Szenen für 10* (DOB), 99
Eberhard, Dennis: *"Especially . . . "* (CFP), 39, 41, 73, 117, 134, 197; *Parody* (MAR), 80–82, 133, 134, 148, 192, 213
Eder, Helmut: *Vox Media* (DOB), 217

INDEX OF COMPOSERS AND WORKS

Eisma, Will: *Affairs II* (DON), 49, 78; *Non-Lecture II* (DON), 64, 150; *World Within World* (DON), 147

El-Dabh, Halim: *Mosaic No. 1* (CFP), 185

Elgar, Sir Edward: *Concerto for Violin and Orchestra* (NOV), 235, 236

Ellis, Merrill: *Mutations* (SHP), 18, 36, 134, 135, 143, 145, 156, 178, 179

Eloy, Jean-Claude: *Equivalences* (HEUG), 177

Encinar, J.: *Abhava* (MS), 11

Englemann, Hans-Ulrich: *Cadenza* (AHN), 82, 85

Erb, Donald: *Basspiece* (MER), 232; *Concerto for Brass and Orchestra* (MER), 9, 17, 19, 22, 52, 59, 148, 182, 184, 189, 232, 236; *Concerto for Solo Percussionist* (MER), 42, 47, 65, 102, 138, 147, 150, 154, 157, 166, 173, 197, 198, 211, 222, 225, 240; *The Rainbow Snake* (MER), 138, 139, 150, 213; *Reconnaissance* (MER), 94, 99; *The Seventh Trumpet* (MER), 16, 19, 26, 28, 42, 47, 67, 69, 81, 102, 105, 134, 150, 156, 157, 164, 173, 178, 193, 197, 235; *String Trio* (APOG), 76, 101, 124, 201, 222; *Symphony of Overtures* (HIGT), 7, 24, 36, 42, 72, 73, 82, 114, 147, 150, 156, 161, 173, 175, 199, 200, 212; *The Tower of Silence* (MER), 125, 126; *Trio for Two* (MS), 92, 135

Erickson, Robert: *General Speech for Solo Trombone* (OKR), 166; *Ricercar à 3* (UCP), 99, 104, 106, 236; *Ricercar à 5* (SEE), 68, 69, 135, 164

Ernst, David: *Rounds* (MS), 244

Ervin, Karen: *Five Little Pieces* (SEE), 25

Evangelisti, Franco: *Aleatorio* (TON), 92, 119, 237; *Ordini* (TON), 78, 173; *Proporzioni* (BRUZ), 65, 153; *Spazio a 5* (TON), 172

Falla, Manuel de: *El Retablo de Maese Pedro* (CHES), 186

Farberman, Harold: *Alea: A Game of Chance for Percussion Ensemble* (MCA), 171, 174, 175, 184, 186

Felciano, Richard: *Background Music* (ECS), 39, 42, 45, 73, 130, 134, 136, 198, 199; *Contractions* (ECS), 130, 135, 154, 156; *Crasis* (ECS), 197, 200, 224; *Ekagrata* (ECS), 217; *Glossolalia* (WLSM), 217; *Spectra* (ECS), 135

Ferneyhough, Brian: *Carceri d'Invenzione III* (CFP), 63; *Cassandra's Dream Song* (CFP), 63, 143, 146, 152, 160; *Etudes Transcendantales* (CFP), 7, 58, 63, 146, 147; *Sonatas for String Quartet* (CFP), 101, 106; *Sonata for Two Pianos* (CFP), 88; *Time and Motion Study II* (CFP), 126; *Unity Capsule* (CFP), 33, 113, 133, 143, 147–49

Ferrari, Luc: *Interrupteur* (MV), 153; *Société II* (MV), 25, 28, 48, 49, 65, 81, 87, 88, 90, 92, 150, 151, 153, 156, 174, 179, 212, 213; *Tautologos III, Version No. 4* (MV), 123, 139

Finney, Ross Lee: *Concerto for Percussion and Orchestra* (CFP), 175, 227; *Divertissement* (BOW), 25, 33, 36, 50, 58, 78, 80, 81, 84, 158, 167; *Nun's Priest's Tale* (CFP), 124; *Three Pieces* (CFP), 174; *Three Studies in Fours* (CFP), 173, 175, 176

Finnissy, Michael: *As When Upon a Tranced Summer Night* (INT), 26, 83, 88, 175, 176; *Song 9* (INT), 210

Fisher, Stephen: *Concert Piece for Doublebass* (CFP), 232

Fokker, Adriaan: *New Music With 31 Notes* (VER), 118

Fortner, Jack: *Quartet* (JJ), 96, 100, 101, 103, 135, 222, 233; *S pr ING* (JJ), 16, 55, 73, 101

Fortner, Wolfgang: *The Creation* (SCHM), 187; *Immagini* (SCHM), 101; *Mouvements für Klavier und Orchester* (SCHM), 187

Foss, Lukas: *Baroque Variations* (CF), 31, 125, 214, 233; *The Cave of the*

Foss (*continued*)
 Winds (SAL), 153, 161; *Echoi* (CF), 22, 25, 119, 130, 146, 167, 179, 185, 188, 224, 233; *Elytres* (CF), 72, 119, 173, 179, 198, 232; *Etudes for Organ* (SOU), 218; *Exeunt* (CF), 178, 190; *For 24 Winds* (CF), 114, 150; *Fragments of Archilochos* (CF), 22, 37, 77, 117, 124, 174, 176, 196, 201; *Ni bruit ni vitesse* (SAL), 47, 83, 87; *Orpheus* (SAL), 42, 49, 50, 53, 88, 130, 150, 161, 198, 222; *Paradigm* (SCHL), 77, 124, 125, 133–35; *Time Cycle* (CF), 176, 185, 224
Fox, Jim: *All Things Fancy* (MS), 9, 63, 64, 67, 133, 146, 151, 161
Frederickson, Thomas: *Music for Five Instruments* (TP), 102, 104, 105
Fulkerson, James: *Now II* (MP), 126; *Patterns III for Solo Tuba* (MV), 64, 69, 137, 150, 157, 164, 166

Gaber, Harley: *Voce II* (APOG), 113, 148, 150, 164
Gaburo, Kenneth: *Antiphony IV* (MS), 92; *Inside* (MS), 106, 136; *Two* (TP), 92, 160
Garant, Serge: *Cage d'oiseau* (BMIC), 87; *Phrases I* (BMIC), 182; *Piece for Piano No. 2* (BMIC), 82
Gerhard, Roberto: *Concerto for 8* (OUP), 59, 95, 201, 202, 227; *Concerto for Orchestra* (OUP), 94, 95, 101, 103, 198; *Epithalamion* (OUP), 206, 226; *String Quartet No. 2* (OUP), 103
Ghent, Emmanuel: *Helices* (OUP), 240
Gielen, Michael: *Musica* (UE), 173
Gilardino, Angelo: *Abrenana* (BER), 117
Gilbert, Anthony, 9; *Brighton Piece* (SCHL), 8, 19, 116, 240; *The Incredible Flute Music* (SCHL), 5–7, 146, 148, 152, 159; *Introit, Gradual and 2 Chorals* (SCHL), 22; *Sonata No. 2 for Piano (2 Players)* (SCHL), 25, 27, 28, 46, 48, 49, 58, 78, 80, 88, 206, 208; *Spell Respell* (SCHL), 7, 84, 123, 161
Gilboa, Jacob: *The Jerusalem Chagall Windows* (IMP), 28, 37, 48–50, 81–83, 183
Ginastera, Alberto: *Bomarzo Cantata* (B&H), 42, 94, 226
Globokar, Vinko: *Accord* (LIT), 19, 64, 66, 67, 92, 101, 106, 146, 147, 150, 164, 166, 176, 179, 222, 226–28; *Airs de voyages vers l'intérieur* (LIT), 123; *Atemstudie für Oboe* (LIT), 33, 65, 146, 156; *Discours II;III* (LIT), 19, 56, 64, 66, 68, 69, 131, 133, 135, 146, 151, 159, 161, 164, 166; *Etude pour Folklora II* (LIT), 64, 114, 116, 143, 147, 150; *Fluide* (LIT), 68, 164; *Vendre le vent* (LIT), 87, 88, 125; *Voie* (LIT), 20, 22, 23, 75, 117, 183, 200
Goeb, Roger: *Fantasy for Oboe and String Orchestra* (AMP), 103
Good, Dennis: *Dialogues* (MS), 167
Gorecki, Henryk: *Canti Strumentali (Genesis II)* (PWM), 222; *Elementi (Genesis I)* (PWM), 53, 222; *Monodram (Genesis III)* (PWM), 53, 119, 120; *Monologhi* (PWM), 40, 70, 200; *Scontri* (PWM), 44, 70
Gould, Morton: *Family Album* (CHAP), 31; *Jekyll and Hyde Variations* (CHAP), 36, 158
Graener, Paul: *The Flute of Sanssouci* (EUL), 31
Grosskopf, Erhard: *Dialectics* (MV), 64, 150
Gudmundsen-Holmgreen, Pelle: *Solo for Electric Guitar* (WH), 11, 203

Hába, Alois, 118; *String Quartets* (PAN;UE), 109; *Suite for ¼-tone Clarinet and ¼-tone Piano* (CHF), 114; *Suite für Vierteltongitarre* (CHF), 117
Halffter, Cristobal: *Anillos* (UE), 69, 92, 101, 156; *Codex I* (UE), 201; *Fibonaciana* (UE), 102, 175, 182, 188, 222, 226, 227; *Lineas y puntos* (UE), 65, 69, 150; *Noche Pasiva del Sentido* (UE), 84, 190; *Planto por las victimas de la violencia* (UE), 82–84, 150, 182,

INDEX OF COMPOSERS AND WORKS 261

190; *Pourquoi für Striecher* (UE), 97, 225–27; *Tiento* (UE), 161, 178
Hambraeus, Bengt: *Introduzione-Sequenze-Coda* (WH), 113, 122, 123
Hannay, Roger: *Fantôme* (HEN), 46, 49, 81, 83, 88, 90, 153, 167, 232
Harris, Donald: *Ludus II* (JJ), 6, 64
Harrison, Lou, 94, 107: *Concerto for Violin with Percussion Orchestra* (CFP), 99; *Concerto in Slendro* (CFP), 27; *Labyrinth No. 3* (CFP), 98; *Suite for Symphonic Strings* (CFP), 92, 94, 100, 103, 104, 226, 240; *Suite for Violin, Piano and Small Orchestra* (CFP), 27
Harsanyi, Tibor: *La joie de vivre* (SAL), 173; *Suite pour Orchestre* (SAL), 5
Hartmann, Karl Amadeus: *1. Symphonie* (SCHM), 187
Hartwell, Hugh: *Soul Piece for 6 or 7 Players* (BMIC), 26, 82
Harvey, Jonathan: *Inner Light III* (NOV), 7, 22, 33, 95, 150, 189, 190, 213, 228, 236; *Persephone Dream* (NOV), 146, 188, 222
Haubenstock-Ramati, Roman: *Chants et Prismes* (UE), 206; *Credentials* (UE), 64, 67, 69, 78, 81, 150; *Interpolation* (UE), 64; *Jeux 6 für zwei Schlagzeuger* (UE), 88, 188, 212, 213; *Multiple 5* (UE), 123, 133, 135, 222, 235; *Petite musique de nuit* (UE), 40, 206; *Séquences* (UE), 40, 232; *Tableau III* (UE), 96, 101
Haufrecht, Herbert: *Square Set* (AMP), 104
Haupt, Walter: *CSS1-Cellosolosonate* (MN), 92, 97, 102, 237; *Volume* (EMOD), 188
Hawkins, John: *Three Cavatinas* (BMIC), 134, 136
Heckster, Walter: *Epicycle I and II* (DON), 201
Heider, Werner: *-einander* (LIT), 19, 29, 67, 123, 150, 164; *Katalog for a Recorder Player* (MV), 151, 160, 164; *Landschaftspartitur* (LIT), 87; *Plakat* (LIT), 222

Heinke, James: *Music for Trombone and Percussion* (CAP), 19, 152, 159, 164
Heiss, Hermann: *Bewegungspiel* (AHN), 46, 49
Heiss, John, 160; *Four Movements for Three Flutes* (B&H), 56, 64
Hellermann, William: *Formata for Trombone and 4 Instruments* (ACA), 22, 26, 48, 78; *One into Another* (ACA), 56; *On the Edge of a Node* (ACA), 202
Henry, Otto: *Do Not Pass Go* (MP), 174, 175
Henze, Hans Werner: *Being Beauteous* (SCHM), 40; *Compases para preguntas ensimismadas* (SCHM), 125; *El Cimarrón* (SCHM), 113, 136, 201; *Heliogabalus Imperator* (SCHM), 44, 56, 72, 98, 123, 159, 161, 168; *Memorias de "El Cimarrón"* (SCHM), 202; *4. Sinfonie* (SCHM), 17, 187; *Sinfonia N. 6* (SCHM), 16, 44, 49, 61, 83, 85, 100, 102, 114, 124, 126, 145, 150, 156, 177, 187, 188, 201, 206, 207, 214, 230
Herder, Ronald: *Requiem II—Games of Power* (AMP), 82
Hespos, Hans-Joachim: *Harry's Musike für Bassclarinette* (EMOD), 8; *Keime und Male* (JJ), 143, 152; *Passagen* (EMOD), 20, 22, 59, 67, 95–97, 150, 152, 164, 222, 228, 239
Heussenstamm, George: *Pentalogue* (SEE), 54, 64, 135, 136, 222, 227, 236, 238, 242, 244; *Poikilos* (SEE), 113, 145, 166, 174; *Seventeen Impressions from the Japanese* (SEE), 21, 83, 174
Hiller, Lejaren: *Machine Music* (TP), 26, 27; *String Quartet No. 5* (TP), 29, 101, 222, 224, 237
Hiller, Lejaren/Isaacson, L. M.: *Illiac Suite* (TP), 101
Hindemith, Paul: *Konzert für Violoncello und Orchester* (SCHM), 20, 174, 187; *Symphonia Serena* (SCHM), 32; *Symphonische Tänze* (SCHM), 11; *When*

Hindemith (continued)
 Lilacs Last in the Dooryard Bloom'd
 (AMP), 31
Hodkinson, Sydney: *Drawings, Set No. 9*
 (MER), 134, 136, 178; *Fresco* (JJ),
 21, 33, 45, 49, 65, 67, 69, 75, 76,
 87, 88, 95, 113, 125, 133, 135, 149,
 150, 154, 156, 157, 171, 173, 190,
 191, 224, 230, 233; *Imagind Quarter*
 (BMIC), 20, 21; *Interplay* (MS), 16,
 65, 103, 113, 146, 148, 158, 165;
 November Voices (MER), 31, 39, 42,
 184, 198
Holab, William: *Woodshedding* (CFP),
 63, 133, 149, 155, 161
Holliger, Heinz: *Glühende Rätsel*
 (SCHM), 23, 42, 196; *"H" for Wind
 Quintet* (SCHM), 9, 63, 64, 69, 149,
 153; *Mobile für Oboe und Harfe*
 (SCHM), 56; *Siebengesang* (SCHM),
 24, 44, 56, 65, 71–73, 82, 155, 172
Honneger, Arthur: *Concertino pour piano
 et orchestre* (SAL), 12
Horvath, Josef Maria: *Die Blinde* (LIT),
 49, 78, 80, 83, 85; *Redundanz 2;3*
 (DOB), 59, 97, 222, 235, 239
Hovhaness, Alan, 236; *Jhala* (SMP), 82
Hrisanide, Alexandre: *À la recherche de
 la verticale* (MS), 65, 154, 155; *Clarinet Sonata* (EMUS), 63; *Directions*
 (GER), 67, 68, 153; *Volumes* (SAL),
 49, 78, 88, 96, 100, 102, 119, 212,
 224, 228, 233
Huber, Klaus: *Alveare Vernat* (SCHM),
 35, 119, 146, 228, 242; *Des Engels
 Anredung an die Seele* (UE), 198; *Tenebrae* (SCHM), 16, 21, 102–04, 114,
 116, 126, 172, 214, 222, 224, 226
Humble, Keith: *Arcade IV* (UE), 76
Husa, Karel: *Apotheosis of This Earth*
 (AMP), 114, 116, 133; *Concerto for
 Trumpet and Wind Orchestra* (GS), 20;
 String Quartet No. 3 (AMP), 11, 61,
 226, 240
Hutcheson, Jere: *Three Things for Dr.
 Seuss* (HMR), 138

Ibert, Jacques: *Suite Symphonique* (CFP),
 149

Ichiyanagi, Toshi: *"Activities" for Brass
 Instruments* (CFP), 17; *Duet for Piano
 and String Instrument* (CFP), 52
Imbrie, Andrew: *Three Sketches for Trombone and Piano* (MAL), 147, 164, 167
Inghelbrecht, D. E.: *Rapsodie de
 printemps* (SAL), 31, 32
Ishii, Maki: *Aphorismen* (ONT), 25, 78,
 80, 87, 90, 95, 100, 102, 222, 227,
 239; *Sieben Stücke für kleine Orchester*
 (ONT), 78
Ives, Charles: *"Concord" Sonata* (AMP),
 206, 208; *Quarter-Tone Chorale for
 Strings* (CFP), 120; *Three Quarter-
 Tone Pieces* (CFP), 117; *The Unanswered Question* (SMP), 31

Jacob, Werner: *Da Pacem* (BRH), 214
Janáček, Leoš: *Sinfonietta* (UE), 7
Janson, Alfred: *Canon* (WH), 47, 83, 90,
 101, 217, 218
Johnston, Ben, 109: *One Man for Trombone and Percussion* (MS), 137; *Sonata for Microtonal Piano* (SP), 118
Jolas, Betsy: *Fusain pour un flûtist*
 (HEUG), 152, 159; *How Now*
 (HEUG), 69, 135; *Tranche pour harpe
 seule* (HEUG), 23, 39, 70, 197
Jolivet, André: *Concerto pour piano et
 orchestre* (HEUG), 37; *Suite transocéane* (HEUG), 36
Jong, Conrad de: *Contact* (GS), 145

Kagel, Mauricio, 186, 214: *Anagrama*
 (UE), 20–23, 25, 37, 42, 58, 70, 71,
 73, 75, 90, 96, 164, 174–76, 179,
 182, 183, 185, 188, 189, 193, 197,
 206; *Heterophonie* (LIT), 88, 145,
 201, 206, 232; *Improvisation ajoutée*
 (UE), 91, 209, 214, 217, 218; *Match
 für drei Spieler* (UE), 59, 92, 96, 100–
 102, 104, 119, 179, 185, 186, 222,
 225, 228, 233, 242, 244; *Metapiece
 (Mimetics)* (UE), 208–10; *Sexteto de
 cuerdas* (UE), 92, 119, 232; *Sonant*
 (CFP), 20, 22–24, 39, 42, 44, 45, 52,
 58, 61, 70–77, 92, 96, 97, 100, 101,
 125, 134, 135, 173–75, 179, 185,
 196–98, 200, 201, 222, 232, 233,

INDEX OF COMPOSERS AND WORKS

239; *Transición II* (UE), 25, 28, 46, 49, 81, 85, 88, 207, 209; *Tremens* (UE), 76, 201, 202
Kam, Dennis: *Rendezvous II* (CAP), 143
Kapr, Jan: *Dialogues* (GEN), 73
Karkoschka, Erhard: *Quattrologe* (TON), 233, 236
Karlins, M. William: *Reflux* (SEE), 126
Kasemets, Udo: $\sqrt[5]{5}$ (BMIC), 139
Kayn, Roland: *Galaxis* (MV), 92, 222, 228, 239
Kelemen, Milko: *Abecedarium* (LIT), 97, 106, 222, 224, 227, 242; *Changeant* (LIT), 39, 42, 52, 69, 70, 87, 95, 96, 100, 196, 233, 237, 239; *Dessins Commentés* (LIT), 206, 210; *Entrances* (LIT), 65, 130, 149, 155; *Equilibres* (LIT), 65, 146; *Olifant* (LIT), 42, 67, 70, 88, 144, 147, 150, 153, 168, 229; *Passionato* (LIT), 5; *Studie für Flöte solo* (LIT), 5, 143; *Surprise* (LIT), 95, 97, 233
Khachaturian, Aram: *Concerto for Piano and Orchestra* (LEED), 7; *Gayne Ballet Suite No. 1; 1-A; 2* (LEED), 7
Kilar, Wojciech: *Diphthongos* (PWM), 81, 96, 97, 237; *Génerique* (PWM), 94, 155, 156; *Riff 62* (PWM), 228
Kirchner, Leon: *Music for Orchestra* (AMP), 138
Knussen, Oliver: *Masks for Solo Flute* (GS), 31, 130, 152
Kohn, Karl: *Son of Prophet Bird* (CF), 197
Kolb, Barbara: *Trobar Clus* (B&H), 18, 125, 236
Kopelent, Marek: *3. Quartetto* (UE), 94, 100, 228, 231
Korte, Karl: *Concerto Mutabile for Piano and Orchestra* (CF), 208; *Remembrances* (EV), 113, 146
Kotonski, Wlodsimierz: *a battere* (MV), 76, 77, 96, 97, 178; *Concerto per quattro* (PWM), 23; *Midsummer* (MV), 36, 123, 125, 126, 240; *Musica per fiati e timpani* (PWM), 57, 113, 116, 173–75; *Oboe Concerto* (PWM), 122, 155, 182; *Pour quattre* (MV), 46, 69, 76, 81, 114, 145, 238; *Spring Music* (MV), 5, 7

Kox, Hans: *Cyclofonie V* (DON), 113; *Passacaglia en Koraal* (DON), 118
Kraft, William: *Configurations* (MCA), 185; *Monumentuum* (SMP), 182; *Suite for Percussion* (MIL), 182, 188, 189
Kramer, Jonathan D.: *Renascence for B♭ Clarinet* (MS), 123
Krenek, Ernst: *Five Pieces for Trombone and Piano* (BAR), 68, 69, 116, 145, 147, 154, 157, 158, 164, 166, 167; *Sonata for Flute and Piano* (BAR), 88
Kroeger, Karl: *Toccata for Clarinet, Trombone and Percussion* (AB), 35, 164
Kruyf, Ton de: *Einst den Grau* (DON), 73, 75; *Mosaico* (B&B), 56, 146, 161; *Quahquahtinchen in Foreign Lands* (DON), 118
Kuhl, Riva: *Dreams Before Dark* (MS), 42, 138
Kunst, Jos: *Ijzer for Violin and Piano* (DON), 49, 84, 85
Kupferman, Meyer: *Infinities 24* (GEN), 97, 98, 233
Kupkovič, Ladislav: *Das Fleisch des Kreuzes* (UE), 20, 173
Kurtz, Eugene: *Improvisations for Solo Contrabass* (JJ), 97, 98, 102, 103, 136, 233

Lachenmann, Helmut: *Dal Niente for Solo Clarinet Player* (GER), 149
Laneri, Roberto: *Esorcismi No. I* (SEE), 16; *L'Arte del Violino* (MP), 126
Lanza, Alcides: *Acufenos I* (B&H), 150; *Cuarteto V para cuerdas* (B&H), 92, 94, 100, 101, 120, 226, 228, 240; *Eidesis II* (B&H), 116, 119, 133–35, 157, 222, 240; *Penetrations VI* (B&H), 127; *Plectros I; II* (B&H), 26, 46, 49, 78, 80–82, 85, 88, 206, 211; *Strobo I* (B&H), 13
Lanzi, Alessandro: *Quattro Pezzi per Arpa* (ZER), 42, 198
Layton, Billy Jim: *Divertimento* (AMP), 228
Lazăr, Filip: *Le Ring* (DUR), 168; *Tziganes* (DUR), 168
Lazarof, Henri: *Espaces* (AMP), 82;

Lazarof (continued)
  Koncordia for String Orchestra (B&B), 135, 232; Textures (AMP), 25, 48, 49, 78, 80
LeBaron, Anne: Memnon for Six Harps (MS), 134, 135
Leeuw, Ton de: The Four Seasons (DON), 24; Second String Quartet (DON), 119; Spatial Music III; IV (DON), 51, 130, 131, 147, 196
Lehmann, Hans Ulrich: Sonata "da chiesa" for Violin and Organ (GER), 222
Leisner, David: Dances in the Madhouse (MER), 77
Lentz, Donald A.: Sermon (MS), 127, 128, 135
Levinson, Gerald: Trio for Clarinet, Violoncello and Piano (MER), 167
Levy, Burt: Orbs with Flute (APOG), 6, 55, 56, 145, 149, 160
Levy, Marvin David: Kyros (B&H), 22, 40, 74
Lewis, Peter: Sweets for Piano (MER), 88, 139
Lidholm, Ingvar: Poesis (UE), 78, 81, 87
Ligeti, György, 214: Apparitions (UE), 18, 53, 64, 69, 87, 96, 100, 149, 154, 155, 173, 210, 233, 238, 239, 242; Atmospheres (UE), 49; Aventures (CFP), 18, 55, 138, 139, 149, 150, 152, 160, 162, 164, 179, 193, 228, 232, 234, 236; Concerto for Violoncello and Orchestra (LIT), 10, 228, 232; Lontano für grosses Orchester (SCHM), 16; Nouvelles Aventures (CFP), 27, 85, 136, 139, 150, 162, 164, 193, 210, 212, 222; Ramifications for Double String Orchestra (SCHM), 119, 233; Requiem (CFP), 7, 16; Ten Pieces for Wind Quintet (SCHM), 10, 151, 155; Volumina (CFP), 214, 217, 218
Loeffler, Charles Martin: Five Irish Fantasies for Voice and Orchestra (GS), 16
Lomon, Ruth: Celebrations (MS), 24, 42, 117; Dust Devils (ARS), 198

Lucas, Theodore: Aberrations No. VII (CAP), 46, 49, 81, 83, 87, 208
Lucier, Alvin: Action Music for Piano (BMIC), 208
Lumsdaine, David: Kelly Ground (UE), 210
Lundquist, Torbjorn: Metamorphoses (HOH), 219; Partita Piccola (HOH), 219
Lunetta, Stanley: Piano Music (SOU), 48, 136, 206, 209, 212
Luti, Vincent P.: Mixed Quintet (BOW), 47, 82, 90, 96, 211
Lutoslawski, Witold: Concerto for Cello and Orchestra (PWM), 119, 183; Concerto for Oboe, Harp and Chamber Orchestra (CHES), 161; Livre pour Orchestre (PWM), 119
Lutyens, Elizabeth: "Go, Said the Bird" (SCHL), 125
Lybbert, Donald: Lines for the Fallen (CFP), 117

Maderna, Bruno: Concerto for Oboe and Chamber Ensemble (BRUZ), 78, 152, 184; Quartetto per archi in due tempi (ZER), 100, 240; Stele per Diotima (ZER), 73, 75, 87, 90; III Concerto pour Oboe et Orchestre (SAL), 21, 25
Mahler, Gustav, 33, 235; Symphonies Nos. 1–9 (B&H), 6, 51, 237
Mamiya, Michio: String Quartet No. 1 (ONT), 95, 96, 242
Mandelbaum, Joel: Ten Studies for 31-Tone Keyboard (MS), 118
Marco, Tomas: Albayalde für Gitarre (ZIM), 76; Aura (SAL), 100; Jetztzeit (MV), 84, 87, 88, 155, 167; Quasi un Requiem (ALP), 227, 236; Rosa-Rosae (SAL), 138
Marie, Jean-Etienne: Le Tombeau de Carrillo (JJ), 118
Maros, Rudolf: Eufonia No. 3 (SMP), 149, 150; Monumentum (SMP), 70
Martino, Donald: B.A.B.B.IT.T (ECS), 7; Cinque Frammenti for Oboe and String Bass (MMX), 16, 232; Concerto for Piano and Orchestra (ECS), 174,

INDEX OF COMPOSERS AND WORKS 265

176; *Concerto for Wind Quintet* (ECS), 56, 145, 149, 151; *Fantasy-Variations for Violin* (IO), 239; *From the Other Side* (DAN), 53, 65; *Notturno* (IO), 5, 15, 82, 103, 104–106, 189; *Parisonatina al'dodecafonia* (IO), 95, 100, 102, 103; *Quodlibets II* (DAN), 5; *Ritorno* (DAN), 18; *Strata for Bass Clarinet* (IO), 33, 63, 65, 114, 144; *Trio for Violin, Clarinet and Piano* (IO), 63; *Triple Concerto* (DAN), 18, 232; *The White Island* (DAN), 8, 20

Martinu, Boguslaw: *Symphony No. 4* (B&H), 173

Matsushita, Shin-ichi: *Fresque sonore* (ONT), 40, 70–73, 75, 92, 94, 100, 103, 196, 197, 226

Maves, David: *Oktoechos* (CFP), 70

Maxwell Davies, Peter: *Eight Songs for a Mad King*(B&H), 80, 161, 175; *Revelation and Fall* (B&H), 44, 119, 124, 126, 191; *Vesalii Icones* (B&H), 46, 119, 133, 189, 194

Mayuzumi, Toshiro: *Metamusic* (CFP), 88, 149; *Pieces for Prepared Piano and Strings* (CFP), 26

McKenzie, Jack: *Paths I* (MP), 20

McLaughlin, John: *Apocalypse* (MS), 125

Meale, Richard: *Clouds Now and Then* (UE), 149, 150, 190

Méfano, Paul: *Interférences* (HEUG), 16; *La cérémonie* (SAL), 124; *Lignes* (HEUG), 126, 136, 156, 172, 226; *Paraboles* (HEUG), 18, 39, 40, 92, 152, 186, 200

Mekeel, Joyce: *The Shape of Silence* (CFP), 5, 113, 130, 149, 159, 165

Mellnäs, Arne: *Aura* (WH), 49, 53, 96, 97, 136, 137, 155, 224, 225; *Capriccio per orchestra* (EDS), 102; *Fixations for Organ* (CFP), 214, 217, 218; *Gestes sonores* (WH), 53, 65, 67, 69, 94, 150; *Per caso* (TON), 94, 226; *Quasi niente* (CFP), 119; *Tombola* (TON), 67, 69, 80–83, 85, 125, 135, 136, 201; *Transparence per orchestra* (EDS), 42

Mestres-Quadreny, Josep Maria: *Double Concerto for ondes Martenot, Percussion and Orchestra* (SEE), 18, 125; *Tramesa a Tapies* (SEE), 20, 22, 175, 176, 179

Meyer, Krzysztof: *Concerto da camera* (MV), 96, 97

Miereanu, Costin: *Finis Coronet Opus* (SAL), 19, 26, 46, 80, 87, 88

Milhaud, Darius, 186; *IIe Symphonie* (HEUG), 5

Mills-Cockell, John: *Fragments* (BMIC), 48, 49, 81, 87

Miroglio, Francis: *Phases* (UE), 65, 149, 152; *Projections for String Quartet* (UE), 130, 131, 224, 225; *Réfractions* (UE), 29, 36, 37, 50, 88, 149, 152, 212, 222, 224, 225, 227; *Réseaux pour harpe et orchestre* (UE), 42, 45, 70, 72, 73, 75, 197, 198, 200; *Tremplins* (UE), 222, 233

Mitrea-Celarianu, Mihai: *Seth* (SAL), 50, 69, 80, 85, 150, 151, 165, 166, 229

Moevs, Robert: *Et Occidentem Illustra* (EBM), 44, 186, 198

Montague, Stephen: *At the white edge of phrygia* (UN), 26, 65, 69, 93, 134, 146, 148, 155, 174, 190

Moross, Jerome: *Paeans* (NME), 173

Morthenson, Jan W.: *Eternes for Organ* (NORD), 214, 218; *Farewell* (WH), 217; *Pour Madame Bovary* (NORD); 214, 218

Moryl, Richard: *Improvisations* (BOW), 152

Moss, Lawrence: *Omaggio* (EV), 84, 209; *Remembrances for Eight Performers* (TP), 18; *Windows* (MS), 61

Moszumanska-Nazar, Krystyna: *Variazioni concertanti* (PWM), 29, 65, 82, 83, 92, 94, 226

Mumma, Gordon: *Hornpipe* (MS), 123, 168

Musgrave, Thea: *Night Music* (WH), 130; *Space Play* (NOV), 130; *Viola Concerto* (NOV), 130, 227, 228

Mussorgsky, Modeste/Ravel, Maurice: *Pictures at an Exhibition* (B&H), 6

Neill, Ben, 168
Nightingale, James: *Entente* (NEO), 124, 134, 136
Nilsson, Bo: *Versuchungen* (UE), 100, 101
Nono, Luigi: *Canti di vita e d'amore* (AVV), 96, 116
Nordheim, Arne: *Partita II* (WH), 125
Nørgård, Per: *Prism* (WH), 53, 96, 151; *Symphony No. 2* (WH), 82, 88, 119, 124, 145, 149, 153, 200, 222, 225; *Waves* (WH), 179

O'Donnell, Rich: *Microtimbre I* (MP), 190
Ohana, Maurice: *Cinq séquences* (JJ), 106; *Si le jour Si le jour parait* (BIL), 76; *Sorôn-Ngô* (SAL), 82, 207, 208; *Tiento* (BIL), 117
Olah, Tiberiu: *Sonate pour clarinette seule* (SAL), 63
Oliveros, Pauline: *Doublebasses at Twenty Paces* (MS), 134; *Theatre Piece for Trombone Player and Tape* (MS), 87, 168; *Trio for Flute, Percussion and String Bass* (MP), 239
Olsen, Poul Rovsing: *Images pour piano* (MV), 78, 87

Pablo, Luis de: *Libro para el pianista* (TON), 80, 83; *Modulos III for Chamber Orchestra* (SAL), 17, 69, 83; *Prosodia* (TON), 136; *Radial* (TON), 70, 96; *Reciproco* (TON), 81, 174, 176, 186, 188, 190
Paccagnini, Angelo: *Gruppi concertanti* (UE), 187; *Musica da camera* (UE), 39, 70, 74, 158
Pärt, Arvo: *Tabula Rosa* (UE), 26
Partch, Harry, 109
Patterson, Paul: *Rebecca* (WEIN), 47, 51, 53, 84, 87, 88, 134
Peck, Russell: *Automobile* (MS), 134; *1 db (1968)* (MS), 134; *Suspended Sentence* (JJ), 45
Penderecki, Krzysztof, 186, 221, 230, 240; *Anaklasis* (MV), 44, 49, 71, 78, 85, 185; *Cantata in honorem Almae Matris* (PWM), 85; *Capriccio per oboe e 11 archi* (MV), 56, 103, 146, 161; *Capriccio per Siegfried Palm* (SCHM), 100, 102, 226, 227, 233; *Capriccio per violino ed orchestra* (MV), 136, 222; *De Natura Sonoris I* (MV), 82, 114, 222; *The Devils of Loudun* (SCHM), 44, 72, 94, 95, 229; *Dies Irae* (PWM), 85, 114; *Dimensions of Time and Silence* (MV), 40, 57, 70, 82, 83, 96, 97, 100, 173, 175, 187, 190; *Emanationen* (MV), 53, 119, 233, 234; *Fluorescences* (MV), 13, 46, 50, 52, 53, 65, 84, 94, 96, 102, 106, 134, 155, 171, 173, 175, 185, 226, 228; *Miniatures for Violin and Piano* (PWM), 119, 245; *Partita* (SCHM), 125; *Polymorphia* (MV), 95, 97, 102, 106, 134, 229; *Quartetto per archi No. 1; 2* (SCHM), 102, 222, 233; *St. Luke Passion* (MV), 218; *Sonata per violoncello e orchestra* (PWM), 50, 78; *Strophes* (PWM), 46, 49, 80, 207; *Threne - aux victimes de Hiroshima* (PWM), 227; *Utrenja I: Grablegung Christi* (SCHM), 85
Perera, Ronald: *Reverberations* (ECS), 214, 217
Perle, George: *Monody II for Solo Double Bass* (TP), 236; *Sonata quasi una fantasia* (TP), 16
Persichetti, Vincent: *Sinfonia: Janiculum* (EV), 22
Peterson, Wayne: *Trialogue* (SEE), 226
Petrassi, Goffredo: *Suoni notturni* (RIC), 201
Phillips, Peter: *Divertimento for Three String Basses* (MUR), 98, 103, 136; *Novasonic for Orchestra* (AMP), 18; *Sonata for String Bass* (MMX), 52, 226, 242
Pijper, Willem: *Six Symphonic Epigrams* (DON), 20
Pinkham, Daniel: *When the Morning Stars Sing Together* (ECS), 217
Piston, Walter: *Symphony No. 2* (ARMP), 7

INDEX OF COMPOSERS AND WORKS 267

Polin, Claire: *The Death of Procris* (SEE), 6, 65, 113, 160, 164; *O, Aderyn Pur* (SEE), 160; *Summer Settings* (LYRA), 70, 71, 196

Poncs, Miroslav: *Suite für zwei Streichengruppen* (MS), 120

Pousseur, Henri: *Honeyrêves* (ZER), 25, 82; *Mobile* (ZER), 208; *Ode pour quatuor à cordes* (UE), 236, 237; *Rimes pour différentes sources sonores* (ZER), 208

Powell, Mel: *Filigree Setting* (GS), 94, 102, 104, 228; *Two Prayer Settings* (GS), 228

Prokofiev, Serge, 3; *Alexander Nevsky* (LEED), 31

Rabe, Folke: *Pajazzo* (WH), 135

Rands, Bernard, 195; *Actions for six* (UE), 40, 42, 45, 71, 100, 150, 151, 175, 197, 199; *Aum* (UE), 73, 125, 198; *Ballad 1* (UE), 130, 134, 135, 150, 164–66; *Canti lunatici* (UE), 20, 174, 176; *Espressione IV* (UE), 25, 45, 87, 209; *Étendre* (UE), 11, 20, 103, 223, 225, 237; *Formantes 1–Les Gestes* (UE), 23, 24, 40, 41, 45, 70, 73, 75, 196, 197, 200; *Memo 1* (UE), 97, 127, 135, 229, 232, 236, 239, 240, 242; *Metalepsis 2* (UE), 154; *Wildtrack 1* (UE), 25, 39, 73, 81, 133, 134, 196, 232, 237

Ravel, Maurice, 35; *Daphnis et Chloé* (DUR), 10, 31, 55; *L'enfant et les sortilèges* (DUR), 27; *Ma mère l'oye* (DUR), 12; *Piano concerto in G* (DUR), 12

Raver, Leonard, 218

Raxach, Enrique: *Estrofas* (TON), 94, 96, 97, 177, 190; *Interface* (DON), 125; *Paraphrase* (HIN), 45, 134, 189, 200

Read, Gardner: *Canzona di notte* (BER), 77, 201; *Diabolic Dialogue* (MS), 30, 54, 61, 96, 103, 106, 138, 173, 174, 185, 226; *Galactic Novae* (MS), 39, 51, 217; *Haiku Seasons* (MS), 39, 40, 42, 45, 71, 73, 78, 82, 138, 173, 175, 176, 182, 185, 187, 190, 191, 196, 197, 207; *Los Dioses Aztecas* (COLE), 20, 21, 173–78, 185, 189; *Phantasmagoria* (MS), 146, 148, 161; *Sonoric Fantasia No. 3* (SEE), 40, 42, 65, 70, 71, 113, 143, 145, 146, 196, 200; *Sonoric Fantasia No. 4* (CF), 214, 218; *Symphony No. 3* (FCOL), 98, 232; *Toccata Giocosa* (TP), 198; *Villon* (MS), 42, 233

Reck, David: *Blues and Screamer* (SOU), 33, 65, 95, 100–102, 113, 119, 133, 144, 145, 158, 173, 233, 234, 240; *Five Studies for Tuba Alone* (CFP), 33, 36, 147, 159, 164, 166; *Night Sounds (and Dream)* (CPE), 135

Rehfeldt, Philip, 160

Respighi, Ottorino: *The Pines of Rome* (RIC), 12

Revueltas, Silvestre: *Sensemayá* (GS), 174

Reynolds, Roger: *Aether* (CFP), 11, 53; *Ambages* (CFP), 65, 113, 165; *Blind Men* (CFP), 25, 46, 48–50, 59, 80, 82, 90, 157, 165, 187, 190, 206, 208; *The Emperor of Ice Cream* (CFP), 25, 28, 47, 48, 50, 58, 82, 83, 87; *Fantasy for Pianist* (CFP), 206, 207; *"From Behind . . . "* (CFP), 134, 137, 147, 151, 177, 182; *I/O: A Ritual* (CFP), 161; *Islands from Archipelago: I. Summer Island* (CFP), 112; *Islands from Archipelago: II. Autumn Island* (CFP), 182, 185; *Mosaic* (CFP), 26, 29, 45, 208; *The Promises of Darkness* (CFP), 12, 134, 147, 190, 209, 222; *Quick are the Mouths of Earth* (CFP), 16, 21, 26, 37, 39, 45, 46, 53, 55, 56, 65, 80, 94, 96, 113, 145, 148, 160, 175, 177, 184, 190, 192, 206, 222, 228, 231, 233; *Shadowed Narrative* (CFP), 233; *Traces* (CFP), 47, 50, 113, 160, 210; *Wedge* (CFP), 39, 48, 49, 80, 81, 88, 90, 145, 184

Richter, Marga: *Blackberry Vines and Winter Fruit* (CF), 18

Riegger, Wallingford: *Study in Sonority* (AMP), 11
Rimsky-Korsakov, Nicolai: *Christmas Eve* (BEL), 53
Rochberg, George: *Apocalyptica* (TP), 33; *Contra mortem et tempus* (TP), 58; *Duo concertante for Violin and Cello* (TP), 119; *Electrakaleidoscope* (TP), 125; *Music for the Magic Theatre* (TP), 103, 113, 114; *Tableaux* (TP), 17, 35, 36, 99, 113, 114, 116, 125, 135, 190, 210, 222
Rodrigo, Joaquin: *Zarabanda lejana y villancico* (ESCH), 29
Roger-Ducasse, Jean Jules: *Le joli jeu de furet* (DUR), 153
Romiti, Richard: *Palingenesis* (MS), 65, 81, 125, 198
Rosenboom, David: *and come up dripping* (CPE), 146, 149, 154, 157, 161
Rosenthal, Manuel: *Les petits métiers* (JJ), 228
Ross, Walter: *Concerto for Trombone and Orchestra* (MS), 20, 150
Rouse, Christopher: *Falcano Luminis* (EAM), 178; *The Infernal Machine* (HEL), 138; *Mitternachtlieder* (EAM), 54, 168; *Ogoun Badagris* (EAM), 134; *Rotae Passiones* (EAM), 133, 167, 178
Roxbury, Ronald: *Aria for Cello and Piano* (CAP), 136, 226
Rubbra, Edmund: *Symphony No. 6* (LEG), 20
Rudzinski, Witold: *Pictures from the Holy-Cross Mountains* (PWM), 52, 65, 69, 92, 100–102, 113, 238
Rudzinski, Zbigniew: *Contra Fidem* (PWM), 46, 49, 155; *Impromptu for Orchestra* (PWM), 21; *Moments Musicaux II* (PWM), 96
Russell, Armand: *Proteus* (ZIM), 242
Russell, William: *Fugue for Eight Percussion Instruments* (NME), 20, 21, 36, 47–50, 82, 179, 182, 185; *Three Dance Movements* (NME), 22, 136, 187, 208
Russo, William: *Three Pieces for Blues Band and Orchestra* (SMP), 17

Sadai, Yizhak: *Nuances* (IMP), 21, 74, 77, 84, 98, 100, 101, 105, 137, 198, 230
Saeverud, Harold: *Peer Gynt* (MH), 240
Sakač, Branimir: *Struktur I* (EMOD), 46, 49, 74, 95, 105, 145, 156
Salzedo, Carlos, 22, 24, 40, 41, 44, 69, 73–75, 196, 198, 200; *Scintillation* (GS), 70, 199; *Sonata for Harp and Piano* (GS), 23, 195
Sandström, Sven-David: *Just a Bit* (WH), 16, 117, 120; *Surrounded* (WH), 117, 203
Santoro, Claudio: *Três Abstrações* (JJ), 105
Sauguet, Henri: *La rencontre* (HEUG), 173
Schafer, R. Murray: *Cortège* (UEC), 131; *The Crown of Ariadne* (ARC), 24, 42, 117, 136, 138, 196; *East* (UEC), 31, 135; *Requiems for the Party-Girl* (BMIC), 72, 96, 133–35, 175; *Son of Heldenleben* (UEC), 150; *String Quartet* (UEC), 232, 240
Schäffer, Boguslaw: *Azione a due* (AHN), 113, 143; *4 Pieces for String Trio* (PWM), 100; *Modell III* (PWM), 25, 78; *Musica per pianoforte* (PWM), 88, 134, 136; *Music for Mi* (PWM), 185; *S'alto* (PWM), 50, 84; *Scultura* (PWM), 21, 33, 53, 80, 87, 96, 97, 100–102, 156, 174, 179, 196, 233; *String Quartet* (AHN), 52, 96, 98, 233; *Trio* (PWM), 101; *Two Pieces for Violin and Piano* (PWM), 234; *Violin Concerto* (PWM), 53
Schat, Peter: *Collages voor 31-toonsorgel* (DON), 118
Schelling, Ernest: *A Victory Ball* (LEU), 31
Schickele, Peter, 169
Schidlowsky, Leon: *Koloth* (IMP), 42, 74
Schifrin, Lalo: *Continuum for Solo Harp* (AMP), 70, 196
Schindler, Alan: *Cirius and Beyond* (MS), 176
Schmidt, Ole: *Toccata No. 1 for Accordion* (HOH), 219

INDEX OF COMPOSERS AND WORKS 269

Schnebel, Dieter: *Versuche* (SCHM), 11, 18, 176, 239
Schneider, John: *Voyage* (MS), 202, 203
Schönberg, Arnold, 92; *Fünf Orchesterstücke* (CFP), 189; *Kammersymphonie I* (PHIL), 236; *String Quartets* (PHIL), 92
Schramm, Harold: *Shilappadikaram* (MS), 96, 97, 101
Schreker, Franz: *Prelude to a Drama* (UE), 201
Schtschedrin, Rodion: *Selbstportrait* (UE), 201
Schuller, Gunther: *American Triptych* (AMP), 35; *Contours for Small Orchestra* (SCHL), 113, 171; *Fantasy for Solo Harp* (AMP), 198, 200; *Five Pieces for Five Horns* (BRUZ), 147; *Journey into Jazz* (AMP), 36; *Music for Violin, Piano and Percussion* (AMP), 139; *Seven Studies on Themes of Paul Klee* (UE), 31, 36, 113; *Sonata Serenata* (MAR), 226; *Spectra* (SCHL), 35, 39, 143, 171; *Study in Textures* (AMP), 18
Schuman, William: *Concerto for Violin and Orchestra* (MER), 18; *Credendum* (MER), 21; *Symphony No. 7* (MER), 21, 22
Schwantner, Joseph: *and the mountains rising nowhere* (CFP), 138; *Canticle of the Evening Bells* (CFP), 18, 134, 138, 140; *Consortium (I)* (CFP), 52; *Elixir* (CFP), 184, 240; *In Aeternum (Consortium IV)*, (HEL), 190; *In Aeternum II* (CFP), 14, 172, 216; *Magabunda* (HEL), 140, 172
Schwartz, Elliott: *Dialogue for Solo Contrabass* (CF), 135; *Essays for Trumpet and Trombone* (AB), 17, 158; *Extended Clarinet* (MS), 123; *Music for Napoleon and Beethoven* (BOW), 26, 29, 35, 36, 81, 82, 90, 130, 131, 134, 135, 167, 213; *Music for Prince Albert* (BOW), 25, 46, 48, 78, 134, 136; *Options I* (MP), 68, 69, 137, 151, 164, 167, 210; *Rip* (MS), 17, 35, 36, 64, 67, 134, 158, 164, 165; *Septet for Voice, Piano and 5 Instruments* (CF), 87–90; *Soliloquies* (BOW), 49, 65, 82, 87–90, 207; *Texture* (AB), 48, 65, 113
Seiber, Matyas György: *Pastorale and Burlesque* (SCHL), 92
Self, George: *Warwick* (UE), 190
Sender, Ramon: *Balances* (MS), 96, 97, 102, 103, 106
Serebrier, José: *Colores mágicos* (SMP), 22, 41, 198; *Momento Psicologico* (SMP), 31
Serocki, Kazimierz, 240; *Continuum for Percussion* (MV), 21, 37, 174, 187, 191, 192; *Episodes for Strings and Percussion* (PWM), 21, 174; *Fantasmagoria* (MV), 28, 39, 49, 78, 87, 191, 192; *Musica concertante* (PWM), 21, 196; *Niobe* (PWM), 40, 41, 44, 46, 80, 81, 186; *Segmenti* (MV), 37, 39–41, 49, 57, 65, 70, 72, 78, 185, 196; *Swinging Music* (MV), 12, 14, 67, 69, 153; *Symphonic Frescoes* (PWM), 17, 41, 67, 69, 70, 81
Shapey, Ralph: *Concerto Grosso for Woodwind Quintet* (TP), 7
Sheppard, C. James: *Garden of Earthly Delights* (SEE), 44
Sheriff, Noam: *"Destination 5'"* (IMP), 158
Shimoyama, Hifune: *Dialog for Violoncello and Piano* (SCHL), 80, 82, 84, 90; *Dialogo No. 2* (SCHL), 11, 203
Shinohara, Makoto: *Relations* (MV), 213
Shostakovich, Dmitri: *Concerto for Violin and Orchestra* (LEED), 20; *Symphonies Nos. 3; 6; 7; 11* (LEED), 7
Sikorski, Tomasz: *Echa II* (PWM), 22; *Prologues* (PWM), 19
Silsbee, Ann: *Spirals* (MS), 48, 50, 51, 59, 78, 225, 236, 239
Silverman, Stanley: *Elephant Steps* (MS), 125
Slonimsky, Nicolas: *My Toy Balloon* (AXP), 136
Smalley, Denis: *Gradual for Tape and Solo Clarinetist* (MS), 168
Smith, Stuart S.: *Two Makes Three* (SP), 182

Smith, William O.: *Variants for Solo Clarinet* (UE), 8, 16, 65, 133, 148
Smith Brindle, Reginald: *Andromeda M.31* (CFP), 160; *Auriga* (CFP), 174; *Concerto "de Angelis"* (SCHL), 203; *Do Not Go Gentle* (ZER), 11, 203; *Orion M.42* (CFP), 37, 184
Sollberger, Harvey: *Grand Quartet for Flutes* (MMX), 65, 113; *2 Pieces for 2 Flutes* (MMX), 55
Spiegelman, Joel: *Morsels* (MCA), 26, 58, 78, 80
Stalvey, D.: *PLC—Extract for Solo Clarinet* (SAL), 147
Standford, Patric: *Notte for Chamber Orchestra* (NOV), 31
Stephan, Rudi: *Musik für Orchester* (SCHM), 168
Stibilj, Milan: *Condensation for Trombone, 2 Pianos and Percussion* (BAR), 67, 147, 157, 174, 175
Stillman-Kelley, Edgar: *Gulliver—His Voyage to Lilliput* (AFMP), 21
Stockhausen, Karlheinz: *Adieu für Wolfgang Sebastian Meyer* (UE), 16, 36, 162; *Gruppen für drei Orchester* (UE), 125, 206; *Hymnen* (UE), 124, 126; *Klavierstücke I - XI* (UE), 58, 206–08, 210; *Kontakte* (UE), 39, 187; *"Kontra-Punkte"* (UE), 70, 74; *Kreuzspiel* (UE), 184; *Kurzwellen* (UE), 124, 126; *Mixtur* (UE), 124, 229; *Momente* (UE), 143, 185; *Punkte* (UE), 17; *Refrain* (UE), 134; *Zyklus* (UE), 39
Stout, Alan: *Study in Densities and Durations* (CFP), 51, 214, 216, 217
Strange, Allen: *Palace* (MS), 244; *Scapes for Trombone Ensemble* (MS), 116
Strauss, Richard: *Also sprach Zarathustra* (EUL), 12; *Don Quixote* (PHIL), 12; *Ein Heldenleben* (EUL), 11; *Elektra* (B&H), 11, 244; *Salome* (FUR), 30
Stravinsky, Igor: *Chant du rossignol* (B&H), 7; *Concertino pour quatuor à cordes* (WH), 236; *The Firebird* (SCHL), 53; *Four Russian Songs* (CHES), 201; *Le sacre du printemps* (ER), 12, 55, 189, 223; *Petrouchka* (ER), 16, 179; *Ragtime* (CHES), 236; *Renard* (CHES), 236; *Symphony in C* (SCHM), 7
Street, Tison: *String Quartet 1972* (GS), 223
Subotnick, Morton: *Before the Butterfly* (MS), 120, 126; *Lamination I* (MCA), 65, 69, 97, 105, 150, 156; *Serenade No. 3* (BOW), 158
Surinach, Carlos: *Feria mágica* (AMP), 41; *Melorhythmic Melodramas* (AMP), 41; *Symphonic Variations* (AMP), 207
Swift, Richard: *Concerto for Piano with Chamber Ensemble* (UCP), 83
Sydeman, William: *Clarinet Duo* (PS), 65; *Concerto da camera No. III* (AMP), 65; *Duo for Trumpet and Amplified Doublebass* (SEE), 99, 126; *For Double Bass Alone* (MMX), 228; *Projections I* (SEE), 92, 97, 98, 103, 126, 131, 224, 228, 232; *Study for Orchestra No. III* (AMP), 174, 239; *Texture Studies for Orchestra* (SEE), 65, 67, 69, 92, 96, 98, 99, 104, 113, 114, 119, 150, 155, 223, 226, 233, 237; *Trio for Flute, Doublebass and Percussion* (MMX), 174, 175, 189
Szalonek, Witold: *Aarhus Music, 1970* (SEE), 16, 55, 114, 150, 151, 161, 165, 166; *Concertino per flauto ed orchestra da camera* (PWM), 65, 72, 96, 100, 101, 106, 144, 156, 171, 197, 223, 236; *Geständnisse* (MV), 173; *Improvisations sonoristiques* (PWM), 153, 156, 167; *Les Sons* (PWM), 55, 56, 80, 143, 144, 151, 156, 211, 212, 222, 223, 236, 237; *Mutanza per pianoforte* (CHES), 28, 49, 50, 85, 89; *1+1+1+1* (PWM), 222, 234, 236, 244; *Proporzioni II* (SEE), 28, 29, 48, 81, 90, 136, 160, 212, 237; *Three Sketches* (SEE), 73, 74, 130

Takahashi, Yuji: *Bridges I* (CFP), 125, 126; *Rosace I* (CFP), 126
Takemitsu, Toru: *Asterism* (CFP), 187, 190, 198; *Cassiopeia* (SAL), 125; *Eu-

INDEX OF COMPOSERS AND WORKS 271

calypts (I); II (SAL), 22, 24, 42, 70, 75, 147, 152, 161, 196, 198; *Green* (CFP), 137, 165, 232; *Masque pour deux flûtes* (ONT), 113; *Ring* (ONT), 67; *Stanza II* (UE), 124, 197; *Star-Isle* (SCHL), 40; *Voice* (SAL) 63, 113, 133, 144, 160, 165; *Waves* (SAL), 56, 161, 167, 229
Tavener, John: *Celtic Requiem* (CHES), 125
Tchaikovsky, Peter Ilyitch: *Symphony No. 3* (BRV), 6
Thomson, Virgil: *Symphony No. 2* (LEED), 20
Tippett, Sir Michael: *Symphony No. 1* (SCHL), 16
Tircuit, Heuwell: *String Quartet No. 3* (AMP), 32, 131, 135
Toch, Ernst: *1st Symphony* (SCHM), 187; *3rd Symphony* (MIL), 187
Tôn-thât Tiêt: *Ngũ Hãnh II* (JJ), 20, 42
Tucker, Tui St. George: *Little Pieces* (MS), 118
Turetzky, Bertram: *Poems, Portraits, Ballades and Blues* (EV), 61, 100, 102, 135, 242
Turok, Paul: *Chartres West* (MS), 41

Ung, Chinary: *Spiral* (CFP), 13, 182

Valcarcel, Edgar: *Dicotomia III* (PAU), 228, 238; *Trio* (PAU), 123, 126
Van Nostrand, Burr: *Ventilation Manual* (MS), 24, 39, 72, 197
Varèse, Edgard, 186; *Ameriques* (COLF), 24, 74, 143, 165, 197; *Arcana* (COLF), 36, 187; *Density 21.5* (COLF), 107; *Déserts* (COLF), 185; *Ecuatorial* (RIC), 36, 185; *Intégrales* (CUR), 174; *Offrandes* (BIR), 39, 197
Vaughan Williams, Ralph: *Sinfonia Antartica* (OUP), 169
Vega, Aurelio de la: *Antinomies for Piano* (MS), 46, 49, 78, 80-82, 87, 207; *Exospheres for Oboe and Piano* (MS), 16, 48, 81, 82, 87, 154, 156; *Interpolation for Solo Clarinet* (MS), 16, 150-52, 161, 165; *Segments for Violin and Piano* (FAC), 94, 226; *Structures for Piano and String Quartet* (MS), 25, 49, 78, 82, 94, 104, 145, 226
Vercoe, Elizabeth: *Herstory II; III* (ARS), 46, 49, 83, 139
Vieru, Anatol: *Clepsidra II* (EMUS), 96, 102, 178
Villa-Lobos, Heitor: *Danses Africaines* (ESCH), 173; *The Jet Whistle* (SMP), 148

Walden, Stanley: *Coronach: A Kaddish* (TP), 113
Walton, Sir William: *Façade* (OUP), 173, 187
Wangenheim, Volker: *Klangspiel I* (LIT), 232
Webern, Anton von: *String Quartets* (PHIL), 92
Weinberger, Jaromir: *Overture, The Bird's Opera* (UE), 56
Welcher, Dan: *White Mares of the Moon* (EV), 70, 73, 113, 148, 198
Welin, Karl Erik: *Nr.3—1961* (AHN), 96, 97, 222
Whittenberg, Charles: *Conversations for Solo Doublebass* (CFP), 101, 135, 233, 236, 237
Widdoes, Lawrence: *From a Time of Snow* (BOW), 48, 50, 81, 101, 113, 146, 147, 151, 160, 232
Wiechowicz, Stanislaw: *Lettre à Marc Chagall* (PWM), 78, 92
Wilding-White, Raymond: *Superball!* (MS), 87; *Whatzit No. 1* (MS), 88, 136
Wilkinson, Marc: *Voices from "Waiting for Godot"* (UE), 152
Wilson, Donald M.: *Decisions, Decisions!* (MS), 25, 42, 70, 134; *Doubles* (CFP), 30, 65, 151; *Seventeen Views* (MS), 101
Wilson, Ervin, 118
Wilson, George Balch: *Concatenations* (JJ), 11, 39, 76, 94, 96, 103, 125, 126, 187, 233
Wilson, Olly: *Echoes for Clarinet and Tape* (MS), 150

Wiszniewski, Zbigniew: *Tre pezzi della tradizioni* (PWM), 39, 40, 71, 196

Wittinger, Robert: *Concentrazione* (BRH), 84; *Concerto lirico per orchestra* (BRH), 39; *Costruzioni* (BRH), 236; *Espressioni* (BRH), 81, 82, 85; *Irreversibilitazione* (BRH), 96; *Om per orchestra* (BRH), 156, 165, 166; *Quartetto per archi No. 3* (BRH), 119

Witzerrmann, Wolfgang: *Dedicazione a Herbert* (MV), 65

Wolff, Christian: *Duet I for Piano 4 Hands* (CFP), 26, 78, 210, 211; *Electric Spring I; II; III* (CFP), 125, 202; *Suite I for Prepared Piano* (CFP), 26

Woodbury, Arthur: *Remembrances* (CPE), 61, 147, 190

Wuorinen, Charles: *Concerto for Amplified Violin and Orchestra* (CFP), 126; *Five* (CFP), 126; *Flute Variations* (MMX), 5, 145, 147

Wyttenbach, Jürg: *Divisions* (AVV), 12

Xenakis, Iannis: *Akrata* (B&H), 114; *Charisma* (SAL), 153, 223; *Eonta* (B&H), 114, 116, 130, 131, 143, 145, 167; *Eridanos* (UE), 226; *Gmeeorh* (UE), 216; *Linaia—Agon* (SAL), 144, 153; *Metastaseis* (B&H), 114, 116, 145; *Nomos* (B&H), 119, 236; *Pithoprakta* (B&H), 102, 103; *Polytope* (B&H), 114, 116; *ST/4-1,080262* (B&H), 11–13, 53, 104, 105, 239; *ST/10-1,080262* (B&H), 24; *Syrmos* (B&H), 52; *Terretektorh* (B&H), 140

Yannay, Yehuda: *Coloring Book for the Harpist* (MP), 72, 124; *preFIX-FIX-sufFIX* (MP), 155, 157, 161, 162, 222

Yuasa, Joji: *Scenes from Bashô* (ZEN), 172, 178, 182, 188; *Triplicity for Contrabass* (ONT), 99

Yun, Isang: *Colloides sonores* (B&H), 238, 240; *Dimensionen* (B&B), 113, 187, 218, 240; *Flukturationen* (B&B), 70; *Images* (B&B), 59, 145; *String Quartet No. 3* (B&B), 233; *Symphonische Szene* (B&B), 72

Zimmermann, Bernd Alois: *Canto di speranza* (SCHM), 20, 21, 173; *Intercommunicazione* (SCHM), 13, 106, 236, 239; *Perspektiven* (SCHM), 208; *Photoptosis* (SCHM), 114, 116, 184, 190; *Sonate für Cello Solo* (EMOD), 234, 238; *Stille und Umkehr* (SCHM), 35, 113, 114, 116; *Tempus loquendi* (SCHM), 64, 113, 150, 160

Zonn, Paul: *Chroma* (SP), 56

Zupko, Raymond: *Fixations* (CFP), 28

LIST OF PUBLISHERS

AB	Alexander Broude, Inc., New York (BBL)
ACA	American Composers Alliance, New York
AFMP	Affiliated Music Corporation, New York
AHN	Ahn & Simrock, Berlin—Wiesbaden (GS)
ALP	Editorial Alpuerto, Madrid
AMP	Associated Music Publishers, Inc., New York (GS)
AMPH	Amphion-Editions Musicales, Paris (TP)
APOG	Apogee Press, Cincinnati (WLSM)
ARC	Arcana Editions, Ontario, Canada
ARMP	Arrow Music Press, Inc., New York (B&H)
ARS	Arsis Press, Washington, D.C. (PMC)
AVM	Avant Music (WIM)
AVV	Ars Viva Verlag, Mainz (EAM)
AXP	Axelrod Publications, Providence
BAR	Barenreiter-Verlag, Kassel (FMD)
BAS	Basheva Music, Newhall, CA
BAY	Barry Editorial, Buenos Aires (B&H)
B&B	Bote & Bock, Berlin (AMP)
BBL	Broude Brothers, Ltd., Williamstown, MA
BDOL	Berandol Music, Ltd., Toronto
BEL	Edition M. P. Belaieff, Paris (CFP)
BER	Edizioni Musicali Berben, Ancona, Italy (TP)
B&H	Boosey & Hawkes, Inc., New York—London
BIL	Gerard Billaudet, Paris (TP)
BIR	C. C. Birchard & Co., Boston
B/M	Belwin/Mills Publishing Corporation, Melville, NY (CPPB)
BMIC	BMI Canada, Ltd., Don Mills (AMP)
BOON	Joseph Boonin, Inc., South Hackensack, NJ
BOS	The Boston Music Co., Boston
BOW	Bowdoin College Music Press, Brunswick, ME
BRH	Breitkopf & Hartel, Leipzig
BRUZ	Edizioni Aldo Bruzzichelli, Florence (MAR)
BRV	Brucknerverlag, Wiesbaden

LIST OF PUBLISHERS

CAP	Composers Autograph Publications, Hamilton, OH
CF	Carl Fisher, Inc., New York
CFP	C. F. Peters Corporation, New York—London
CHAP	Chappell & Co., Ltd., London—New York (INT)
CHES	J. & W. Chester, London (MMB)
CHF	Cesky Hudebni Fond, Prague
COLE	M. M. Cole Publishing Co., Chicago
COLF	Colfranc Music Publishing Corp., New York (KER)
CPE	Composer-Performer Edition, Sacramento, CA
CPPB	CPP/Belwin, Inc., Miami
CUR	J. Curwen & Sons, Ltd., London
DAN	Dantalian, Inc., Newton, MA
DOB	Ludwig D. Doblinger Verlag, Vienna (FMD)
DON	Donemus, Amsterdam (TP)
DUR	Durand et Cie., Paris (TP)
EAM	European American Music Distributors Corp., Valley Forge, PA
EBM	Edward B. Marks Music Corp., New York (HL)
ECS	E. C. Schirmer Music Co., Boston
EDS	Edition Suecia, Switzerland
EMOD	Edition Modern, Munich
EMUS	Editio Musica, Budapest (TP)
ER	Edition Russe de Musique, Paris
ESCH	Max Eschig Editions, Paris
EUL	Ernst Eulenburg, Ltd., London (EAM)
EV	Elkan-Vogel, Inc., Bryn Mawr, PA (TP)
EX	Experimental Music Catalogue, London
FAC	Facimile Edition (Composer)
FCOL	Franco Colombo Publications, New York (CPPB)
FMD	Foreign Music Distributors, Nutley, NJ
FOS	Mark Foster Music Co., Champaign, IL
FUR	Adolf Fürstner, Ltd., Berlin (B&H)
GAL	Galaxy Music Corp., New York (ECS)
GEN	General Music Publishing Co., New York (BOS)
GER	Edition Hans Gerig, Cologne (MCA)
GS	G. Schirmer, Inc., New York
HAN	Hänssler-Verlag, Stuttgart (FOS)
HAR	Harms, Inc., New York
HEL	Helicon Music Corp., New York (EAM)
HEN	Henmar Press, New York (CFP)
HEUG	Heugel & Cie., Paris (TP)
HIGT	Highgate Press, Inc., New York (ECS)

LIST OF PUBLISHERS

HIN	Hinrichsen Edition, Ltd., London (CFP)
HL	Hal Leonard Publishing Corp., Milwaukee, WI
HMR	HaMaR Percussion Publications (B&H)
HOH	Matth. Hohner A. G., Musikverlag, Trossingen
IMP	Israeli Music Publications, Ltd., Tel Aviv (TP)
IMPR	Impero Verlag, Wilhelmshaven (TP)
INL	International Music Publications, London
INT	International Music Co., New York
IO	Ione Press, Inc., Boston (ECS)
JJ	Editions Jean Jobert, Paris (TP)
KER	E. C. Kerby, Ltd., Toronto
LED	Alphonse Leduc et Cie., Paris (TP)
LEED	Leeds Music Corp., New York (MCA)
LEG	Alfred Legnick & Co., Ltd., London (TP)
LEU	F.E.C. Leukart, Munich
LG	Lawson-Gould Music Publishers, Inc., New York
LIT	Henry Litolff's Verlag, Frankfurt (CFP)
LYRA	Lyra Music Co., New York
MAL	Malcolm Music, Ltd., New York (SHP)
MAR	Margun Music, Inc., Newton Centre, MA
MCA	MCA Music, New York (HL)
MER	Merion Music, Inc., Bryn Mawr, PA (TP)
MH	Musikk-Huset, A. S., Oslo, Norway
MIL	Mills Music, Inc., New York (CPPB)
MMB	MMB Music, Inc., St. Louis, MO
MMX	McGinnis & Marx Music Publishers, New York
MN	Musikedition Nymphenburg, Munich (CFP)
MP	Media Press, Champaign, IL
MS	Manuscript (Composer)
MUR	Murbo Music Publishing Co., New York
MUZ	Editura Muzicala, Bucharest, Romania
MV	Moeck-Verlag, Celle, Germany (EAM)
NEO	Neofonic Music and Recording Co., New York
NME	New Music Edition, New York (TP)
NORD	Nordiska Musikförlaget, Stockholm (GS)
NOV	Novello & Co., Ltd., London (TP)
OKR	Okra Music Corp., New York (SEE)
ONT	Ongaku-no Tomo Sha, Tokyo (TP)
OUP	Oxford University Press, London—New York

PAU	Pan American Union, Washington, D.C. (PS)
PD	Pietro Diero Publications, New York
PHIL	Philharmonia Partituren, Vienna (EAM)
PS	Peer-Southern Organization, New York (TP)
PWM	Polskie Wydawnictwo Muzycne, Warsaw—Cracow (EBM)
RIC	G. Ricordi & C., Milan (HL)
SAL	Editions Salabert, Paris (GS)
SAM	Samfundet til udgivelse af dansk musik, Copenhagen (CFP)
SCHL	Schott & Co., Ltd., London (EAM)
SCHM	B. Schott's Soehne, Mainz (EAM)
SEE	Seesaw Music Corp., New York
SEN	Editions Maurice Senart, Paris (GS)
SHP	Shawnee Press, Inc., Delaware Water Gap, PA
SK	Son-Key, Inc., Aurora, CO
SMP	Southern Music Publishing Co., New York (PS)
SOU	Source: Music of the Avant-Garde (TP)
SP	Smith Publications, Baltimore, MD
TON	Edition Tonos, Darmstadt (SEE)
TP	Theodore Presser Co., Bryn Mawr, PA
TR	Tritone Press, Bryn Mawr, PA (TP)
TRMP	Transcontinental Music Publications, New York
UCP	University of California Press, Berkeley, CA
UE	Universal Edition, A. G., Vienna—London (EAM)
UEA	Universal Edition, Australia (EAM)
UEC	Universal Edition, Canada (EAM)
UN	United Music Publishers, Ltd., London
VER	Verlag der Gesellschaft zur Foderung der Systematischen Muzikwissenschaft, Germany
WAT	Waterloo Music Co., Ltd., Ontario, Canada
WEIN	Josef Weinberger, Ltd., London (B&H)
WH	Wilhelm Hansen Edition, Copenhagen (MMB)
WIM	Western International Music
WLSM	World Library of Sacred Music, Cincinnati, OH
ZAI	Zaiks, Warsaw, Poland
ZEN	Zen-on Music Co., Tokyo (EAM)
ZER	Edizioni Suvini Zerboni, Milan (B&H)
ZIM	Musikverlag Wilhelm Zimmermann, Frankfurt, Germany

About the Author

GARDNER READ, a noted American composer, is Professor of Music Emeritus at Boston University and a scholar of erudition and originality. His books include *Thesaurus of Orchestral Devices, Music Notation: A Manual of Modern Practice, Contemporary Instrumental Techniques, Modern Rhythmic Notation, Style and Orchestration, Source Book of Proposed Music Notation Reforms* (Greenwood Press, 1987), and *20th-Century Microtonal Notation* (Greenwood Press, 1990).